SPEED DREAMS

A Guide to America's 23 NASCAR® Tracks

JAY AHUJA

CITADEL PRESS
Kensington Publishing Corp.
www.kensingtonbooks.com

CITADEL PRESS BOOKS are published by

Kensington Publishing Corp.
850 Third Avenue
New York, NY 10022

All Kensington titles, imprints, and distributed lines are available at special quantity discounts for bulk purchases for sales promotions, premiums, fund-raising, educational, or institutional use. Special book excerpts or customized printings can also be created to fit specific needs. For details, write or phone the office of the Kensington special sales manager: Kensington Publishing Corp., 850 Third Avenue, New York, NY 10022, attn: Special Sales Department, phone 1-800-221-2647.

The photo that appears on pages 11 and 207 is by Howie Hodge. Used with permission.

Citadel Press and the Citadel logo are trademarks of Kensington Publishing Corp.

First Kensington printing: March 2002

10 9 8 7 6 5 4 3 2 1

Printed in the United States of America

Library of Congress Control Number: 2001098930

ISBN: 0-8065-2243-7

To race fans, whose enthusiam, loyalty, and support of the sport
is nothing short of remarkable.

CONTENTS

ROAD COURSES

INTRODUCTION

"I'm not a big fan of running the same racetrack in different cities. Part of what makes racing fun is going to a lot of different racetracks."

—JEFF BURTON

I don't always let on, but these past few years have been like my own personal racing fantasy camp. Traveling to the nation's premier cities—Las Vegas, Miami, Chicago, Los Angeles, Sonoma, Fort Worth, Atlanta, Indianapolis, and Phoenix—as well as the classic racetracks in more unassuming southeastern towns such as Bristol, Richmond, Martinsville, Darlington, and Rockingham has been an experience I will not soon forget.

Witnessing unforgettable races at Daytona, Watkins Glen, Talladega, Dover, and Texas, not to mention my hometown track, Lowe's Motor Speedway, has enabled me to catch up with old friends, fall headlong into the excitement of Winston Cup stock car racing, and meet some remarkable individuals along the way. Visiting the pits and garages, talking to pit crews, drivers, photographers, writers, and all kinds of fans, has been a remarkable awakening to the teamwork, skill, and all-out competition required to excel at the nation's fastest-moving and fastest-growing sport. Watching the Coca-Cola 600 for four hours and seeing "the losers" roar to the finish line one-tenth of a second too late is astounding. That's roughly the equivalent of driving from my hometown in North Carolina to the Poconos in Pennsylvania. To work so hard and lose by such a small margin is unfathomable.

I moved to Charlotte, North Carolina, in 1986 and was struck by the fervor of racing fans. Serious fans know where next week's race will take place and precisely how their favorite driver is doing in the season-long Winston Cup points chase. The personal cars and trucks of race fans proudly display decals with the number of

1

their favorite driver. They wear hats, T-shirts, and jackets touting the DuPont Chevrolet, Home Depot Pontiac, or Havoline Ford and pack the sports bars on any given Sunday afternoon (and an occasional Saturday night) from February to November. Tens of thousands more fans furnish their homes with giant-screen TVs and satellite systems that allow them (and their friends) to watch races uninterrupted and commercial-free. And nearly all of them will gladly travel to every race they can get to.

To see how far the sport has come in a relatively short time is staggering. I grew up following baseball, football, basketball, and nearly any other worthwhile sport. I occasionally saw a NASCAR race on *ABC's Wide World of Sports* and rooted for Cale Yarborough year after year in the Daytona 500—the only race shown live from start to finish in those days—while my best friend pulled for David Pearson. As a kid, I remember A. J. Foyt's short-lived yet moderately successful NASCAR career, because he was my favorite Indy car driver. But when I moved to Charlotte in 1986, I was primarily a "stick and ball" sports fan with a modest interest in racing. Davey Allison became my new favorite when I met him at an event in May 1990. He was as kind and personable an athlete as I have ever encountered.

Stock car racing was slow to take over my life. First it was a trip to see qualifying for the Winston Select. Then I went to the Winston, NASCAR's winners-only, all-star race, and then the Coca-Cola 600. A road trip to Rockingham, with my good friend Bill, fell into place the following year. A journey to stock car racing's Super Bowl, the Daytona 500, came the next season—two buddies and I bought tickets through an ad in the local newspaper and camped in the backyard of a fraternity house for a long race weekend at the beach. Ever since then, it's been a new track nearly every weekend during the Winston Cup season.

Instead of camping I try to stay at nearby hotels or with friends. I bring my wife or a buddy or two, and on occasion, I travel alone. I get pit passes every chance I can and tour tracks whenever possible. I visit racing Internet sites like jayski.com, thatsracing.com, and goracing.com, watch videotape of the race if I was at that weekend's race in person, read the racing section of every newspaper I come across, and subscribe to a weekly stock car racing magazine. I've been amazed by the fans of racing, who are as knowledgeable, friendly, intense, raucous, and fun as those of any sport in the world. And infinitely more dedicated.

I've gone to races as a "fan in the stands" and as a credentialed writer. I'm not sure which I enjoy more. I have been in team transporters, in skybox suites, and atop the roof. I watched in awe inside the track garage as crews attempted to pull an engine out of a wrecked car, install it in a backup car, and get the driver back on the track in time to compete in a nonpoints race. I've been to drag strips, dirt tracks, road courses, short tracks, old tracks, new tracks, and everything in between.

On those weekends that I stay home to write, instead of traveling to see a track I've already visited, I genuinely miss the thrill of being at the track on race day. If the race is a short drive away in Bristol, Richmond, Darlington, or Rockingham, I can almost always find a buddy willing to make a day-long road trip.

I've gone so far as to join ESPN's online racing fantasy league. Sadly, my team, the DNF Kings, lived up to their moniker. I knew I was in deep last summer when I was watching videotape of a race that I had been to just a few days earlier. Even though I knew who had won the race, I was on the edge of my seat for the wild finish. On many a race day I've lugged around my cooler full of ice and beer for what seems like miles. I've sat on the frontstretch, the backstretch, in the infield, on the turns, in photo towers, hospitality suites, the press box, and in the pits. I was even invited to join some fans atop their converted school bus in the infield at Watkins Glen, the "Woodstock" of Winston Cup.

I have paid what some might consider far too much money for tickets and gotten others absolutely free from gracious fans at the track on the day of the race. I've bought tickets in advance and bought tickets from scalpers. I've tailgated before and after races, waited in traffic for hours, and even come home from Martinsville with some Ford Taurus "scrap metal" that occupies a good portion of my garage. My buddies knew I was hooked when I bought a $500 scanner, intercom, and head-phone set that allows a friend and me to talk to each other as we watch the race and listen to the drivers and crew members communicate. Once you've tried it, there's no better way to watch a race. My wife gave me a certificate to take part in the Buck Baker driving school program at Rockingham, which may be the coolest gift I have ever received.

As I visit new tracks all over the country, I'm thrilled for fans in those areas because they don't have to travel very far to see a race in person. I also recognize that the sport gains exposure in new and important markets with these new venues. I wonder, however, why so many of the newer tracks—ChicagoLand, Kansas City, Las Vegas, Miami, and Texas—seem to be clones of Lowe's Motor Speedway and the remodeled Atlanta Motor Speedway. Don't get me wrong: the track at Charlotte is among the best on the circuit, especially when it comes to fan amenities and traf-fic management, but unique facilities with their own quirks and nostalgia make any sport better.

Major League Baseball made the same mistake decades ago when stadiums like Veterans in Philadelphia, Fulton County in Atlanta, Three Rivers in Pittsburgh, Riverfront in Cincinnati, and Busch in Saint Louis were nearly indistinguishable from each other. At some point, I would hope that the powers-that-be would rec-ognize that the fans think Bruton Smith has a good thing going in Bristol. I'm not suggesting that every new track should be a half-mile concrete oval surrounded by

140,000 seats, but tracks like Richmond, Dover, Martinsville, and Bristol are what really make stock car racing interesting and worth the occasional road trip. If they all look the same, why not stay home and watch the races on TV?

I would also hope that in the future, Winston Cup race dates are not taken away from these classic ovals, as happened to North Wilkesboro a few years ago. I know the sport will continue to survive, and perhaps even thrive, but it's diminished nevertheless when a part of the sport's history is tossed aside for newer, sleeker, more profitable tracks that cater to corporations at the expense of the fans who made the sport what it is today.

Lifelong friends, who have been race fans for as long as I've known them, give me a hard time for not having joined them at the track earlier. This book is for them and everyone else who gets a rush when forty-three 750-horsepower engines roar to life at the command of "Gentlemen, start your engines" or zoom by at nearly 200 miles per hour when they drop the green flag to start a race.

I've also learned that two people can go to the same race and have very different experiences, which explains the heated debate that ensues when you ask fans which is their favorite track. Some tracks and cities are unquestionably better than others. Some tracks are brand-new, and others have a sense of history and nostalgia that cannot be duplicated. Some are great for families, while others are strictly for hard-core fans. I hope this book will encourage you to venture across this great country of ours with friends and family to see a few racetracks and experience them for yourself. And I hope, perhaps because of something I've shared in the pages ahead, that you are able to do it better than ever before.

Work, common sense, and finances get in the way sometimes, but you can be sure that on any given Sunday between Valentine's and Thanksgiving, I'd rather be at the racetrack than just about anywhere else. I'll be the one drinking a cold brew, smiling from ear to ear, watching the race with good friends, new and old, and trying to decide who should take Cale Yarborough and Davey Allison's place as my favorite driver. Hope to see you there.

A Dozen Favorite Racing Experiences

12 Standing inches away from the cars as they came through turn eleven at Sears Point.

11 Tailgating with friends at the 1995 Winston Select in Charlotte, my first Winston Cup track experience.

10 Hanging out with my wife and the local rowdies in the infield and under the pedestrian bridge at Dover.

9 Camping in the backyard of my friend Mark's fraternity house in Daytona.

8 Scoring a free ticket to the spring night race at Richmond.

7 Spending some time atop a converted school bus in the infield of Watkins Glen.

6 Watching Dale Jarrett cross the finish line from the infield photo tower at Darlington.

5 Seeing Tony Stewart spin out Jeff Gordon on pit road in Bristol after Gordon knocked Stewart sideways on the final lap.

5a Seeing Tony's smirk as he left the track on a golf cart that afternoon.

4 Bringing home the front end of the #11 car from Martinsville.

3 Meeting Davey Allison. I've met several drivers since then, but none impressed me more.

2 Any race at Bristol. Especially a night race.

1 Standing in the garage watching as Jeff Gordon's crew scrambled to pull an engine out of their wrecked car in the 2001 Winston. The teamwork between his crew and the UAW-GM crew was phenomenal. Even though they ended up not switching engines, Gordon went on to win the race.

PLANNING YOUR TRIP

There are a few things you must do as you embark on your racing road trip.

Rule number one: Buy a local map or, better yet, stop at the state visitor center on your way to a race and pick up a free one. These maps are far more detailed than the typical multistate maps that your travel club furnishes and will enable you to find shortcuts or, more important, recover more easily when traffic control personnel at various tracks invariably force you to head away from your destination as you leave a race.

Rule number two: Purchase the local daily newspaper. The newspaper and the local entertainment weekly will prove to be invaluable for planning activities. Smaller towns may not have a worthwhile entertainment tabloid, but they will have a daily paper. If you want to learn where driver appearances will be held, what the local traffic patterns are, and what frequency drivers will be using to communicate to their crew and spotters, these newspapers are often your best source.

This brings me to rule number three: Be aware that the newspaper's suggested route is generally the one that most other folks will be taking. As my buddy David says, "Not every track has a shortcut, but most of them do." He offers several wonderful suggestions when it comes to getting to and from a Winston Cup race. First, look for cars with special permits hanging from their rearview mirrors and follow them. Second, the best way to avoid traffic on race day is to go to the track on the Thursday before the race, with your map in hand. Find out where you need to park on race day and work your way back to wherever it is that you are staying after the race. This will better acclimate you with your surroundings in case you are forced by the highway patrol to head away from your desired route. Living in Charlotte, I have the advantage of following a transporter home from the races. Transporter drivers know all the shortcuts and have yet to steer me wrong.

Did you ever wonder why so many race fans take recreational vehicles to the race and why they seem to have more fun than anybody else? It's not because their spots atop the RVs are the best seats in the house. Oftentimes they are no better than grandstand seats. RVs have become so popular because traffic after the race is brutal and hotel prices during race week in some cities are almost criminal. RV race fans know that they don't have to deal with either. They simply spend the night at the track, continue partying with all the creature comforts of home, and leave the following morning when 90 percent of the fans have already cleared out. But you don't have to drive an RV to the race to have a good time. It certainly helps, but if you plan ahead you can have a great time with or without an RV.

If you are driving to a race, pack as if you were going camping. Bring collapsible chairs, bottled water, a grill, your favorite meat and side dishes, a tent and sleeping bags, a tarp, and of course a cooler full of ice and your favorite beverage. Plan to tailgate for hours after the race and let the traffic (and the drunk drivers) clear out. I've eaten some elaborate meals prepared at the track, and few things are more enjoyable than a good meal after a long day at the race. You may be planning to head home after a race or have a hotel room reserved, but it can't hurt to have these things on hand.

If you are flying to a race, chances are you will not be able to use frequent flyer miles. Airlines are becoming as savvy as hotel chains when it comes to race weekends. Consider flying into nearby airports rather than directly into race cities. Fly in and out of Greensboro for races in Charlotte, Bristol, or Martinsville. Fly through Indianapolis to get to Chicago and vice versa. Fly into Philadelphia for Dover or Pocono races. In 2001, I flew into Pittsburgh, saw a ball game at the brand-new PNC Park with some buddies on Saturday, and drove to Watkins Glen after the game. I saved hundreds of dollars in the process.

As soon as you secure tickets to a race, book a hotel or reserve a campsite. At tracks like Daytona, Rockingham, Pocono, and Dover, nearby hotels are often booked by the same folks year after year, so you may find that you'll be forced to stay an hour or more from the track. There is no magic solution to this other than perseverance and luck. A good travel agent may be helpful, but be sure that they are familiar with hotels they arrange. Just because a place costs $139 a night doesn't mean it's a nice place. Don't bother calling a hotel's nationwide toll-free numbers, because most hotels black out race weeks and handle those reservations directly. If you strike out with a particular place listed in this book, your best bet is to ask the person at the reservation desk if they know of comparable places that might have availability. I found a brand-new Spring Hill Suites hotel with no minimum-stay requirements on race weekend in Richmond that way.

Most importantly, bring along your family and friends. Just like any other sport, it's that much better when you can share it with others. Perhaps the best thing about this past year is that I've caught up with so many old friends in cities across the country as I've traveled to NASCAR races. There's no better way to see a city than with a host who knows the town inside and out. Other cities, such as Indianapolis, Daytona, and Dover, I discovered together with friends for the first time.

I've been to some Winston Cup cities many times and others only once, so if I've missed something important I hope you'll let me know by e-mailing me at jahuja@carolina.rr.com. If I've learned anything on my trips to America's Winston Cup tracks, it's that race fans are a social bunch. The common bond of supporting stock car racing brings people together in ways I could not have imagined just a few years ago. Once fans learned that I was writing about their favorite sport, they were quick to point out places I should visit, restaurants I should eat at, and vantage points at various tracks I should be sure not to miss.

What follows is everything I learned along the way. As new tracks are potentially added to the schedule, you can bet I'll be there in the years to come.

A Dozen Things to Bring into the Track

12 A seat cushion. Seats range from cement bleachers to padded plastic chairs, but none of them can be described as comfy. A jacket or sweatshirt can serve this same purpose until you get cold. Indy rents padded chairs with backs that hook to the bleachers for just $7. Every track that subjects fans to benches should offer the same service.

11 A seating chart. If you're buying tickets at the track, know where the good seats are before you pay a scalper big bucks for those "great seats" on the front row of the backstretch or some other such travesty.

10 A can hugger. Five hundred miles can make for a long, hot day at the races, and a can hugger will help you pace yourself as you empty your cooler of frosty beverages.

9 Bottled water and snacks. For the very same reason. Save some room in your cooler. You might enjoy the race more, and you'll definitely feel better the next day.

8 Earplugs. Every track is loud, but short tracks are notoriously loud. If you don't use a scanner or radio headset, buy a $3 set of earplugs at the track. My buddy Jamie bought a pair in Daytona, not for the race, but so he wouldn't have to listen to me snoring in the tent after the race that night. He claims it was the best money he ever spent, so I bought my wife a pair.

7 **A digital stopwatch.** Time your favorite driver's laps or pit stops. If you are on the frontstretch, consider timing drivers from the time they enter pit road until they exit onto the track. There's usually a painted line at each end of pit road and the total time—from leaving the track to returning—is often more telling than the time a crew works on the car in the pit stall.

6 **A camera.** Especially if you have a pit pass. Ideally, you'll want an auto-focus 35-millimeter camera with at least a 200-millimeter zoom lens. A point-and-shoot or disposable will do in a pinch. Binoculars are also very worthwhile.

5 **A ticket holder.** For less than $5 you can get the kind you wear over your neck or one that pins to your belt loop. It keeps your tickets handy and in good shape as a souvenir afterward.

4 **Friends and family.** A race is infinitely more fun when you have somebody to hoot and holler with. At least one of you should also bring a felt-tipped pen, because drivers are famous for autographing nearly anything you ask to have signed.

3 **A scanner and headset.** Once you use a scanner, especially at a short track, you'll never want to go to a race without one. Hear the drivers and crew chiefs communicate or listen to the race broadcast, while saving your hearing. I prefer one with an intercom system, so I can talk with a friend, but I opted not to buy the custom-fitted earpieces the drivers use.

2 **A ball cap.** Preferably related to racing, to prevent sunburn and to show which driver you are pulling for. Matching T-shirts, jackets, coolers, can huggers, sunglasses, and tattoos are optional, albeit growing in popularity. Sunscreen is always good to have as well.

1 **A 14-inch-tall cooler full of ice and your favorite beverages in cans.** But be sure you know which tracks allow you to bring a cooler in with you. These days you can even find collapsible coolers with pop-up handles and wheels. It doesn't get any more convenient than that!

Another Dozen Things to Bring for Tailgating

12 Everything from the previous list plus this book.

11 Horseshoes or crateball. Nothing passes the time better while you're tailgating. Crateball, a game consisting of a pair of plastic crates and two softballs, is less dangerous than horseshoes to those parked nearby.

10 Cellular phone or walkie-talkies. As much as I despise the things on the road, they are a big help in finding your buddies before, during, and after a race.

9 The local newspaper. Not just for traffic routes and scanner frequencies, but also to do a driver pool for the race.

8 A tarp. Rain or shine, you'll be glad you brought it.

7 A boombox. Listen to the prerace or postrace show, or jam some tunes. On race day there may be a shortage of Lynyrd Skynyrd, Allman Brothers, Marshall Tucker Band, and .38 Special CDs and tapes at area stores, so be sure to bring plenty of your own.

6 Camping supplies. A tent, sleeping bag, and pillow can come in very handy. But also think about a flashlight or lantern, propane grill, and cooking kit. Some places, such as Talladega, offer free primitive camping spots within walking distance of the track. Area hotels often jack up their rates and still sell out quickly, but don't let that keep you from seeing new tracks.

5 Cash. Tickets, parking, race programs, hats, T-shirts, speeding tickets, bail money—they all require cash, and lots of it. There's plenty to buy at the track. While some vendors take credit cards, lines are often massive, and charging stuff really slows things down.

4 Collapsible camping chairs. Some tracks will even let you bring them into the infield, so you and your buddies can set up a spot to watch the race, but they are absolutely essential for tailgating.

3 A grill, charcoal, lighter fluid, and matches. Tailgate after the race. Traffic is almost always a nightmare, and you are going to wait forever either way. Eat something and let the state troopers clear the road of drunk drivers before you head home.

2 **A giant cooler.** Full of ice, plenty of bottled water, steaks or burgers for the grill, side dishes, and, of course, beer.

1 **An RV.** Nobody enjoys a race more than the folks who know that they have all the comforts of home in their recreational vehicle, just a short walk from the track.

▪ *BRISTOL MOTOR SPEEDWAY* ▪

Bristol, Tennessee

"If you can imagine banks like Talladega on a half-mile track and obviously when you have that much bank with these big ole heavy cars, you get up some pretty good speed up around there. And every now and then you run into people."

—MICHAEL WALTRIP

Ask a dozen hard-core race fans which Winston Cup track is their favorite, and don't be surprised if ten of them say Bristol. Veterans contend that the only thing better than a day at Bristol is a night race at "The World's Fastest Half-Mile." This track is home to a pair of points races: the Food City 500 is generally held in late March or early April, while the Goody's 500 is run under the lights near the end of August.

Bristol has expanded relentlessly upward over the years and resembles a giant, 150,000-seat college football stadium from a distance. Aerial views of the facility, with the stands encircling the .533-mile oval, confirm that uncanny resemblance. Skybox suites are atop the stands from turn three all the way through turn one. The tallest section of stands is between turns one and two, where the steep climb to the upper elevations keeps even the hardiest fan from making too many trips to the concourse area. Team spotters occupy a spot above the stands in turn three. Seats in the upper rows of this section offer a near-total perspective of the half-mile oval.

The surrounding grandstands and mountainous setting contribute to Bristol's "Thunder Valley" reputation as the circuit's loudest track. If you generally neglect to use a race scanner and headphones at the track, this is one place you should seriously consider renting a set, if for no other reason than to protect your hearing.

Even in the highest seat in the house, there is no escaping the roar of forty-three 750-horsepower automobiles charging around the track. The track's 36-degree turns are five stories tall, easily the steepest in Winston Cup racing. The 650-foot-long straightaways are banked at 16 degrees, helping to create the sense of racing inside a massive tub. In fact, the straightaways at Bristol are steeper than the turns at ten Winston Cup speedways, including much longer ovals in Las Vegas, Homestead, Indy, California, Kansas City, and Pocono.

Many upper sections in turns one, two, and four at Bristol offer comfortable red plastic seats. Most sections have metal bleacher benches, including the uppermost seats in turns one and two. The backstretch has a massive section of cement bleachers in the very bottom rows. The relatively short scoring tower, near the winner's circle and testing area, lists the current lap and the top seven cars. The scoring tower is slightly closer to the seats in turns three and four but is visible from practically any seat in the track.

A pedestrian tunnel is in the works, but there is no vehicle tunnel to Bristol's infield and pit area, so get there early if you plan to cross the track and check out the pit area. Once the green flag drops, visitors are there for the duration of the race, and folks in the grandstand are unable to enter the garage and pit area. For that matter, drivers who are eliminated early in a race must wait until the race is over before they can get in their motor coaches and head home. This may explain why drivers tend to stay angry about incidents at Bristol.

Infield fans at Bristol may want to bring a collapsible chair and settle down between the turns to watch the tops of cars as they negotiate the incredible banks. Either set of turns offers a tremendous view. The infield's best-kept secret, however, may be the deck that sits above the media center. From this comfortable perch, about a dozen fans are treated to a perspective that overlooks the trailers, pit row, and the start/finish line.

The pits at Bristol are split between the front and back straightaways. The first twenty-one pit stalls are on the front side, while the remaining pits are along the back straightaway. For races with forty-three cars, two crews share one pit along the backstretch until an alternate pit space becomes available through attrition. Earning a starting position with a corresponding frontstretch pit stall is a significant advantage at Bristol. In more than eighty Winston Cup races at Bristol, only eleven winners have started worse than tenth. Cars pitting on the backstretch during a green flag lap tend to lose four to seven positions each time they pit. During single-file restarts following caution flags at BMS, cars at the back of the pack can be half a lap behind the lead car. Accordingly, a driver starting out among the top fifteen positions has won all but four races here. Dale Earnhardt earned two of those four victories and is the only driver to have won each of the Bristol Winston Cup races from a starting position with a backstretch pit stall.

Lights were added at Bristol in August 1978. The first Winston Cup race run at night was that year's Volunteer 500, in which Cale Yarborough and his Oldsmobile beat out Benny Parsons and Darrell Waltrip. That race was a huge success for Bristol Motor Speedway, and they have been running Bristol's second Winston Cup race of the season under the lights ever since.

Bruton Smith purchased Bristol Motor Speedway for $26 million in 1996 and has been adding seats and fan amenities ever since. Upgrades under Smith's guidance have exceeded $50 million and the track has become a fan favorite, often labeled "the toughest ticket in motorsports." The track is less than a tenth of a mile longer than Martinsville, while seating capacity is about double, but this is short track racing heaven, so if you get the opportunity to see a race here, jump on it. Camp, get a hotel, or do it as a day trip, but definitely go.

HISTORY

Built on the site of a former dairy farm, the track originally had seating for just 18,000 fans and was called Bristol International Speedway. The track was exactly half a mile long and had 22-degree banked turns. The straightaways were 60 feet wide, and turns broadened to 75 feet wide. At the time the speedway covered just 100 acres and offered parking for 12,000 cars. Bristol's 500-mile races took too long to finish, so the track was reconfigured to its current length and banking in 1969. With the completion of the Kulwicki Terrace and Tower in time for the 2000 season, total seating capacity has reached 147,000, and there are nearly 100 luxury skybox suites overlooking this incredible half-mile concrete oval.

Since July 30, 1961, NASCAR has been heading to the northeast Tennessee hills. Jack Smith owned and drove the car that won the first SouthEastern 500 at an average speed of 68.37 miles per hour. Forty-two cars started that race, but only nineteen finished. In fact, after 290 laps Jack Smith was relieved by Johnny Allen and the two drivers split the $3,225 purse. The inaugural race at Bristol featured a pair of father-and-son competitors: Lee and Richard Petty as well as Buck and Buddy Baker. Joe Weatherly broke the 70-mph barrier with his victory in that year's second cup race at Bristol, the Volunteer 500. In 1964, Fast Freddy Lorenzen took first place with a last-lap pass to sweep that season's Winston Cup Bristol races. It was the only lap Lorenzen led all day, but it was the one that counted most, as he became the first driver to win three straight races here. They were his only Bristol victories.

In 1968, David Pearson became the next driver to sweep on his way to five Winston Cup Bristol victories in five seasons. Between the two races in 1969, Bristol was reconfigured to its current size and banking. The new track agreed with Pearson, as he won the first race in the fall of 1969. In 1971, Pearson became the first driver to average more than 90 mph at Bristol, with a mark of 91.704 mph. On July 11 of that same season, Charlie Glotzbach, and his relief driver Raymond Hassler, topped that by averaging 101.074 mph in the Volunteer 500. That race is the only caution-flag-free race in the track's history, and Glotzbach's mark remains as the track's top average race speed. The NASCAR Winston Cup record for most caution flags during a race is twenty. Not coincidentally, it happened at Bristol, twice.

Bobby Allison won four times at Bristol. All four of his victories came within four years, concluding with a season sweep in 1972. Cale Yarborough took the pole position a remarkable nine times at Bristol. He won the SouthEastern 500 in 1973 from the pole position and led all 500 laps, the only time that has happened in NASCAR history. The race was postponed after 52 laps, because of rain, and finished two weeks later. That was the first of nine Winston Cup point wins for the Yarborough/Junior Johnson team at Bristol. Yarborough swept the races in 1974, 1976, 1977; and in the 1977 SouthEastern 500, he became the second and last driver at Bristol with an average race speed of better than 100 mph. Richard Petty broke up Yarborough's incredible run of season sweeps with his own sweep in 1975. Petty's only other victory at Bristol had come nearly a decade earlier in 1967.

Darrell Waltrip earned his first Bristol checkered flag in the 1978 SouthEastern 500. He went on to win a track record twelve times, including seven straight cup races from 1981 to 1984. Seven straight Winston Cup victories at one track is a NASCAR record that "D. W." shares with Richard Petty, who took seven consecutive races at Richmond in the early seventies.

Dale Earnhardt gained his first career Winston Cup victory at Bristol on April 1, 1979, in the SouthEastern 500. Earnhardt outraced Bobby Allison, Darrell Waltrip, Richard Petty, and Benny Parsons, none of whom were known to willingly let somebody finish ahead of them. In the mid- to late 1980s, Earnhardt dominated Bristol with sweeps in 1985 and 1987. Earnhardt earned five wins in four seasons on his way to nine Winston Cup wins at Bristol. The Intimidator placed in the top ten thirty times and had twenty top-five finishes over his career. The 1987 Busch 500, which Earnhardt won, was also significant because Janet Guthrie came in sixth, the best-ever Winston Cup finish for a female driver at a track still in use.

Rusty Wallace won his first Winston Cup checkered flag here and has nine career victories at Bristol, taking his first in the 1986 Valleydale 500. Wallace is second only to Yarborough with seven poles at Bristol and continued his success with a sweep of the 2000 season races. Four of Wallace's wins have come from the pole, a track record he shares with Yarborough. In 1990, in his sixty-fifth career start, Ernie Irvan earned his first pole position. That same season, in his seventy-ninth start, he won his first Winston Cup race, the Busch 500 at Bristol. The asphalt racing surface was ripped up and replaced with concrete in the summer of 1992. Darrell Waltrip won the ensuing race, his twelfth and final checkered flag at Bristol.

Elliot Sadler celebrates his first Winston Cup win. *(Photo by Keith Wilson)*

Jeff Gordon had a streak of his own with four consecutive wins in the Food City 500 from 1995 to 1998. Rusty Wallace broke that streak in the first Bristol race of 1999. Dale Earnhardt took the Goody's 500 that season with a dramatic last-lap pass. Earnhardt won the race despite qualifying twenty-sixth, breaking his own record of winning at Bristol from the twenty-fourth spot in 1994.

Steve Park set the track qualifying record of 126.370 mph (a blazing 15.184-second lap) on March 26, 2000. One year later, in his eightieth career start, Elliot Sadler won his first Winston Cup race in the Food City 500, gambling late in the race that he could finish without pitting for gas and tires with the leaders. Remarkably, it was the Wood Brothers' first-ever victory at Bristol despite ninety-six previous Winston Cup wins as a team. The Wood Brothers team had been going through a brutal victory drought, not winning a points race since March 1993 in Atlanta. The feat is that much more incredible when you consider that Sadler started the day from the thirty-eighth position, the worst starting position ever to win at Bristol.

Teams are well aware of the importance of winning at Bristol. In the first thirty-eight years of Bristol's existence, twenty-one season points champions have won at least one race at Bristol that same year. Bobby Labonte defeated the odds in 2000 by winning the season championship without a Bristol victory. Jeff Gordon, on his way to winning the 2001 points championship, led the most laps in the fall race, but Tony Stewart captured his first Bristol victory on the night of August 25 of that year. Stewart passed Gordon late in the race and held off Kevin Harvick for the win. The race featured a race-record sixteen caution flags, and nearly every car in the field was banged up.

GETTING TO THE TRACK

Bristol is surprisingly easy to get to, considering that 150,000 fans converge on this tiny Tennessee town via a handful of minor highways and nearly all of the parking is along Highway 11E or near the dragstrip off Highway 394. The only major highway that leads to Bristol is Interstate 81. Interstate 181 intersects I-81 southwest of the track.

Parking is available all along 11E and prices range from $5 to $10, depending on how far you are willing to walk uphill toward the track. Parking close to the track has its downside. Traffic on the way out is brutal, so if you don't mind walking half a mile or so, you can avoid much of the confusion and congestion right outside the track when the race ends. Route 75 and Interstates 421 and 19 are excellent back ways to avoid the majority of out-of-town traffic, but I-81 will be slow going for miles after a race.

WHAT TO SEE AND DO

The **Morgan McClure Motor Sports Museum** offers 15,000 square feet of race memorabilia at 26502 Newbanks Road in Abingdon, Virginia, just off I-81 at exit 22. You'll find race cars, including Sterling Marlin's Daytona 500 winner, three Daytona 500 trophies—Ernie Irvan's from 1991 and Sterling Marlin's back-to-back trophies from 1994 and 1995—a cutaway chassis, video footage of races, and pit equipment that you would not generally get to see without a pit pass. Admission is free. **Abingdon** is a quaint town nestled in the Blue Ridge Mountains. The Abingdon historic district is home to the **Barter Theatre, William King Regional Arts Center**, and the **Fields-Penn 1860 House**. Call (800) 435-3440 for more information.

Abingdon is also the finish point of the **Virginia Creeper**, a wonderful 34-mile downhill bike trail beside cool streams, through wide-open valleys, over old railroad bridges, and overlooking incredible farmland that is particularly scenic in the fall. Bring your own bike and arrange for transportation back up the hill or call **Blue Blaze Bike & Shuttle Service** at (800) 475-5095. The ride is not particularly rigorous but does require some work, especially where the trail flattens out below Damascus. A short and simple version of the Creeper runs for 18 miles from Whitetop, at 3,700 feet above sea level, to Damascus about 2,000 feet below.

Bristol sits on the Tennessee/Virginia border, and the state line runs through the center of town along State Street. Downtown Bristol's main attraction is the **Train-station Marketplace**, a collection of shops and eateries occupying the turn-of-the-century station house. Country music fans will want to stop by the **Country Music Mural and Monument** at 500 Gate City Highway. Bristol is said to be the site of the first commercially taped country music recordings in 1927, so this outdoor mural and monument pay tribute to country music pioneers the Carter Family, the Stonemans, and Jimmie Rodgers. Country fans may also want to visit the birthplace of Tennessee Ernie Ford in a quaint neighborhood on the outskirts of downtown Bristol.

Bristol Dragway hosts the NHRA Drag Race Nationals in late April and other drag races every week throughout the spring and summer. If you have never been to a drag race before, it is definitely worth experiencing. The sound and raw power produced by Top Fuel Dragsters and Funny Cars that reach more than 300 mph is incredible. For ticket information, call (423) 764-DRAG.

Bristol Caverns, said to be 200 million years old, are less than 6 miles southeast of town on U.S. 421. The largest caverns in the Smoky Mountains feature an asphalt trail winding through several levels, including a stretch alongside an underground river. The caverns are open 9 A.M. to 5 P.M. daily during the race season. Admission is just $8 for adults. Call (423) 878-2011 for additional information.

At 100 West Poplar Street, in Johnson City, Tennessee, may be the world's most enthusiastic Jeff Gordon fans. The house and yard of Walter and Dianne Witt comprise a virtual shrine to the boy wonder. A 1990 Cavalier painted to look like the #24 Dupont Chevrolet and signed by Gordon in his rookie year sits outside. A go-kart with flame paint job sits in front of a fountain, and a golf cart with a Monte Carlo shell and rainbow warrior paint job occupies the yard. Inside, the entry is tiled in black and white checkers and you'll find a museum-worthy collection of Gordon memorabilia. There's even a Pepsi room and a two-and-a-half-foot green macaw, named Gordon of course, who is trained to say "green, green, green" and "Go Gordon." The Witts encourage fans to stop by. If you can't get by their house, stop by their camper on race day. Just look for the tallest Gordon flag in the campgrounds. You can't miss it. The camper has a Jeff Gordon awning and the Monte Carlo golf cart will be out front.

Golfers will want to check out **Clear Creek Golf Club**, a picturesque public course at 732 Harleywood Road in Bristol, Virginia. Other courses open to the public include **Cedars Golf Course** and **Steele Creek**, located in Steele Creek Park, a public park with recreational fields, fishing, paddleboats, and a nature center. Serious fishermen should visit one of the area's outstanding lakes. Marinas located along South Holston Lake and Boone Lake allow boaters to drop in and check out Tennessee's incredible scenery by water. Particularly scenic and race-fan-friendly is **Observation Knob Park**, 8 miles southeast of Bristol via U.S. 421, with boat ramps, picnic areas, and campsites.

NIGHTLIFE IN THE TRI-CITIES AREA

There are a handful of bars and nightclubs in Bristol to choose from but none that I'd call a full-fledged sports bar or nightclub. Many of the bars are associated with restaurants or hotels. Race fans who camp at or near the track tend to create their own nightlife or head to Johnson City and Kingsport.

O'Malley's Lounge, at 1514 Weaver Pike, is beside the bowling alley and has a friendly staff, plenty of beers on tap, and a few TVs scattered about the place. **Mr. Gatti's** is a small, race-fan-friendly bar with a couple of televisions that's just up the street from the track.

Nashville Sound, at 1121 North Roan Street in Johnson City, is a popular country music club that hosts live rock and country entertainers on the weekends. Expect a good-sized crowd and cover charge on race weekends. **Poor Richard's** has two locations in Johnson City, one downtown and the other on Walnut Street near the East Tennessee State campus. Either place offers good food and a fun environment. **The Planet** is another worthwhile club on Walnut Street.

WHERE TO EAT

BRISTOL

Applebee's   425 Volunteer Parkway (423) 968-1855   I'm reluctant to include a chain restaurant in this listing, but there are only a few places to choose from near the track. This one is right on 11E, a few miles northeast of the track. Stop on the way out, enjoy a meal, and let the traffic pass you by.

Athens Steak House   105 Goodson Street (540) 466-8271   A Bristol institution serving Greek and American fare in a warm, friendly atmosphere. Steaks are paramount here and the desserts are legendary. Save some room for the apple pie.

Bonfire   1020 Volunteer Parkway (423) 968-5991   This place has been around forever, serving good country cooking in a laid-back setting minutes from the track.

Bonnie's Family Restaurant   3002 Lee Highway (540) 669-3361   A small, family-style restaurant that serves home-cooked breakfast and lunch. Located just over the Virginia border beside the Wal-Mart; take exit 5 off I-81.

Brooklyn Grill   2125 Euclid Avenue (540) 669-1900   A casual place specializing in steak, seafood, prime rib, and pasta. Open for lunch Monday through Friday and dinner Monday through Saturday. They pack 'em in for race week, but they do accept reservations.

Chop's   Within the Holiday Inn at 3005 Linden Drive (540) 466-4100   As hotel restaurants go, this is a worthwhile choice. They offer steaks, seafood, chicken, and fajitas, but the filet with mushrooms and onions is their specialty.

Simply Delicious Marketplace Deli   2600 Volunteer Parkway (423) 764-3354   This modest deli offers specialty sandwiches galore just a half mile north of the track. In addition to deli choices, they offer barbecue sandwiches, salads, and appetizers to eat in or to go.

The Vinyard   603 Gate City Highway (540) 466-4244   Yes, that's how they spell it. This casual bistro specializing in southern Italian fare made from scratch is just over the Virginia border. Reservations are suggested for race weekends.

JOHNSON CITY

Galloway's   807 North Roan Street, near exit 35 off I-181. (423) 926-1166   Open for lunch and dinner, Galloway's occupies a 1920s-era home with a nice open, outdoor patio. Moderately priced fare ranges from simple sandwiches to hearty dinner entrees.

Grady's   North Roan Street across from the Mall at Johnson City. (423) 282-2722   About thirty minutes from the track, this American grill specializes in steaks, ribs, pasta, and seafood in a casual atmosphere and offers a full bar.

Makato's   3021 East Oakland Avenue (423) 282-4441   A popular Japanese steakhouse that prepares your meal tableside. Teriyaki steak, sesame chicken, and tuna grill are among the house specialties.

Peerless   2531 North Roan Street just off I-181; take exit 35. (423) 282-2351   This cozy place has been around for decades. The staff is friendly and the food— pasta, steaks, and seafood—is worth the trip. This is also a popular place with drivers and their crews on the nights leading up to race day.

The House of Ribs   3100 North Roan Street (423) 282-8077   A casual café with a surprisingly chic decor, located near the park and lakes. They offer much more than ribs, but if you like your baby backs to fall off the bone, this is the place for you. Reservations are suggested.

The Ridgewood   900 Old Elizabeth Highway, Bluff City (423) 538-7543   Another popular place with teams and officials, this humble barbecue place is worth going out of your way for.

LOCAL MEDIA

The two newspapers are the *Bristol Herald Courier* and the *Johnson City Press*. Radio broadcasts of the races can be heard on Motor Racing Network (MRN)— WFHG 980 AM.

WHERE TO STAY

HOTELS

The only downside to a race at Bristol is that there are very few hotels in the immediate vicinity and those within a short drive of the track are often booked for years in advance. Cancellations do occasionally occur, but it may be wise to call the hotels directly rather than use their toll-free numbers. Johnson City, Kingsport, Abingdon, Virginia, Boone, North Carolina, and Asheville, North Carolina, are not too far away. Bristol Motor Speedway maintains a hotel hotline at (423) 764-2730 or you can call **Race Lodging LLC** (423) 764-5454.

Best Western   111 Holiday Drive (423) 968-1101 or (800) WESTERN   Near the Medical Center, just 12 miles from the track. One of the larger hotels in the area, but they still sell out a year in advance. The Bristol Bar and Grill, on premises, packs with race fans during race week.

Comfort Suites   3118 Brownsmill Road, Johnson City, TN (423) 610-0010 or (800) 517-4000   Just 10 miles from the track. They offer complimentary continental breakfast, and there's also a Cracker Barrel and Outback Steakhouse nearby.

Days Inn   536 Volunteer Parkway (423) 968-2171 or (800) DAYS-INN   Well-kept accommodations, just 7 miles from the track. This affordable hotel is just 5 miles from the caverns and 1 mile from a number of worthwhile restaurants. Amenities include continental breakfast and an outdoor pool.

Regency Inn   975 Volunteer Parkway (423) 968-9474   A newly refurbished hotel just 3 miles from the track. Located across the street from the Bonfire restaurant.

Howard Johnson   2406 North Roan Street (423) 282-2161   Fifteen miles from the speedway. The Rocky River Grill and outdoor pool are on the property.

Holiday Inn & Suites   3005 Linden Drive, Bristol, VA (540) 466-4100 or (888) 466-4141   Despite being in Virginia, this ten-story hotel is just 17 miles from the track. They offer a pool, hot tub, and on-property restaurant but book up for race week very quickly. This is a popular place with teams and officials.

Holiday Inn   101 West Springbrook Drive, Johnson City, TN (423) 282-4611 or (800) HOLIDAY   About 17 miles from the track. Outdoor heated pool, lounge, and restaurant on site.

Holiday Inn Express   4234 Fort Henry Drive, Kingston, TN (423) 247-7853 or (800) HOLIDAY   Overlooking the Holsten River, just 16 miles from the track. There are a handful of restaurants nearby, and the hotel offers a complimentary continental breakfast.

Ramada Inn 2122 Euclid Avenue, Bristol, VA (540) 669-7171 or (800) 2RAMADA
Six miles from the track. They offer a complimentary breakfast, and the inn is
also within walking distance of several worthwhile eateries.

CAMPSITES

In the event that area hotels are completely booked, you may want to consider
camping near the track. **Thunder Valley Campground** is located at 2623 Volunteer Parkway, on the same side of the street, just half a mile from the Speedway.
Built by Randy Moore, son of Carl Moore, the track's original owner, it offers level
campsites, hookups for electric and water, shower facilities, twenty-four-hour security, and a shuttle bus to the track. Spaces range from $150 to $400 a week during
race weeks. Call (423) 652-CAMP for reservations. For more primitive campsites on
race weekends, make plans to stay at **All American Campground**, located on the
back side of the Speedway. For more information, call (423) 764-9454. Call as early
as possible, as both campsites get packed. **Green Spring Sport Center**, in Abingdon, offers race rentals of campers set up on site. Call (540) 623-5240 for details.

Good to Know
- To charge tickets, call (423) 764-6555; for additional race information, call
  (423) 764-1161.
- Mail orders can be sent to P.O. Box 3966, Bristol, TN 37625.
- The Bristol Convention & Visitors Bureau can be reached at (423) 989-4850.
  The events line is (540) 645-4238.
- A worthwhile city Web site is www.bristolchamber.org.
- ➤ The official racetrack Web site is www.bristolmotorspeedway.com.

NEARBY WINSTON CUP RACE CITIES

Martinsville: 144 miles (three hours)
Lowe's/Charlotte Motor Speedway: 177 miles (three hours, thirty minutes)
Atlanta: 250 miles (four hours, twenty minutes)
Rockingham: 250 miles (five hours)

IN THE VICINITY

Asheville, North Carolina, is an absolute jewel of a town, just two hours from Bristol. **The Biltmore House**, an astounding 250-room mansion built by the Vanderbilt
family in 1889, is surrounded by 8,000 acres of gardens and rolling hillside. The

house has thirty-four master bedrooms yet was never inhabited by more than three members of the Vanderbilt family. Worth visiting at any time of year; admission is $32.

The **Grove Park Inn** is a truly grand hotel that's a favorite mountain getaway for celebrities, politicians—including eight presidents—writers, and the well-to-do. Built in 1913 from boulders and timbers hauled up the mountain by wagon train, this magnificent inn overlooks a spectacular valley and boasts a world-class golf course, an unbeatable Sunday brunch, and a brand-new health and fitness spa. Even if you decide not to stay at the hotel, stop by for a meal and enjoy a drink in front of the giant fireplace or on the deck overlooking the valley below. High above the city of Asheville, the Grove Park has tremendous restaurants, galleries, and activities, just a short drive from the cafés, clubs, and shops of downtown.

Nightlife in downtown Asheville is surprisingly diverse, and the selection of worthwhile restaurants is equally vast. **Be Here Now** is a superb live music club. This mid-sized venue has terrific sight lines, good acoustics, and a regional- or national-caliber headline act nearly every weekend. Be sure to check their schedule if you find yourself in the area. **Magnolia's Raw Bar & Grille** has it all: wonderful lunch and dinner options, a great downtown location, and live entertainment later at night. **The Windmill** is off the beaten path, tucked away downstairs in the nondescript Innsbruck shopping center on Tunnel Road, but offers outstanding international fare ranging from German to Italian to Indian. It's all good, but their steaks are legendary.

To the west, **Knoxville** is the first good-sized Tennessee town a short drive from Bristol. **Pigeon Forge** and **Dollywood** are a little more, 135 miles southwest of Bristol. **Gatlinburg**, on the edge of **Great Smoky Mountains National Park**, is just 6 miles south of Pigeon Forge. If you cannot find a hotel room closer to Bristol, day trips from any of these tourist towns would be conceivable.

The Smoky Mountains **NASCAR Café**, at Governor's Crossing between Pigeon Forge and Sevierville, has a tremendous collection of Bristol Motor Speedway memorabilia, including a gallery of photographs, trophies, helmets, and uniforms. Bobby Labonte's Interstate Batteries Pontiac sits outside the front entrance. Full-scale model cars—including the rides of Dale Earnhardt, Jeff Gordon, Rusty Wallace, Tony Stewart, Terry Labonte, Mark Martin, Dale Jarrett, and Dale Earnhardt Jr.—are displayed inside. If you'd rather strap yourself into a go-kart, Richard Childress's **Race World** in Pigeon Forge is among a handful of go-kart facilities in the area. Call (865) 429-2030 for hours of operation.

A Dozen Favorite Tracks to Watch a Race

12 Atlanta—almost always a close finish.

11 ChicagoLand—this place could move way up on the list as it develops.

10 Rockingham—a classic track with lots of worthwhile seats.

9 Sears Point—as good as a road course gets. And it keeps getting better.

8 Texas—bigger can be better. This place has it all.

7 Darlington—intimacy and tradition rule at this vintage speedway.

6 Daytona—another track with tons of tradition and nostalgia.

5 Charlotte—nobody puts on a better show than Humpy and Bruton.

4 Dover—this track is tough on cars, tires and drivers, but the action is tops.

3 Martinsville—unlike any other track on the circuit. I'll be going here for years to come.

2 Richmond—a great track in a great town. Nothing beats a night race.

1 Bristol—the Wrigley Field of racing. If you can't enjoy a race here, stay home.

■ *DOVER DOWNS INTERNATIONAL SPEEDWAY* ■

Dover, Delaware

"This place is the Monster Mile—it chews up cars, it spits out trucks, whatever it is, this is the toughest place. It was almost intimidating looking at it the first time."

—KURT BUSCH

Nobody appreciates their hometown track more than the good folks of Delaware, and with good reason. Like other Winston Cup tracks, Dover Downs contributes handsomely to the local economy, but races here also take on a festival atmosphere that I've seen nowhere else. For my first race at Dover, I spent the majority of my time in the infield and watched as fans enjoyed the day with their friends and family. Some watched the race atop makeshift platforms, others played catch and soccer while listening to the race on headphones or watching one of the giant-screen TVs, and still others partied with groups that were seemingly oblivious of the race that was happening all around them.

Fans in the stands are treated to a track that offers the best of both worlds. Grandstands are nicely elevated yet close to the track. The track is long enough to allow drivers to exceed 155 mph in qualifying but intimate enough that during a race the leaders zoom by your seat about every twenty-five seconds. This intimacy also allows fans in the upper rows to easily follow the action around the entire track. Since 1997, races here have been 400-milers. Because of the relatively high speeds and mid-sized track, races here can be over almost before you know it.

The "Monster Mile" is a 1-mile concrete speedway that can be described as a true oval. All four turns are banked at 24 degrees, while the identical straightaways are sloped at 9 degrees and equidistant at 1,076 feet long. Except for the grandstands, the entire place looks symmetrical. When Atlanta Motor Speedway was reconfigured in 1997, Dover Downs assumed the title of longest and fastest perfect oval among

View from the infield of pit road and turn four. *(Photo by Karen Ahuja)*

Winston Cup tracks. The concrete surface, installed in 1995, is tough on tires and drivers, so pit crews are careful to monitor the right front tires in particular.

Pay attention early in the race, as the track starts off loose for the first fifteen or twenty laps until rubber builds up on the track and good grip is established. Drivers know it's critical to qualify well at Dover, not only to help avoid early wrecks, but also because only a dozen races have been won from outside the top ten starting positions. Qualifying well also enables teams to choose a better pit stall along one of the narrowest pit roads on the circuit.

The Monster Mile, with its high banks and short, narrow straights, is among the most treacherous in all of Winston Cup racing. Turn two is considered the trickiest part of the track and can be the site of a lot of mayhem. The track is fairly tight, 48 feet wide in the straights and 58 feet across through the turns, so there's not much room for error. Cars that get too low in the turns' asphalt safety aprons often shoot back up into traffic. Under normal conditions, the speedway offers about a groove and a half of racing room until the track tightens up around 200 laps into the race.

Dover Downs has been expanding steadily over the years. In 2001, 7,000 seats were added, on top of the 15,000 seats added in 2000, and seating capacity is currently about 140,000. Plans for expansion to 170,000 seats are in the works and may be completed as soon as 2004. Seating sections on the frontstretch start at the start/finish line and increase in number toward turn four, through turn three and the backstretch, all the way around the second and first turns, and back to the start/finish line. So don't despair if you find yourself with tickets in section 251. These are among the best at the track.

Seats in the Richard Petty grandstand are generally thought to be the most desirable—the east, northeast, and Allison grandstands are also very good—but there really are very few seats along the frontstretch that are not worthwhile. Another good place to sit is the northeast grandstand overlooking the exit of pit road and the entrance to the first turn. Grandstands in turns three and four are among the tallest at the track, but lower-level seats here are not as elevated as those in turns one and two, which start about 20 feet up from the track.

A pedestrian bridge, added in 1995 before the spring race, is situated over the track where turn two exits into the backstretch. This walkover bridge allows credentialed personnel access to the infield area, garages, and pits. The bridge was constructed and positioned so that it does not block the view of the track from much of the grandstands. It does, however, interfere with the view of the backstretch for some fans seated in the middle rows of sections 190 through 200 of the north grandstand. Seats in the higher rows are largely unaffected. It also blocks turn two for some fans in the reserved bleacher seats. Bear in mind, we are talking about a split-second of obstruction in either case.

Giant-screen TVs face the frontstretch as well as both sets of turns. Fans in the infield may want to consider bringing a collapsible chair and joining the crowds on the grassy area between the Busch Garages and turn four. This is a terrific spot to settle in and watch the cars negotiate their way onto the frontstretch. Fans with pit passes can sit along a grass-covered hill overlooking the pits. These spots fill up quickly, so show up well in advance of the race if you want to occupy some real estate in this area.

The track is more than thirty years old, but it has been expanded consistently over the years, so facilities are not as dated as you might expect. A few years ago, slot machine gambling was legalized in Delaware and a slots casino was added to the complex. The slots building is also home to the Garden Café Restaurant and the Gazebo Bar. You must be twenty-one years old to partake of these restaurants. Air-conditioned, indoor grandstands are adjacent to the casino, overlooking the backstretch. The Winner's Circle Buffet is served on the third floor of the air-conditioned grandstand at lunch and dinner during race week. A hotel is being built along the backstretch near turn three and should be completed before the 2002 spring race. Historically, Dover hosts the first and final Winston Cup season points races in the Northeast.

HISTORY

Dover Downs opened on July 6, 1969, as a harness-racing facility surrounded by a 1-mile speedway. Richard Petty won the 300-mile event by six laps, averaging 115.772 mph, in the only season he drove a Ford. Petty repeated the feat the following year, beating out Bobby Allison, this time driving a Plymouth. In 1971, Dover Downs began hosting two points races per year. Allison upped the ante in the track's first 500-mile race, setting a new track record of 123.254 mph. Allison was the only driver to finish on the lead lap in a caution-free race. Petty and Allison continued their dominance at Dover, winning the first five races here, until David Pearson swept the next three races in his Wood Brothers Mercury. Pearson became the first driver to win at Dover from the pole in 1973. In fact, he did it at both Dover races that season, and once again in 1975. Petty, Allison, and Pearson top the all-time win list at Dover. Petty and Allison had seven wins each, while Pearson had five.

Cale Yarborough won back-to-back races at Dover in 1976 and 1977. Yarborough won from the pole in the 1976 Delaware 500 and eclipsed Petty's track record for fastest average speed in the 1977 Mason-Dixon 500. In 1981, rookie driver Jody Ridley beat out Bobby Allison in the Mason-Dixon 500 for his first and only career win. Ridley was five laps down at one point, but engine trouble eliminated leaders David Pearson, Neil Bonnett, and Cale Yarborough at various stages late in the race and Ridley pulled off the miracle win. Ridley started eleventh and became the first driver to win at Dover from a starting position outside the top ten.

The early eighties saw the return of the old guard to Dover Downs' victory lane as Allison and Petty won four out of five races from 1982 to 1984. Allison won the spring race in 1982 and swept the Dover races in 1983. Richard Petty won his seventh and final Dover race in the 1984 Budweiser 500. Petty, the old master, edged out up-and-coming superstar Tim Richmond for his 199th and penultimate career victory. Harry Gant won the second Dover race of the 1984 season and repeated with wins in 1985, 1991, and 1992. Gant is tied for third with Bill Elliott, Ricky Rudd, and Jeff Gordon on the Dover career win list. Elliott won at Dover in 1985, swept the 1988 races, and won again in 1990. His victory in 1990 came from the pole. Ricky Rudd won back-to-back Delaware 500s in 1986 and 1987 and revisited the winner's circle at Dover in 1992 and 1997.

Dale Earnhardt finally took the checkered flag at Dover in 1989. He liked it so much, he did it twice that season. In the 1991 Peak 500, Gant pulled off his third consecutive win of the season as only sixteen cars were running at the end of the day. Earnhardt finished fifteenth, an uncharacteristic 53 laps behind. Rusty Wallace became the second driver in Dover Downs' history to win three consecutive races by winning the Splitfire 500 in 1993 and sweeping the 1994 races. Not to be outdone, Jeff Gordon won three straight races by taking the 1995 MBNA 500 and sweeping the 1996 races. Gordon led 400 of 500 laps in the 1995 victory.

In 1997, races at Dover were shortened to 400 laps and, of Ricky Rudd's four Dover wins, only the 1997 victory came in the spring race. Rudd beat Mark Martin, Jeff Burton, and Jeremy Mayfield as Ford swept the top four spots. That fall, Mark Martin improved upon his good showing earlier in the season and set the track record in winning the MBNA 400 with an average speed of 132.719 mph. The race lasted just three hours and fifty seconds. Martin won the MBNA 400 again in 1998 and 1999.

Matt Kenseth got his first career start at Dover on September 20, 1998, subbing for Bill Elliott. Kenseth finished sixth and began to prove he's one to watch at the Monster Mile. He returned as a regular for Roush Racing and finished fourth in 1999. Things got even better for Kenseth as he managed a second-place finish behind Tony Stewart in 2000. Stewart won again at Dover that season, beating out Johnny Benson and Ricky Rudd this time. Jeff Gordon prevented Stewart from joining Bobby Allison, Rusty Wallace, and himself as the track's only back-to-back-to-back winners, as Gordon won the 2001 spring race at Dover. Gordon led a remarkable 381 of 400 laps for his fourth career win at Dover. In the fall race, Dale Earnhardt Jr., and his co-pilot Wilson, a volleyball similar to the one that kept Tom Hanks company in the movie *Castaway*, took the checkered flag for Junior's first win at Dover. The race also featured a skirmish between Ricky Rudd and Rusty Wallace's lapped car. Rudd recovered to finish third but the animosity between him and Wallace continued throughout the season.

GETTING TO THE TRACK

Sandwiched between U.S. 13 and State Route 1, traffic can be brutal on race day. Routes to the track are not plentiful, so fans tend to get to Dover as early as Wednesday or Thursday and leave on the Monday after the race whenever possible. Traffic does not really bog down before the race until you get within a few miles of the track. In fact, I found the drive there to be fairly easy.

Leaving, on the other hand, can be trying, especially if you are heading north on U.S. 13 or State Route 1. Two alternate routes are available for travelers heading north. Route 9 is well east of the track and winds through some incredible countryside. It's a two-lane road, but it moves and eventually links with I-95 near Wilmington. I also noticed many of the team transporters heading west on Route 42, presumably taking 300 to Interstate 301 across the Chesapeake Bay Bridge or 15 North, which intersects with 896 and eventually with I-95 near Newark, Delaware.

Parking at the track is free for preliminary races but costs $5–10 for Winston Cup races. Infield parking is $25 per car and $30 for a pickup truck or van. There is no RV parking in the infield at Dover. Several businesses along U.S. 13 also offer parking for $10–20 on race day. Spots at some of these businesses may be easier to exit after the race.

A shuttle bus runs from Christiana Mall near Route 1 in Wilmington. Call (302) 652-DART for price and schedule of this and other DART shuttles. Another shuttle is offered from Delaware Technical Community College. For $20 you can park here and everyone in your vehicle is provided with round-trip transportation to Dover Downs. Call (302) 857-1700 for schedule information.

RV lots at Dover Downs are south and east of the track off Leipsic Road. The spots cost just $30 and the best spots, especially those in lots 5 and 6, are taken quickly. Lot 2 offers the only reserved RV parking. Call (302) 734-7223 for details.

If you live north of the track, you can also get to Dover Downs via Amtrak. Special **Monster Mile Express** trains serve New York's Penn Station, Newark, Trenton, Philadelphia, Washington, D.C., Baltimore, and Wilmington, Delaware, on the morning of the race. Fans arrive in Dover around 10 A.M. and take a shuttle bus to the track. Once the race is done, the shuttle returns to the train station and you'll be back home that night. Call (877) 835-8725 for details.

WHAT TO SEE AND DO

The **Dover Downs Slots**, a casino that shares the west parking lot with the track, offers 2,000 video slot machines to choose from. The casino often presents nationally known entertainers in its performance hall. They also have a handful of restaurants to choose from, smoking and nonsmoking gambling areas, and a gift shop.

The **Sewell Biggs Museum of Art** is a former courthouse at 406 Federal Street. In addition to a collection of paintings, drawings, and sculpture spanning 200 years, the museum boasts a collection of fine silver, clocks, and furniture from the Colonial period. The museum is open Wednesday through Sunday and admission is free. Dover has a huge military presence and is home to the **Air Mobility Command Museum**. The museum is home to a sizable collection of vintage aircraft as well as World War II artifacts. Located at the Dover Air Force Base, the museum is open daily and admission is free.

For something completely different, check out the **Kent County Theatre Guild**, an acting troupe that performs plays and skit comedy on Friday and Saturday evenings. The intimate **Patchwork Playhouse**, at 140 East Roosevelt Avenue, offers a cabaret atmosphere with snacks and drinks, including wine, beer, and cocktails, available before the show. Admission is $12.50 per person. Call (302) 674-3568 for details on upcoming shows.

One of the fastest-growing participant sports in the country is paintball, a battle-simulation game based on capture-the-flag that's played with airguns that shoot paintballs. **Delaware Paintball** is located north of the track, along Route 13, in Smyrna. They offer gun rentals, ammo sales, a regulation speedball course, and wooded courses if you book a group in advance. For about $60–75 you can play four to six hours, if you don't go through your ammo too quickly. Call (302) 659-5140 for details.

About 7 miles south of Dover, you'll discover one of the nation's few remaining drive-in theaters. The **Diamond State Drive-In Theatre**, on Route 13 South in Felton, shows first-run movies at dusk every weekend.

NIGHTLIFE IN DOVER

This is a college town, so there are a few places to go out at night. Quite a few places are near the track, while others are in downtown Dover.

Froggy's Bar & Grille is a good-sized place that features live rock bands and DJ music, just five minutes south of the track on Route 113. They present a full casual menu of appetizers, burgers, sandwiches, and ribs and have food and drink specials nightly. For race week they offer a shuttle bus on Friday and Saturday nights to and from the track's RV camping area. **Rack's Bar & Billiards** is a short walk from the track and offers plenty of pool tables and video games.

Spanky's is an intimate tavern about a mile and a half from the track in downtown Dover at 132 West Loockerman Street. Spanky's is a typical college hangout/sports bar with a foosball table, darts, pinball games, and a solid jukebox. **W. T. Smithers**, also in downtown Dover at 140 South State Street, is a comfortable club with decent bar food and folk, rock, and blues bands on the weekends. There's also pool, darts, foosball, and an occasional cover charge, but why not support the live music scene and hang with the locals? For sports fans who enjoy wings, cheese steak hoagies, ribs, and pasta, check out **J. W.'s Restaurant & Sports Lounge**. This place has thirty-four TVs, plenty of pool tables, fifteen beers on tap, a decent pub menu, and live music on the weekends. Located at 1035 Walker Road, in the Hamlet Shopping Center, they are open daily until one in the morning.

Pizzeria Uno–Chicago Bar & Grill, on Route 13 next to the Dover Mall, is probably more restaurant than bar, but they offer some worthwhile happy hour specials from 4 to 7 P.M. and after 9 P.M. seven days a week. They also have a few televisions scattered around the bar to watch the race highlights.

WHERE TO EAT

If you don't mind driving a few miles away from the track for some killer Italian food in a casual atmosphere, head to **Franco's**. The servings are huge, the Peroni beers are reasonable, and the service is friendly. A little closer to the track, at 2463 South State Street, **Cool Springs Fish Bar and Restaurant** is a more upscale place that's also off the beaten path but worth the drive. Their specialties include fresh seafood, steaks, and chicken.

The **Hollywood Diner** is an authentic, old-style diner that has been around for ages. This may very well be the best place in town for late-night grub after the bars close. The wait staff is friendly and patient, while their affordable breakfast menu is everything you'd expect.

The **Iron Gate Inn** is an upscale establishment on Route 113, south of the track, that specializes in prime rib served in a casual, inviting atmosphere. The **Blue Coat Inn** is a casual place on the lake at 800 North State Street. The seafood, steaks, and veal are all popular choices at this friendly American bistro. Live acoustic music is presented on the weekends. The **Lobby House** is another place on the water at 9 East Loockerman Street. This laid-back lunch and dinner establishment has patio seating, a happy hour barbecue, and live entertainment, as well as terrific steaks and seafood. Within a short walk of the track, at the corner of Loockerman and Route 13, you'll find **Where Pigs Fly**, a casual, friendly BBQ joint.

While you are so close to the Atlantic Ocean, you may feel the need for some fresh seafood. **Pleasanton's Seafood** offers inexpensive take-out seafood, cheese steak hoagies, burgers, crab cakes, and fried seafood platters. They are open only Thursday through Sunday for lunch and early dinners. **Sambo's**, on Front Street in Leipsic, has been serving fresh seafood since 1953. The restaurant is open for lunch and dinner and specializes in steamed crab, shrimp, clams, and oysters. The bar serves up live music and affordable beers until 11 P.M. every night except Sunday. On nights leading up to race day, this may be the single best place on the Winston Cup circuit to see drivers cutting up with their crews. **Shucker's Pier 13** is another worthy seafood eatery at 889 North DuPont Highway.

Roma Italian Restaurant is a dark, classic place just up the street from Dover Downs on Route 113 that's been serving traditional Italian fare for ages. **Paradiso's** on Route 10, south of the track, has more of a fine-dining atmosphere. The Italian entrees are absolutely top-notch, but they are legendary for their homemade Caesar salad dressing.

There are also a number of franchise restaurants, such as **Olive Garden, Lone Star, Red Lobster, TGI Friday's, Hibachi Japanese, and Applebee's**, a short drive from the track.

LOCAL MEDIA

The local newspaper is the *Dover Post*. The *Delaware State News* is somewhat less helpful regarding Dover events but does offer a sports section with NASCAR news. The race is broadcast on MRN Radio via 92.9 FM WDSD.

WHERE TO STAY

HOTELS

All the hotels near the track are along DuPont Highway, so there is no significant advantage to staying at one versus another. Finding one with availability is the trick. Hotels in Dover, even the less desirable ones, are notorious for jacking up their rates for race week and requiring minimum stays of three days or more. Consider places in Wilmington or Rehoboth Beach, to the north and south, respectively. Staying to the south will make your commute more tolerable on race day. For a more complete list of area hotels, call Kent County Tourism at (302) 734-1736.

Sheraton Dover   1570 North DuPont Highway (302) 678-8500   Just five minutes north of the track, this is among the nicest and largest hotels in the area surrounding the track. Tango's restaurant and a pair of lounges are on site.

Hampton Inn   1568 North DuPont Highway (302) 736-3500   Nicely appointed rooms just minutes from the track. This place books quickly, so call well in advance of the race. No restaurant or lounge on premises, but the Sheraton is next door and several places are within walking distance.

Comfort Suites   1654 North DuPont Highway (302) 736-1204   Reasonably priced hotel just 1 mile north of the track. This three-story hotel offers clean, comfortable rooms and free continental breakfast but sells out year after year for race weekend, so call early.

Holiday Inn Express   1780 North DuPont Highway (302) 678-0600   One of the newest hotels to open near the track. About a mile and a half north of the track, this place offers an outdoor pool, game room, fitness center, and convenient in-room microwaves and refrigerators.

Ramada Inn   348 North DuPont Highway (302) 734-5701   Overlooking Silver Lake, this hotel is one of the largest in the area. Nevertheless, they fill up quickly during race week.

Howard Johnson   561 North DuPont Highway (302) 678-8900   A moderately priced place, just two and a half blocks from the track, with an outdoor pool, free breakfast, and a gym on site.

Days Inn   272 North DuPont Highway (302) 674-8002   Perhaps the most inexpensive accommodations within walking distance of the track, this modest motel has been a favorite with Dover race fans for ages.

Comfort Inn   222 South DuPont Highway (302) 674-3300 or (800) 228-5150   A recently renovated hotel, three and a half miles from Dover Downs, with an outdoor pool, free continental breakfast, and local calls.

CAMPSITES

Camping at Dover Downs is strictly first come, first served. There is no tent camping at the track, and RVs must be self-contained units. The RV camping lot opens ten days before the race weekend, and the best spots fill up quickly. RV spots cost $30 per day.

Good to Know

- To charge tickets or for additional race information, call (800) 441-7223 or (302) 734-7223.
- Mail orders can be sent to Dover Downs, P.O. Box 843, Dover, DE 19903.
- Call the Central Delaware Chamber of Commerce at (302) 734-7514. The Delaware Visitor Center can be reached at (302) 739-4266.
- A worthwhile city Web site is www.cdcc.net.
- ➤ The official racetrack Web site is www.doverdowns.com.

NEARBY WINSTON CUP RACE CITIES

Pocono: 165 miles (three hours)
Richmond: 255 miles (four hours, thirty minutes)
Watkins Glen: 320 miles (five hours, thirty minutes)
Martinsville: 470 miles (eight hours)

IN THE VICINITY

Rehoboth Beach is less than 50 miles south of Dover. Not only will you find white sandy beaches, a beautiful boardwalk, and several restaurants to choose from, but it's also possible to camp at the scenic **Delaware Seashore State Park**. Rehoboth offers nature cruises, dolphin- and whale-watching tours, waterslides, golf, kayaking, museums, and even parasailing to choose from. **Midway Speedway** on Route 1 is an outdoor go-kart track that's a hit with race fans.

When you need to refuel at dinnertime, stop by the **Blue Moon Restaurant**, located in a handsome beach house just two blocks from the ocean. The casual atmosphere belies the quality fare and solid service offered nightly. **Jake's Seafood House**, on First Street between Baltimore and Maryland Avenues, is a casual place with outstanding Baltimore-style crab cakes, fresh shrimp, lobster, and seafood dishes. If you find yourself on Dewey Beach, just south of Rehoboth, be sure to stop by the **Northbeach Restaurant and Bayside Bar** at 125 McKinley Street.

The **Boardwalk Plaza Hotel** is an elegant Victorian-style inn overlooking the beach and ocean. Area hotels pack quickly in the summer months, especially for race weeks. Other suitable places to overnight include the **Admiral Motel**, **Brighton Suites Hotel**, the **Oceanus Hotel**, and the **Sea Witch Bed & Breakfast**.

The **Rehoboth Beach Chamber of Commerce and Visitor Center** can be reached at (800) 441-1329 or via their Web site, www.beach-fun.com.

▪ *MARTINSVILLE SPEEDWAY* ▪

Martinsville, Virginia

"I don't think it should be a cookie-cutter series, I think there should be a wide variety, and Martinsville is at the extreme. A track like this is sort of the foundation and grass roots of our sport."

—JOHN ANDRETTI

Unlike any other track on the circuit, Martinsville is shaped like a paper clip with twin 800-foot, unbanked straightaways and tight 12-degree banked turns. The track in Loudon, New Hampshire, has some similar characteristics but is not nearly as intimate or beloved by race fans and drivers. The .526-mile Martinsville oval is the shortest on the NASCAR Winston Cup circuit and has often been described as a pair of drag strips with tight turns at each end. Martinsville is tough on brakes and drivers, as caution flags can come out fifteen times a day despite race speeds that often average 75 to 85 mph. More often than not, yellow flags seem to wave at Martinsville because a driver has spun out exiting turn two or four, rather than violently run his car into the wall or a competitor.

In addition to being the shortest and slowest NASCAR Winston Cup track, Martinsville is also the oldest, and the only track still on the circuit that hosted a race for the 1949 inaugural season, now that North Wilkesboro Speedway no longer has a points race. The pits at Martinsville are unusual because the forty-three pit stalls begin in turn three and wrap all the way around through the frontstretch to turn two. Drivers enter pit row at the end of the backstretch and exit the pits at the start of the backstretch. The pole sitter earns the first pit stall, near the beginning of the backstretch, while the second qualifier will often opt for pit number 11, along the frontstretch, because it offers the slight advantage of a car length's space between that stall and the pit directly in front of it.

The track is 55 feet wide all the way around, allowing some room to pass, but drivers rarely venture away from the groove that runs along the outside wall in the straightaways and low on the apron in the turns. While it seems that every car on the track has significant sheet metal damage after just a few laps, don't expect to see a lot of "three-wide" racing here until the final laps. Even then, drivers can be reluctant to open the way for a long line of cars behind them to draft past. Track position and pit strategy are often the keys to winning here, as infrequent lead changes are common during 263-mile/500-lap Winston Cup races. Through the 2001 season, more than half of all Cup races at Martinsville were won by a car starting within the top four positions, and one-third of the first forty-five Cup races at this classic Virginia track were won from the pole position.

The first thing that strikes you as you enter the stands is how long and narrow the track seems. There are only 71,000 seats at Martinsville Speedway, and from either end you can see almost the entire track, so you see every bit of action whether it happens in the turns nearest you or clear down at the opposite end. It also seems odd that the straightaways have absolutely no bank, as opposed to the 16-degree straightaways at Bristol, Winston Cup's other "half-mile" track. The

Single file through turn one as seen from the Old Dominion Grandstands.
(Photo by Author)

stands are not as vertical as those at Bristol, nor do they completely surround the track, so the noise does not seem nearly as deafening as at Bristol.

Seats at Martinsville vary greatly. Prices range from $40 for lower rows of the backstretch to $70 for seats in the Old Dominion Tower in turns one and two. Because of the unique pit row at Martinsville, pit action can be seen from nearly any seat that isn't in the middle of the backstretch. Frontstretch grandstand seats cost $55 for lower rows, $60 up to row 44, and $65 for tower seats rows 45 and higher. The highest rows in the Blue Ridge Tower sit under the skybox seats and are protected from rain and sun. A family section near turn three has $5 seats for kids ages six to twelve when accompanied by an adult paying $40. Kids under six get in free for this section. Concessions at Martinsville are among the most affordable on the circuit. I know of no other Winston Cup track that serves $2 hot dogs, $3 barbecue sandwiches, $1 cans of Pepsi, and $2 bottles of water.

If at all possible, purchase seats in the Old Dominion Tower in sections 101 to 108. They cost a little more than frontstretch sections, but these seats offer a great perspective of the track with the sun behind you, so you can get some shade later in the afternoon and your photos will come out better. At the base of the Old Dominion Tower, a press gate opens to the grassy area between the stands and the track. This is where drivers exit the infield area toward their helicopters, so if you want to get close to your favorite driver, wait here after the race. Seats in the Winston Tower, especially the upper rows of section EE, are also quite good. Except for the backstretch, no matter where you sit at Martinsville you can be relatively close to the action with a sweeping view of much of the track. Backstretch seats are not undesirable, but for $15–30 more you can sit in a terrific seat elsewhere and overlook some of the pits as well.

For years, the infield area at Martinsville was accessed solely by crossing the racetrack between the Richard Petty stands at the start of the frontstretch and the Bill France Tower in turns three and four. There is still no automobile tunnel to the infield, but there is a brand-new pedestrian tunnel that allows those with infield passes to access the pits and garage area. Once the race starts, there is no other way to get in or out of the infield area, so drivers who are knocked out of the race early generally spend the remainder of the day in the infield. Other recent improvements at Martinsville include a garage area that is sunken to minimize interference with sight lines of fans in the stands. Drivers and their crews are thrilled with the new garages as compared to the old facilities, which forced crews to work on cars out in the elements.

Unlike superspeedways in Charlotte, Daytona, Indianapolis, and Texas, the souvenir-vending area at Martinsville is unspectacular. The track's primary drawback is the rest rooms, especially those along the front- and backstretches, which, along with those at Watkins Glen, may be the worst in all of Winston Cup racing.

HISTORY

H. Clay Earles originally built the speedway as a dirt track in 1947, before NASCAR was formed. Red Byron won the first race, a 50-lap race of "modified stock cars" that attracted a crowd of 6,013 fans to a facility with just 750 seats. Asphalt was added in 1955. Speedy Thompson won what was then a 200-lap, 100-mile race. The first official 500-lap points race at the track was the Virginia 500, won by Buck Baker on May 20, 1956. Baker won from the pole, averaging 60.950 mph in his Dodge.

Lee Petty won the Virginia 500 in 1959. Remarkably, Petty started in the twenty-fourth position, the worst starting position ever to win at Martinsville. Richard Petty followed in his daddy's tire tracks one year later, driving his #43 Plymouth to the first of a track-record fifteen victories, despite earning the pole at Martinsville only twice. Fred Lorenzen won four consecutive races at Martinsville from 1963 to 1965, including a sweep in 1964. Lorenzen won the Old Dominion 500 in 1966, but Richard Petty dominated Martinsville between 1967 and 1973, winning ten points races, and "The King" earned season sweeps in 1967, 1969, and 1972. Petty was the first driver to break the 70-mph barrier with an average speed of 72.159 mph in 1970. Petty led a track-record 480 of 500 laps on his way to victory lane. Tom Wolfe's classic stock car racing movie based on the life of Junior Johnson, *The Last American Hero*, was filmed at Martinsville in 1973 and includes footage of Petty's victory in the Old Dominion 500.

Rookie driver Earl Ross won the Old Dominion 500 in 1974. This is significant because Ross was the only driver other than Cale Yarborough, Richard Petty, David Pearson, or Bobby Allison to win a race the entire thirty-race season. Ross, a Canadian who drove for Junior Johnson and earned Rookie of the Year honors that season, never won again. On September 28, 1975, Dave Marcis got his first career victory in his 255th start by winning the Old Dominion 500. Cale Yarborough enjoyed some serious success at Martinsville, winning six times including three straight races from 1976 to 1977. Those wins were sandwiched between a pair of Darrell Waltrip victories. Waltrip won eleven series races at Martinsville and dominated the 1980s with nine wins in a decade. When Waltrip wasn't winning at Martinsville during the 1980s, it seems that neophytes were. As a rookie in 1981, Morgan Shepherd earned his first victory at Martinsville in the Virginia 500.

Harry Gant won his first Winston Cup race at Martinsville on April 25 of the following year. In the 1984 Sovran Bank 500, Geoffrey Bodine earned his first career victory at Martinsville. Harry Gant drove his Buick back to victory lane at Martinsville in 1986 and 1991. His victory in September 1991 was his fourth consecutive win of the season. The streak started in Darlington, continued through Richmond and Dover Downs, and concluded with a narrow victory over Brett Bodine and Dale Earnhardt at Martinsville.

Rusty Wallace took three straight races from 1994 to 1995, including a sweep in 1995. He was the first driver to average better than 80 mph at Martinsville, with a mark of 81.410 mph in a victory in the 1996 Goody's 500. Wallace has furthered his reputation as a short track master by taking six checkered flags at Martinsville. Dale Earnhardt also had six wins at Martinsville. His first victory came in 1980 and his last in 1995. Remarkably, the only time Earnhardt Sr. ever started on the pole at Martinsville was when time trials were rained out for the 1995 Old Dominion 500.

Jeff Gordon set the race record in the Old Dominion 500 on September 22, 1996, averaging 82.223 mph in a race that lasted just three hours, eleven minutes, and fifty-four seconds. The following spring, he went on to win the 1997 Goody's 500 in record style by leading 432 of 500 laps. In the 1999 NAPA 500, Gordon led just 29 laps, on his way to victory. John Andretti set a track record by winning the 1999 Goody's 500 despite leading just 4 laps all race. Tony Stewart set the Goody's 500 qualifying record of 95.275 mph in 1999 and the NAPA 500 mark of 95.371 in 2000. Stewart went on to win the 2000 NAPA 500 from the pole. Earlier that year, Mark Martin took the Goody's 500 by staying out on the track while the leaders pitted with 64 laps to go. Martin held off Jeff Burton in a race that featured a Martinsville 500-lap race record, seventeen yellow flags, and 112 laps under caution.

In 2001, Dale Jarrett won the Virginia 500, his third win of the season and his first ever at Martinsville. The win was the twenty-seventh of his career but was a milestone of sorts because Martinsville was the site of his first career Winston Cup start in 1984. Jarrett has fourteen top-ten finishes in his first twenty-eight starts at Martinsville.

GETTING TO THE TRACK

About equidistant from Roanoke, Virginia, and Greensboro, North Carolina, the speedway is 2 miles south of Martinsville and notorious for traffic bottlenecks once you get within 20 miles of the track. Get there very early or expect to spend a great deal of time on U.S. 220. And I mean a ridiculous amount of time in bumper-to-bumper traffic! After the race I'd suggest you fire up a grill, cook dinner, read a book, take a nap, and leave as late as possible.

An access road to U.S. 220/58 Bypass was built in 1995, so traffic is not as maddening as it once was, but it's still among the worst on the Winston Cup circuit. Martinsville accommodates just 86,000 fans. Nevertheless, local access roads, if you can call them that, simply cannot support that sort of traffic. Since 1988, seats have been added every year except 1995. In the last fifteen years, fan capacity has increased 44,500 at Martinsville. Fortunately, 100 acres of parking were also added. Parking at track-owned lots is free. Off-track parking can be a long way from the track but is inexpensive by Winston Cup standards, usually $10 or less.

The problem is that there is no easy way to get to Martinsville, and once you get near the track there is nothing but two-lane and one-lane roads leading to the track. Anticipate at least an extra hour of drive time on race day, or get there a day early and camp. Be especially early if you want to visit the pits and garage areas. Unless you despise short track racing to begin with, a trip to Martinsville is worth the hassle. Be sure to check it out while they still have two race weekends. Tickets may become scarce and crowds could grow if this "old school" track loses a race date.

WHAT TO SEE AND DO

To say Martinsville has little to do is an understatement. Your best bet may be to bring a bunch of friends or family, secure a decent hotel room or campsite, and make your own entertainment.

The **Wood Brothers Racing Shop and Museum** is located on Performance Drive in Stuart, Virginia, about 30 miles from the track. For more than fifty years the Wood Brothers have fielded a team in Winston Cup racing. Wood Brothers drivers include Curtis Turner, Junior Johnson, Fast Freddy Lorenzen, Tiny Lund, Cale Yarborough, David Pearson, Buddy Baker, Neil Bonnett, Dale Jarrett, and others. The Wood Brothers team has won ninety-seven Winston Cup races, 116 poles, and run in more than 1,000 races. A visit to their shop is unlike any other I've seen. Instead of sitting behind a giant glass wall, tours allow you to get a behind-the-scenes look and listen to the action as the crew prepares cars for upcoming races. The museum has three stock cars, trophies, uniforms, and a collection of classic photos. Admission is free, and the shop and museum are generally open weekdays from 8:30 A.M. to 5 P.M. with a one-hour break for lunch at noon. During Martinsville race weekends, the shop and museum are also open on Saturday. Call (540) 694-2121 for directions.

The **South Boston Speedway**, about an hour east of Martinsville, offers ASA and late-model stock car racing on a .4-mile, semibanked, asphalt oval. This is a happening place on Winston Cup weekends. In addition to late-model stocks, you'll see superstocks and modifieds. Call (804) 572-4947 for race schedule and directions.

Outdoors enthusiasts and fishermen will enjoy **Fairy Stone Park**, **Smith River**, and **Philpott Lake**. The park, about 20 miles northwest of Martinsville, offers camping, hiking, and fishing spread out over 4,750 acres. Tent camping and RV hookups are available but disappear quickly on race weekends. The trout fishing, in Philpott Lake and along the Smith River, is among the best in the region. Boat rentals are available and Virginia fishing licenses are required. The fall Martinsville race generally takes place around prime leaf season along the **Blue Ridge Parkway**. The parkway runs through the Blue Ridge Mountains and wonderfully scenic countryside of Virginia, North Carolina, and Tennessee. Don't expect to cruise around the winding two-lane roads of the parkway as if you were navigating a road course, because they get crowded this time of year. The same can be said of better hotels along the parkway, so book a place early.

Martinsville is home to the Astros, an Appalachian League affiliate of the Major League Houston Astros. They play home games at **Hooker Field**, an intimate 3,200-seat stadium at Commonwealth Boulevard and Chatham Heights. Call (540) 666-2000 for schedule and ticket information.

The **Virginia Museum of Natural History**, at 1001 Douglas Avenue in Martinsville, is open until 5 P.M. seven days a week. Permanent exhibits feature dinosaurs, mammals, geology, insects, and more. Admission is $4 for adults. Call (540) 666-8600 for additional information.

NIGHTLIFE IN MARTINSVILLE

The very concept of nightlife here might seem unlikely, but it does actually exist. For years, the **Dutch Inn**, at 2360 Virginia Avenue in nearby Collinsville, was just about the only place to eat, drink, and be merry on race weekend in Martinsville. Sadly, the Dutch Inn restaurant burned to the ground about a month before the 2001 Virginia 500, but it should be rebuilt in time for the 2002 spring race.

Duffer's Bar & Grill, at 730 Church Street, is more of a casual, hilltop restaurant than a sports bar. The golf-themed menu has a nice variety of steaks, seafood, burgers, and sandwiches. There are a couple of TVs—generally showing sports—a small outdoor patio with a view of speedway fireworks, and a DJ playing tunes on weekends. Dinner is served until 10 P.M., but after 9 P.M. you must be twenty-one or older to enter. They are open Monday through Saturday. **Time Out** is a bona fide sports bar in nearby Collinsville, beside the Dutch Inn. They offer fourteen TVs and three big screens and serve everything from steaks to boneless hot wings. They also have a dance floor with a DJ spinning tunes on weekends. **Peter's Lounge**, adjacent to the Hong Kong Restaurant in the Patrick Henry Mall, is a popular place with the locals on Saturday nights.

WHERE TO EAT

The **Dutch Inn** was famous for attracting a big race crowd and serving a mean prime rib. That is sure to be the case when they return, but there are a few other places in town to check out. **Dixie Pig Barbecue** is an old-style drive-in place that has been around since the fifties. Located at 817 Memorial Boulevard in Martinsville, this humble place keeps it simple but fills you up without busting your budget. Also in Martinsville, **Pigs-R-Us** at 1014 Liberty Street has slow-cooked barbecued pork smoked for thirteen hours, hickory-smoked barbecued chicken, home-made beans, coleslaw, and potato salad. Race fans will appreciate the race car hood and autographed photos of drivers on the wall.

Captain Tom's Seafood is an inexpensive place to grab your favorite fried fish and shrimp served with hush puppies, slaw, french fries, or a baked potato. Located on Highway 220 South in Martinsville, they also offer oysters, scallops, and crab but do not serve alcohol of any kind. For surprisingly good Chinese food, head to **China Buffet** at 609 Memorial Boulevard. The staff is outgoing and mindful while the massive buffet features dozens of fresh entrees to choose from, including all your favorites.

Michael's Steak & More is an affordable family restaurant, serving seafood, chicken, pasta, and sandwiches, in addition to their trademark steaks. This recently remodeled local establishment, on U.S. 220 North in Collinsville between the Dutch Inn and Hampton Inn, also features a large-screen TV and a small bar serving drinks, beer, and wine. You could do worse than **Texas Steakhouse and Saloon** for after-race grub. This franchise establishment, at 283 Commonwealth Boulevard, also offers a separate bar where you can down a cold pop while you wait for a table. **Clarence's Steak House**, about a mile south of the track on U.S. 220 in Ridgeway, is another good-sized family place with steaks, barbecued chicken, pork chops, and sandwiches—a great place for lunch and dinner. You can expect hearty portions and friendly service. About a decade ago this place burned to the ground, but it has come back bigger and better than ever. This place is way beyond race-fan-friendly; they go so far as to sponsor race teams in the Late Model Sportsmen division.

LOCAL MEDIA

The *Martinsville Bulletin* is the local paper. Race broadcasts are carried on Motor Racing Network—WMVA 1450 AM.

WHERE TO STAY

HOTELS

Al Groden's Dutch Inn   2360 Virginia Avenue (540) 647-3721   Minutes from the track, this is one of the larger and nicer hotels within a short drive of the track. The staff has been catering to race fans for years and goes out of their way to help.

Best Western   1755 Virginia Avenue, Martinsville (540) 632-5611   A clean, comfortable hotel with a wading pool, an exercise room, and Marigold's, an adjacent restaurant and lounge.

Days Inn   U.S. 220 Business, Ridgeway (540) 638-3914   Less than a mile from the track; you could conceivably walk to the track from here and avoid the hassle of parking at the track. Also within a short walk of several fast food restaurants.

Hampton Inn   50 Hampton Drive, Collinsville (540) 647-4700   Also among the better accommodations minutes from the track, albeit somewhat short on amenities.

Holiday Inn Express   1895 Virginia Avenue, Martinsville (540) 666-6835   A mid-sized, two-story hotel with large rooms and a convenient location.

Jameson Lodge   378 Commonwealth Boulevard, Martinsville (540) 638-0478   Simple accommodations a short drive from the track and within walking distance of several restaurants. Free continental breakfast and local calls.

CAMPSITES

Because there is so little to do, Martinsville is an ideal place to go RV camping. Drive in a day early, set up the satellite dish, bring some comfortable chairs and a cooler full of cold pop, play horseshoes or crateball, and avoid the traffic by walking to the race.

Primitive camping sites at the track are located behind the backstretch stands and cost just $30 for your entire stay. Reservations are not accepted and there are no water or electrical hookups. Wood fires, bikes, ATVs, golf carts, and dirt bikes are not allowed. Charcoal and gas grills are permitted.

Good to Know

- To charge tickets or for additional race information, call (877) RACE-TIX or (540) 956-3151.
- Ticket inquiries and mail orders can be sent to P.O. Box 3311, Martinsville, VA 24115.
- The Martinsville–Henry County Chamber of Commerce can be reached at (866) 632-3378 or (540) 632-6401.
- A worthwhile city Web site is www.martinsville.com.
- ➤ The official racetrack Web site is www.martinsvillespeedway.com.

NEARBY WINSTON CUP RACE CITIES

Rockingham: 135 miles (three hours)
Lowe's/Charlotte: 140 miles (three hours, thirty minutes)
Bristol: 141 miles (three hours, fifty minutes)
Richmond: 173 miles (four hours, ten minutes)
Darlington: 175 miles (five hours, five minutes)

IN THE VICINITY

Roanoke, Virginia, is a neat little town about 50 miles north of Martinsville. Greensboro, North Carolina, is about the same distance to the southeast, but traffic from Greensboro can be heavier. Unfortunately, neither is particularly easy to get to from Martinsville. Roanoke, also known as "Star City" because of a 100-foot lighted star situated atop Mill Mountain, has a little more charm and character than Greensboro, so it may be a better bet. **Center in the Square** is an arts theater beside the outdoor farmer's market area in downtown Roanoke. The entire area hosts cafés, breakfast places, live-music nightclubs, and several quaint shops and galleries. The **Virginia Museum of Transportation** is housed in a vintage freight train station and is home to historic trains, including a J Class 611 steam locomotive, rail cars, cabooses, antique cars, trucks, carriages, and model trains. Admission is $6 for adults.

The **Patrick Henry Hotel** is a wonderful historic hotel in the heart of Roanoke. This place features top-notch service, clean rooms, and a friendly, mahogany-paneled bar tucked in the corner of the main lobby.

If you decide to stay in **Greensboro** there are a handful of hotels—La Quinta, Courtyard by Marriott, AmeriSuites, Shoney's Inn, and others—near the intersection of I-40 and Wendover Road. The **O'Henry Hotel**, at 624 Green Valley Road, is a fairly new hotel that looks like it's been around for centuries. Within walking distance of several worthwhile eateries and a shopping mall, this upscale, European-style hotel is a wonderful place to stay for just a little more than you might pay for lesser accommodations in some Winston Cup cities on race weekend.

On the other end of the spectrum, more than one race fan has recommended **Harper's Exotic Car Wash**, a topless car wash in Greensboro. Located just off I-40 at exit 213, two or more ladies will clean your car topless for $15, as you sit back and enjoy a beer or soft drink. Greensboro also has a number of worthwhile eateries and sports bars to choose from. **Jack Astor's**, at 3031 High Point Road, is one of the area's preeminent sports bars. You'll find plenty of TVs as well as food and beer specials. Just up the street, **Blue Marlin** is a terrific seafood restaurant that also offers steak, pasta, and chops, all presented with a southern flair. Rumor has it a **NASCAR Café** will be coming to Greensboro in 2002. In nearby Winston-Salem, the oldest NASCAR-sanctioned track can be found at **Bowman Gray Stadium**. This quarter-mile, flat asphalt oval hosts NASCAR Modifieds, Sportsmen, Street Stocks, and Stadium Stocks on Saturday nights. The track has been around for more than fifty years and doubles as the Bowman Gray campus football stadium, as well as the track and field facility, but still packs them in on race nights. Call (336) 724-7932 for schedule and ticket information.

■ *PHOENIX INTERNATIONAL RACEWAY* ■

Phoenix, Arizona

*"I really like this racetrack. The first time I was ever here,
I finished in the top ten in a Winston Cup car. The big thing
here . . . is getting the car to handle in the corners."*

—JIMMY SPENCER

Nestled among the arid hills of the Sonoran Desert, PIR has a number of quirks that set it apart from other tracks on the Winston Cup circuit. It is one of only two speedways with a backstretch that's longer than the front straightaway. In fact, the backstretch, at 1,551 feet, is bent while the 1,179-foot frontstretch is straight, so the track is laid out opposite of most D-shaped ovals. Neither straight has any banking. The track is also relatively flat through the turns with 11-degree banking in turns one and two and a 9-degree slope in turns three and four. Turns one and two are tighter while three and four are more sweeping. This fact creates challenges for the crew setting up a car's chassis for the race and generally results in a compromise that works well for one set of turns and requires the driver to compensate through the opposite turns.

Pit road at Phoenix is unique in that it exits the track as turn four meets the frontstraight and returns to the track on the backstretch. Pit stalls begin about a third of the way into the frontstretch and curl around into turn one. Perhaps the most unusual quirk at Phoenix is the tiered hillside seating overlooking the third and fourth turns. Fans on the hill bring their own chairs, blankets, and pop-up awnings to watch the race among the cacti. A walkover bridge, connecting the infield with the hillside area, crosses the track near the entry to turn four.

The track was originally conceived as a road course in the early sixties. In the middle of construction, the owners were persuaded to add a closed 1-mile oval that was incorporated in the road course. As a result, Phoenix was built as a hybrid

accommodating both tracks so some quirks became necessary. One of those quirks is a noncontinuous retaining wall that ends suddenly near the exit of turn two heading into the back side tri-oval.

Emmett Jobe purchased the track in 1985 with the intention of bringing NASCAR races to the track. Jobe emphasized the asphalt oval, making a host of additions to the stands and garage areas to accommodate a larger NASCAR crowd. ISC bought the track in 1997 and made additional improvements including luxury suites, expanded grandstands and parking, and infrastructure improvements. The track is still outdated in appearance, but the changes and additions are ongoing. While PIR may never compare to the circuit's finest tracks, it has enough quirks and individuality that it is certainly worth checking out.

Drivers like going to Phoenix, especially in late October or early November when the weather is wonderful, even though they find the track to be very demanding. From a fan's point of view, the track is not generally thought of as among the most competitive, because the bottom of the track is the fastest line and there is rarely much racing up top. Cars tend to spread out quickly along the mile-long asphalt oval, and single-file racing is the order of the day until very late in the race when a second groove develops, particularly coming out of turn two. Winston Cup races here are just 312 laps, or roughly 500 kilometers, and generally finish in less than three hours. Races at PIR also tend to feature long stretches of green flag racing, so it can be difficult for drivers to recover from mistakes made early in the race. As the sun sets, drivers can find themselves staring into the sun as they drive down the backstretch, so expect to see plenty of dark helmet shields and strips of tape across the top of the cars' windshields late in the race.

The grandstands at PIR are not exactly state-of-the-art, but they do offer a decent view of the entire track from the highest rows. If any place needs luxury suites atop the main grandstands, if for no other reason than to provide some much-needed shade, this is it. Sadly, there is almost no shade to be had at the track except for seats on the right side in the top rows of the Bobby Allison grandstand. That shade extends to the lower rows as the race goes on and the sun sets behind the Allison grandstand.

The Jimmy Bryan grandstands are situated at the start/finish line and, as such, are some of the most expensive seats at the track. The Bobby Allison grandstands in turn two are among the newest seating sections at the track and are much taller than other grandstand sections. Seats in the top rows here offer the best perspective of the track but do not overlook the pits very much, although they do oversee the exit from pit road to the track. Seats here, even in the lowest rows, are more expensive than anywhere else at PIR. The Richard Petty stands near turn four on the frontstretch may have the most complete view as cars come around turn four and head into the frontstretch. Seats here, as well as those in the A. J. Foyt section near turn one, are the most affordable on the frontstretch. The Petty section is set back from the track and may offer a better value. Backstretch seats are simple bleacher stands with a limited view of the track. The 76/Circle K hillside seating is a better option if you hope to see more than just a small portion of the track, but it faces into the sun for much of the day.

A three-sided scoring tower sits in the middle of the infield and lists the current lap as well as the top five drivers. The track offers some interesting amenities for folks who stay in the infield or camp just outside the track in **Estrella Regional County Park**. In addition to the standard rest room and shower facilities, a temporary grocery store sits in the RV parking lot. There's also a retail store, a restaurant/sports bar, and an entertainment deck. Live concerts are held throughout race weekend. The track has one major drawback: you cannot bring your own beer into the track. To make matters worse, you can purchase only two beers at a time, so a good deal of your day could be spent in line instead of in your seat watching the race. As a good friend once said, "You really have to be a fan to watch a race here."

HISTORY

The first Winston Cup race held at PIR in 1988 was a milestone for several reasons. Alan Kulwicki won the race, his very first Winston Cup victory, in just his third season as a Winston Cup driver. Ricky Rudd dominated the race but lost his engine with sixteen laps remaining. Kulwicki started twenty-first but held off Terry Labonte, Davey Allison, Bill Elliott, and Rusty Wallace for the win. As a result, the "Polish victory lap" was introduced to the sport as Kulwicki turned his Ford around and saluted the crowd with a counterclockwise lap around the track. Remarkably, Kulwicki won as an independent driver. Kulwicki remained an independent through his 1992 Winston Cup championship season and was still independent the day he died in an airplane crash in 1993.

NASCAR drivers returned to Phoenix in 1989, and Bill Elliott took the checkered flag for the second Winston Cup points race at PIR as Ford swept the top three spots. Elliott became the first driver to average more than 100 mph with a mark of 105.683 mph. Dale Earnhardt's first top-five finish at PIR was a win in the 1990 Checker 500. Earnhardt, driving a Chevy to its first win at Phoenix, started third to become the first driver to win from inside the top ten qualifying positions.

Davey Allison outpaced Darrell Waltrip, Sterling Marlin, and Alan Kulwicki on his way to victory lane in 1991. Allison started thirteenth and became the second driver to average better than 100 mph with a speed of 103.885 mph. Allison repeated in 1992 by beating Mark Martin, Waltrip, and Kulwicki. With the win Allison, who started from the twelfth position, became the track's first two-time winner.

Mark Martin, who runs well at Phoenix, continued Ford's dominance and got his first win at PIR in 1993 by beating out Ernie Irvan, Kyle Petty, and Dale Earnhardt. Martin was just the second driver to win with a starting position inside the top five. Terry Labonte, who had settled for second-place finishes twice before, beat Martin and Marlin to the checkered flag in 1994. Labonte paced his Chevrolet around the track at an average speed of 107.463 mph to set a track record. Ricky Rudd finally received some solace for his misfortune in the inaugural race with a win in 1995. Rudd started twenty-ninth to set the record for the worst starting position to win at Phoenix. Bobby Hamilton earned his first career Winston Cup victory at Phoenix, beating out a hard-charging Mark Martin and Terry Labonte on October 27, 1996. Labonte had wrecked his car in practice, breaking his thumb in the process. Despite driving a backup car with a fractured thumb, he scrambled to a third-place finish. Hamilton's victory was also the first win for Pontiac at Phoenix and Richard Petty's first win as an owner of a car he was not driving. Fittingly, seven years earlier Hamilton started his first Winston Cup race on this same track.

Dale Jarrett, driving a Robert Yates Ford, won the Dura Lube 500. It was the third win for Yates at Phoenix. Remarkably, Jarrett came from a lap down to win the race without the benefit of a caution flag. Rusty Wallace finished second for his fourth top-five finish at Phoenix. Wallace earned his first win the following season with Mark Martin and Dale Earnhardt on his trail in a race shortened to 257 laps because of rain. That remains the only rain-shortened race in the track's history.

Tony Stewart blew away the track record with a pace of 118.132 mph on his way to victory in 1999. Like most winners at Phoenix, Stewart started outside the top ten.

In 2000, Ryan Newman started his first Winston Cup race in the Dura Lube 500. As first races go, it was a disappointing one because he blew an engine in lap 176 and finished forty-first. Rusty Wallace earned the pole for that race with a record qualifying speed of 134.178 mph and became the all-time leader at Phoenix with three pole-position starts. Jeff Burton, who started beside Wallace and ran well all day, grabbed the lead from Mark Martin with five laps remaining and took the checkered flag—the first winner at Phoenix to start from the front row.

The following season, rookie Casey Atwood won his first Winston Cup pole for the Checker Auto Parts 500 driving a Ray Evernham–owned Dodge and was clearly the one to beat until a blown tire put him a lap down late in the race. On lap 279, Jeff Burton took the lead from Mike Wallace, who got to the front by swapping two tires while everybody else was taking on four during a yellow flag pit stop. Burton held on to become just the second driver in track history to win a second race at Phoenix. He and Davey Allison both won back-to-back races at PIR. Burton's win was also the third victory for Jack Roush Racing at Phoenix and the fiftieth career win for Roush Racing. Burton, who finished 2.645 seconds ahead of Wallace, led Ford to a sweep of the top four spots, with Ricky Rudd and Matt Kenseth close behind Wallace.

Oddly, through the 2001 season, no driver has won from the pole at PIR. Another statistical quirk at Phoenix is the fact that Jeff Gordon has never won at Phoenix, the only Winston Cup track on which he has started more than six races and not earned a win. In fact, he has never finished within the top three. He managed a fourth-place finish, a lap down, in 1994 and back-to-back fifth-place finishes in 1995 and 1996.

GETTING TO THE TRACK

Getting to Phoenix International on race day is difficult to say the least. The track is well west of Phoenix, yet authorities direct nearly all traffic to approach the track from the west, so unless you have a parking pass or ride on a bus, you must loop around the track and head back east toward the parking lots. Most automobile parking lots are west of the track. Complimentary trams run regularly throughout the parking lots, so you should not have to walk more than a few blocks before encountering a tram stop.

From Phoenix, you can take Interstate 10 west to Estrella Parkway South. Take a left on Vineyard Road and follow it to the track. Alternative exits off I-10 include 99th Avenue, 115th Avenue, and Litchfield Road. Widening of 115th Avenue should improve this route, but all roads from I-10 are narrow and congested.

Your best bet may be to take the Desert Sky Pavilion Park 'n Ride shuttle. Buses are given priority entering and exiting the facility and park close to the track. The Park 'n Ride lot at Desert Sky is just north of I-10 at 83rd Avenue. At just $7 per carload it's a bargain.

WHAT TO SEE AND DO

Keith Hall's **Manzanita Speedway** offers eleven different divisions of racing including midget, sprint, modified, and street stock car racing on their half-mile and one-third-mile dirt ovals every Friday and Saturday night. The converted dog track is located just below the Salt River southwest of downtown Phoenix where Thirty-fifth Avenue meets Broadway Road. Call (602) 276-7575 for details.

The **Firebird Raceway** is a quarter-mile drag strip that hosts NHRA and other competitions east of town on the Gila River Indian Reservation near I-10 at the Mariposa exit. Call (602) 268-0200 for upcoming race schedules. The **Gila River Casino** is also nearby.

Phoenix is packed with attractions to see while in town. **Waterworld Safari**, at 4243 West Pinnacle Peak Road, has 20 acres of water slides and wave pools to offer a break from the Arizona heat. **Salt River Recreation** is among a handful of outfits that offer shuttle service and tube rentals for a long, lazy ride down the Salt River. Outdoor enthusiasts will find plenty to do in **Encanto Park**. This city park at 2705 North Fifteenth Avenue has an abundance of walking trails, paddleboats, tennis, basketball and volleyball courts, and an affordable public golf course. Serious golfers may want to check out the **TPC at Scottsdale**. This Tom Weiskopf–designed course, at 17020 North Hayden Road in Scottsdale, hosts the PGA Phoenix Open every year and is open to the public. Another worthwhile golf course, minutes from the track in Goodyear, Arizona, is the **Estrella Mountain Ranch Golf Club** designed by Jack Nicklaus II.

Papago Peaks Park, at Galvin Parkway and Van Buren Street, offers simple bouldering and hiking trails with a number of caves and terrific views of the surrounding valleys. The **Desert Botanical Garden** and **Phoenix Zoo** are also located within the park. The zoo occupies 125 acres and is home to more than 1,300 animals. Admission is $7 for adults. The botanical gardens showcase more than 150 acres of desert foliage. Admission is just $6 for adults.

The **Arizona State Capitol Museum** is in the heart of downtown at the corner of West Washington Street and Seventeenth Avenue. Built in 1900, this tuff stone and granite building served as the state capitol until 1974, when the adjacent capitol building was opened. The legislative chambers are open to the public from 8 A.M. to 5 P.M., Monday through Friday. Admission to the museum and legislative hall is free. Guided tours are available 10 A.M. to 2 P.M. Monday through Saturday. The **Heard Museum**, at 22 East Monte Vista Road, is the area's premier cultural attraction. The emphasis here is on southwestern Native American art and history.

Admission is just $5 for adults. Entry is free for everybody on Wednesdays. The **Phoenix Art Museum** is two blocks south of the Heard, at 1625 North Central Avenue. The museum boasts an extensive collection of nineteenth- and twentieth-century art including work by such artists as Frederic Remington and Georgia O'Keeffe. Admission is $4 for adults. Like the Heard, admission is free on Wednesdays.

The **Arizona Center**, a massive indoor mall in downtown Phoenix at Third Street and Van Buren, offers restaurants, shopping, and entertainment seven days a week. In addition to the **Phoenix International Raceway Ticket Office and Race Shop**, the Arizona Center is home to various race-related festivities during race week. Baseball fans will want to stop by **Bank One Ballpark**. Even after the season, this is a remarkable ballpark with a removable roof and wall panels that slide open to give it an outdoor feel. The area surrounding the park has a number of sports bars and restaurants.

NIGHTLIFE IN PHOENIX

The number of solid sports bars and nightclubs in the Phoenix area is astounding. Minutes from the track, **Driver's Sports Grill**, at 14175 West Indian School Road in Goodyear, is an authentic racing bar with excellent food as well. Photos of well-known drivers adorn the walls, and sheet metal from various cars is suspended from the ceiling. There are plenty of games, a pool table, ample cold beer on draft, and a staff that is as friendly and helpful as they can be. In downtown Phoenix, near the ballpark, **Cooperstown** is a combination sports bar and live music venue owned by Alice Cooper. The emphasis here is on hot waitresses, good food, and plenty of TVs. A side patio is a nice retreat at night. Just up the street, **Jackson's on Third**, at 245 East Jackson Street, is another sports-oriented place with a decent crowd and a solid bar menu.

The **Rhythm Room** at 1019 East Indian School Road offers live blues seven days a week and books better-known national acts on the weekends. **Warsaw Wally's** is a live music venue at 2547 East Indian School Road that generally hosts regional acts and offers a separate billiard room. The **Mason Jar** is a dark yet popular alternative and rock music club at 2303 East Indian School Road. Country music fans will want to stop by **Roman's Oasis** at 16825 West Yuma Road in Goodyear. This rustic place is minutes from the track and presents live country bands throughout race week. **Roman's County Line**, at 10540 West Indian School Road, has been around about as long as NASCAR/Winston Cup drivers have been coming to Phoenix. They feature live country music on Friday and Saturday evenings and karaoke other nights.

One of the city's most popular sports bars is **Majerle's Sports Grille** at 24 North Second Street. If you decide to stop by the Arizona Center, **America's Original**

Sports Bar is another place worth visiting. They offer fifty-three TVs and seven giant screens, or you can join the action on their outdoor volleyball court. **Sports Fever** is another giant sports bar at 2031 Peoria Avenue. Sports Fever offers satellite sports on thirty-eight TVs and four large screens. They also have a sports memorabilia room, pool tables, darts, basketball, a DJ, and a dance floor.

Scottsdale Road in downtown Scottsdale has a few clubs to choose from. **Axis/Radius** is really two clubs in one with dance music and a dance floor on one side and radio-driven pop music on the other side. **Famous Store** is a more down-to-earth bar with occasional live music. Other clubs include the **Velvet Room** and **Six**. The Biltmore area, at the intersection of Camelback Road and Twenty-fourth Street, also has a number of nightclubs to choose from.

WHERE TO EAT

Dan Ryan's Sports Grill 2121 East Highland Avenue Don't let the name fool you; this restaurant in Phoenix's affluent Biltmore neighborhood is more bistro than bar. The menu ranges from steaks to pasta while the crowd dresses to impress. Step down into the bar for a slightly more casual experience.

Don & Charlie's 7501 East Camelback Road, Scottsdale This upscale place has a reputation for catering to athletes and local dignitaries. Expect to come off the hip for dinner, but the ribs here are truly unforgettable.

Macayo Mexican 4001 North Central Avenue This is as good a Mexican place as I have ever eaten at—anywhere. It's not particularly fancy; it's just good food in an authentic, casual atmosphere. The tortilla soup is out of this world, but it's hard to go wrong with anything on the menu. There are several locations throughout the Phoenix area, so look for the one near you.

Pink Pony 3831 North Scottsdale Road, Scottsdale A classic restaurant with a baseball theme. The steaks here are near legendary, and don't be surprised to see a driver, broadcaster, or other such celebrity dining in a nearby booth.

Pinnacle Peak Patio 10426 East Jomax Road, Scottsdale A casual, cowboy steakhouse with outdoor dining on the patio. The menu features steaks, chicken, ribs, and burgers. There's also live country music seven nights a week.

Raul & Teresa's 519 West Main Street, Avondale This casual place features affordable Mexican and American entrees just minutes from the track. It is also one of the most kid-friendly restaurants in the area.

T-Bone Steakhouse 10037 South Nineteenth Avenue About halfway up South Mountain, overlooking the city, this casual steakhouse keeps it simple. Choose a T-bone, porterhouse, or top sirloin, tell them how you want it cooked, and prepare to be sated. Beans and bread are the standard sides, and a trip to the salad bar is included in your meal.

LOCAL MEDIA

The *Arizona Republic* is the local daily newspaper. Race broadcasts can be heard on MRN via KGME 550 AM or Xtra Sports 910 AM.

WHERE TO STAY

HOTELS

To avoid traffic hassles it may help to stay in Goodyear, west of the track. Most of what you will want to do and see is in downtown Phoenix, so if that is a priority for you, there are a number of very nice hotels in Phoenix.

Budget Suites   2722 North Seventh Street, Phoenix (888) 915-5656 or (800) 932-0044   Don't be fooled by the name. If you are planning to stay for an entire week, this is a quality place to stay. The one-bedroom suites have an equipped kitchen, and the pool is a great place to chill on nonrace days.

Courtyard by Marriott   2101 East Camelback Road (602) 955-5200   A moderately priced place in the heart of the Biltmore nightlife district.

Comfort Inn   1770 Dysart Road, Goodyear (623) 932-9191   A terrific location west of the track at I-10 and Dysart Road. This is one of the more affordable, yet comfortable places to stay in the Goodyear area.

Embassy Suites Biltmore   2630 East Camelback (602) 955-3992   Luxury accommodations with good-sized suites, in the Biltmore area, not far from the nightlife district.

Hampton Inn and Suites   2000 North Litchfield Road, Goodyear (623) 536-1313   Unlike any Hampton Inn I've ever seen. The place looks like a high-dollar resort from the street and inside the lobby. Minutes from the track and within a short drive of several notable restaurants.

Holiday Inn   1313 Litchfield Road, Goodyear (623) 535-1313   Another notable place within a short drive of the track. This place features a heated swimming pool, complimentary breakfast, and nicely appointed rooms.

The Phoenix Inn   2310 East Highland Avenue   Very nice, moderately priced accommodations in the Biltmore area of Phoenix.

Not-so-nearby towns with suitable lodging during race week include Scottsdale, Mesa, Tempe, Sedona, and Tucson. For a more complete list of hotels call the **Arizona Office of Tourism** at (800) 842-8257.

Good to Know

- To charge tickets or for additional race information, call (602) 252-2227.
- For campsite information, call (602) 252-3833.

- Mail orders can be sent to Ticket Office, 7602 South 115th Avenue, Avondale, AZ 85323.
- The Phoenix and Valley of the Sun Convention & Visitors Bureau can be reached at (602) 254-6500.
- Worthwhile Web sites include www.arizonaguide.com and www.azcentral.com.
- The official racetrack Web site is www.phoenixintlraceway.com.

NEARBY WINSTON CUP RACE CITIES

Las Vegas: 295 miles (five hours)
Fontana: 370 miles (six hours, thirty-five minutes)

IN THE VICINITY

Take a forty-five-minute drive north of Phoenix and you'll find the make-believe Wild West town of Cave Creek. In the heart of town is the **Black Mountain Brewery** and **Crazy Ed's Satisfied Frog Saloon**. Black Mountain Brewery produces several outstanding brews including Frog Light, Black Mountain Gold, and a chili beer. All three can be sampled next door at the Satisfied Frog, where they are served ice-cold in mason jars. The saloon also offers terrific barbecue, steaks, ribs, and Mexican entrees. The town itself is a little cheesy, but the food and beer at the Satisfied Frog make it well worth the trip.

The **Grand Canyon** is three and a half hours north of Phoenix. The canyon is by far the most impressive natural wonder in the United States, perhaps in the world. Be sure to get up early to see the sunrise, as the canyon is at its colorful best when the sun rises and sets. You can spend your days hiking or riding a mule to the basin, aboard a helicopter riding through the interior, or taking a guided raft down the mighty Colorado River, far and away the best whitewater ride in the nation. Accommodations within the national park range from rustic cabins along the southern ridge to luxury rooms with fine dining in the main lodge. Make your reservations well in advance as cabins, mule rides, and rafting trips sell out quickly.

Sedona, a popular spot between Phoenix and the Grand Canyon, offers a wealth of incredible desert scenery that approaches the natural beauty of the Grand Canyon. Sedona was originally an artist community and has since become something of a retirement mecca with an abundance of shops, galleries, restaurants, and some terrific bed-and-breakfast lodges. **Red Rock State Park**, just west of Sedona, offers five hiking trails of varying degrees of difficulty through some of the area's prettiest countryside. **Slide Rock State Park** has a plunge pool at the bottom of a natural rockslide that is a lot of fun for the whole family.

■ *RICHMOND INTERNATIONAL RACEWAY* ■

Richmond, Virginia

*"The neat thing about Richmond that is different from most
tracks is that it has a lot of grooves. You can run the bottom,
you can run the middle, and you can run the top."*

— JEFF BURTON

There is some dispute as to when NASCAR drivers first raced at Richmond, 1948 or 1953. The "official" story is that Richmond first hosted NASCAR-sanctioned races in 1953 at Strawberry Hill Raceway, a half-mile dirt track on the site now occupied by RIR. Fifteen years later the track was renovated into a .542-mile paved oval and continued to host sanctioned races. Finally, wanting to create a speedway that was unique within the Winston Cup circuit, Paul Sawyer, the track's owner, built the current .750-mile, D-shaped paved track in 1988. The raceway features a 60-foot-wide asphalt racing surface with relatively flat 14-degree banked turns and some of the finest racing action on the NASCAR schedule. Drivers work to avoid trouble and spins, driving along the bottom line early in the evening, but really get busy with fifty to sixty laps remaining as the race takes on the strategy of an all-out war for track position, not unlike Charlotte's night race, the Winston. Because both Winston Cup events here are 400 laps (only 300 miles) around a moderately sized three-quarter-mile track, the race will often be over before you know it.

RIR offers the proximity of a short track, with lots of sheet-metal-shredding action, and the exciting speeds and passing of a larger speedway because it's a true "two-groove" track. Turn two is particularly challenging and is generally the site of lots of rubbing, racing, and spins. Much of the passing occurs as drivers exit turn two and head into the backstretch. Turn three also gets tight, as drivers exit the short 860-foot back straightaway that's banked at just 2 degrees, work the brakes, and negotiate the flat turns. The frontstretch at RIR is 1,290 feet long and banked at 8 degrees, which allows drivers to open 'em up a little between turn four and the entry to the first turn.

Richmond is often the site of Winston Cup's first night race of the season, the Pontiac Excitement 400. Dubbed the "Saturday Night Fight Under the Lights," this race sells out quickly and lives up to its nickname, especially as the night gets later and the track gets tighter. Flying sparks and glowing brake rotors are a common sight on race night and add to the overall race experience. The track has not been repaved since its reconfiguration and has a reputation of starting off slick, especially in the entries and exits of the flat turns. While speeds do exceed 120 mph, mishaps here tend to be spins and single-car run-ins with the retaining wall, as opposed to the massive wrecks that eliminate a half dozen cars or more that you're likely to see at superspeedways. Unlike most short tracks, drivers choose a groove based on their car's setup, and side-by-side racing is not uncommon.

The key to success at Richmond seems to be qualifying and track position, as more races have been won from the pole position than any other starting position. Nearly half of all points races run here have been won from the top three qualifying spots, and only sixteen of the first eighty-one Winston Cup races at Richmond were won from outside the top ten starting positions. Horsepower and brakes are also essential, as the track has characteristics of both a superspeedway and a short track.

The entrance to pit road is at the base of turn three, and the exit is between turns one and two. Pit stalls extend from the exit of turn four to the end of the frontstretch, so seats all along the frontstretch offer a good view of pit action. Richmond International Raceway is also unique because the stands are on a single deck nearly all the way around the track. A walkway beside the track allows you to circle the oval and see the facility from every angle. Virginia state troopers are stationed about every 50 feet or so and discourage you from stopping and standing too long in any one spot, but it's nice to be able to walk the circumference, especially if you have seats along the backstretch. There are very few seats that don't offer a terrific perspective of the race. Two sections to avoid are the lower rows of Colonial sections A and B and Old Dominion sections J and K. The walkway around the track gets particularly wide in front of these sections, so large portions of the track are obscured by the constant crowds of people walking past.

Seats in the upper rows of the Winston and Commonwealth sections are among the best at the track, but the Dogwood section is also worthwhile, especially sections A and B, which face down the frontstretch and pit road. Suites occupy the highest area of the sections A–I in turn one, but Dogwood sections J–M offer some of the highest available seating at the track. If possible try to get seats in row 22 or higher for a view of the entire track. Tickets range from $75 to $80 for Winston Cup races, so order early and spend the extra $5 if you know you are going to Richmond for a race. A four-sided scoring tower, listing the laps completed and the top seven cars,

Under the lights on the backstretch near turn two. *(Photo by Tom Mills)*

is situated near the center of the infield. There's also a pleasant shortage of advertising billboards at the track. The only signs you'll notice are those on the track's cement retaining walls. The pedestrian tunnel from the grandstands to the infield is located near turn one, and the vehicle tunnel is at the end of the backstretch near turn three.

Once you settle into your seat, the track has few drawbacks. The seats are aluminum benches with seatbacks and can get somewhat cramped. There are only two ticket sales booths, both on the front side, and lines can be remarkably long and slow. Concession stands, souvenir booths, and other facilities are certainly adequate. I was surprised that there were no giant-screen TVs in the infield, but there is almost no need for them because the track is small enough that you can follow the action without them.

A friend and I once showed up for the spring night race without tickets and got one free and a second for $20 less than face value, twenty minutes before the race started. Plenty of tickets for the Henrico grandstands, along the backstretch, were available for sale along the streets and in the parking lot on the day of the race. We held out for better seats and scored big time. Based on this experience, I might not suggest buying seats in advance for two people or fewer, unless they were quality seats in the Winston, Commonwealth, or Dogwood sections.

HISTORY

In April 1953, Buck Baker earned the very first pole on the half-mile dirt track at Richmond with a qualifying speed of just 48.5 mph. Despite qualifying his Oldsmobile up front, Baker settled for third place in the Richmond 200. Lee Petty took the checkered flag in the track's inaugural NASCAR-sanctioned event, a 100-mile race, and was the only driver on the lead lap. The Flock brothers, Tim and Fonty, finished first and second respectively in the 1955 Richmond 200. Lee Petty finished third and Chrysler swept the top three positions. Buck Baker finally won the race in 1956, becoming the first driver at Richmond to win from the pole position. In the fall of 1960, Speedy Thompson won the Capital City 200, beating out Junior Johnson, Ned Jarrett, and Richard Petty. It was the twentieth and final win of his career.

Richard Petty tops the win list at Richmond with a remarkable thirteen victories. His first Richmond checkered flag came in 1961, the final 100-mile race held at Richmond. Joe Weatherly won the Capital City 300 in the fall of 1962 and followed that with a victory in the 1963 Richmond 250, becoming the first driver to win back-to-back races at Richmond. David Pearson did him one better by sweeping three consecutive races at Richmond in 1965 and 1966. Pearson won six points races at Richmond over his illustrious career, tied for third most with Rusty Wallace and Darrell Waltrip.

Richard Petty swept the 1967 races. The track at Richmond was asphalted in 1968, and Petty continued on a tear that may never be matched in NASCAR Winston Cup racing. The King won twelve points races at Richmond in nine seasons between 1967 and 1975. Petty won five of those races from the pole. He also came in second four times during that same time frame. His most dominant stretch at Richmond was seven consecutive wins from the 1970 Capital City 500 through the same race in 1973. Petty shares the NASCAR record with Darrell Waltrip, who won seven straight points races at Bristol. Bobby Allison ended Petty's win streak in the 1974 Richmond 500 as Petty finished second, the only other driver on the lead lap. Petty also earned the distinction of winning from the twenty-eighth starting position. No other driver has ever won from that far back at Richmond.

Bobby Allison earned seven victories at Richmond, despite competing during the same era as Petty. In fact, Allison qualified for the pole six consecutive times between 1971 and 1974 but had to watch Petty celebrate in victory lane for each of those races, until he won the 1974 Richmond 500. Allison added to his success at Richmond by winning three consecutive races from 1982 to 1983.

Kyle Petty won the Miller High Life 400 in 1986, his first career Winston Cup victory, and became the third Petty generation to visit the winner's circle at Richmond. Dale Earnhardt swept the 1987 season races on his way to his third Winston Cup points championship. Earnhardt won five races over his career at Richmond.

The track was rebuilt as a .750-mile facility in 1988. Davey Allison won the first race at the new and improved Richmond International Raceway from the pole that year. Rusty Wallace swept the 1989 races at Richmond and has more wins than any other driver since the track was lengthened to its current configuration. Wallace has won six races to date, all of them after the remodeling.

Early in the 1990 season, Mark Martin edged out Dale Earnhardt for first place at Richmond but was found to have an illegal half-inch aluminum spacer between the carburetor and the intake manifold in his engine. Martin forfeited forty-six points that day, the difference between first and tenth place, and was fined $40,000 for the violation. At season's end, Martin finished second to Earnhardt in the Winston Cup championship by twenty-six points, so this race proved critical to both drivers. The following year, Dale Earnhardt became the first driver to average better than 100 mph at Richmond when he paced his Chevrolet around the track at an average speed of 105.397 mph. Later that year, lights were added to the track, and Richmond has been running at least one night race every season since that time. Harry Gant won the first race under the lights at Richmond, passing Davey Allison with nineteen laps to go in the 1991 Miller 400.

Terry Labonte won back-to-back races in 1994 and 1995. Labonte won again in 1998 to join Cale Yarborough and Joe Weatherly as three-time winners at Richmond. In 1997, Rusty Wallace led the way as Ford swept the top three positions. It was the first top-three sweep at Richmond since Earnhardt led Chevrolet to a sweep in 1985. On September 6, 1997, Dale Jarrett set the track record with an average race speed of 109.047 mph. Tony Stewart gained his first career Winston Cup win, on September 11, 1999, in the Exide Batteries 400. Dale Earnhardt Jr. beat out Terry Labonte to win the second race of his rookie year in the Pontiac Excitement 400. Tony Stewart returned to victory lane in the Pontiac Excitement 400 in May of 2001. The fall race at Richmond that year, also held at night, was one of the most exciting races of the season. Rusty Wallace dominated much of the Chevrolet Monte Carlo 400 only to relinquish the lead to Ricky Rudd with twenty-three laps to go. Rookie Kevin Harvick bumped Rudd aside on the backstretch a few laps later and assumed the lead. Rudd managed to save his car from spinning into the wall and chased Harvick down. With four laps to go, Rudd nudged Harvick in turn four, reclaimed the lead, and held on for the win.

GETTING TO THE TRACK

The track is located on what was the State Fairgrounds near the intersection of I-95 and I-64. These two highways stay surprisingly clear on race day, but the minor arteries that lead to the track back up once you get within 5 miles of the track. Expect 2-hour delays if you don't arrive four to five hours in advance of the race. From the west, Meadowbridge Road is particularly slow, as are Mechanicsville Turnpike, Carolina Avenue, and Laburnum Avenue. It may help to approach the track from the east, but there are few options leading to the track.

A shuttle bus for Winston Cup races is available from downtown Richmond. The bus costs just $5 and can be picked up at the Greater Richmond Convention Center parking deck at Marshall and Fifth Streets or at the parking lot at Fifth and Jackson Street, near I-95. Buses have an assigned parking lot near the track and are given priority exiting the race, so this can be an efficient way to get to and from the race. Parking at the track in official lots is free. Other lots cost $10 and allow for quicker egress after the race. Trams are available for those who park in annex lots. Trams begin running forty-five minutes after the race ends and continue running for two hours. Parking in annex lots can also help avoid long traffic delays after the race.

WHAT TO SEE AND DO

Richmond may be one of the most established NASCAR Winston Cup cities in the Southeast, but unlike Darlington, Rockingham, and Martinsville, Richmond is a decent-sized city that offers plenty to see and do outside of a weekend at the track. Virginia's capital city has a long and storied history as a hotbed of Colonial leadership and the capital of the Confederacy during the Civil War.

The **Donlavey Racing** team garage is at 5011 Old Midlothian Pike, about twenty minutes south of the track. This is home to Hut Stricklin and the Hills Brothers Coffee Ford, but Benny Parsons, Ken Schrader, Ernie Irvan, Dick Trickle, and Mike Wallace have driven for Junie Donlavey over the years. The shop is open from 8 A.M. to 5 P.M. during the week. Don't expect to see a big museum and fancy gift shop. This is a simple, no-frills race shop. The only memorabilia you'll find here are the photos lining the walls of a 20–30-foot hallway. Call (804) 233-8592 for details.

The **Maymont House** was the home of Major James Dooley. Situated on 100 pristine acres overlooking the James River, this Victorian estate was built in 1893 and is open to the public. Guests are invited to stroll through the formal gardens, check out the carriage collection, visit the new nature center, Children's Farm, see the Virginia wildlife exhibit, and tour this magnificent home. There is no admission charge, but donations are appreciated. Call (804) 358-7166 for exhibit information and hours of operation. The **Virginia Museum of Art** has a remarkable permanent art collection and attracts outstanding traveling exhibits as well. More than half a million people visited the museum in 1999 alone. Expect to see paintings by Degas, Sargent, and Monet, works by Fabergé and Tiffany, and more modern creations by the likes of Andy Warhol. Admission is just $5. The museum is located at 2800 Grove Avenue, near North Boulevard.

The **Richmond Braves**, the top farm team for the big-league Atlanta Braves, play AAA baseball at the Diamond, located near the intersection of I-95 and 195, at 3301 North Boulevard. Over the past decade this has been one of the top minor-league franchises, and a day at the ballpark makes for a fun, inexpensive day of entertainment. Call (804) 359-4444 for schedule information.

Saint John's Church, at Broad Street and Twenty-fourth, was the site of the 1775 Virginia Convention, attended by George Washington, Thomas Jefferson, and Benjamin Harrison, among others. The church was also where Patrick Henry proclaimed, "Give me liberty or give me death," just weeks prior to the start of the Revolutionary War. Tours are available every half hour for $2. Call (804) 648-5015 for details. **Monument Avenue**, so called for its many statues, is a scenic street lined with historic old homes, churches, and towering trees. You'll find monuments dedicated to Robert E. Lee, Stonewall Jackson, Jefferson Davis, J.E.B. Stuart, and others. Arthur Ashe, the U.S. Open Tennis Champion who was born in Richmond, is among the latest additions to the collection of sculptures.

Civil War buffs will want to visit the **Museum of the Confederacy**. The museum, located just two blocks north of Broad Street at 1201 East Clay Street, features one of nation's largest collections of Confederate artifacts, paintings, military equipment, and clothing. Admission is $6. The museum is open daily. Other Civil War attractions include the **White House of the Confederacy**, next door to the museum, and the **Civil War Visitor Center at Tredegar Iron Works**, down by the James River. A combination ticket to the Museum of the Confederacy and the White House is just $9.50.

Families traveling with small children will want to check out the **Children's Museum of Richmond**. This recently renovated and enlarged museum features hands-on exhibits for kids ages two through twelve that encourage them to have fun while learning. Located at 2626 West Broad Street, the museum is open daily and admission is $5. A short walk away, at 2500 West Broad Street, the **Science Museum of Virginia** is housed in a former train station that was built in 1919. The museum features a five-story, domed IMAX theater. The museum is open daily during the race season. Call (800) 659-1727 for exhibit information.

The **Richmond Visitors Center** offers the **Richmond Pass** for $15. The pass allows visitors to check out five of twenty cultural institutions and includes a weekend shuttle service. Among the participating attractions are Maymont, Science Museum of Virginia, Lewis Ginter Botanical Garden, the Virginia Museum of Fine Arts, and the Virginia Aviation Museum. Call the Richmond Visitors Center at (804) 358-5511 for details.

NIGHTLIFE IN RICHMOND

Breakers Sports Grill   9127-V West Broad Street (804) 270-1461   A good-sized place in the West End with thirty-eight televisions, two pool tables, darts, and foosball. They also serve a pretty mean sandwich, wings, and ice-cold beverages.

Legend Brewing Company   321 West Seventh Street (804) 232-8871   A handsome brewery and pub on the south side with a comfortable patio, a better-than-average pub menu, and a friendly staff.

Mulligan's Sports Grille   8006 West Broad Street (804) 346-8686   A better-than-average sports bar chain with four area locations. In addition to plenty of TVs, pool, darts, and video games, this place books quality regional and national bands on the weekends. They are open every day and have some remarkable happy hours. Call for the location near you.

Paper Moon and the Platinum Club   6710 Midlothian Turnpike (804) 674-0790   An upscale gentlemen's club that seems to be popular with the race crowd. Open from 8 P.M. to 2 A.M. Tuesday through Saturday.

WHERE TO EAT

One of the nicest surprises Richmond has to offer is the diversity of restaurants. No matter what you are in the mood for, you can find it in Richmond.

Joe's Inn   205 N. Shields (804) 355-2282   This place is legendary with the locals. In the the heart of the historic Fan District, Joe's is known for their huge plates of baked spaghetti, but the entire menu is top-notch.

Awful Arthur's   101 North Eighteenth Street (804) 643-1700   A carefree establishment that features crab legs, oysters, shrimp, and other seafood specialties in a casual setting. The all-you-can-eat crab leg special is a highlight. They have a second location on West Broad Street.

Old Original Bookbinder's   2306 East Cary Street (804) 643-6900   Perhaps as nice a restaurant as you'll find in all of Richmond. This cozy place specializes in fresh crab cakes, huge, mouthwatering lobsters, and fine cuts of steak. The staff is wonderfully attentive, the setting is first class, and the desserts are out of this world.

Sally Bell's Kitchen   708 West Grace Street (804) 644-2838   A simple place that locals might just as soon keep to themselves. This humble eatery has been around for ages and can be counted on for affordable hearty meals that taste like homemade.

Skilligalee's   5416 Glenside Drive (804) 672-6200   About twenty minutes from the track, this massive two-story seafood place has been around for more than thirty years. The warm atmosphere is especially inviting in the non-smoking area upstairs, but the downstairs bar is also generally packed during race week.

The Tobacco Company Restaurant   1201 East Cary Street   (804) 782-9555   Located in a historic warehouse, this massive, four-level establishment has a good-sized bar on the first floor, a two-tier restaurant above that, and a nightclub in the cellar. The upscale restaurant presents steaks and seafood prepared with a southern flair. The casual bar is popular with race fans and offers live music Monday through Saturday nights. The nightclub features DJ dance music and has a separate entrance and cover charge.

Topeka's Steakhouse and Saloon   1776 North Parham Road (804) 346-3000   If you are staying in the Regency Mall area, head to Topeka's for fresh-cut steaks and salmon in a country-and-western atmosphere. They specialize in steaks, especially the New York strip, ribs, and pork chops. This casual steakhouse seats more than 300 people but fills up quickly during race week.

Zeus Gallery   201 North Belmont Avenue (804) 359-3219   An intimate, moderately upscale bistro in the Museum District that offers nicely presented seafood and steaks, as well as mindful service. Call ahead or get there early because seating is limited.

LOCAL MEDIA

The local newspaper is the *Richmond Times-Dispatch*. MRN race broadcasts of the race can be heard via WRXL 102.1 FM.

WHERE TO STAY

HOTELS

The Berkeley Hotel   1200 East Cary Street (888) 780-4422 or (804) 780-1300   Located in the heart of historic Shockoe Slip within a short walk of nightlife and restaurants. This upscale European-style inn is just 6 miles from the track.

Springhill Suites   9701 Brook Road in Glen Allen (804) 266-9403   One of the newest area hotels, just a few miles from the track. It's within a short drive of several restaurants, the rooms are surprisingly comfortable, and the staff is very helpful.

The Jefferson 101 West Franklin Street (804) 788-8000 or (800) 424-8014 A historic hotel with 274 rooms, quite possibly the finest in Richmond. You can be sure that many celebrities who attend a race at Richmond will be staying and dining here.

Holiday Inn–Central 3207 North Boulevard (804) 359-9441 Less than 2 miles from the speedway, this hotel offers the Magnolia restaurant/lounge on site, a pool, and is next door to the Richmond Visitors Center.

Holiday Inn–Crossroads 2000 Staples Mill Road (804) 359-6061 High-rise hotel with a pool, restaurant, and lounge, conveniently located about 5 miles from the track.

Good to Know

- To charge tickets or for additional race information, call (804) 345-RACE.
- To get on the campsite waiting list, call (804) 345-7223 or send a postcard with your name, address, home and work phone numbers, and the size of the camper you'll be using to NASCAR Camping, P.O. Box 9257, Richmond, VA 23227.
- Mail orders can be sent to Richmond International Raceway, P.O. Box 9257, Richmond, VA 23227 or 600 East Laburnum Avenue, Richmond, VA 23222.
- Call the Convention and Visitors Bureau at (800) 370-9004 or (804) 782-2777. The Chamber of Commerce can be reached at (804) 648-1234.
- Worthwhile city Web sites www.richmond.com and www.richmondva.org.
- ➤ The official racetrack Web site is www.rir.com or www.richmondraceway complex.com.

NEARBY WINSTON CUP RACE CITIES

Martinsville: 175 miles (three hours, ten minutes)
Dover Downs: 255 miles (four hours, twenty minutes)
Charlotte/Lowe's Motor Speedway: 280 miles (five hours)
Pocono/Long Pond: 335 miles (six hours, twenty minutes)

IN THE VICINITY

Paramount's Kings Dominion is a 400-acre theme park with more than 200 rides, shows, and attractions just half an hour north of Richmond at exit 98 off I-95. Highlights are the 19-acre WaterWorks water park, a 332-foot replica of the Eiffel Tower, and eleven outrageous roller coasters. NASCAR fans will appreciate the Hyper-Sonic XLC roller coaster, which accelerates from zero to 80 mph in 1.8 seconds.

The park is open daily between Memorial Day and Labor Day. Kings Dominion is also open on weekends from late March to Memorial Day and Labor Day through early October. Call (804) 876-5561 or (804) 876-5000 for more information.

A little farther away, but certainly worth the drive, is **Busch Gardens–Williamsburg.** Less than an hour's drive from Richmond, Busch Gardens re-creates European landmarks and is home to some of the nation's best amusement park rides. **Water Country USA** is an adjacent water park. A two-day, two-park pass is $49.99. Call (800) 343-7946 or (757) 253-3350 for hours of operation.

History buffs will appreciate **Colonial Williamsburg.** Families with young children should not miss the opportunity to spend an afternoon at this genuine eighteenth-century village comprising eighty-eight government buildings, homes, shops, barns, and the local jail. Military re-enactors, costumed citizenry, and craftspeople perform daily. Call the Convention and Visitors Bureau at (800) 368-6511 for additional information.

SPEEDWAYS

▪ *ATLANTA MOTOR SPEEDWAY* ▪

Atlanta, Georgia

*"It's fast—there's no doubt about it. And the bad part
about a fast racetrack is the width of the racetrack. . . .
Here you blow a right front [tire] and you're going to go
60 to 80 feet and you're still going to be hauling the mail,
and the impact angle is going to be bad."*

— TODD BODINE

Like Lowe's Motor Speedway near Charlotte, Atlanta Motor Speedway does not
look more than forty years old. Bruton Smith bought the track in 1990 and has
spent a great deal of time, energy, and money improving the track—so much that,
from the exterior at least, you'd think it was just a few years old. In 1997, the track
was completely overhauled from a 1.522-mile true oval to a 1.54-mile quad-oval.
The start/finish line and pit road were relocated to the opposite side of the track. A
pair of pedestrian tunnels were added to the frontstretch and a host of other additions were made, including new garages and scoring towers.

The track retained its 24-degree banking in the turns, while the frontstretch was
lengthened to 1,415 feet. The backstretch is slightly shorter at 1,320 feet. Both
straights are banked at 5 degrees. These changes and the new asphalt surface have
resulted in some incredible speeds being posted at AMS. In the late nineties,
speeds were so fast that NASCAR considered requiring restrictor plates for races at
Atlanta. Drivers were not always enamored of AMS, but most like it these days as
it has more than one groove and they feel like they can run fast, yet have the room
to race. One drawback is that late in the day the sun can cause a serious glare as drivers enter the first turn.

The track looks a great deal like Smith's other tracks in Texas and Charlotte but
also has its own character. The Petty Garden features a statue of Richard Petty

signing an autograph for a young girl. The statue is situated in a small gated, grassy area in front of the gift shop and ticket offices, near turn four. The statue was dedicated on November 13, 1992, the same weekend of Petty's last Winston Cup race. At both ends of pit road, massive scoring towers—nicknamed the twin towers—list the current lap and top twenty drivers. The old scoreboard, listing the number of laps completed and the top five drivers, is still in operation near the middle of the infield.

Atlanta Motor Speedway is notoriously tough on engines because drivers drive so fast for so long that "hanging RPMs" can cause engines to seize late in a race. Atlanta can be tough on fans as well. In recent years, weather on race day has ranged from brutally hot to freezing cold. In fact, NASCAR has changed the schedule for coming seasons, so Atlanta's second race of the season is earlier in the year when bad weather is less likely to be a factor. Brand-new grandstands were erected, so stands on the current frontstretch are among the newest in Winston Cup racing. The backstretch, completed in 1960, offers a worthwhile view of the track from the higher rows and is not as woefully outdated as many other tracks.

The track seats 124,000 fans, yet ticket prices at AMS remain reasonable by big-city, Winston Cup standards. I don't mean to say good seats can be had cheaply, but the high-end seats are not outrageous. The Champions grandstand overlooks the start/finish line and costs $105 for seats in row 29 and higher. Seats in row 28 and lower cost just $5 less, so if you come across a seat in the higher rows it is generally worth the difference in price. There are seventy-one rows of seats in the adjacent Earnhardt section, just like the Champions grandstand, but all seats in this section cost $95. The Richard Petty grandstand overlooks turn four and the entry into the frontstretch. Section 113 of the Petty section is a nonalcoholic family section. Most seats within the Petty section are exceptional, but they cost $95 no matter what row you are in, and there is no discount offered for kids sitting with their families here. Kids can get in at a discount in General Admission areas.

Seats on the east turn offer a terrific perspective of the track. They don't come cheaply at $95 for rows 21–39, but in lieu of seats high on the frontstretch consider the upper rows here. Seats in rows 1–20 cost $90, but the first row in this section is fairly elevated. The only problem with seats here is that the setting sun can be staring you in the face all afternoon. One section to avoid is the lower rows of the Weaver stands along the backstretch. Seats at the top of the Weaver section are worthwhile at $60, but the bottom rows are $30 and don't offer much of a view of the front side. On the other end of the price spectrum, fans can spend $300 for a seat in a suite. The price includes food and beverages, as well as a great view of the Winston Cup race from an air-conditioned skybox with a private rest room.

Camping is available at the track. Reserved RV camping is $75. Unreserved spots in the Coleman Campground are just $30. The infield opens to cars and RVs at 2 P.M. on the Thursday before the race. All infield spots are reserved. The infield area offers showers, rest rooms, concessions, and souvenir stands. Unreserved tent and pop-up trailer camping is available outside the track, near the intersection of 19/41 and Richard Petty Boulevard. There are rest room and shower facilities available within these campgrounds.

Nineteen eighty-seven was the first year that the season's final race was held in Atlanta instead of Riverside, California. Since then it has been the site of several big races.

HISTORY

On July 31, 1960, Atlanta International Raceway, as it was called in those days, hosted its first sanctioned race, the Dixie 300. Fireball Roberts took the pole and averaged 112.653 mph to beat out Cotton Owens in the innagural race. Pontiac swept the top four spots that day.

The 1961 Dixie 500 at Atlanta featured one of the wildest finishes of all time. With five laps to go, Banjo Matthews blew an engine and relinquished the lead to Fireball Roberts. Roberts ran out of gas with two laps remaining. Bunkie Blackburn, driving in relief of Junior Johnson, inherited the lead on the final lap, but he ran out of gas on the backstretch and coasted across the finish line. David Pearson passed Blackburn's Pontiac before reaching the checkered flag, but the race was initially awarded to Blackburn. Upon further review it was determined that Pearson was on the lead lap and had won the race despite leading just one lap all day, the final lap. Pontiac ended up sweeping the top four positions yet again.

Fast Freddie Lorenzen won the Festival 250 in 1961 and followed that with three consecutive Atlanta 500 wins from 1962 through 1964. Rex White won the Dixie 400 in 1962. He led just the final three laps to clinch his only superspeedway victory and the final win of his career. Marvin Panch, driving a Ford owned by the Wood Brothers, became the first driver to sweep the season races at Atlanta in 1965. Cale Yarborough earned a trio of wins in the Atlanta 500 from 1967 through 1969. They were his first wins here. All told, Yarborough won seven times at Atlanta. While Cale was dominating the spring races at Atlanta, LeeRoy Yarbrough won back-to-back Dixie 500s in 1968 and 1969. They were his only two victories in Atlanta.

Richard Petty won consecutive Dixie 500s in 1970 and 1971. Bobby Allison swept the 1972 races, and David Pearson duplicated the feat in 1973. Buddy Baker qualified fastest eight times at Atlanta, edging out Cale Yarborough for the most poles, but Baker won just twice at Atlanta. Those wins came in the 1975 Atlanta 500 and 1979 Dixie 500. In 1978, Donnie Allison led the way as Chevy swept the top four positions in the Dixie 500. It was the final Winston Cup win of Allison's career.

Dale Earnhardt won the 1980 Atlanta 500, early in the season, for his first superspeedway victory and proceeded to win his first Winston Cup championship that

The leaders motor through turn four during a single-file restart at the 2001 NAPA 500 in Atlanta. *(Photo by Karl Golden)*

season. The win at Atlanta that year came from the thirty-first qualifying position, which at the time was the record for worst starting position to win at Atlanta. Rusty Wallace finished second that day in his first Winston Cup start. Cale Yarborough won again in 1983, sixteen seasons after his first Atlanta win. Benny Parsons took his twenty-first and final checkered flag on March 18, 1984, in the Coca-Cola 500.

Earnhardt revisited victory lane in the fall of 1984, on his way to a track record of nine checkered flags in Atlanta. Earnhardt's nine wins were spread out over twenty-one seasons. Remarkably, he never swept races in a single season or won the same race in consecutive seasons. In the 1986 Atlanta Journal 500, Earnhardt lapped the field on his way to victory, locking up his second Winston Cup championship. It was the first time in eight years that the title was clinched before the final race of the season. Atlanta has also been kind to Bill Elliott over the years. Elliott swept the 1985 Atlanta races, won from the pole in 1987, clinched the Winston Cup championship with an eleventh-place finish in 1988, and swept the season again in 1992.

Jeff Gordon got his first Winston Cup start on November 15, 1992, in the Hooters 500. This was also the 1,177th and final career start for Richard Petty. Heading into the landmark race, Davey Allison was leading the season points chase by 30 points over Alan Kulwicki and was 40 points ahead of Bill Elliott. Allison got tangled up with Ernie Irvan late in the race and his championship hopes were dashed. Elliott and Kulwicki traded the lead for much of the race, and it became apparent that even if Elliott won the race, he would also need to lead the most laps and receive the 5 bonus points in order to overtake Kulwicki for the points championship. Elliott won the race, but Kulwicki led 103 laps versus Elliott's 102, so Kulwicki won the championship 4,078 points to 4,068. Had Elliott led more laps than Kulwicki, they would have tied on points for the season and Elliott would have won because he finished first in five races versus Kulwicki's two victories. To date, that remains the tightest finish in the Winston Cup championship.

Going into the final race of the 1995 season, Jeff Gordon had a nearly insurmountable lead in the Winston Cup points chase. Dale Earnhardt was 147 points behind and gave it his all by winning the NAPA 500. Earnhardt set a track record by averaging 163.633 mph and led the most laps in a race that took just three hours and three minutes. Gordon, however, led a single lap despite finishing in thirty-second place, 14 laps behind Earnhardt. That was enough for Gordon to earn the championship with a 34-point margin. It was Gordon's first championship season. Just a few seasons later, Gordon won his third championship and tied Richard Petty's modern-era record of thirteen wins with a victory in the 1998 NAPA 500. Gordon took the lead in that race with 7 laps to go and edged out Dale Jarrett by .739 seconds in a race shortened by rain to 221 laps.

Bobby Labonte has been a force to reckon with at Atlanta in recent years. Labonte won the NAPA 500 from the pole in 1996. He won the fall race again in 1997, the first race on the redesigned 1.54-mile track, and followed that with a win in Atlanta the next spring. The new track configuration also saw Geoffrey Bodine set the track qualifying record of 197.478 mph, a sizzling 28.074-second lap around the newly paved track. In 1999, Labonte won the NAPA 500 again, this time from the thirty-seventh starting position, the worst starting position to win here.

Dale Earnhardt won the 2000 Cracker Barrel 500 from the thirty-fifth position. The victory was one of the closest margins of victory in NASCAR history, as Earnhardt edged out Bobby Labonte by .010 seconds. It was also Earnhardt's penultimate win. On November 20, 2000, Jerry Nadeau got his first career victory in the NAPA 500, his 103rd Winston Cup start. Nadeau was just the fourth driver to earn his first-ever checkered flag in Atlanta.

The very next year, Kevin Harvick topped that by holding off Jeff Gordon by .006 of a second to win his first race in the Cracker Barrel 500. The race could have been won by any of five drivers—Earnhardt Jr., Dale Jarrett, Jerry Nadeau,

Gordon, and Harvick—running neck and neck in the final laps. In just his third Winston Cup start, Harvick powered the very same Goodwrench Chevrolet that Dale Earnhardt drove to victory lane in Atlanta a year earlier to one of the most hotly contested and emotional victories of the season. It was also the very first Winston Cup race in which Harvick led a lap. That fall, in what ended up being the second-to-last race of the 2001 season because the New Hampshire race was rescheduled to be the season finale, Bobby Labonte took the checkered flag once again. Jerry Nadeau led the race when the white flag was waved but ran out of gas with half a lap to go. Nadeau crossed the start/finish line, but not before Labonte, Sterling Marlin, and Kevin Harvick passed him. Labonte started thirty-ninth to break his own record for worst starting position to win a race at Atlanta. Had Nadeau not run out of gas, he would have won easily from the forty-first qualifying position. Jeff Gordon finished sixth that afternoon to clinch his fourth Winston Cup championship.

GETTING TO THE TRACK

It seems that all roads in Georgia lead to Atlanta. Unfortunately, only one road leads to the track. The speedway is about 27 miles south of downtown Atlanta in Hampton, Georgia. Parking at the track is free in track-owned lots. Most of those lots are along Speedway Boulevard or along Highway 19/41. Lots on Bear Creek Road may offer the quickest exit from the track after the race. Regulars will tell you that traffic on race day is among the worst in NASCAR Winston Cup racing. The road behind the track has been widened to five lanes, alleviating some of the trouble, but there is one major road, Highway 19/41, that leads from Atlanta to the track and it backs up for miles near the track. After my first race at Atlanta, I spent three hours waiting to exit the track parking lot; two of those hours were with my keys out of the ignition because traffic was going nowhere.

Route 20 is a worthwhile back-road alternative to I-75 to the east, but Route 20 is a winding two-lane road that can be nearly as bad on race day. I-85 is well west of the track, but 92 to Woolsey Road, the route between I-85 and the back side of the track, is no picnic either. Traffic is worst from downtown Atlanta and all points north of the track, so your best bet may be to approach the track from below. Route 16 runs between I-75 and I-85 and intersects with 19/41 south of the track. Locust Grove Road (exit 212) is another way to take from I-75. None of these routes qualify as a well-kept secret, however, and you should expect serious delays on the way to the track. This is another track for which fans should pack a tailgate barbecue and wait out the traffic before leaving. Fans heading north on I-85 should simply follow a team transporter. They head back toward Charlotte after a race and generally know all the shortcuts.

You can also fly a private plane into Clayton County Airport/Tara Field, which is adjacent to the speedway. Atlanta's MARTA rail system is among the most convenient and widely used mass transit systems in a Winston Cup city. Unfortunately, it is not an option for trips to the racetrack. It is, however, very convenient for folks staying in downtown Atlanta and the nearby suburbs as they head to major attractions and nearby restaurants.

WHAT TO SEE AND DO

Atlanta has a wealth of things to keep race fans busy. One of the city's more popular attractions is the **CNN Center/CNN Studio Tour**, which offers a behind-the-scenes look at TBS's world headquarters and production facilities. It's located in the heart of downtown across from Centennial Olympic Park. The tour takes a little less than an hour and costs $6 for adults. In addition to touring the studio you can join the audience of a live TV show. Call (404) 827-2300 for tour reservations or (800) 410-4266 to attend a show. Another Atlanta original is the **World of Coca-Cola**. Downtown, adjacent to Underground Atlanta at 55 Martin Luther King Jr. Drive, this three-story tribute to America's favorite soft drink is open seven days a week. Expect to spend about an hour and a half on a self-guided tour. Tickets are $3.50 for adults and reservations are recommended.

Atlanta is also home to **Road Atlanta**, a 2.52-mile, twelve-turn road course on Georgia 53 near I-85 northeast of downtown Atlanta. Road Atlanta hosts the Nissan Grand Prix each spring. The **Atlanta Dragway**, farther north at I-85 and U.S. 441, is a quarter-mile drag strip that hosts NHRA races and lesser events. Call (404) 335-2301 for race schedules. Baseball fans should try to see an Atlanta Braves game at **Turner Field**. The ballpark, opened in 1997, is a vast improvement over the old Fulton County Stadium. If the Braves are out of town, tours are available. During the baseball season, tours leave every half hour and generally include the Braves Hall of Fame and Museum, a luxury suite, broadcast booth, press box, clubhouse, and the dugout. Tours cost $7 for adults. Call (800) 326-4000 for game tickets or (404) 614-2311 for tour information.

North of downtown Atlanta, at 11000 Alpharetta Highway in Roswell, the **Andretti Speed Lab** is home to a host of classic cars, authentic racing gear, go-kart tracks, video racing games, a state-of-the-art sports bar with a glass floor overlooking the go-kart tracks, and much more. A race around the go-kart track is $18 for adults. Another racing oriented attraction is **SpeedZone**, at 3505 George Busbee Parkway in Kennesaw. Here you'll find four tracks—a 140-yard drag strip that features dragsters that accelerate to 70 mph in less than four seconds, Grand Prix racing, sprint track racing, and an 1,100-foot road course track. There's also a restaurant, a bar, and a game room that features pool tables and dozens of simulators.

Malibu Grand Prix, off I-85 at Indian Trail, offers outdoor go-kart racing and putt-putt golf as well as an indoor arcade with racing games.

Atlanta also has several fine museums. Two of my favorites are the **High Museum of Art** and the **Sci/Trek—Science and Technology Museum of Atlanta**. The High, at 1280 Peachtree Street NE, has an impressive collection of twentieth-century art and photographs but has become a great place to see world-class traveling exhibits as well. Open Tuesday through Sunday, it's free after 1 P.M. on Thursdays. Otherwise, admission is $5 for adults. Sci/Trek is a hands-on museum at 395 Piedmont Avenue that's a big hit with kids. The museum features more than 150 exhibits for kids of all ages. Call (404) 522-5500 for additional information. The **Atlanta Cyclorama & Civil War Museum**, in historic Grant Park, re-creates the battle of Atlanta, a pivotal Civil War battle. This multimedia display has been entertaining visitors since before the turn of the century.

Stone Mountain Park is just 16 miles east of Atlanta on U.S. Highway 78. The park is open daily at 10 A.M. during the Winston Cup season. Admission is free, but a one-day parking permit costs $7. The park is best known for the giant granite mountain and Confederate Memorial carving, but you'll also discover hiking trails, an open-air railroad, a sky lift that takes you to the top, museums, campgrounds, a beach, and a waterslide park. You can also board the paddlewheel riverboat, attend concerts and festivals, check out the Saturday-night laser light show, or take on the thirty-six holes of championship golf. Robert Trent Jones Sr. designed the Stonemount golf course. Call (800) 317-2006 or (770) 498-5690 for prices to individual Stone Mountain attractions and other details.

Six Flags over Georgia, just west of Atlanta, is an amusement park with more than 100 rides, shows, and attractions, including nine roller coasters. Déjà Vu, the newest coaster, takes riders through two twenty-story freefalls, once backward and once forward. Other highlights include Batman: The Ride, The Georgia Scorcher, Ninja, Viper, and a pair of classic wooden coasters, the Great American Scream Machine and the Georgia Cyclone. The park is not generally open during the first Atlanta race, but with the new Winston Cup schedule it is open for the weekend of the fall race. Call (770) 739-3400 for schedule and general park information.

NIGHTLIFE IN ATLANTA

Atlanta ranks among the best Winston Cup cities for nightlife. Buckhead and Virginia Highlands are two outstanding nightlife districts that rival those of much larger cities. Buckhead is home to **Lulu's Bait Shop**, where drinks are served in giant 96-ounce fishbowls accented with rubber alligators. Tables on Lulu's patio are highly coveted and offer a great view of revelers as they pass by on the street. **Fado** is an authentic Irish pub and restaurant at 3035 Peachtree Road. This dark and friendly place has a wonderful selection of brews from across the pond. Another worthwhile Buckhead establishment is **ESPN Zone**. This massive sports bar features 165 TVs, loads of sports memorabilia, decent bar chow, and hundreds of interactive games.

Virginia Highlands has a more indigenous selection of clubs. **Blind Willie's**, at 828 North Highland Street, is about as good as a blues club gets. The place has a classic feel, great sight lines and acoustics, and legendary blues acts just about every weekend. Seats are limited, so get there early. Nearby, you'll find the **Highland Tap**. This dark basement bar is a great place to grab a cold beer, but don't overlook the restaurant. For the money, it's tough to beat their steaks.

Sports fans looking for something on a smaller scale should check out **Frankie's** in Sandy Springs. The emphasis here is on good bar food, a fun atmosphere, sports trivia, and wall-to-wall sports memorabilia. There are more than 170 TV monitors, indoors and out on the patio, so no matter where you sit, you'll have a good view of whatever games or races are being shown. Nearby, **Five Seasons Brewing Company**, at 5600 Roswell Road, has a pub setting as well as pool tables, darts, and an Old World–style biergarten. If you are into theme bars and restaurants, Atlanta is also home to an All-Star Café, a Planet Hollywood, and a Hard Rock Café. All three are downtown on Peachtree Street NW, near International.

WHERE TO EAT

One of my favorite Atlanta eateries is the **Three Dollar Café** in Buckhead. The food is good, affordable, and piled high on your plate. The bottled beer selection is outstanding and reasonably priced. What more could you ask for? Not quite as inexpensive, **Ray's on the River**, at 6700 Powers Ferry Road, is a comfortable waterfront café with terrific seafood, steaks, and chops. The outdoor deck overlooking the Chattahoochee River offers a nice retreat for lunch. Call (770) 955-1187 in advance to get on the waiting list for a riverfront table.

Sotto, Sotto, at 313 North Highland Avenue in the Inman Park neighborhood near Virginia Highlands, is a wonderful northern Italian bistro with outstanding entrees, friendly, considerate service, and a dressy casual atmosphere. **McKinnon's**, at 3209 Maple Avenue, is minutes from Buckhead and serves some of the best Louisiana cuisine you'll find this side of the bayou. They offer an upscale atmosphere in the main dining room or a more casual setting in the Grill Room.

The Varsity, at the corner of North Avenue and Spring Street, has been a bastion of burgers, hot dogs, and onion rings in Atlanta for more than seventy years. Legend has it that a Georgia Tech business student was told by his professor that he was so incompetent that he couldn't operate a hot dog stand. The student decided to prove his teacher wrong, and the Varsity has since become an Atlanta institution. **Max Lager's** is a brew pub and restaurant in downtown at 320 Peachtree Street. They specialize in steaks, seafood, and wood-fired gourmet pizza. The outdoor patio is a great place to enjoy a cold, handcrafted beer and a moderately priced lunch or dinner.

For delicious, affordable Mexican food, stop by **El Ranchero**. There are several locations around town, but the Jonesboro restaurant at 7919 Tara Boulevard is closest to the track. Just up the street, **Sports Café**, at the corner of Tara Boulevard and Robert E. Lee Street, is one of the better sports bars near the track. Jonesboro is also home to Hooters, Longhorn Steakhouse, Sonny's BBQ, and a Winn-Dixie grocery store, so this is a convenient place to stay during race week.

Manhattan's, about 10 miles south of the track at 1707 North Expressway in Griffin, is a casual steakhouse that also offers seafood and pasta specialties. This mid-sized place jams them in during race week and is a popular place with officials and race teams on nights leading up to the race.

LOCAL MEDIA

The *Atlanta Journal Constitution*, the local daily newspaper, takes its racing seriously and does a good job of listing racing-related events. *Creative Loafing*, the weekly entertainment tab, is a good source for nightlife and dining options. Races are broadcast on the Performance Racing Network, which is broadcast on WYAY 106.7 FM.

WHERE TO STAY

HOTELS

There's no shortage of hotels in Atlanta. Unfortunately, few of them are located near the track. There are, however, plenty of hotels in downtown Atlanta within walking distance, MARTA ride, or a short drive of many of the city's major attractions and restaurants. Decide what's important to you—proximity to the track or downtown—and choose a place that fits your budget.

Country Hearth Inn   1078 Bear Creek Boulevard, Hampton (770) 707-1477
  One of the closest hotels to the track is also one of the newest. Just 1 mile from the track, this may be one of the best bargains for race weekend.
Best Western   805 Industrial Boulevard, McDonough (770) 898-1006   A clean, moderately affordable hotel with several fast food restaurants within a short drive.
Comfort Inn   80 Highway 81 West, McDonough (770) 954-9110   Among the better hotels in McDonough, just 10 miles from the track.

Days Inn 744 Highway 155, McDonough (770) 957-5261 Comfortable accommodations within a modest drive of the track and minutes from several restaurants.

Hampton Inn 759 Pollard Boulevard (404) 658-1961 An affordable place across the street from Turner Field, minutes from downtown and a reasonable drive to Atlanta Motor Speedway.

Holiday Inn 930 Highway 155 South, McDonough (770) 957-5291 Just 10 miles east of the track near I-75, this one-story hotel has an outdoor pool and a fitness center.

Holiday Inn Express 140 Lanier Avenue E, Fayetteville (770) 461-5600 A handsome southern-style hotel with an elegant lobby and wraparound porch about 10 miles north of the track. Complimentary breakfast and local phone calls.

Ramada Limited Suites 357 Lee Street, Forest Park (404) 768-7799 Just 4 miles from the airport and a modest drive to the track, this property is within walking distance of a Denny's and Riley's Irish Pub.

Regency Suites Hotel 975 West Peachtree Street (404) 876-5003 or (800) 642-3629 A reasonably priced hotel near downtown Atlanta. The hotel is 30 miles north of the track, but it's adjacent to MARTA and just 3 miles from Turner Field.

Shoney's Inn 6358 Old Dixie Highway, Jonesboro (770) 968-5018 Just 14 miles from the track, this amiable hotel features reasonably priced king-size rooms with microwaves and refrigerators.

Westin Peachtree 210 Peachtree Street NW (404) 659-1400 Luxury accommodations in the heart of the downtown nightlife and restaurant district. Not particularly convenient to the track, but there is nothing of this caliber close to the speedway.

Houseboats

For something completely different, rent a houseboat on Lake Lanier, a wonderfully scenic 38,000-acre lake just north of Atlanta. Available houseboats sleep up to ten people. Call **Lake Lanier Houseboat Rentals** (770) 271-3596 for additional information.

Good to Know

- To charge tickets or for additional race information, call (770) 946-4211.
- For infield and camping information, call (770) 707-7904.
- Mail orders can be sent to Ticket Office, Atlanta Motor Speedway, P.O. Box 500, Hampton, GA 30228.
- The Atlanta Convention & Visitors Bureau is at 233 Peachtree Street, Suite 2000, Atlanta, GA 30303. Call (404) 521-6600 or (404) 222-6688.

- Call 1-800-VISIT GA for information on additional attractions, hotels, and restaurants in Georgia. The Georgia Department of Industry, Trade and Tourism can be reached at P.O. Box 1776, Atlanta, GA 30301.
- Worthwhile city Web sites include www.atlanta.com.
- ➤ The official track Web site is www.atlantamotorspeedway.com.

NEARBY WINSTON CUP RACE CITIES

Talladega: 105 miles (one hour, thirty minutes)
Charlotte: 235 miles (four hours)
Bristol: 250 miles (four hours, twenty minutes)
Darlington: 295 miles (five hours)

IN THE VICINITY

Thunder Road USA, Georgia's Racing Hall of Fame is the new 40,000 square foot home to the Bill Elliott Museum. Opened in May 2002, the hall includes all of the memorabilia that was housed at the Bill Elliott Museum and much more. You'll find dozens of vintage cars, including a rotating exhibit of a 1939 Ford coupe, a 1976 Torino, and a 1969 Plymouth Superbird, a pair of theaters—one emulates a drive-in movie theater, while the other has 125 seats and shows a twenty-minute film on Georgia racing history—and a tribute to the Elliott family and other home-grown racing heroes, including Smokey Yunich and Buckshot Morris. There are also state-of-the-art racing simulators, an exhibit on Georgia racetracks, the Champion's Café Diner, an arcade with plenty of racing games, and, of course, a gift shop. Thunder Road is located in Elliott's hometown of Dawsonville, Georgia, at 415 Highway 53 East, about 50 miles north of Atlanta. Call (706) 216-7223 for details.

Golf fans will want to check out the **Chateau Elan Golf Club**. The resort offers four courses to choose from—three eighteen-hole courses and a nine-hole par-three walking course. The Chateau course is one of the absolute finest public courses in the state. The course is located northeast of downtown Atlanta at exit 48 off I-85 in Braselton. Call (770) 271-6050 for tee times and additional information. For a list of other area golf courses visit www.golfatlanta.com.

A Dozen Favorite Winston Cup Race Cities—
Things to Do Away from the Track

12 Richmond—history buffs will absolutely love this town.

11 Daytona—the beach is just the beginning.

10 Atlanta—nightlife and pro sports are why it's also known as "Hotlanta."

9 Las Vegas—if you like casino gambling, this city moves way up the list.

8 Miami—South Beach nightclubs and Miami Beach bikinis. What more can you ask for?

7 Fort Worth—area museums, attractions, nightclubs and restaurants are astounding.

6 Indianapolis—as vibrant a downtown as there is on the circuit.

5 Kansas City—another surprising race destination with plenty to do and see.

4 Phoenix—the Grand Canyon alone makes this a trip worth making.

3 Charlotte—nowhere else has as many race-related attractions.

2 Sonoma—San Francisco is a short drive away and wine country is a great excuse to leave the kids at home.

1 Chicago—an unbelievable city with world class museums, attractions, restaurants and nightlife.

■ *CALIFORNIA SPEEDWAY* ■

Fontana, California

"It's a fast track, but it's a forgiving racetrack and one that is extremely fun as a driver because you have to have a combination of a good handling car and a lot of horsepower."
— DALE JARRETT

This track is often compared to Michigan Speedway because the wide, sweeping racing surface presents two or three grooves and side-by-side racing is not uncommon, but this 2-mile monster has its own distinct personality. The track was built on the site of a former Kaiser steel mill that is said to have been the film location for the Arnold Schwarzenegger movie *Terminator II*. A 137-foot water tower emblazoned with the track logo is the lone remnant from the old steel plant. The racing surface is smooth, 75 feet wide, and fairly flat with 14-degree banking in all four turns, an 11-degree slope through the tri-oval, and a mere 3 degrees along the 2,500-foot backstretch. Palm trees dot the immaculate grounds at California Speedway, and the grandstands form a giant arch that sweeps alongside the 3,100-foot frontstretch.

Races here are 500 miles and 250 laps long, as opposed to the 400-milers at Michigan, so engine failures and tire trouble are anticipated late in the race, especially if long green flag runs are the order of the day. The track has wide-open areas along the infield on both the front- and backstretches, so drivers can often recover from spins exiting the turns and caution flags appear infrequently. One spot on the track that collects its share of wrecks is the exit of turn four, where the track can get slick and cars tend to push out toward the wall, especially if cars stay three wide heading into the straight. The track is fairly weather-sensitive and as it gets hotter, the track can get slicker. Those teams that adapt to the changing conditions are generally the most successful. These weather changes are best illustrated by the sudden appearance of the San Gabriel Mountains beyond the backstretch in the middle of the afternoon as it warms up and Los Angeles's trademark haze burns off.

You can expect speeds to exceed 200 mph at California Speedway, but the fastest car doesn't always win here. The speedway has become known as a fuel-mileage racetrack. The pit window is around fifty laps, and on more than one occasion pit strategy has enabled a middle-of-the-pack car to steal a win by staying out when others were forced to pit for gas. Other teams have finished well by taking two tires and fuel or a daring "splash and go" pit stop under a green flag. On the flipside, this is a bad track for crews to guess wrong at and run out of fuel, because it's a long way around to pit lane and they can lose a bunch of track position. Fontana has been described as a patient man's race because drivers must concentrate on hitting their marks, beating the track as well as the competition. It's also possible to recover from early mishaps, because the races are 500 miles long and engine failures can take out the leaders at any time.

The track has a number of unique qualities. Palm trees are spaced along the backstretch between a dozen or so giant billboards in turns two and three. A wide roadway sits between the track and the stands, and the seating sections are well elevated, so the first row of seats is about 8 feet off the ground. The long red press box and luxury suites sit atop the grandstand and provide some shade for the very top rows of seating near the start/finish line. The long, wide pit road has large pit boxes and ample room for drivers to negotiate during mass pit stops. A tall scoring tower, reminiscent of Indy, sits between pit road and the track. The tower lists forty-two drivers and the current lap. A sea of campers occupies the infield all weekend long, and the track has wide-open spaces of green grass that give it an unspoiled feeling found at very few tracks. This is especially impressive when you consider the harsh, industrial surroundings from which this site was recovered.

California Speedway is the only Winston Cup track with its own mass transit depot. The Metro stops beyond the backstretch near gate 4. Trams deliver fans to the front side of the track from the Metro station. A vehicle tunnel runs beneath turn four. The tunnel is best accessed via gate 6 off San Bernardino Avenue. A colorful racing mural featuring the #2 Miller Lite car occupies the wall near the tunnel outside the facility. A crossover bridge, outside the track, allows pedestrians to easily access the grandstands from the parking lot. With a crowd approaching 120,000 fans, the Winston Cup race here is the largest sporting event in California. In a state that hosts the Rose Bowl every year, that's quite an accomplishment. Tickets can be hard to come by on race day; 93,000 seats and 1,700 reserved infield RV spaces were presold for the 2001 race.

Drivers note that they are driving into the sun as they head down the backstretch late in the day. The track has a long row of terrace suites in the infield running

(Photo Courtesy of California Speedway)

parallel to pit road. These buildings obstruct the view of fans in the lower rows of the main grandstand. Cars tend to spread out along the 2-mile oval, and races here can be uneventful for long periods of time, especially in the first 150 laps. The track's greatest flaw is the rule against bringing your own beer to the track. You can bring the standard 14 × 14 × 14 cooler with food and nonalcoholic beverages. Concessions are unspectacular at the track, with your standard offerings of hot dogs, burgers, pizza, nachos, pretzels, peanuts, lemonade, bottled water, soft drinks, and, of course, beer. One exceptional concession stand is near pit road and offers deli sandwiches, burritos, and juices.

Seating at the track is relegated to the frontstretch and turn one. Seats in turn one have a nice view down the frontstretch and pit road but face the sun late in the day. Many seats overlooking the start/finish line were sold as season ticket packages and are the most coveted at the track. These seats are individual stadium-style seats, while most sections feature aluminum bleachers with seatbacks. Prices range from $39 to $105 for grandstand reserved seating, but season tickets can be as much as $189. Infield wristbands are $40 dollars. After the race a concert is held in the infield, and the scene is reminiscent of a giant tailgate party. Prerace pit passes, good Friday through Sunday, cost $45, over and above the cost of a grandstand ticket.

HISTORY

West Coast fans have been attending NASCAR races in the Golden State at more than a dozen different racetracks since 1951. The current speedway site is located just 20 miles from the old Riverside International Raceway, a 2.62-mile road course that hosted such legends as Richard Petty, Marvin Panch, Dan Gurney, Fred Lorenzen, Junior Johnson, and A. J. Foyt in the late fifties and sixties. In later years, Bobby Allison, Cale Yarborough, David Pearson, and Darrell Waltrip found their way to victory lane at Riverside.

In 1981, Riverside was actually the site of three Winston Cup races, one 400-miler and a pair of 500-mile events. DW earned the pole for all three and won the 400-mile race. Bobby Allison won both the 500-milers. In 1982, Tim Richmond earned his first Winston Cup victory at Riverside. He won again that season in the year's final race at Riverside to complete a sweep in just his second full season. Winning again in 1986 and 1987, four of Richmond's thirteen career wins happened at this southern California road course. Rusty Wallace won the final two sanctioned races at Riverside in 1987 and 1988. Bill Elliott and Ricky Rudd are among the drivers who earned their first career victories at Riverside.

The former Ontario Motor Speedway, a 2.5-mile quad-oval that was the site of nine sanctioned races from 1971 to 1980, was even closer to the new California Speedway. A. J. Foyt won the first two races from the pole, beating fifty other drivers as each race started with seventeen rows of cars lined three abreast at this Indy-style track. Bobby Allison, Benny Parsons, David Pearson, Buddy Baker, and Neil Bonnett completed the celebrated list of winners at Ontario. Allison and Parsons joined Foyt as the track's only two-time winners. Parsons won the track's final two events in 1979 and 1980. The following year Riverside held three races, so except for 1973, the Los Angeles area actually supported three Winston Cup races annually from 1971 through 1981.

After an extended absence, Winston Cup stock car racing returned to southern California when Roger Penske opened California Speedway in 1997. Joe Nemechek earned the first pole of his career in the inaugural race, but Jeff Gordon, the Golden State's Golden Boy, edged Terry Labonte and Ricky Rudd to take the checkered flag in a race that featured twenty-one lead changes. It was the second time Gordon won a track's inaugural Winston Cup race, as he also won at Indy in 1994. His winning average speed of 155.012 mph at California has held up as the track record.

Gordon, further demonstrating that he knows his way around this track, earned the pole the following year. Mark Martin, driving a Jack Roush Ford, beat out Jeremy Mayfield, Terry Labonte, Gordon, and Darrell Waltrip that Sunday afternoon in a race that featured a track record of six caution flags. In 1999, time trials were rained out. Nevertheless, Jeff Gordon, who started fifth in his Rick Hendrick–owned Chevrolet, employed better fuel-mileage strategy to return to victory lane and became the track's first two-time winner, finishing ahead of Jeff Burton, Bobby Labonte, Tony Stewart, and Dale Jarrett. The 1999 California 500 set a Fontana record with twenty-eight lead changes.

On April 28, 2000, Mike Skinner averaged 186.061 mph as he set the track qualifying record with a 38.697-second lap. Jeremy Mayfield won the race that season, despite decreasing oil pressure in the race's final laps. By winning from the twenty-fourth starting position, Mayfield's second career victory was one for the California Speedway record books, as he became the first driver to win from outside the top five qualifying spots. The win also enabled Roger Penske to visit victory lane as owner of the winning car at the speedway he had built just a few years earlier.

A Penske-owned Ford returned to the winner's circle the following year, as Rusty Wallace, who started nineteenth, dominated the second half of the race and survived six caution flags. The final restart came with just nineteen laps remaining. Jeff Gordon, Dale Earnhardt Jr., Tony Stewart, Jeremy Mayfield, and Ricky Rudd were in his rearview mirror as Wallace took the checkered flag for the first time in twenty-one races. The win was Wallace's fifty-fourth career win and extended his streak to sixteen consecutive seasons with at least one win. Rusty's victory lap holding the #3 flag was one of the more poignant tributes to Dale Earnhardt in a season full of memorable moments.

GETTING TO THE TRACK

In a part of the country known for frustrating traffic, California Speedway has a better traffic plan than most tracks, with twenty-five separate routes to and from major freeways. Of course, getting to a freeway does not mean it's clear sailing from that point on. The track is near the intersection of I-10 and I-15 and is also easily accessed from Interstate 215 or Route 60. Most race fans coming from L.A. will take I-10 to the Valley/Etiwanda exit or the Cherry Avenue exit and proceed north to the track. If I-10 is bogged down with race traffic, an alternative route is to take Route 60 to Etiwanda Avenue North. Signs and highway patrol will direct you to the track and one of the free parking lots. Lots 2, 3, 5, 8, 9, 10, 11, and 12 are general parking. Lot 1 is for Speedway Club guests and handicapped parking, lot 4 is for hospitality chalet guests, and lot 8 is for oversized vehicles. Lots 7 and 8 are for infield fans. Parking gates open at 6 A.M. and admission gates open an hour later.

And, as mentioned earlier, the track has its own Metro train stop. In fact, more than 9,000 fans took the train from Orange County, Santa Barbara, Los Angeles Union Station, and other stops along the way for the 2001 race. Call (800) USA-RAIL for ticket and schedule information. The track is also just 5 miles from Ontario International Airport.

WHAT TO SEE AND DO

There are a few things to do in the immediate vicinity of the track, but the area's landmark attractions are spread throughout southern California. **Ontario Mills Mall** is one of the largest malls in the nation and attracts race fans for a few reasons. It is designed in an oval shape, not unlike a racetrack, and **Dave & Buster's**, the giant bar/restaurant, features a video game room with hundreds of interactive racing video games. Race fans from the Carolinas will appreciate the **Krispy Kreme Donuts** location just outside the mall on Fourth Street. The mall features hundreds of shops, a giant food court, and a handful of specialty restaurants. The mall is minutes from the track near the intersection of I-10 and I-15. Golfers will want to hit the links at **Empire Lakes**, a challenging eighteen-hole course and golf academy designed by Arnold Palmer. This stunning course sits at the base of the mountains in Rancho Cucamonga and weaves its way through the foothills around four scenic lakes. Call (909) 481-6663 for details.

Not particularly close to the track, but well worth the drive, **Universal Studios** has become equal parts amusement park and movie studio, attracting five million visitors a year. The studio occupies more than 400 acres, which you can see via guided tram and a walking tour. Along the way, you'll pass by several familiar backdrops and sets, see the star's dressing rooms, and come upon a number of catastrophes and calamities, re-creating scenes from some of Universal's more memorable movies and

TV shows. You may also get the chance to be part of an audience during the taping of a TV show. The amusement park rides, especially Back to the Future and Jurassic Park, are some of the best I've ever been on but also have some of the longest lines I've ever had to endure. If possible, go to the park during the week when lines are shortest.

Warner Brothers Studios takes a much more subtle approach, offering small group tours (twelve people or less) of the actual moviemaking process. This allows visitors to get a genuine behind-the-scenes look at various processes involved in making a movie. It's a lot less glitzy but offers an authentic glimpse into the industry's goings-on. Admission is $24 for adults. Because tours are limited to just two a day, it's suggested that you call at least a week in advance to reserve a spot for you or your group.

Disneyland is the area's premier family attraction and occupies 82 acres, which means you can expect to do a lot of walking around. The parking lot accounts for another 102 acres, so be certain to remember where you parked. Disneyland is divided into eight different areas, with rides and attractions for both kids and adults. My favorite rides include the Matterhorn, a great indoor/outdoor roller coaster with wild 45-degree turns that will scare the pants off you, and Space Mountain, an indoor roller coaster that features planetarium effects and a simulated space launch. Lines here are also ridiculously long. The newest addition to Disneyland is **California Adventure**, a theme park with re-creations of several Golden State attractions. Multiday passes for both parks are available.

Knott's Berry Farm is the area's other amusement park, in Buena Park at 8039 Beach Boulevard. The park offers hundreds of rides and attractions in six themed areas covering 150 acres. One of the park's more recent attractions is the Boomerang, a roller coaster that is more than 110 feet tall and turns you upside down six times. In nearby Yorba Linda, the **Richard Nixon Library and Birthplace** is visited by hundreds of thousands of people each year. The museum and library, dedicated to one of the most controversial U.S. presidents, includes the humble home Nixon lived in as a child, a rose garden, and a main gallery, which contains the artifacts of his scandal-shortened presidency.

Venice Beach has become a major tourist draw and one of the city's trendiest areas. You may have seen Venice Beach in the movie *White Men Can't Jump*. The basketball courts are pretty much as depicted in the movie, with lots of incredible athleticism and hotdogging, highlighted by a stream of never-ending trash talking. I could have spent the entire afternoon watching these guys play hoops if it weren't for the equally impressive talent milling about on the beach and boardwalk. The beach is not especially crowded, as much of the people-watching seems to take place on the boardwalk. Jammed with shops and cafés overlooking the ocean, the boardwalk is a nonstop parade of gorgeous women, muscle-bound men, in-line skaters, and street entertainers. Just taking a seat with your friends at an open-air café and watching the crowd is an entertaining way to spend a few hours. **Figtree's** is my favorite place along Venice's Ocean Front Walk to grab a cold drink or a bite to eat and people-watch.

The **Walk of Fame** runs for about a mile along Hollywood Boulevard, between Gower Street and La Brea Avenue, and continues along Vine Street just south of Hollywood Boulevard. Each month a new name, along with a terrazzo and brass star, is added in a public ceremony. To date, nearly 1,900 stars have been embedded in the world's most famous sidewalk. **Mann's Chinese Theatre** is a short walk away, at 6925 Hollywood Boulevard. Here you'll find the handprints and footprints of stars from the past and present in the concrete of the courtyard in front of the theater.

The **Petersen Automotive Museum** is in Los Angeles at 6600 Wilshire Boulevard, at the corner of Fairfax Avenue. The museum has a permanent collection of more than 150 vehicles including several classic race cars. In addition to the permanent collection, special exhibits are often featured. The museum is open from 10 A.M. to 6 P.M. Tuesday through Sunday. Admission is $7 for adults. Car enthusiasts can spend hours here, so plan accordingly. Drag racing fans will want to check out the **NHRA Motorsports Museum** at the Los Angeles County Fairgrounds. The museum features dozens of dragsters and funny cars from the past and present. You'll also see trophies, photos, uniforms, helmets, and gear from throughout the history of NHRA racing. The museum is open Wednesday through Sunday. Admission is $5 for adults. Call (909) 622-2133 for details.

NIGHTLIFE IN FONTANA AND SOUTHERN CALIFORNIA

There are a handful of places near the track, including the Dave & Buster's at Ontario Mills Mall, but the lion's share of worthwhile nightlife is in Los Angeles along Sunset Strip. There are also a few places to check out in Anaheim.

The **Palomino Sports Lounge**, at 450 North Mountain Avenue in Ontario, is possibly the biggest and best pure sports bar near the track. They offer four pool tables, live music on Fridays, and plenty of TVs to watch the race or other sporting events. **Beer Hunter** is another good-sized sports bar, with fifty-four televisions, ten satellite dishes, and 200 different beers. The walls are covered with sports memorabilia with one wall dedicated to racing. The menu includes pasta, seafood, steaks, sandwiches, and burgers. They are located at 12809 Foothill Boulevard and open at 9 A.M. on weekends. The **Compass Creek Brew Pub** is just down the street at 11837 Foothill Boulevard. This 10,000-square-foot brew pub is a friendly place that features an extensive menu, with outstanding margaritas, ten televisions, and a giant-screen TV. In addition to bottled beers, there are eight beers on tap, all of them brewed on site, as well as two pool tables, darts, video golf, and an outdoor patio. They offer live music on the weekends and there's never a cover charge.

The **Riverside Brewing Company**, at 3397 Mission Inn Avenue in historic downtown Riverside, is another worthwhile brewery, with seven handcrafted beers on tap and a diverse, reasonably priced menu with burgers, seafood, and wood-fired pizzas. The pub area features five televisions and a giant-screen TV, a covered patio, and a pair of outdoor seating areas. They present live music on Thursdays with a $3 cover charge.

In Los Angeles there is no end of places to go at night, but they are very spread out. Your best bet for barhopping is in West Hollywood, along Sunset Boulevard. Also known as Sunset Strip, it's home to many of the city's best-known nightclubs. Santa Monica also has several less trendy places within walking distance of each other. To help plan your evening's entertainment, check out *L.A. Weekly*, *Los Angeles View*, and *Los Angeles Reader*. The list below barely scratches the surface when it comes to the outstanding area clubs worth visiting.

The **House of Blues**, at 8430 Sunset Boulevard, hosts national acts ranging from blues to reggae and seventies pop. The restaurant offers generous portions of above-average chow and a terrific view of the city from its patio dining area. If you can't get in at night (the club's $25–30 cover charge may also discourage you), check out their Sunday Gospel Brunch. The **Whisky a Go Go** is an L.A. institution and is still a great place to catch some of the area's hottest music. On days that they don't have a national act, you can generally see four or five local bands for $10–12. The Whisky's sister club, the **Roxy Theater**, is just up the street at 9009 Sunset Boulevard. The Roxy books a solid mix of regional and local acts, usually presenting three or four bands each night. The cover charge varies with the quantity and quality of talent booked.

Dublin's Irish Whiskey Pub, a relative newcomer at 8240 Sunset, is as close to a local watering hole as you'll find in West Hollywood. Dublin's has a good selection of beer and cigars; a friendly, helpful staff; pool tables; several TVs; and darts. Sunset Strip also offers two of the area's better-known comedy clubs, the **Comedy Store** and the **Laugh Factory**. The Comedy Store, at 8433 Sunset Boulevard, has three different comedy showcases—the Main Room, the Belly Room, and the Original Room—under one roof. The Original Room generally hosts nationally known headliners on the weekends. Cover charge and prominence of comedians vary, so be sure to call in advance. The Laugh Factory, at 8001 Sunset Boulevard, also offers top-notch stand-up comedy with several show times each night, as well as dinner and valet parking. Both clubs have a two-drink minimum.

Another great choice for nationally known stand-up comedy is the **Improvisation**, where Robin Williams is said to have gotten his start. The Improv is located at 8162 Melrose Avenue in West Hollywood.

B. B. King's is really two bars in one. The main hall is a restaurant that serves classic Delta cooking, seats more than 400 people, and hosts some of the best blues in the area. B. B.'s is not-so-conveniently located at City Walk, in Universal City at 1000 Universal Center Drive, but offers a gospel brunch every Sunday at noon that is said to be the best in town. I'm not sure which was better—the buffet or the show. Either way, it's two hours and $25 well spent. Make reservations in advance and show up around 11:30 for the best seats. City Walk is also the site of two dozen other restaurants, a **Jillian's Sports Bar**, and **NASCAR Silicon Motor Speedway**. NASCAR Silicon allows you to compete in a simulated race against a dozen competitors. The .85-scale simulators mimic the motion of turns, speed changes, and the impact of wrecks. After a short safety briefing, drivers strap into a simulator lined up beside opposing cars and take on a virtual Winston Cup track. All told, the experience lasts less than half an hour, but you're sure to exit all smiles.

In Anaheim, the brand new **ESPN Zone** is in Downtown Disney, directly across from the Disneyland Hotel. This place is loaded with sports memorabilia and has a 14-foot big-screen TV, a pair of virtual reality race cars, a 30-foot climbing wall, and 163 televisions, so every seat has a great view of the race or game. Across the street, there's a second **House of Blues** location, and Downtown Disneyland has eleven bars and restaurants to choose from. Also in Anaheim, the **Improv Comedy Club** has a location at 945 East Birch Street in the Brea Marketplace.

WHERE TO EAT

There are a handful of dependable places near the track, especially along Valley Boulevard in Fontana and Foothill Boulevard in Rancho Cucamonga, where you'll find franchise establishments such as Old Spaghetti Factory, Applebee's, Macaroni Grill, and Chili's as well as a handful of notable local eateries. Ontario Mills Mall, just minutes away from the track, offers **Wolfgang Puck's**, **Market Broiler**, Dave & Buster's, and others to choose from. The restaurant options in neighboring Los Angeles, San Bernardino, and Anaheim are practically endless.

Race fans can't go wrong for breakfast, lunch, or dinner at **Millie's Country Kitchen**, minutes from the track at 17039 Valley Boulevard in Fontana. The simple home-cooked menu is prepared and served by friendly folks in a comfortable setting. A little farther away in Ontario, **Crabby Bob's Seafood Grill**, at 36660 Porsche Way, is a casual regional establishment with affordable salads, sandwiches, ribs, and pasta, fresh snapper, mahi mahi, swordfish, trout, and yellowtail tuna prepared one of four ways. Practically next door, **Stuart Anderson's Black Angus** is an upscale, white-linen steakhouse open for lunch and dinner that locals rave about.

Burger lovers looking for nothing more than a quick and delicious fast food meal should stop by the **In & Out**, at 12599 Foothill Boulevard in Rancho Cucamonga.

In & Out restaurants can be found throughout southern California, and once you've enjoyed a burger here, no other fast food place will do. If that's not your style, **Claim Jumper** has a California mining camp motif and specializes in steaks, ribs, and chicken entrees. It's just down the street, in the Foothill Marketplace, at 12499 Foothill Boulevard. **DiCenso** and **Vince's Spaghetti** are a pair of worthwhile Italian restaurants on Foothills Boulevard. The **Cask 'n Cleaver** is another good choice for lunch or dinner in Rancho Cucamonga. Located at 8689 Ninth Street, this casual western steak and seafood place packs them in, especially for race week.

The Catch in Anaheim is a top-notch seafood restaurant that has been around since 1979. Located at 1929 State College Boulevard, this place is popular with local athletes and celebrities. **Charlie Brown's**, just down the street at 1751 South State College Boulevard, has a more modest atmosphere and menu, with affordable food and drinks, a notable sports memorabilia collection, and a dozen TVs scattered about the place.

LOCAL MEDIA

The *Fontana Herald News* is the local newspaper, but you'll also find useful race information in the *Los Angeles Times* and *Orange County Register*. Race broadcasts can be heard on MRN Radio via KVVQ, 910 AM.

WHERE TO STAY

HOTELS

There are plenty of places to stay in southern California; it's just a matter of finding a place that balances your need to be near the track and the area's landmark attractions. There are a few places near the Ontario Airport, others between the track and downtown Los Angeles, and thousands of hotel rooms in the Anaheim area.

Amerisuites　4760 East Mills Circle, Ontario (909) 980-2200　Located half a mile south of Ontario Mills Mall and 10 miles west of the track, they offer an outdoor pool, exercise room, and proximity to a number of solid restaurants.

Best Western　8179 Spruce Avenue, Rancho Cucamonga (909) 466-1111　Less than 20 miles from the track, this reliable, moderately priced hotel is surrounded by franchise restaurants and offers in-room refrigerators, as well as a pool, Jacuzzi, and fitness room.

Comfort Inn　16780 Valley Boulevard, Fontana (909) 822-3350　This is one of very few hotels in Fontana. This modest inn is among the closest and most affordable places to stay for a race at California Speedway.

Country Suites 1945 East Holt Boulevard, Ontario (909) 390-7778 Near I-10, the rooms here are complete with refrigerator and microwave kitchenettes. There's also an outdoor pool. If they are full, be sure to ask about their other two nearby locations.

Embassy Suites 1211 East Garvey Street, Covina (626) 915-3441 This all-suites hotel is less than 20 miles from the speedway. They offer an outdoor pool, a complimentary happy hour in the lounge every evening from 5 P.M. to 7 P.M., and a full cooked breakfast in the morning.

Fairfield Inn 3201 East Centrelake Drive, Ontario (909) 390-9855 This is among the most affordable brand-name chain hotels in the immediate vicinity. Aside from a heated pool, they are somewhat short on amenities, but you can expect a clean room and helpful staff.

Holiday Inn 3400 Shelby Street, Ontario (909) 466-9600 Located near the Ontario International Airport, this hotel has suites and whirlpool rooms available. There's a heated pool, whirlpool, and fitness room on site.

Hilton 700 North Haven Avenue, Ontario (909) 980-0400 Less than 20 miles from the track, this is a good-sized hotel near the airport with a restaurant and lounge on site, as well as a pool, whirlpool, and workout room.

Marriott 2200 East Holt Boulevard, Ontario (909) 975-5000 Across from the Ontario Convention Center, this place is among the largest area hotels and is convenient to the airport and interstates.

Mission Inn 3649 Mission Inn Avenue, Riverside (909) 784-0300 Located in a historic downtown neighborhood, this is a stunning hotel that was built at the turn of the century with domed ceilings, stained glass windows, and wrought iron balconies. They have two outstanding restaurants and a pair of lounges on premises, as well as an Olympic-size pool. If you want stay in style, this is the place.

CAMPSITES

There is no tent camping at the track, but **El Monte RV** offers a rental package with an RV and a spot at the track. RV spaces are good from Wednesday evening until Monday morning. Call (800) 367-3687 for details. **Silverwood Lake** is less than 20 miles northeast of the track in the San Bernardino National Forest. Call (800) 444-7275 for more information. **Hurkey Creek Park** has ninety-one campsites a modest drive from the track. Call (800) 234-7275 for details. Tent camping sites at nearby California state parks can be reserved by visiting www.cal-park.ca.gov or www.reserveamerica.com.

Good to Know

- To charge tickets or for additional race information, call (800) 944-7223 or (909) 429-5000.
- Mail orders can be sent to California Speedway Ticket Office, 9300 Cherry Avenue, Fontana, CA 92335.
- For more information on area hotels, attractions, and restaurants, call the Fontana Chamber of Commerce at (909) 822-4443 or the Ontario Chamber of Commerce at (909) 984-2458. The Los Angeles Convention & Visitors Bureau can be reached at (213) 624-7300. For more information on Anaheim destinations, call the Convention & Visitors Bureau at (714) 999-8999.
- A worthwhile city Web site is www.lacvb.com.
- ➤ The official racetrack Web site is www.californiaspeedway.com.

NEARBY WINSTON CUP RACE CITIES

Las Vegas: 230 miles (three hours, forty minutes)
Sears Point: 420 miles (seven hours, twenty minutes)

IN THE VICINITY

The drive to northern California along U.S. 1 is a meandering road that is a blast to drive. Starting out near San Luis Obispo and heading north through Santa Cruz, the view of the Pacific Ocean meeting the cliffs of the California coast is absolutely incredible and well worth going out of your way. It adds several hours to the trip, but it's a drive you won't soon forget. If you are planning to stop for a night between Los Angeles and San Francisco, try to split the drive up over two days. The additional time goes unnoticed, and you'll have time to stop along the way to enjoy the surroundings. There are several scenic overlooks and an occasional restaurant worth pulling over for.

One word of caution: The roads are very curvy and the cliffs very steep, so drive carefully and plan to stop before nightfall, because you don't want to miss any of the scenery. You'll probably want to fill your tank before you leave San Luis Obispo because gas stations along U.S. 1 tend to jack up their prices considerably.

▪ *CHICAGOLAND SPEEDWAY* ▪

Joliet, Illinois

"When they laid this racetrack out, they put a lot of thought into how to design a track that is friendly to the drivers. I think that maybe their thought process was that if they get everybody real comfortable, they'll see better races out here."

— RICKY RUDD

This racetrack is certainly driver-oriented, but it's also as fan-friendly a track as I've visited. The place was built with fans in mind. The stands are elevated about 15 feet, the infield sits well below the stands, and infield buildings are no taller than 14 feet, so the backstretch can be seen from seats in the very lowest rows. A wide road between the stands and the track is not open to fans, so there is no constant stream of fans walking along the safety fence and blocking the view of fans in the lowest rows. There are two tiers of stands, which allows for a second level of concession stands and rest rooms, while eliminating the need for exceedingly long walks to the very highest seats, about sixty-five rows up in some sections. Seats in the Founders' section are wide, comfortable plastic chairs with individual cupholders, similar to those you'd find at a football stadium. Seats elsewhere are aluminum bleachers with seatbacks.

The 900-acre site, situated 38 miles southwest of town amid rolling farmland, complete with barns and cornfields, has all the amenities a fan or corporate sponsor could ask for. A four-sided scoring tower sits in the very middle of the infield and can be seen from every vantage point. For fans with pit and garage passes, a pedestrian tunnel runs below turn one. A wide tunnel for RVs and cars parking in the infield runs below turn three. The fan midway, with souvenir trailers on either side of the main entrance road, is among the biggest in racing.

The track is considered a "racer's racetrack" with a smooth asphalt surface, wide turns, an 11-degree banked frontstretch, 18-degree turns, gradual entries into the turns, and a bowed backstretch that is unique to ChicagoLand. The bowed, 5-degree backstretch serves two purposes. It allows for smoother transition into the turns and, when stands are eventually built along the back of the track, the safety fence will be easier for fans in the lower rows to see through. Drivers describe the track as a giant circle because it never really straightens out and they can maintain remarkable speeds all the way around the track. Going into turn one, speeds approach 200 mph and don't generally drop below 160 mph in the turns.

For the inaugural race, ChicagoLand Speedway offered 75,000 seats and sold out in advance, despite requiring fans to buy a package of tickets to four days of racing over two weekends, including Busch, ARCA, and Indy Northern Lights series races, in addition to the single Winston Cup race. I expect that 25,000 to 50,000 seats could be added before the 2003 Winston Cup race is held here. In its current configuration, there are thirty-two corporate suites, 250 infield RV spots, and eighty RV spots outside the track overlooking the backstretch. These Speedway Ridge RV spots are atop a berm and allow fans to drive right up to the edge of the track and watch the race through their windshield or from atop the RV. These spots cost $2,300 and include four Speedway Ridge admission tickets. Other RV parking spots range from $500 for infield and raceway village spots to $650 for trackside infield spots but do not include the cost of tickets. These prices include all four ChicagoLand races spread out over two weekends.

Purists will fuss that ChicagoLand is yet another sterile, D-shaped, 1.5-mile tri-oval that caters to corporations and well-to-do, Johnny-come-lately fans. They may also say that the track has just one groove, so track position and fuel economy will become the keys to victory at ChicagoLand, as opposed to the sheet-metal-banging, side-by-side racing seen at some of the classic ovals. While there's truth to all of this, ChicagoLand is a world-class venue that will develop a second groove through its 55-foot-wide turns as the years go by—just as Las Vegas, Charlotte, Texas, and Atlanta have. Over the years, Chicago winters will tear up the smooth driving surface and races, big and small, will lay down enough rubber that side-by-side racing will become more commonplace.

Because all the seats are located along the frontstretch, the track really has no bad seats, but rows 25 and higher may be worth paying a premium for. Seats in the middle six sections overlooking the start/finish line have the sun to their backs and are almost completely shaded by the skybox suites and press box halfway through the race. Seats here are among the most desirable at the track, but those in the upper rows toward either end of the main grandstand may present a more sweeping view of the track. Seats near turn one offer an up-close view of the trickiest section of the track, as drivers slow down exiting the 2,400-foot frontstretch and queue up for the first turn. Drivers often attempt to stay out wide going into turn one to avoid the subtle bumps there but must protect the bottom line to avoid getting passed.

Turn three has a relatively flat entry and presents the best place for drivers to pass, because the groove is slightly wider here. Cars that get too high in turn three often push up toward the wall, and mishaps are not uncommon between three and four. The apron onto pit road is also difficult to navigate, as the surface is slicker when cars get onto pit road, which has less grip than the track. For now, the track has a tendency to blister tires, but that may lessen with time. Only time will tell, but unusually high attrition may become a factor at ChicagoLand as single-car wrecks, blown engines, and tire wear were common in the first weekend of stock car racing. The inaugural race featured ten yellow flags and fifty-six laps run under caution.

For the inaugural race, food and beverages could not be brought into the track, so the stands took a while to fill up. Fans attempted to save a few bucks by enjoying their own snacks and beverages before passing through one of the three turnstile entrances and shelling out $3 for bottled water or $5 for a beer. Concessions range from typical track fare of burgers, pizza, and barbecue ($4.50–6) to regional specialties like roasted corn and Italian beef ($3–6). There's an abundance of beer vendors roaming the stands, so fans are not obligated to get in line at the concession stands if they are willing to pay an extra quarter for the convenience.

The staff is remarkably friendly, helpful, and, considering they are all rookies, fairly knowledgeable. Once inside the track, you'll notice few flaws. There was no concession stand in the infield, which was surprising since you could not bring in your own cooler. I was somewhat disheartened by this, especially when you consider that tickets start at $175 and range up to $290. One would hope that at a minimum, ChicagoLand would offer buckets of beer and ice, like Talladega, so fans could spend more time in their seats and less time in lines. Concession-stand lines were not terrible for the first race at ChicagoLand, although ATM and rest room lines were about what you'd expect at a superspeedway. The track offers pass-out privileges for fans who get their hand stamped and keep their ticket stub, so it's possible to return to your vehicle after going inside.

Tent camping and overnight parking are nonexistent at ChicagoLand. Things may change as the years go by and seating sections are added, but there were virtually no tickets for sale on the day of the race. Reselling of tickets is prohibited on track property, and the only scalper activity I witnessed was alongside Route 53 and Laraway Road. For the next few years, races here may be among the toughest tickets in Winston Cup, because the market is so massive, the event is still brand new, and, at this point, the track has just 75,000 grandstand seats.

HISTORY

Not surprisingly for a first-year speedway, cars that qualified later in the day tended to run better as the track got more grip. Todd Bodine earned the pole for the 2001 Tropicana 400 with a speed of 183.717 mph. Fords swept the top three qualifying spots as Jimmy Spencer and Ricky Rudd drove the only other cars to exceed 183 mph. Not unlike the inaugural race at Texas in 1997, there was concern that because the track had a single groove with good grip, there might be trouble on the first lap under green as cars on the outside row dove down into the lower line. Aside from Andy Houston's inability to get his car going, the first lap went off without incident.

The race saw the field spread out quickly into a single file along the low groove, but the first caution flag appeared on lap 23 as Mike Skinner slammed into the wall of turn one at 180 mph and his car burst into flames. Skinner walked away with the assistance of medical staff and was later diagnosed with a mild concussion and a broken ankle. Pole sitter Todd Bodine brought out two caution flags as he lost control of his car twice. Each time he managed to avoid the wall and spun toward the infield across the track without contact.

Rookie Kevin Harvick dominated the race in his Richard Childress Chevrolet, leading 113 laps that day, including 101 of the last 130 laps. About two-thirds of the way through the race, Buckshot Jones hurtled into the wall as he slipped on some oil on the track, and the race's sixth caution flag came out. After another yellow appeared on lap 229, when Jeff Burton's car blew the right front tire and spread debris on the track, the race looked like it might become a fuel-economy finish, as several cars opted to pit while others stayed out to maintain track position. All that changed when Tony Stewart tangled with Sterling Marlin and crashed hard in turn two, with 10 laps to go.

Harvick had retaken the lead from Mark Martin on lap 242 and never looked back. The late restarts made the race seem much closer than it really was, as Harvick had a far superior car. Robert Pressley harassed Harvick on the final restart by bumping him as they headed toward the green flag but clearly had nothing for him once they got under way. The real excitement was taking place behind them, as Ricky Rudd drove low and passed Mark Martin on the apron when Martin's car hesitated on the restart near the first turn. Rudd challenged Pressley with 2 laps remaining but could not get by him. Kevin Harvick became just the seventeenth driver to win an inaugural race at one of Winston Cup's twenty-three tracks currently in use. Lee Petty, Buck Baker, and Richard Petty have all won two inaugural races. Jeff Gordon has won three inaugural races.

With the win at ChicagoLand, Harvick also became just the fourth driver in the modern era to win more than one race in his rookie season. The victory was Harvick's second win of the year and catapulted him to seventh in the Winston Cup

Start/finish line at the
Tropicana 400. *(Photo
by Darren Mullahey)*

points standings. More remarkable was the fact that Jeff Gordon, who had engine trouble late in the race and fell from fourth place to a seventeenth-place finish, dropped into a first-place tie with Dale Jarrett in the season points chase at the season's halfway point. Jarrett finished fourth in the race and gained fifty-one points on the day.

The 2001 Tropicana 400 was not the first NASCAR race held in Chicago. Throughout the 1950s stock car races were held at Soldier Field. On July 21, 1956, racing legends such as Buck Baker, Curtis Turner, Jim Paschal, and Ralph Moody participated in the only sanctioned race ever run at Soldier Field. Fireball Roberts drove his Ford to victory that day before a crowd of 60,000 fans. The only other

NASCAR-sanctioned race held in Illinois was on July 10, 1954, in Willow Springs. Dick Rathman won that afternoon at Santa Fe Speedway, one of three wins he managed that year, and among his 13 career victories accumulated in 128 starts over a five-year career.

GETTING TO THE TRACK

Located near the intersection of I-80, Highway 53, I-55, and Highway 52, there is no direct way to the track from downtown. Traffic gets thick early and stays slow for hours after the race. It's nowhere near as bad as the most notorious Winston Cup tracks, but five hours before the green flag dropped, we encountered slow traffic approaching from the north, taking I-80 and Highway 53. Traffic from the north (Chicago and the suburbs) tends to be worse than driving from the south (Bloomington or Champaign), but the surrounding infrastructure of two-lane roads, narrow bridges, and simple intersections without traffic lights is not suited to handle the traffic associated with Winston Cup races. This will be addressed as track officials learn where the problems are, but for now expect slow going and get there very early.

After watching Kevin Harvick make history, we got home by exiting the parking lot behind the main grandstand and driving away from the main entrance (and counter to traffic) toward the back side of the track, near Lot F. From there, we followed a line of cars to Laraway Road. This exit is shown as a dotted line on the *Fan Guide* track map and is worth going out of your way for. We were actually in the parking lot of a hotel at exit 127 of Highway 53 within a half hour of getting under way. A colleague of mine had the opposite experience at ChicagoLand and was stuck in traffic for hours after the race, despite having waited for nearly three hours after the checkered flag to head out. Hence the 2001 event's snide nickname of the "Trafficana 400."

Highway 53 may be an alternative route for folks arriving from the western suburbs of Chicago. Taking Route 45 south from I-80 and approaching the track from the south may be helpful for fans coming from the east and south Chicago suburbs.

The track has 700 acres of parking that accommodates 50,000 vehicles. Parking is free on the track property. Paying for parking spots outside track property will require a very long walk and wouldn't seem to be worthwhile until there are many more fans and cars at races here. A complimentary trolley transports fans from lot F to spots near the north and south turnstile gates. The vast majority of parking lots are not yet paved. The weather cooperated for the first races here, but a week of bad weather before race week could turn the parking lots into a sloppy mess if they are not paved at some point.

If you'd like to avoid traffic altogether, contact Henry Aviation for a helicopter ride to the track. Park at O'Hare Airport and fly to the same heliport that the drivers use beside the track in Joliet. Call (800) 925-9339 for details and reservations. It's not inexpensive, but time is money.

WHAT TO SEE AND DO

Chicago is the third-largest market in the United States, so there is no shortage of things to do here. On the same weekend of the first running of the Tropicana 400, the Cubs were playing the White Sox at **Wrigley Field**. This can be one of the toughest tickets in all of baseball, as Chicago fans are fervently divided between their two teams. This inter-city rivalry leads to sold-out games and exorbitant prices outside the stadium on game day. It's not likely that this rivalry will be scheduled opposite the race often, but any series at Wrigley should sell well during race week, so if you want to see Wrigley Field while in Chicago, order your tickets well ahead of time. **Wrigleyville**, the area surrounding the "Friendly Confines," is a great place to grab a meal or a few drinks. Games at **Comiskey** are less likely to sell out, but lower-level seats are not always easy to come by.

The **Shedd Aquarium** is the largest indoor aquarium in the world. It's home to sharks, dolphins, otters, sea turtles, and even a few beluga whales. All told, there are 700 different species of aquatic life and more than 6,000 marine animals under one roof. Admission to both the aquarium and oceanarium is $8 for adults; admission to just the aquarium is $4. You can visit the aquarium for free on Thursday. Advance tickets are recommended. The **Navy Pier** extends for half a mile into Lake Michigan and is home to several amusement rides including a Ferris wheel and carousel. The pier offers a great view of Chicago's skyline and is a great place for a jog, bike ride, or picnic. **Grant Park**, right on the shores of Lake Michigan, is another great place for a walk or jog. There are miles of walking paths and a spectacular light show held every night at **Buckingham Fountain** from 9 to 11 P.M.

Chicago is home to five of the world's twenty-five tallest buildings. The most recognizable is the **Sears Tower**. On a clear day, the view from the 103rd-floor skydeck is phenomenal. Adult admission to the observation deck is $6, with discounts available for children and senior citizens.

The **Field Museum of Natural History**, located near Soldier Field at Roosevelt Road off Lake Shore Drive, is one of the finest in the nation. The museum's centerpiece is the world's largest mounted dinosaur, a brachiosaurus. Admission is $5, except Thursday, when it's free. The **Art Institute of Chicago**, at 111 South Michigan Avenue, is also among the best of its kind. The extensive permanent collection of paintings and sculpture is well worth the $6 admission. Admission is free on Tuesday. The **Museum of Science and Industry**, at Fifty-seventh Street and Lake Shore Drive, features thousands of hands-on exhibits that demonstrate basic scientific principles. There's also the **Henry Crown Space Center** and **Omnimax The-ater**. Admission is $5 for adults. Parking here is free and there is no charge to enter the museum on Thursday.

The **Chicago City Pass** allows you to visit six of the city's finest attractions—Field Museum, Shedd Aquarium, Museum of Science, Adler Planetarium, Art Institute, and Sears Tower—for just $33.75. Call (707) 256-0490 or purchase a City Pass, which is good for nine days, at any of these attractions. The **Chicago Cultural Center** is home to the **Chicago Office of Tourism Visitor Information Center**, and a great place to start any trip to the Windy City.

The town of Joliet has become a destination in its own right for race weekend. **Harrah's Casino Pavilion**, in downtown Joliet, is a remarkable hotel and casino with all the games you'd find in Las Vegas or Atlantic City. **The Empress** is another casino, consisting of a pair of riverboats and a riverside pavilion with three restaurants, off Route 6. The casino offers an Egyptian theme and, more important to race fans, an RV park with complete hookups, rest rooms, and a laundry facility. Call (888) 436-7737 for reservations or additional information. Adjacent to the Empress you'll find the 20-acre **Splash Station Waterpark**.

Challenge Park Xtreme, 4 miles west of the track at 2903 Schweitzer Road, is the Disneyland of paintball facilities. For $49 they will outfit you with a mask, gun, air refills, and 500 rounds of ammo and set you loose on any of their themed game fields. They also offer a giant skate park, two mountain-bike courses, and a BMX racing track. Call (815) 726-2800 for details.

The brand new **Joliet Ballpark** is the home to the Joliet Jackhammers, a Northern League baseball franchise. For a more complete list of area hotels and attractions, call the **Joliet Chamber of Commerce** at (815) 727-5371.

NIGHTLIFE IN CHICAGO

Chicago is home to some of the best nightlife (and my favorite sports bar) in the nation. Nightlife in Chicago is not relegated to one central area but can be found just about anywhere. Wrigleyville, Rush and Division Streets, and Old Town are known for their proliferation of nightclubs, but no matter where you are staying in Chicago you're likely to be just a short cab ride away from a worthwhile nightclub, sports bar, or watering hole.

First and foremost, Chicago is known for its blues clubs. Legendary musicians such as Buddy Guy, Koko Taylor, and Eddie Clearwater own clubs in town. Most folks know that Rush and Division Streets are home to many of the city's premier nightclubs. There are far too many outstanding nightclubs to list here. For a more complete list, pick up a copy of Chicago's excellent alternative weekly, *The Reader*.

Blue Chicago   937 State Street (312) 642-6261   Regularly hosts nationally known blues talent. Not far from Rush Street. Get there early for a good seat.

Buddy Guy's Legends   754 Wabash Avenue (312) 427-0333   The Grammy-winning musician occasionally takes the stage with a headliner. On most nights you can expect to see top-name acts and even a few celebrities in the crowd. Live blues seven days a week.

Cubby Bear   1059 West Addison (773) 327-1662 or 477-SHOW   Across the street from Wrigley Field, but this place is not just for before and after the game. They regularly host a wide variety of top musical acts.

Double Door   1572 North Milwaukee (773) 489-3160   A dark, cavernous place with live music on the main floor, a balcony upstairs, and billiards downstairs. Closed-circuit TVs downstairs keep you in tune with what's happening on stage.

ESPN Zone   43 East Ohio Street (at Wabash) (312) 644-3776   You'll catch all the racing action on their 16-foot giant-screen TV or the 150 smaller monitors. No racing memorabilia to speak of, but baseball fans will appreciate the model of Wrigley Field constructed entirely of chewing gum wrappers.

Kingston Mines   2548 North Halsted (312) 477-4646   Live music seven days a week with a second stage on weekends. Open until 4 A.M. except Saturdays, when they are open until 5 A.M. This place is a favorite spot for celebrities when they are in town.

Koko Taylor's Celebrity   1233 South Wabash (312) 566-0555   An intimate supper club with great acoustics and sightlines. Live gospel brunch on Sundays is outstanding. Get there early for the best tables.

Slow Down, Life's Too Short   1177 North Elston Avenue (773) 384-1040   On the river, this place doesn't look like much from the outside. Inside you'll find dancing, patios overlooking the river, Ping-Pong, pool, and beautiful people pulling up to the dock in their sleek power boats. The line of cars parked up and down the street for blocks is a good indication of the crowd inside.

Mothers   26 West Division Street (312) 642-7251   One of the places that make Division Street famous. For twenty-five years this has been one of Chicago's best-known clubs. After midnight, consider crossing the street to check out the Lodge.

Murphy's Bleachers   3655 North Sheffield Avenue (773) 281-5356   Right across the street from Wrigley Field, this may be my favorite sports bar on the planet. Not because it has tons of TVs or cheap beer, but because of the enthusiastic crowd and friendly staff.

Old Town Ale House   219 West North (312) 944-7020   A neighborhood bar said to be the haunt of Second City comedians Belushi, Aykroyd, et al. They offer inexpensive beers by Chicago standards and a solid jukebox.

Second City   1616 North Wells Street (312) 337-3992   Chicago's best-known comedy troupe is essentially a farm team for the *Saturday Night Live* TV show.

You're likely to see tomorrow's stars hamming it up on stage at Second City. Call for reservations, as shows tend to get packed, especially on weekends.

Sheffield's Beer & Wine Garden 3258 North Sheffield Avenue (773) 281-4989 A cozy place with a terrific beer and wine selection, best enjoyed under the cottonwood trees that shade the beer garden.

The Wild Hare (and Singing Armadillo Frog Sanctuary) 3530 North Clark Street (773) 327-HARE Claims to be the reggae capital of the United States, which is hard to dispute. The atmosphere is 100 percent fun, and the place is definitely worth stopping by.

Zanies 1548 North Wells Street (312) 337-4027 The top national stand-up acts in Chicago can usually be found here. Many of the better-known comedians have plied their craft here at some point.

WHERE TO EAT

There are plenty of wonderful places for steaks, ribs, and deep-dish pizza all around town. Don't settle for the hotel restaurant if you can get out to one of the places listed below. If you are staying near the track, consider eating in Naperville.

Al's Steak House 1990 West Jefferson Street, Joliet (815) 725-2388 Among the finest upscale establishments in the immediate vicinity of the track, this place has been around for decades but was recently remodeled. The steaks are legendary, and their Sunday brunch is also worth checking out.

Berghoff Restaurant 17 West Adams Street (312) 427-3170 A Chicago institution offering German specialties as well as steaks, poultry, and fresh fish since 1989. Home of Berghoff Dortmunder beers.

Bogarts Char House 17344 Oak Park Avenue, Tinley Park (708) 532-5592 Not far from the track, this place offers outstanding steaks, friendly service, and a warm, inviting atmosphere. Try the filet or New York strip and you won't go wrong.

Gino's East 160 East Superior (312) 943-1124 The Chicago-style pizza by which all others should be judged. Dark, cozy atmosphere with friendly, attentive service. Expect to wait during lunch and dinner hours.

Harry Caray's 33 West Kinzie at Dearborn (312) HOLY-COW A great baseball atmosphere packed with fans. You don't have to be a baseball fan to enjoy their prime steaks and classic Italian dishes. As you might expect, Budweiser is the beer of choice here.

Heroes & Legends Sports Bar 2400 West Jefferson Street (815) 741-9207 About ten minutes from the speedway in Joliet. This place has twenty-five TVs, fifteen beers on tap, and an outdoor patio. What more could you ask for? They offer a decent menu of burgers, ribs, wings, and more.

Morton's of Chicago   1050 North State Street (312) 266-4820   This is where it all began. A favorite with athletes and celebrities, they specialize in prime, aged steaks and whole Maine lobsters.

Nick's Fishmarket   1 First National Plaza (312) 621-0200   Locals will tell you it's Chicago's best seafood. Classy atmosphere and attentive wait staff are what set this place apart. Not inexpensive, but you only live once, so what the heck— splurge! Reservations are required.

Pizzeria Uno   29 East Ohio Street (312) 321-1000   The originator of Chicago's deep-dish pizza. Renovated a few years ago, perhaps taking away some of the original charm, but the pizza remains the same. Pizzeria Due is just down the block and offers the same menu with a shorter wait.

Rodity's   222 South Halstead (312) 454-0800   In the heart of Greektown. There are bigger and perhaps better-known places nearby, but you'll be hard pressed to find a better meal served by a friendlier staff. They'll keep the house wine coming and you are certain to leave satisfied.

Ruth's Chris Steak House   431 North Dearborn (312) 321-2725   Another favorite with athletes and celebrities. Ruth's began in New Orleans but are now located in major cities across the country. They feature huge cuts of steak, lamb, veal, pork chops, and live lobster.

LOCAL MEDIA

Chicago has two fine newspapers, the *Chicago Tribune* and the *Chicago Sun-Times*. For entertainment and restaurant information pick up *The Reader* or *Chicago* magazine. Race broadcasts can be heard on Motor Racing Network 850 AM WAIT. Traffic and race updates can be heard on 1340 WJOL-AM. One of the leading sports talk radio stations is 1000 WMVP-AM. WGN-AM 720 also carries sports.

WHERE TO STAY

HOTELS

If you stay near the track, you're a long way from the downtown restaurants, nightlife, and attractions. If you stay downtown, you're 35 miles from the track. Decide which is important to you and go with that. There really is no compromise, unless you want to be 15–20 miles from both.

Baymont Inn and Suites   7225 West 183rd Street, Tinley Park (708) 633-1200   A new hotel not far from the track in an area with a handful of quality restaurants and a neighborhood pub just a short drive away.

Best Western   4380 Enterprise Drive, Joliet (815) 730-7500   A fairly new hotel within 7 miles of the track. They offer an indoor pool, whirlpool, and complimentary breakfast.

Comfort Inn   8800 West 159th Street, Orland Park (708) 403-1100   About halfway between Chicago and Joliet, this affordable hotel offers a pool, spa, game room, and Alexi's Restaurant on site. A shopping mall and several franchise restaurants are a short drive away.

Comfort Suites   18400 Spring Creek Drive, Tinley Park (708) 342-1425   The spacious suites here feature an in-room refrigerator and microwave. The hotel is just off I-80 near the quaint downtown of Tinley Park. A Cracker Barrel restaurant is a short walk away.

Fairfield Inn South   1501 Riverboat Center, Joliet (815) 741-3499   A short drive from area casinos and just 7 miles from the track, this convenient inn offers an indoor pool and whirlpool on the premises. A Cracker Barrel restaurant is adjacent to the hotel.

Harrah's Hotel and Casino   151 North Joliet Street, Joliet (815) 740-7885   It may not be Vegas, but this top-notch hotel and casino is a short drive from the track and offers plenty of gaming and restaurants to keep you entertained when you are not at the track.

Holiday Inn Express   411 South Larkin Avenue, Joliet (815) 729-2000   A short drive from the casinos and ChicagoLand Speedway, this is among the most affordable hotels during race weekend. The hotel offers an outdoor pool, a game room, and fitness center on site.

Ramada Limited   1520 Commerce Lane, Joliet (815) 730-1111   This is among the first places to book for race weekend. This affordable property has an indoor pool and spa, but relatively few amenities compared to surrounding hotels.

The **Heritage Corridor Convention & Visitors Bureau** offers a hotel reservation system representing more than 100 nearby hotels. Call (800) 746-0531 or access the system online through the track Web site.

Good to Know

- To charge tickets or for additional race information, call (815) 727-RACE.
- To get on the campsite waiting list, call (815) 727-7223.
- Mail orders can be sent to ChicagoLand Speedway Ticket Office, P.O. Box 3339, Joliet, IL 60433.
- The Chicago Office of Tourism can be reached at (877) CHICAGO.
- A worthwhile city Web site is www.ci.chi.il.us/tourism.
- ➤ The official racetrack Web site is www.chicagolandspeedway.com.

NEARBY WINSTON CUP RACE CITIES

Indianapolis: 190 miles (three hours, thirty minutes)
Michigan: 230 miles (four hours, ten minutes)
Kansas: 505 miles (eight hours, twenty minutes)

IN THE VICINITY

Milwaukee, Wisconsin, 90 miles to the north, is home to the **Milwaukee Mile** at the Wisconsin State Fair Grounds and much more. On the shores of Lake Michigan, you'll find **Maier Festival Park**, home to countless festivals throughout the summer. Summerfest, billed as "The World's Greatest Music Festival," is the largest, but there are others celebrating the heritage of nearly every ethnic group you can conceive of. The relatively new **RiverWalk** was expanded at a cost of $9.6 million and is similar to the riverside area in San Antonio, Texas. Baseball fans may want to check out the brand-new **Miller Park**, the spectacular new home field of the Milwaukee Brewers.

Milwaukee also has some remarkable restaurants and nightlife. The **Safe House**, at 779 North Front Street, is a unique restaurant that could be straight out of a James Bond movie. You'll have to know the password to gain entrance through the "International Export Office" or be subjected to an entertaining "security check." **Mader's German Restaurant**, a Milwaukee institution at 1037 North Old World Third Street, is equal parts restaurant, bar, and museum. The dining hall is reminiscent of a medieval castle with vaulted ceilings and a $2 million collection of knight's armor and Old World art. The adjoining bar offers a long list of imported and domestic beers and more than 200 wines to choose from. It houses hand-carved oak tables and chairs that once furnished Baron von Richthofen's castle in Germany.

Water Street, downtown just east of the Milwaukee River, is a great place to barhop. **Luke's of Milwaukee** is a three-level sports bar, at 1225 North Water Street, with something for everyone on their forty-two televisions. The **Water Street Brewery** is an outstanding brew pub with a spectacular view of the city and a cozy atmosphere. They offer an impressive array of beers brewed on site and a nice selection of appetizers, bratwursts, sandwiches, and dinner entrees. **Lucci's** is one of the hot nightspots in the area near the Bradley Center. This multilevel bar is at 1135 North Water Street.

The drive from Chicago to Milwaukee is not always an easy one, as construction, tollbooths, and accidents along I-94 often slow things down considerably. Give yourself at least an hour and fifty minutes for the trip, more if you're coming from the south side of Chicago. The **Milwaukee Convention & Visitors Bureau** at (800) 231-0903 offers more detailed information on local attractions, restaurants, and nightlife.

A Dozen Favorite Winston Cup Race City Nightlife Scenes

12 Sonoma

11 Phoenix

10 Fontana

9 Kansas City

8 Daytona

7 Charlotte

6 Fort Worth

5 Indianapolis

4 Atlanta

3 Miami

2 Chicago

1 Las Vegas

■ *DARLINGTON RACEWAY* ■

Darlington, South Carolina

"To put the whole 500 miles together, that's the hard part of this sport. It takes such a team effort. It takes pit stops, making the right calls on the chassis, the driver not making mistakes. It takes the whole package."

— TODD BODINE

Darlington is the stop on the Winston Cup circuit they call "The Lady in Black." The keys to victory here are tire management, avoiding the seemingly requisite wreck that collects the middle of the pack at some point in the day, and qualifying well. In fact, through the track's first ninety-seven points races, only a dozen have been won from outside the top ten qualifying positions. The track has also earned the moniker of "The Track That's Too Tough to Tame." To illustrate this point, through the 2001 season only three active drivers, Jeff Gordon, Bill Elliott, and Dale Jarrett, have more than two wins at Darlington. Gordon and Elliott have visited victory lane at Darlington five times each, while Jarrett just earned his third trip to the winner's circle in the spring of 2001.

Stock car racing's prototype asphalt superspeedway has a colorful history that dates back to 1950. The Southern 500 was run at Darlington on Labor Day weekend of that year. As the story goes, Harold Brasington had attended the Indy 500 and decided to build a paved speedway for a 500-mile stock car race. Upon purchasing the land in the heart of South Carolina tobacco fields, he agreed not to disturb an existing minnow pond, so one end of the track had to have a narrower radius than the other end. As a result, the egg-shaped Darlington Raceway was created to fit in the space allowed and is unique among tracks used in the NASCAR Winston Cup series today. The track was built at a cost of just $250,000, unheard of by today's standards.

Labonte leads the way through turn one at the "Lady in Black." *(Photo by Steve Fink)*

These days, turns one and two make up the wider end of the track with a 600-foot radius, 79-foot-wide turns, and 25-degree banking. The identical 1,229-foot straightaways are 90 feet wide and banked at just 2 degrees. Turns three and four are banked at 23 degrees and are considerably tighter than their counterparts at 62 feet wide and a radius of just 525 feet. Because the turns are so different, and because of the tendency of the race surface to tear up tires, this 1.366-mile track is one of the most challenging on the Winston Cup circuit. Black "racing stripes" on the wall going into turns two and four are all too common until drivers find a sufficient groove. Perhaps to accentuate Darlington's best-known hazard, track personnel does not repaint the wall before the Winston Cup race on Sunday, proudly showing off the "Darlington Stripe" in turn two. The groove at Darlington is as high as or higher than any other track on the circuit. In fact, some veteran drivers claim they utilize a "four-wheel slide" and intentionally graze the wall in early laps, thereby compacting their cars and giving themselves an extra half inch of room on the track.

In 1997, the track was inverted so the start/finish line is now on the south side of the track. New grandstands and parking lots were added to create a more enjoyable race experience for the fans. Darlington is in many ways an antiquated track with dated facilities on the backstretch, but it's still a terrific place to see a race. Few places on the Winston Cup circuit allow fans to get this close to the action yet provide such a worthwhile view of the entire track at an affordable price.

The best bargain at the track may be the upper rows of the Wallace Grandstand, which sell for just $80 and overlook the pits and start/finish line. The Pearson Tower, situated outside turn four, is another great place to sit if you can get a seat in rows 15 and higher. The Tyler Tower along the frontstretch offers the track's most expensive tickets at $110.

In 2000, the pits were consolidated onto the same side of the track for the first time. The pits at Darlington are split up into three sections along the frontstretch and are easily viewed from almost any seat in the Wallace Grandstand and Tyler Tower. The scoring tower is near the very center of the track and lists the current lap and top ten positions. The three-sided tower is visible from any place in the track. Three giant-screen TVs are positioned in the infield, so fans can view replays from most seats throughout the track. One TV faces the main grandstand along the frontstretch, another is similarly set in front of the backstretch, while the third faces the Pearson Tower. The Pearson Tower, located in turn four, is the tallest section at the track.

The Brasington Grandstand, near turn two, is covered and offers some much-needed shade for the summer race at Darlington. The Pearson Tower also offers some shade in the late afternoon. If you can't get good seats in the grandstands, the Palmetto Terrace inside turns one and two is a worthwhile place to park the truck, van, or car and watch the race. This single row of vehicles is a great place for the families with kids and has an unobstructed view of one of the most treacherous stretches of track in all of stock car racing. Fans with infield access also head to the backstretch area that used to serve as the pits near turn two, plop down in a collapsible chair, and watch as cars exit turn two and head down the back straightaway. Few places on the circuit allow you to get this close to the action.

Fans may want to check out the **NMPA Stock Car Hall of Fame and Joe Weatherly Museum** located on the north side of the track, along Highway 151/34, behind the backstretch grandstands. The museum houses more than a dozen stock cars, ranging from the 1950 Plymouth that was driven to victory in the very first NASCAR superspeedway event—the 1950 Southern 500 at Darlington—to the wrecked 1991 Chevy Lumina that Darrell Waltrip rolled eight times along the backstretch at Daytona. My favorite cars in the collection were Buddy Baker's 1969 Dodge Daytona and Curtis Turner's 1956 Ford convertible that is said to be the winningest car in NASCAR history. The Hall of Fame is decidedly low-tech and consists of pencil drawings of legendary drivers, team owners, and track owners and memorabilia from each, as well as an audio presentation of their career highlights. There's also a smattering of racing art, trophies, model cars, car parts, and racing memorabilia throughout the museum. The museum and Hall of Fame are open daily from 8:30 A.M. to 5 P.M. Admission is just $3. Call (843) 395-8821 for more information.

The track oozes a sense of history and tradition, but despite its age, Darlington has few flaws. Surprisingly, there is only one ATM at the track, and it's located outside near the ticket booths along Richard Petty Boulevard. ATMs can be few and far between on the way to the track and are often depleted of funds on race day. So plan ahead or expect to endure a long line outside the track (at the end of Petty Boulevard across from the Ticket Office) if you show up at the track without cash and want to shop for souvenirs or buy concessions. Available concession and rest room facilities are dated but far better than at some other tracks.

HISTORY

In 1950, Johnny Mantz won the very first Southern 500 in a race that featured just four race leaders. Mantz drove a Plymouth owned by Bill France and averaged only 76.260 mph. The key to his victory was a lighter car than the Cadillacs, Hudsons, and Oldsmobiles of other drivers, and the use of hard rubber tires that allowed him to avoid long pit stops other drivers needed when the asphalt tore up their tires. Remarkably, Mantz won the inaugural race from the forty-third starting position in a seventy-five-car field vying for $25,000 in total prize money. The race took six hours and thirty-eight minutes to complete.

The following year, eighty-two cars entered the race, and Herb Thomas drove a '51 Hudson to victory with an average speed of 76.900 mph. Thomas repeated the feat in 1954 and 1955, achieving an average speed of 94.930 mph in his '54 Hudson. The first driver to top the 100-mph average speed barrier at Darlington was Fireball Roberts, who drove his Ford 107.540 mph in the 1957 Rebel 300. That same year, Bobby Myers was killed in a crash during the Southern 500. Myers' car crashed into Fonty Flock's car head-on and flipped several times along the backstretch. Tragically, the following year, Myers' older brother Billy died of a heart attack while driving in a modified sportsman race in Winston-Salem.

Fred Lorenzen earned his first NASCAR victory in the 1961 Rebel 300. Lorenzen passed the legendary Curtis Turner with two laps to go and held on for the win. Joe Weatherly won the 1963 Rebel 300, a race run without a caution flag. In the 1965 Southern 500, Ned Jarrett set the NASCAR record for the greatest margin of victory, finishing fourteen laps and more than 19 miles ahead of second-place finisher Buck Baker.

Richard Petty earned three Darlington victories from 1966 to 1967, sweeping the Rebel 400 and Southern 500 in 1967. Surprisingly, Petty never returned to the winner's circle again at Darlington. After his sweep, Petty came tantalizingly close to winning again with six second-place finishes, five thirds, two fourths, and one fifth-place finish. In 1969, LeeRoy Yarbrough completed a sweep of the season's big three races—the Daytona 500, World 600 in Charlotte, and Southern 500 (Talladega opened that year and was not yet considered one of the major races). David Pearson was leading on what turned out to be the race's final lap when Yarbrough passed him on the third turn of the rain-shortened race. It was the first time a driver had swept the big three races in a single season.

David Pearson captured a track-record twelve poles and is the all-time winningest driver at Darlington with ten victories. Those ten victories were spread out between 1968 and 1980, with his only season sweep occurring in 1976. Seven of Pearson's ten victories came in the spring race. It's only fitting that, on April 13, 1980, Pearson's final career victory came at "The Lady in Black." On September 1, 1980, Terry Labonte won the first Winston Cup race of his career in the Southern 500, beating out David Pearson, Harry Gant, and Benny Parsons as Chevy swept the top four positions. Coincidentally, Labonte got his first Winston Cup start at Darlington, almost two years earlier to the day, on September 4, 1978.

Darlington was the scene of NASCAR's first million-dollar payday as Bill Elliott cashed in with a victory in the 1985 Southern 500. Elliott won the Daytona 500 and Winston 500 earlier in the season but finished poorly in the Coca-Cola 600. In order to collect the "Winston Million" bonus for winning three of NASCAR's four major races, Elliott needed a win at Darlington. Driving a Ford Thunderbird, he passed Cale Yarborough with forty-four laps to go to take the lead and earn the nickname "Million Dollar Bill." The car is part of the permanent collection at the Joe Weatherly Museum. If you visit the museum, take a close look at the roof number decal. Elliott's crew applied the number 9 upside down and it looks like a lower case "e" or a backward 6, depending on which side it's viewed from.

On September 6, 1992, Darrell Waltrip won the Mountain Dew 500 for the eighty-fourth and final victory of his career. Dale Earnhardt set the race record with an average speed of 139.958 mph in the 1993 TranSouth 500. Earnhardt has the second most Darlington Winston Cup victories with nine, including a dominating stretch between 1986 and 1990 when "The Intimidator" won six races in five years.

Jeff Gordon had a similar streak from 1995 through 1998, when he won five out of seven races at Darlington. In 1997 the track was flopped so the start/finish line was on what had been the backstretch. It did not affect Gordon, as he became the first driver to win three consecutive Southern 500s. He won the race again the following year to become the only driver in NASCAR history to win an individual superspeedway race four straight times. Ward Burton, driving a Pontiac, set the track qualifying record of 173.797 mph on March 22, 1996. Dale Jarrett won the TranSouth 400 in 1997 and 1998 to join Burton as the only other winners at Darlington during Gordon's streak. Having won at Daytona and Charlotte already, Gordon collected the Winston Million-Dollar Bonus with his victory at Darlington in 1997.

Jeff Burton drove his Jack Roush Ford to victory lane for both races in 1999. The Burtons kept up their winning ways as Ward took the spring race in 2000.

Bobby Labonte won the 2000 season Pepsi Southern 500 on his way to the Winston Cup points championship in a rain-shortened race of 448 miles. Labonte qualified thirty-seventh for the race that fall, to become just the third winner in race history to qualify worse than fifteenth, and the first since Herb Thomas won from the twenty-third position in 1954. Dale Jarrett visited Darlington's winner's circle again in the spring of 2001, beating out Steve Park for his first win of the season. On September 2, 2001, Ward Burton duplicated Bobby Labonte's feat of winning from the thirty-seventh starting position in a race that ended under a caution flag. The win was his second at Darlington and his third career Winston Cup victory. He also became the year's fifteenth different winner, a NASCAR Winston Cup season record. A day earlier, Ward's younger brother Jeff won the Busch race at Darlington for a rare sibling sweep of the weekend's races.

GETTING TO THE TRACK

Darlington seats only 57,000 fans, so this may be the easiest Winston Cup track to drive to on race day, especially if you get an early start. The track is just 2 miles west of downtown Darlington near the intersection of Highway 151/34 and U.S. Highway 52. It is easily accessed from I-20 by taking exit 131 and driving east on Highway 401 to 52 North and west on 151/34. From I-95 take exit 164 and travel north to Highway 151/34. Aside from I-95, none of these roads are major highways, so pedestrian and automobile traffic gets very dense near the track both before and after a race. Coming from Florence, Rogers Road is a very worthwhile shortcut to the back side of the track. If you are approaching from the west, the grandstand parking area, near Ramsey's Pond at gate 40, is often the best parking lot to use. Bear in mind that because the frontstretch is now where the backstretch used to be, you may have to drive away from the main drag, 151/34, to get to the parking lots near the Tyler and Wallace grandstands or walk a long way to your seats.

Leaving, on the other hand, is no picnic. If you are parked in the infield or on the frontstretch side of the track, anticipate spending a great deal of time going nowhere. The parking lot on the frontstretch side of the track is little more than a hilly field with narrow entrances that do not allow for quick exits. Also, you may very well find yourself forced to travel miles in the wrong direction to get away from race traffic. Expect South Carolina Highway Patrol to set up roadblocks for license checks and such, before and after a race along any of the minor arteries that lead to the track from I-95, Route 74, or I-20. Towns such as Jefferson and McBee are notorious speed traps during race weekends, so be sure to pay attention to speed limits.

Parking in track-owned lots is free. Most of the parking lots can be found along Indian Branch Road near the frontstretch, but a handful are scattered along Highway

151/34. To shorten your drive time home, consider parking in a lot that will exit to the right and enable you to more easily head back the way you came. One of the track's biggest flaws is the lack of pedestrian walkways and crossovers that would facilitate automobile egress after the race.

WHAT TO SEE AND DO

I can't even pretend there's a great deal to do in Darlington. With a population of 7,300 people, there's simply no reason to spend much time in Darlington other than the track, its adjoining Stock Car Hall of Fame, and the **Winston Walk of Fame**. In downtown Darlington, a half block from the Square at Pearl Street, the Walk of Fame consists of handprints in a concrete walkway of several drivers who have won a race at Darlington, including Richard Petty, Dale Earnhardt, Cale Yarborough, David Pearson, Jeff Gordon, and others. The **Southern 500 Parade** is held nearby on Saturday at 9:30 in the morning before the fall races. The parade has been held since the mid-fifties and features a host of retired drivers, vintage racecars, floats, horses, and marching bands. For details on the parade, call (843) 398-4035.

The nearest city of any significant size is Florence, which is still a relatively small town with fewer than 30,000 residents. If you are not able to see a race in Darlington as a day trip, you may want to spend a night or two in Florence, have a few meals there, and head to the beach for the rest of your vacation.

If you have sense of humor, stop by **South of the Border**, a tourist trap like no other in the nation. You'll see billboards for miles along highways in every direction as you approach the small town of Dillon, South Carolina. The place is little more than a collection of motel rooms, a hole-in-the-wall restaurant/nightclub, and a gift shop. The rooms are tolerable, the restaurant is decent enough and serves as an adequate watering hole if you're with the right group of friends, while the gift shop is full of overpriced, hokey kitsch plastered with South of the Border logos. Call (843) 774-2411 for additional information.

NIGHTLIFE IN DARLINGTON

Honestly, go to the beach. There are worthwhile places throughout North Myrtle Beach just a short drive away. Some that I can recommend firsthand include the **Spanish Galleon**, a beachside dance club with a sandpit volleyball court set up during the day; and **Pirate's Cove**, just across the street from the Galleon, which offers a scenic rooftop deck with a casual crowd and good music at night. **Murphy's** is a solid sports bar/restaurant with plenty of TVs that has been packing them in for ages on Route 17 in North Myrtle Beach. Just across the street you'll find **Champions**, a newer, two-level sports bar with a considerable collection of sports memorabilia and a good-sized crowd for big games and races.

Not nearly as indigenous, but still worth checking out, **Broadway at the Beach**, in Myrtle Beach, has several nightclubs, including an **All-Star Café** and **Hard Rock Café**, in one location at 17 Bypass and Twenty-first Avenue.

WHERE TO EAT

DARLINGTON

B & B Restaurant   1536 South Main Street (843) 393-9534   Minutes from the track, at South Main and West McIver, this humble place specializes in southern country cooking and friendly service. McIver is also a handy back way to the front side of the track.

Cromers Pizza   103 Pearl Street (843) 393-3626   A casual Italian restaurant with a full bar, lunch buffet, wings, pasta, and of course, pizza. This may be the closest thing to a bar in Darlington.

Dairy Bar   318 Pearl Street (843) 393-4531   A simple place serving burgers and hot dogs about a mile from the track. I was surprised to learn that despite the name, they don't serve ice cream.

Jewel's Deluxe   32 Public Square (843) 393-5511   A country cooking establishment, right on the square in downtown Darlington, that's been around forever. Open for lunch only; the menu changes daily, but expect a meat and three home-style veggies or two veggies and dessert.

Joe's Grill   306 Russell Street (843) 393-9140   Two blocks from the square, this short-order eatery has been in business for fifty years. Open for lunch and dinner only.

Raceway Grill   Highway 151/34 (843) 393-9212   Located at the track, this modest eatery has surprisingly tasty burgers, sandwiches, and salads. The chicken salad sandwich is my favorite. Needless to say, they are mobbed on race weekends.

Taki's   639 Pearl Street (843) 393-8979   A diner located between the track and downtown Darlington, 2 to 3 miles from the track. One of the few places in town to serve breakfast, lunch, and dinner; their specialties include burgers, sandwiches, and salads.

FLORENCE

Cracker Barrel   1824 West Lucas Street (843) 662-9023   A popular place with crews and drivers on days leading up to the race.

PA's   Southpark Shopping Center, 1534 South Irby Street (843) 665-0846   About as nice a place as you'll find in Florence, this place offers a remarkable atmosphere and tremendous seafood.

P & M Steakhouse   (843) 669-1611   A casual, family-oriented place that the locals might just as soon keep to themselves. They are open only for dinner, but the steaks, in particular the prime rib, are well prepared while the service is prompt and attentive.

Percy's & Willie's   2401 David McLeod Boulevard (843) 669-1620   Open for lunch and dinner. The reasonably priced menu offers some wonderfully diverse choices, but they are known for their rib-eye steaks, which are seasoned and prepared to perfection. This is a popular place with teams and officials.

Red Bone Alley   1903 West Palmetto Street (843) 673-0035   One of the few places I've come across in Florence with a separate cocktail lounge. Located in the Florence Mall, one might not expect the tasteful decor and eclectic menu. In years past, this has been a popular place with race teams in the evenings leading up to the race.

Victor's European Bistro   829 South Irby Street (843) 662-6311   This formal Old World establishment is open for dinner only. Expect a courteous staff, succulent regional European and American entrees, and rich, tempting desserts.

LOCAL MEDIA

Local newspapers include the *Darlington News and Press* and the *Florence Morning News*. Races are broadcast by MRN on 92.9 FM WEGX.

WHERE TO STAY

HOTELS

Area hotels sell out weeks in advance of race week because nearby rooms are few and far between. Most folks traveling great distances for a race at Darlington stay in surrounding towns such as Florence, Bennettsville, Camden, Sumter, Dillon, and Hartsvile. Camping at the track is also an option.

Holiday Inn Express   U.S. Highway 15/401 Bypass, Bennettsville (843) 479-1700   This well-kept hotel offers an outdoor pool and complimentary breakfast about forty minutes from the track.

Best Western   1808 West Lucas Street, Florence (843) 678-9292   A surprisingly well-appointed roadside inn with a small pool, complimentary breakfast, and free local calls.

Comfort Inn   1739 Mandeville Road, Florence (843) 665-4558 or (800) 882-3840   Another solid choice for a race at Darlington. Cracker Barrel restaurant is a short walk away.

Fairfield Inn   140 Dunbarton Drive, Florence (843) 669-1666   Clean, comfortable motel not far from a local shopping mall and a handful of restaurants.

Hampton Inn 1826 West Lucas, Florence (843) 662-7000 Worthwhile accommodations with amiable rooms on the north side of Florence.

Hampton Inn Suites 3000 West Radio Drive, Florence (843) 629-9900 Modest-sized place next to the Civic Center, but considerably nicer than many local hotels in this price range.

Holiday Inn Express 150 Dunbarton Road, Florence (843) 664-2400 Reasonably priced place with a pool and a convenient location near the Civic Center.

Holiday Inn Hotel & Suites 1819 W. Lucas Street (843) 665-4555 One of the larger and nicer area hotels. The bar is popular with race crews on nights leading up to race weekend.

Ramada Inn I-95 and U.S. 52 (843) 669-4241 A quality place for the money on the north side of town with a restaurant, whirlpool, and sauna on site.

Red Roof Inn 2690 McLeod Boulevard, Florence (843) 678-9000 One of the most economical places to stay in the city. Short on amenities, but the staff is certainly race-fan-friendly.

CAMPSITES

Camp Darlington, a recent addition to the track, is a fenced area for tent camping and overnight parking near turn four, behind the Pearson Tower. Reserved spots are 15′ × 30′ and are renewable year after year. Spots are free with some race ticket packages. Call (843) 395-8499 for details. An alternative camping option is the **Florence KOA Campground** at 1115 East Campground Road. Call (843) 665-7007 for reservations.

Good to Know

- To charge tickets or for additional race information, call (843) 395-8499.
- To get on the campsite waiting list, call (843) 395-8499.
- Mail orders can be sent to P.O. Box 500, Darlington, SC 29540-500.
- For information on local attractions and lodging, call the Darlington/Lamar Department of Tourism at (888) 427-8720 or (843) 393-2641. The Pee Dee Tourism Commission can be reached at (800) 325-9005 or (843) 669-0950.
- ➤ The official racetrack Web site is www.darlingtonraceway.com.

NEARBY WINSTON CUP RACE CITIES

Rockingham: 47 miles (one hour)
Charlotte: 92 miles (two hours)
Martinsville: 175 miles (three hours, ten minutes)

IN THE VICINITY

Myrtle Beach, also known as the Grand Strand, is just an hour and a half away from Darlington and offers a wealth of nightlife, restaurants, deep-sea fishing, arcades, shows, more than 100 golf courses, and a pair of NASCAR attractions. For more information on Myrtle Beach activities, call the Myrtle Beach Convention and Visitors Bureau at (800) 356-3016 or Myrtle Beach Key Attractions at (800) 819-2282. The Convention & Visitors Bureau has a worthwhile Web site at www.mbchamber.com.

Broadway at the Beach, between Twenty-first and Twenty-ninth Avenues on U.S. 17 Bypass, is a dining, shopping and entertainment complex that offers laser light shows nightly and fireworks on Tuesday nights during the spring and summer months. You'll also find nightclubs and movie theaters, a butterfly pavilion, Treasure Hunt: Pirates of the Carolina Coast, one of several amusement rides, Ripley's Aquarium, Dragon's Lair miniature golf, as well as a shuttle boat that ferries folks back and forth across the lake.

NASCAR Café at 1808 Twenty-first Avenue in North Myrtle Beach is the original location of this growing chain. This location has the standard bar and food offerings, as well as an astounding collection of memorabilia, simulators, and a game room. The memorabilia features tributes to Darlington and legendary South Carolina drivers. Call (843) 946-7223 for more information. **NASCAR SpeedPark** is right next door and offers go-kart racing for every skill level. They open at 10 A.M. every day and an all-day race ticket is just $24.95 for adults. Call (843) 918-8725 for details.

▪ *DAYTONA INTERNATIONAL SPEEDWAY* ▪

Daytona Beach, Florida

"The Daytona 500 is the biggest race we run. . . . If you had to pick a race to win, this would be the one."

— TERRY LABONTE

Opened in 1959, this monstrous tri-oval track with steep 31-degree turns, twin 1,900-foot chutes that form the angled frontstretch, and a 3,000-foot backstretch is the granddaddy of NASCAR speedways. Beginning in 1982, the stock car season has started each February with the Daytona 500, a.k.a. "the Super Bowl of racing," and nearly 200,000 folks attend the sport's ultimate speedweek. Winston Cup's "opening day" is eagerly anticipated as the twelve-week off season ends and fans from all over the country descend upon the sunny shores of Daytona Beach.

From a distance, the track looks brand new, but once inside, the tradition and nostalgia of a place where countless racing legends were spawned is instantly apparent. Talladega Superspeedway is the only track on the Winston Cup circuit that is longer than Daytona International Speedway. The tracks at Indianapolis and Pocono are the same 2.5-mile length as Daytona but have very different layouts. The unique D shape at Daytona allows for outstanding views of the track from various seating sections at the track, particularly along the frontstretch.

Scoring towers at each end of pit row display the current lap and the top nine cars, as do a pair of horizontal scoreboards facing the backstretch. There are also two giant-screen TV monitors facing both sets of grandstands, so fans can follow the action when the leaders are on the other side of the track. Replays can be seen from most seats.

I've seen races at Daytona from seats along both the front- and backstretch. The most coveted seats are generally considered to be those in the Winston Tower, but the Earnhardt and Petty sections to either side also offer sweeping views of nearly

Let the season begin as the Daytona 500 gets underway. *(Photo by Jamie Fink)*

the entire track. Closer to the track, the Weatherly and Roberts Towers and the Campbell section, at the start/finish line just below the Winston Tower, are terrific sections as well. The Segrave Tower, sections E and above, are worthwhile, especially in rows 20 and higher. If seats in the frontstretch have a disadvantage, it's that there are too few rest rooms and concession stands. Facilities nearby are dated and not as fan-friendly as the ones on the backstretch.

Veteran Daytona fans won't settle for seats anywhere on the backstretch, but seats here in rows 52 and higher are padded and protected from the sun and rain by the skyboxes above. They also offer a view of the notorious half-mile backstretch, where cars occasionally drive four across and many exciting passes are attempted—some more successfully than others. Trams deliver fans to and from the front side of the track to seats along the backstretch, allowing them to check out Daytona USA and other attractions before heading to their seats. A giant area of souvenir trucks selling scanners, earplugs, programs, and driver paraphernalia sits just outside the backstretch.

HISTORY

In 1959, Lee Petty won the first Daytona 500 in a photo finish with Johnny Beauchamp. Petty's Oldsmobile averaged just 135.5 mph in the inaugural race. The 1959 race was the only caution-free Daytona 500 ever. Three days after the race, newsreel footage helped race organizers determine that Petty was the winner. Richard Petty won the Daytona 500 in 1964, pacing his Plymouth around the speedway at more than 154 mph. Petty was the only driver to complete all 200 laps. A. J. Foyt, winner of four Indy 500s and seven Indy-car championships, won his first sanctioned race in his second NASCAR season, taking the checkered flag in the Firecracker 400 in July 1964 by outpacing Bobby Isaac. He won the same race again the following year, this time beating out Buddy Baker. In 1967 Mario Andretti became the first and only rookie to win the Daytona 500. Cale Yarborough set the track record with an average speed of 167.247 mph, driving a Wood Brothers Mercury, in the 1968 Firecracker 400. That record stood for more than a decade.

Pete Hamilton won the Daytona 500 in his third year on the circuit in 1970. Hamilton passed David Pearson with nine laps to go and held on for the win in a Plymouth Superbird. In 1972, A. J. Foyt won the Daytona 500 averaging 161.550 mph in his Mercury. Richard Petty became the first driver to win back-to-back Daytona 500s in 1974. He was the only driver to finish on the lead lap in 1973 and beat out Cale Yarborough in 1974, a race that was shortened to 180 laps because of the energy crisis. From 1971 to 1974, Richard Petty placed second in the Firecracker 400. David Pearson won three consecutive Firecracker 400s from 1972 through 1974. It wasn't until 1975 that Petty finally visited the winner's circle for the 400-miler at Daytona.

The 1979 Daytona 500 was the first stock car race covered from start to finish by a national TV network. The exciting race, carried by CBS, featured a crash involving the two leaders, Donnie Allison and Cale Yarborough, along the backstretch on the last lap and propelled the sport into the national spotlight. Richard Petty managed to avoid the wreck and took his sixth victory at the Daytona 500. Petty won the Daytona 500 seven times, three more than any other driver.

Buddy Baker won his first and only Daytona 500 in 1980 with an average speed of 177.602 mph, a record that still stands as the race's best average speed. In 1982, Bobby Allison won the Daytona 500 and the Pepsi 400 in the same season, the last driver to do so. In 1984, Cale Yarborough was the first to break the 200-mph barrier in qualifying at Daytona. Richard Petty won his 200th points race in the 1984 Pepsi 400. It was the final win of his career. In 1987, Bill Elliot set the record for the fastest lap (210.364 mph) in his Ford Thunderbird. Bobby Allison won the 1988 Daytona 500, edging out his son Davey, who finished second, by two car lengths. Bobby was fifty years old at the time and the victory turned out to be the final Winston Cup win of his career. In the same race, Richard Petty's car collided with A. J. Foyt's, and Petty's Pontiac went airborne and flipped several times along the backstretch.

Derrike Cope, in his seventy-first career start, won the Daytona 500 in 1990 for his first career victory. Dale Jarrett won his first of three Daytona 500 victories in 1993 while his dad, Ned Jarrett, urged him on from the television booth in one of the most memorable race broadcasts. D. J. won again in 1996 and 2000 driving a Robert Yates Ford. Dale Jarrett leads all active drivers with three Daytona 500 victories.

Sterling Marlin won his first career Winston Cup race in grand style on February 20, 1994, beating Ernie Irvan, Terry Labonte, and the rest of the field in the Daytona 500. Later that same season, Jimmy Spencer earned his first career victory in the Pepsi 400, edging out Irvan and Earnhardt. In 1997, Jeff Gordon became the first driver in nearly two decades to win the season opener at Daytona and go on to become the Winston Cup points champion. Gordon beat out Terry Labonte and Ricky Craven for his first Daytona 500 victory, as Chevy swept the first three positions at Daytona. On July 5, 1997, John Andretti won the Pepsi 400, the first Winston Cup victory of his career.

Dale Earnhardt Sr., won three points races at Daytona (two summer races and one Daytona 500) culminating with his only Daytona 500 victory in 1998. It came with a million dollar payoff and was his twentieth start in a Daytona 500. The outpouring of emotion from other teams congratulating Earnhardt for the win was one of the most remarkable scenes to ever take place at Daytona. Jeff Gordon visited victory lane again at the Daytona 500 in 1999, beating out Dale Earnhardt as he won from the pole. Gordon has two other cup wins at Daytona, taking the Pepsi 400 in 1995 and 1998. Coincidentally, the 1995 Pepsi 400 is the last Winston Cup points race that two drivers tied for the most laps led. Jeff Gordon and Sterling Marlin each led seventy-two laps, so they both earned five bonus points for that race. Gordon's Pepsi 400 win in 1998 was the first to be run at Daytona under the lights. The race was delayed more than three months because wildfires were raging across Florida in July of that year.

Dale Jarrett won the Daytona 500 from the pole position in February 2000. Jarrett is one of just seven drivers to win the Daytona 500 from the pole, joining the likes of Fireball Roberts, Richard Petty, Cale Yarborough, Buddy Baker, Bill Elliott, and Jeff Gordon. Yarborough and Elliott are the only drivers to accomplish the feat twice.

On February 18, 2001, Dale Earnhardt crashed into the wall of turn four on the Daytona 500's final lap, just a quarter mile from the finish, and died from the impact. Michael Waltrip won that race in a car owned by Earnhardt. It was Waltrip's first career win in 463 starts. Dale Earnhardt Jr. took second place that afternoon and did not realize his father was involved in a tragic wreck until after he had crossed the finish line. Fittingly, Dale Jr. won the Pepsi 400 on the night of July 7,

2001. Junior dominated the entire race, leading 116 of 160 laps, but was forced to come back from seventh place with six laps to go because of a late caution flag. It was NASCAR's first race at Daytona following the wreck that took Dale Earnhardt Sr.'s life. Cynics cried conspiracy, but the win went a long way toward healing the sport's grieving fans. Michael Waltrip finished second for a Dale Earnhardt Inc. sweep of first and second place. It was Junior's first trip to the winner's circle for the 2001 season and just the third Winston Cup victory of his career. The win came eleven years to the day after his dad's first points race victory at Daytona.

GETTING TO THE TRACK

Near the intersection of I-95 and Route 92, just 4 miles from the Atlantic Ocean, Daytona is not an easy place to get to or from on race day. The majority of traffic utilizes I-95, which can become incredibly congested for the 500 and other Winston Cup events. Your best bet is to approach from the south on U.S. 1, as much of the traffic is coming from Orlando, to the southwest on I-4, and cities north of the track. Parking can cost up to $40 at the track. Local businesses along International Speedway Boulevard open up their lots as early as 4 A.M. and can sell out in twenty minutes despite a $35 fee. Wherever you decide to park, get there early and situate yourself so you can get back to the main roads easily.

There are a number of free parking lots available a few miles from the track, with complimentary shuttles that deliver fans to and from the track. The downside of these lots is that you can spend a great deal of time waiting for shuttles and in traffic when you get back to your vehicle.

The best-kept secret in leaving the track is not to go immediately west toward I-95, but to head east toward U.S. 1 and take U.S. 1 to I-95. Folks heading north are better served taking U.S. 1 all the way to Saint Augustine before jumping back on I-95. Southbound visitors can take U.S. 1 south to Highway 44 to access I-4 West or take Highway 442 to access I-95 South.

WHAT TO SEE AND DO

February speedweeks offer nine different races at DIS, starting with the Rolex 24 at Daytona and ending with the Daytona 500. Between those races, there's plenty to do in town. Years ago, Daytona Beach warned revelers with a roadside sign proclaiming, "Come on Vacation, Leave on Probation," because the town had developed a reputation for wild times. Things have changed a little since then, but the 23 miles of beaches are still Daytona's biggest attraction. At low tide, the beach here can become as wide as 500 feet, allowing plenty of room for families to spread out among the many oceanside parks that make up Daytona Beach. The beaches are open all day, every day, and most areas allow cars to drive right onto the beach. Be sure to take note of the tide; many a tourist has had the ocean swallow their vehicle while they were off enjoying the sights.

Oceanfront Park, just east of the Adam's Mark Hotel, is a popular beach that offers the **Boardwalk Amusement Area**, with a castle-shaped bandshell and the **Salute to Speed** consisting of more than thirty granite plaques recognizing Daytona's storied place in motorsports history. There's also the **Main Street Pier** with the revolving "Space Needle" tower and a gondola ride that extends out over the ocean. Oceanfront Park has a wide-open grassy area and a public volleyball court, as well as proximity to businesses along Atlantic Avenue. Just to the south is **Sun Splash Park**, with beach access ramps, picnic areas, volleyball courts, and public rest rooms.

Bicentennial Park, another popular beach just north of Granada Boulevard, has a boardwalk, basketball courts, a public fishing dock, and a picnic area. The park is open from sunrise to sunset. **Lighthouse Point Park** is at the south tip of the beach at Ponce Inlet. This pristine spot offers 52 acres of nature trails and is home to a wealth of wildlife. The park is open from 8 A.M. to 9 P.M. and charges an admission fee of $3.50 per vehicle. The Ponce de Leon Lighthouse is 175 feet tall—the second-tallest lighthouse in the United States—and has a 203-step spiral staircase to the top where you'll be rewarded with a sweeping view of Daytona Beach. The lighthouse is open from 10 A.M. to 4 P.M. daily. For more information on all area beaches, call (904) 239-SURF.

Adventure Landing, on the beachfront at 601 Earl Street in Daytona Beach, offers some serious waterslides, a twenty-seven-hole miniature golf course, and a go-kart track. For more intense go-karting action, check out **Go Kart City**, 7 miles from the speedway at 4114 South Nova Drive, near U.S. 1 in Port Orange. The wide, quarter-mile road course is the largest in the area and popular with race crews during speedweek. The twisting track accommodates up to fifty-three go-karts at one time. Races are four laps each and cost $5.50 per person. They offer a number of multirace packages; the best buy is an eight-race deal for $28. They also have batting cages and a challenging eighteen-hole miniature golf course. A full-size driving range is located adjacent to Go Kart City. This place is a zoo during speedweek, so if you have a group of ten or more, you may want to call (336) 761-2882 in advance to reserve the track.

Race fans also flock to a pair of area tracks during speedweeks. Saturday nights at 7:30, **New Smyrna Speedway** hosts open-wheel modifieds, late-models, mini-stocks, and strictly stocks on their dirt oval, while the **Volusia County Speedway** has both a dirt track and an asphalt oval. VCS hosts races every night for two weeks leading up to the Daytona 500. Daytona Beach is home to one of the world's largest Harley Davidson dealerships. Just minutes from the beach, **Daytona Harley Davidson** is at

290 North Beach Street and offers the latest and greatest in Harley apparel, gear, and bikes. The Motor Racing Network hosts the **"Daytona 500 Preview"** at area malls during speedweek. MRN radio personalities interview top drivers each night before a live audience. Admission is free to the public. Refer to the local newspapers for locations and additional details. The **Stock Car Racing Fanfest** and the **Circle Track Racing Expo**, at the Ocean Center in Daytona Beach, are also held during Speedweeks in February, generally Wednesday through Friday, just before the 500. Admission is $9 for both shows on Wednesday when a handful of Busch and Winston Cup drivers are available for autograph sessions. For more information, visit their website at www.stockcarfanfest.com.

Daytona USA, billed as the ultimate motorsports attraction, is beside turn four of the track at gate 1. Adult admission is $12 and can be combined with a tour of the track for just $4 more. Equal parts motorsports museum and arcade, this place allows fans to call a famous race in a simulated broadcast booth, race the clock in a pit stop challenge, or take a virtual reality lap around Daytona Speedway. A fifteen-minute movie simulates Daytona 500 racing, and kids of all ages will enjoy video games in the Speedplay Arcade. Added in 2001, the new IWERKS TurboRide Theater is thirty-two-seat simulator that gives fans the feel of traveling 200 mph in a 750-horsepower stock car. The actual winning car from the previous Daytona 500 is housed in Daytona USA's Gatorade Victory Lane. Daytona USA is open every day except Christmas and has extended hours during race weekends.

Smokey Yunick's Garage, billed as "The Best Damn Garage in Town," has been a landmark destination for "old school" race fans for decades. Yunick, who passed away in 2001, was a legendary, straight-shooting mechanic who invented countless racing components and safety devices throughout a colorful career. Yunick's cluttered, low-tech garage is located at 957 North Beach Street in Daytona Beach. Admission is free, but be sure to call (866) 766-5392 to see when they are open, as operating hours vary.

NIGHTLIFE IN DAYTONA BEACH

Boot Hill Saloon is a classic biker bar on Main Street in downtown Daytona Beach. A Daytona institution, they feature inexpensive domestic brews and never charge a cover despite offering top-notch bands on weekends. The "world's steepest motorcycle track," beside the outdoor patio, presents daredevil shows regularly. The **Bank Blues Club** is just down the street and offers national and regional blues acts during race week. This roomy, well-appointed place has plenty of tables but gets full after 10:30 P.M. The extraordinary acoustics and sight lines make this place worth a visit, despite the modest cover charge after 9:30 P.M.

The **Oyster Pub**, located on Seabreeze, has a college/sports bar atmosphere. An enthusiastic crowd generally surrounds the giant bar and partakes of a few drinks as they watch their favorite sports on TV. This place also features a terrific, moderately priced menu of burgers, sandwiches, and appetizers. There are plenty of TVs to satisfy folks spread out between the three main dining areas. A friendly wait staff works hard to get you seated and served quickly while inviting you to stay as long as you like.

Nearby, **Baja Beach Café** and **Razzles** on Seabreeze attract younger, alternative dance crowds. Razzles has a $10 cover charge. On weekends, if you show up before 10 P.M. you receive a souvenir cup that they'll refill with draft beer at no charge until midnight. They also feature an amateur wet T-shirt contest on weekends.

WHERE TO EAT

In addition to the Oyster Pub, there are a number of outstanding indigenous Daytona area eateries. **Chart House**, at Halifax Harbor Marina in Daytona Beach, has fresh-off-the-boat seafood and mouth-watering steaks. In the days leading up to the February race, you'll find drivers and their teams here regularly. **Julian's** at 88 South Atlantic Avenue in Ormond Beach is another popular spot with officials and race teams. This casual, family-oriented place has been around for decades and specializes in prime steaks and fresh seafood. **Billy's Tap Room** on Granada Boulevard serves seafood and perfectly prepared aged steaks at lunch and dinner in a genuine pub atmosphere. This casual place has tons of vintage racing memorabilia and is popular with race teams, officials, and Daytona regulars. It's bound to be packed throughout Speedweeks, so be sure to get there early. **Sophie Kay's Waterfall Restaurant**, west of A1A in Daytona Beach Shores, offers lunch and dinner seven days a week and is popular with the locals. The **Inlet Harbor Marina and Restaurant**, at 133 Inlet Harbor on Ponce Inlet, overlooks the water and is a great place to catch the sunset. They have a giant patio and present live music daily. One of the largest restaurants in the area, they specialize in Caribbean seafood and fine steaks. They serve lunch and dinner a short walk from the Ponce de Leon Inlet Lighthouse.

Cruisin' Café is very affordable and a fun place to take the kids. This place offers authentic race car tables and a NASCAR motif, serving burgers, sandwiches, pizzas, and salads. They are located on the corner of Atlantic Avenue and Main Street in the heart of Daytona Beach. Not far away, at 401 North Atlantic Avenue, the **Starlite Diner** has tasty inexpensive burgers, meatloaf, and homemade desserts.

The area along International Speedway Boulevard has sprouted numerous franchise restaurants including **Hooters, Cracker Barrel, Carrabba's, Hopp's, Rio Bravo, Pizzeria Uno, Bob Evans, Outback**, and **Olive Garden**. The **Daytona Ale House** is an exceptional place to eat, drink, and be merry near the Holiday Inn along Route 92 at I-95. This place offers microbrew beers and a superior pub menu of burgers, steaks, and salads. Another worthwhile stop is **Bucca di Beppo**, a chain restaurant that manages to stand out with what they like to call "immigrant Italian family style" lunches and dinners. They also offer a nice outdoor patio.

One of the best bargains available during race week is parking at **Denny's** on International Speedway Boulevard for just $10. Call ahead to reserve a parking spot, enjoy a quick breakfast, and walk over to the track. Next door is **Sonny's Bar-B-Q**, where parking is $25 with $5 refunded toward your food bill. Across the street, a track-owned parking lot costs $25 per day.

In Port Orange, south of Daytona on Route A1A, you'll find a pair of restaurants that locals may be reluctant to point out to tourists. **Aunt Catfish's on the River** offers casual patio dining overlooking the Intracoastal Waterway and has a wonderful southern menu of seafood, steaks, and ribs. This place can get busy, especially during Sunday brunch. **J. C.'s Oyster Deck** is just across the river and offers a fun, indoor/outdoor dining experience that's a little more laid back.

LOCAL MEDIA

The local newspaper, *The Daytona Beach News Journal*, is sold outside the track and lists driver/crew chief frequencies for that day's race. This is the least expensive way to know which frequencies to listen to on your scanners. Souvenir programs are sold outside the track and at concession stands inside for $15 and offer the same information and much more.

The race is broadcast on the radio by MRN on WKRO-FM 93.1 in Daytona Beach.

WHERE TO STAY

HOTELS

Hotels sell out well in advance for the Daytona 500 speedweek. In fact, some area hotels impose a ten-day minimum stay. As soon as you have tickets to the race you should call to get a room. Two hotels that are close to the track are the **Hampton Inn** and the **Hilton Garden Inn**. They are both within walking distance of the track on the same side of International Speedway Boulevard.

The **Adam's Mark Resort** is a sixteen-story hotel right on the beach with 437 oceanfront rooms in the heart of Daytona Beach. On site you'll find a huge heated pool, whirlpool, beach volleyball court, playground, and, of course, the beach. The **Hilton Resort**, to the south in Daytona Beach Shores, is another luxury place right on the ocean, with many of the same amenities. The **Palm Plaza**, at 3301 South Atlantic Avenue in Daytona Beach Shores, is a relative newcomer with spacious, well-appointed rooms overlooking the Atlantic. One of the area's most established elegant hotels is the **Plaza Resort and Spa** at 600 North Atlantic Avenue. This historic hotel is located right on the ocean and offers a good-sized pool, rooms with optional whirlpool suites, and a well-equipped exercise room and is within walking distance of the nightclubs and restaurants along Seabreeze Boulevard.

The **Howard Johnson Ocean Front Hotel**, at 2560 North Atlantic Avenue, is considerably more affordable than those places mentioned above and a good distance from the revelry of the strip's clubs and restaurants. The eight-story HoJo fills up quickly during race weeks and offers plenty of well-kept beachfront or beach-view rooms with balconies, beach access, a pool, and whirlpool. There are kitchens in many units.

Chances are some of these hotels will be sold out nearly a year in advance of the Daytona 500. To have a complete list of area hotels sent to you, call the Daytona Beach Area Convention and Visitors Bureau at (800) 854-1234 or (904) 255-0415. In the event you can't get a place in Daytona, try to find a hotel south of the track to minimize your traffic hassle before and after a race. **Titusville** is a decent-sized town, near the Kennedy Space Center, that has a **Best Western**, **Days Inn**, **Holiday Inn**, and **Ramada Inn**.

CAMPSITES

Because the track is surrounded by the local airport, a major highway, and commercial development, there are surprisingly few campsites surrounding the track. Campsites near the track include **Nova Family Campground**, about 4.5 miles away in Port Orange at 1190 Herbert Street; the **Daytona Beach Campground**, also in Port Orange at 4601 Clyde Morris Boulevard; and the **Town and Country RV Park** at 3003 U.S. Highway 92 in Daytona Beach. Area campsites fill quickly and often don't take reservations during race weeks, offering sites on a first-come-first-served basis instead. They may also require a three- or four-day minimum stay.

Good to Know

- To charge tickets or for additional race information, call (904) 253-7223.
- Mail orders can be sent to P.O. Box 2801 Daytona Beach, FL 32120-2801.
- The Daytona Beach Area Convention and Visitors Bureau can be reached at (800) 854-1234.
- A worthwhile city Web site is www.info@daytonabeach-tourism.com.
- ➤ The official racetrack Web site is www.daytonainternationalspeedway.com.

NEARBY WINSTON CUP RACE CITIES

Miami/Homestead: 260 miles (five hours)
Atlanta: 297 miles (six hours)
Talladega: 403 miles (seven hours, thirty minutes)

IN THE VICINITY

Walt Disney World is an hour and fifteen minutes to the southwest, in Orlando. I've encountered several families who combine a trip to Daytona with a trip to the Magic Kingdom, often because it's the closest place they can find a hotel on race weekend. A one-day admission to one of Disney's four theme parks, **Epcot, Animal Kingdom, Disney-MGM Studios,** or the original **Magic Kingdom** park, is $46 for adults and kids age ten and older. Combination passes are available and parking is $6 per vehicle. **Richard Petty Driving Experience** allows fans to ride along in a Winston Cup–style stock car for about $95. For $350 you can attend driving school and take a few laps of your own around the **Walt Disney World Speedway,** a 1-mile tri-oval with banking from 7 to 10 degrees in the turns. Call (800) 237-3889 or (407) 939-0130 for reservations and details.

The **Kennedy Space Center** is just an hour south of Daytona at the Merritt Island National Wildlife Refuge. Tours of the space center offer a behind-the-scenes glimpse of the launch facility, actual and replica spacecraft, robots, a moon rock, and a pair of IMAX theaters showing films about space exploration. An all-inclusive ticket costs $24 for adults. Expect to spend four to six hours, especially if you don't show up early to avoid the crowd. Call (321) 449-4444 for more information. **Cape Canaveral** and the **U.S. Astronaut Hall of Fame** are also nearby and worth visiting.

▪ *HOMESTEAD-MIAMI SPEEDWAY* ▪

Homestead, Florida

"As much as I hate to see the smaller tracks go by the way-side, I think it is great how the new tracks can seat more people and have nicer amenities for the race fans, as well as the competitors."

— JEFF GREEN

A new track, Homestead is often lumped in with other 1.5-mile speedways but has some significant differences that set it apart from Texas, Charlotte, Atlanta, Chicago, and Kansas City. The track is considerably flatter than the aforementioned speedways with 6-degree banking in the turns and just 4 degrees of slope through the straights. In fact, Homestead is the flattest oval on the Winston Cup circuit. One noteworthy difference is that Homestead has identical 1,760-foot straightaways as opposed to the tri-oval configurations found at other mile-and-a-half tracks. Pit road at Homestead is also unusual because drivers enter pit road near turn three and exit pit road on the backstretch, near turn two. Another quirk here is that the fourth pit stall is often the first one chosen because it has about a car length of room in front of it, allowing the driver to accelerate out of the pits unimpeded by a car and crew directly in front of them.

The most striking aesthetic difference between Homestead and other 1.5-mile tracks is the pristine pastel blue-and-yellow buildings that make up the infield and grandstand structures. The **Brugal Rum Pavilion** outside the track, near section 220, is party central. This shaded pavilion area features an island bar serving frozen drinks, an open-air area of tables and chairs, live steel drum musicians, and a view of the giant-screen TV showing the race. I didn't imbibe but discovered that most concessions are reasonably priced at the track. A convenient area with round plastic tables and benches sits beneath the grandstands near sections 211–213. The entire facility is kept spotless, and the fan-friendly amenities are among the best in the sport. The track and grounds are surrounded by more than 800 palm trees and feature a pair of man-made lakes in the infield. The larger infield lake is spacious enough that it actually accommodates an occasional jet ski or water-skier during race weekend. The smaller infield pond, near turn one, has a picturesque fountain in the middle of it. Some of the track's premium RV spots are situated beside the large infield lake.

The grandstands at Homestead seat more than 70,000 fans and stretch from turn one through the frontstretch with a small section of luxury suites occupying an area overlooking turn four. The beauty of this track's design is that fans do not face into the sun for any of the race. All seating sections have aluminum bleachers with seatbacks, except the club seats, which are plastic, fold-down stadium-style seats. A fan in the know was kind enough to point out that the walkway at the very top of the grandstands, between the start/finish line and turn one, is a good place to loiter if you're not thrilled with your ticketed seats.

Most tickets are sold as part of a package, but single-day tickets are available. The last to go are generally those in the lower rows of turn one in and around section 181. Seats in the first ten rows cost $65, while rows 11 through 21 are $75. Two-day

Frontstretch at Homestead-Miami. *(Photo by Author)*

packages range from $90 to $150. Seats below row 11 are the cheapest, rows 11–21 cost $110, rows 22 through 32 are $120, and the highest rows, 33 through 48, account for the most expensive seats. Seriously well-to-do fans can get a two-day package in the club section with the very best seat available and a prerace pit pass, as well as separate rest rooms and concessions, for $400. Stands are elevated 15 to 20 feet, so the entire track can be seen from rows 10 and higher. Flags atop the the infield garage terraces can obscure the view of the backstretch for fans seated in the very lowest rows. My favorite place to sit at Homestead is in the upper rows of sections 187 and 188. Seats here offer a terrific view of the frontstretch without having to look through the retaining fence, and they receive some shade from the TV tower above. Sections 196 and 197 have a similarly decent view of the track and face a giant-screen TV located in the infield.

Homestead-Miami is among the most scenic tracks on the circuit, but it does have a few drawbacks. Drivers can exceed 175 mph heading into turn one and 115 mph through the turns, yet some lament that the track's flat-oval configuration does not allow the drivers to drive into the corners two or three cars wide. From a fan's standpoint, the track's downfall may be the rule against bringing beer and large coolers into the track, because lines for concessions can get very long as the day goes on. Even in mid-November it can get blistering hot on race day, and there is also very little shade within the grandstands at the circuit's southernmost track, so be sure to bring your sunscreen. Seats in turn one are the first to get shade in the afternoon, but it's still scarce. The only other shortcoming I noticed was that the three-sided scoring tower, which sits atop the infield garage terraces and lists the top five drivers, is difficult to read from either end of the grandstands.

The track has been open since 1995 when Dale Jarrett won the Jiffy Lube Miami 300 in the NASCAR Busch Series, but it remains a predominantly one-groove track where drivers find it difficult to bring the cars into the corners. For this reason, the track is said to drive a lot like Phoenix. The weather, wind, and sandy soil surrounding the track have deteriorated the racing surface over the years, and cars have a tendency to slip and slide going into the corners. The symmetrical oval design, as opposed to a tri-oval, and the lack of banking are often mentioned as reasons that races here are not as exciting as they could be. The track is simply not conducive to side-by-side racing, it's difficult for drivers to complete passes on the track, and the pack tends to spread out into a single file as the race goes on.

HISTORY

More than two years before the track hosted its first Winston Cup race, John Nemechek, driving in a NASCAR truck race, died of head injuries when he hit the wall on March 21, 1997. Remarkably, his brother Joe, who grew up in Florida, bravely returns every season to compete in the Winston Cup race at the track that claimed his younger brother's life.

Through the 2000 season, the Winston Cup history at Homestead could be summed up in two words: Tony Stewart. On November 14, 1999, Stewart won the inaugural race in his rookie season with an average speed of 140.335 mph. David Green surprised just about everyone when he earned the pole, while Stewart, driving the Joe Gibbs–owned Pontiac, qualified seventh and started on the fourth row. Bobby Labonte, Stewart's teammate, got tangled up with the Home Depot Pontiac as Stewart exited pit road with less than 20 laps to go. Up to that point, Labonte had dominated the race by leading 174 of 267 laps, but almost ended up in the wall. He managed to recover and finished second, while Jeff Burton, Mark Martin, and Dale Jarrett rounded out the top five that afternoon in a race that featured ten different leaders and took just two hours, fifty-one minutes, and fourteen seconds to run. Jarrett's fifth-place finish earned him the 1999 points championship.

Almost a year later, Steve Park set the track record with a qualifying lap of 156.518 mph. For just the second pole of his career, Park took a mere 34.518 seconds to traverse the 1.5-mile oval. Stewart returned to victory lane at Homestead, however, joining Richard Petty as the only drivers to win the first two Winston Cup races at a track still in use. Petty accomplished the feat at Dover in 1969 and 1970. Stewart edged out Jeremy Mayfield, Mark Martin, Bobby Labonte, and Jimmy Spencer for his ninth career Winston Cup victory. Labonte's fourth-place finish at Homestead in 2000 wrapped up the Winston Cup points championship for the 2000 season.

In 2001, Tony Stewart looked strong in the late stages of the race but finished nineteenth after being penalized for entering pit road improperly and sent back to the end of the longest line. While Stewart's streak came to an end, Bill Elliott ended a streak of his own. Elliott, driving a Dodge, started from the pole and won, for his first Winston Cup victory since 1994, a run of 226 starts without a victory. It was the first time a Winston Cup race was won from the pole at Homestead and Ray Evernham's first win as a team owner. Elliott's average speed was just 117.449 mph, the slowest ever for a winner at Homestead, in a race that featured nineteen lead changes among seven drivers. After the sixth and final caution flag, Elliott passed his teammate Casey Atwood for the lead with just five laps to go. Michael Waltrip took second place as Atwood's tires lost their grip and he wound up third, his best finish as a Winston Cup driver. Jeff Gordon, who has never finished in the top five at Homestead, failed to clinch the 2001 championship because of a twenty-eighth-place finish, marking the first time in the track's brief history that the season title was not decided by the Pennzoil 400. In 2002, Homestead will host the series finale for the NASCAR truck, Busch, and Winston Cup series on the same weekend.

GETTING TO THE TRACK

The track is located southeast of downtown Homestead near the intersection of U.S. 1 and the West Dade Expressway. Homestead is about 20 miles southwest of Miami. From the north, take the Florida Turnpike (be sure to bring a bunch of quarters for tollbooths on the turnpike) to Speedway Boulevard, a.k.a. SW 137th Avenue (exit 6), then travel east for 3 miles to the main entrance. From Florida City and points south, take U.S. 1 to SW 344th Street (Palm Drive), make a right turn and head east for 2.5 miles, then go left on 142nd Street, heading north to the track. The vehicular tunnel to the infield crosses under the backstretch, east of 137th Avenue/Speedway Boulevard, off Palm Drive.

The turnpike backs up on race day, so even if you are staying north of the track, it is often quicker to approach from the south. If possible, get off the turnpike early and circle around to the back side of the track. One way is to take the turnpike to SW 112th Avenue, head south until you make a left on 268th Street, followed by a right onto 107th Avenue. Follow 107th Avenue until you make a right on 308th Street, a left on 112th Avenue, a right on 316th Street, and a left on Colonial Drive, which becomes 117th Avenue. Take 117th to Palm Drive. Make a right on Palm Drive (also known as 344th Street) and follow the signs to the track.

An alternate route from the north is to take U.S. 1 to 162nd Avenue South and turn left on Alex Muxo Jr. Boulevard, which heads east directly into Speedway Boulevard. This is often a better route for exiting the track than for getting there.

There's also a convenient free shuttle to the track for folks staying in Homestead or Florida City. The shuttle stops at the **Prime Outlet Mall**, a handful of RV parks, campsites, and other places in Florida City and downtown Homestead. The shuttle runs from 8 A.M. to 10 P.M. on Friday, Saturday, and Sunday of race weekend. The entire route takes about thirty minutes under ideal circumstances.

WHAT TO SEE AND DO

Two of the more significant landmarks in Homestead include the **Fruit and Spice Park**, which really needs no explanation, and the **Coral Castle of Florida**, a shelter built from 1923 to 1940 by a single Latvian immigrant using simple tools. It's said that he built the place because he was jilted by a woman he wanted to marry. Not to knock either of these unique attractions, but I saved my money for other things, because between South Beach, the Everglades, Key West, and the track itself, there's plenty for race fans to do and see during race week.

The **Tropical Fun Center** offers a quarter-mile go-kart road course, an outdoor, lighted paintball field that's about the size of two football fields with all kinds of obstacles and bunkers to hide behind, and a challenging miniature golf course. Located at 27201 South Dixie Highway, next door to the Winn-Dixie about 4.5 miles from the track, this place is said to be popular with race crews on the nights leading up to the race.

The **Everglades Alligator Farm** offers guided airboat tours of their massive farm with more than 2,500 alligators, countless other reptiles, and a wealth of indigenous wildlife. They also offer hourly alligator and snake shows. Airboat tours cost

$14.50 for adults and $8 for kids. You can also see local wildlife by taking a boat tour of **Everglades National Park**. Tours cost just $16 per person and depart from the ranger station near Everglades City. Tours leave every half hour and do not require reservations. Call (800) 445-7724 for details.

The **Flamingo Lodge, Marina and Outpost** offers kayaks, canoes, bikes, fishing poles, binoculars, and coolers for rent. The lodge opens in November when the weather and mosquitoes are more tolerable. Call (800) 600-3813 for additional information. The Homestead area is a short drive from terrific dive spots that scuba and snorkeling fans will want to visit. The **Biscayne National Underwater Park**, minutes from the track at 9710 SW 328th Street, offers scuba diving, snorkeling, and glass bottom boat tours at Biscayne National Park in Homestead. Call (305) 230-1100 for reservations. The area also has a number of deep-sea fishing and scuba-diving charter boats. Two local outfits worth mentioning are **Hit 'n' Run Charters** in Homestead, for fishing, and **Mike's Charters** in Marathon, for scuba diving. Key Largo is a short drive away and has a wealth of deep-sea fishing, snorkeling, and scuba-diving opportunities. For a more complete list of area marinas and boat captains, call the Chamber of Commerce.

It would be a shame to be in south Florida in November and not spend some quality time at the beach. **Miami Beach** offers a 300-foot-wide beach that stretches for more than 10 miles along the Atlantic Ocean. Dozens of pastel-colored, luxury oceanfront hotels are situated on Collins Avenue. A 2-mile boardwalk overlooking the beach was built between Twenty-first and Forty-sixth Streets. South of that, both above and below **Lummus Park**, are a number of public beaches. For $15 (plus tip), many beaches offer the use of a pair of lounge chairs and a good-sized umbrella. These are well worth the investment. I enjoyed the beaches between Tenth and Fifteenth Streets. They had plenty of volleyball nets, concession stands, public rest rooms, and a good crowd. I was told that certain beaches are reserved for nude sunbathing, but you are likely to see some topless tanning no matter where you go, although there is supposedly a pretty hefty fine for women caught without both halves of their suit on.

NIGHTLIFE IN HOMESTEAD-MIAMI

A trip to the greater Miami area without a visit to South Beach is just about unheard of. The South Beach nightlife district is ever evolving, but one thing that never changes is its ranking among the wildest and most outrageous club scenes in the country. That can hardly be said about the area immediately surrounding the track, but there are a handful of places that attract a crowd during race week.

The **Sports Page Lounge**, at 113 South Homestead Boulevard, is a fairly happening place with an accommodating staff, a handful of televisions, pool tables, and a solid sports bar menu of wings, sandwiches, and steaks. Next door, The **Peachtree**, located at the Days Inn, serves as the local late-night dance club. Florida City has the Wharf Lounge, King Richard's, and Gusto's mentioned below. **Redland Tavern** has a Miami address, but it's minutes north of the track at 17701 SW 232nd Street. There's not much to the place other than three pool tables, occasional bands, and a friendly staff. They serve burgers and such at lunch and dinner and offer a pork barbecue with live music on Sundays.

South Beach is the place for area nightlife, and the *Miami New Times* is a good source for up-to-date club listings. Bear in mind that things don't really get hopping in Miami until eleven at night, so you may want to grab a late dinner before heading out to spend a night on the town. Many of the best-known clubs are within walking distance of each other along Ocean Drive or Washington Avenue. There are countless open-air clubs and restaurants along Ocean Drive, where people-watching could last all night. My favorites are the **Delano**, a funky hotel and bar with a hip, sophisticated crowd at 1685 Collins Avenue, and **Wet Willie's**, an open-air club and a great place to watch the beautiful people stroll by at 760 Ocean Drive. A few blocks away, at the corner of Tenth Street, you'll find an **All-Star Café** in the Edison Hotel at 960 Ocean Drive.

Miami's dance clubs seem to come and go, and it's difficult to say what's hot and what's not. The **Shadow Lounge** is an elegant two-story club at 1532 Washington Avenue. This upscale spot is open Thursday through Saturday until five in the morning. There is a cover charge on the weekends and a fairly strict dress code. **Cristal** offers an incredible display of lights, a state-of-the-art sound system, and a crowd that is dressed to impress. There's almost always a line to get in, despite the hefty cover charge. Cristal is located at 1045 Fifth Street and occasionally features live music.

In downtown Miami, the **Bayside Marketplace** is home to several bars and nightclubs. Located on Fourth Street at the Bay, **Hard Rock Café** and **Crocodile Cantina** are among the clubs you'll find here. **CocoWalk** in Coconut Grove has the **Improv Comedy Club**, **TuTu Tango**, and **Fat Tuesdays**, among other bars and restaurants. **Planet Hollywood** is just a short walk away.

WHERE TO EAT

No matter where you are staying, you'll find a number of standout eateries to choose from. In Homestead, there are some fine Mexican places, as well as a number of solid local establishments and national chain restaurants along the Dixie Highway and Krome Avenue. **El Toro Taco** is an affordable, family-oriented place where everything is made from scratch, the servings are huge, and the prices are modest. Generally considered the best Mexican food in town, they're located at 1 South Krome Avenue. They offer indoor and outdoor dining for lunch and dinner.

Casita Tejas is another choice for Mexican cuisine at 27 North Krome Avenue that presents Tex-Mex specialties in a casual setting.

Tiffany's is a fairly fancy place for breakfast and lunch and offers an outstanding Sunday brunch buffet. They're located at 22 NE Fifteenth Street in Homestead, but don't count on going here the day after the race because they're closed on Mondays. **Angie's**, on the other end of the spectrum, is a small diner that serves a mean southern breakfast and hearty lunch specials at 404 SE First Avenue in Florida City.

King Richard's Room at 935 Krome Avenue in Florida City has been around for forty-three years. This place has an actual throne inside and packs 'em in for race week, but it has nothing to do with Richard Petty. Richard, the restaurant's owner, has a keen sense of humor and a way with steaks, stone crabs, lobster, and Italian specialties. The adjacent **Capri Restaurant**, specializing in hand-tossed pizza, lasagna, and Parmesan dishes, shares a bar with King Richard's. The bar stays open as late as the dining rooms; for race week that can be late in the evening. **The Mutineer** is another restaurant with a bar scene of its own. Located in Florida City, at 11 SE First Avenue, this comfortable restaurant specializes in seafood ranging from lobster to alligator tails and, as the name implies, has a nautical theme. There's generally live music inside the adjoining **Wharf Lounge** for race weekend. **Gusto's**, on Strano Boulevard, is Florida City's newest sports bar with a pool table, a limited food menu, ice-cold beers, and a handful of televisions to view.

The **Farmer's Market Restaurant** is inside the local produce market at 300 North Krome Avenue in Florida City. Open daily, this casual place is popular with the locals and features good-sized portions at an affordable price. The **Main Street Café**, at 128 North Krome Avenue in Homestead, is open for lunch and serves dinner Thursday through Saturday. The entrees and sandwiches have a healthy, organic flair, and they offer live acoustic music at night on the weekends. The **Redland Rib House** is on the northern fringe of town at 24856 Krome Avenue. This moderately priced place specializes in Saint Louis baby back ribs, chicken, and homemade side dishes in a very casual setting. **Valentino's Pizza**, located in the same shopping center at the corner of Coconut Palm Drive and Krome Avenue, serves pizza, subs, and Italian specialties for lunch and dinner. If you are staying nearby, they offer free delivery.

Miami has far too many worthwhile restaurants to list here. **Bayside Marketplace**, in downtown Miami between Biscayne Boulevard and Biscayne Bay at Fourth Street, has a number of restaurants to choose from. **CocoWalk** at 3390 Mary Street in Coconut Grove is another spot with an assortment of restaurants. For a place that is legendary as an indigenous Miami eatery, check out **Joe's Stone Crab** at 227 Biscayne Street in Miami Beach. This place has been around since 1913, the food is out of this world, and the service is as friendly and attentive as you'll find anywhere. They are open only from mid-October to mid-May, so race fans should be sure to take advantage of being there at the right time of year. Expect a wait on weekends and be sure to save room for the key lime pie.

LOCAL MEDIA

The *Miami Herald* is the dominant daily newspaper. The *South Dade News Leader* is another source for local information on race weekend. Race broadcasts can be heard via MRN on WINZ 940 AM.

WHERE TO STAY

HOTELS

Miami and Miami Beach have an abundance of hotels to choose from. Florida City, just southwest of Homestead, is another option worth exploring. Traffic is generally less of a hassle approaching the track from the south. A little farther south, Key Largo is the first of the Florida Keys and a terrific destination for race week. North of the track, the town of Kendall has a handful of solid hotels located a short drive from a number of nightclubs and restaurants.

Bay Harbor Inn   9660 East Bay Harbor Drive, Miami (305) 868-4141   Clean, convenient, and affordable, the inn is a short drive from the beach and within walking distance of several worthwhile restaurants.

Baymont Inn & Suites   10821 Caribbean Boulevard, Cutler Ridge (305) 278-0001   This is a fine compromise location about 10 miles from the track and 28 miles from downtown Miami. The hotel has an outdoor pool and offers a complimentary breakfast and newspaper in the morning. They also have a new location about 18 miles from the track near the Miami International Airport.

Best Western   1 Strano Boulevard, Florida City (305) 246-5100   A modest place less than 3 miles from the track. Every room offers a refrigerator and microwave oven. Located across the street from Denny's and a short walk from the Mutineer restaurant.

Comfort Inn   333 East First Avenue, Florida City (305) 248-4009   On the same block as the Best Western, this place has similar amenities, including a pool and complimentary continental breakfast, and sells out quickly on race weekend.

Days Inn   51 South Homestead Boulevard, Homestead (305) 245-1260   This is one of the first places to book up on race weekend. There's a restaurant and lounge on premises, refrigerators in the rooms, and free continental breakfast in the morning.

Hampton Inn   124 East Palm Drive, Florida City (305) 247-8833   Located near the two Florida City hotels listed above, this hotel has an outdoor pool on site and the same selection of restaurants nearby.

Ocean Pointe Suites   500 Burton Drive, Tavernier (305) 853-3000 or (800) 882-9464   Small groups or families would do well to check this place out for race week. The suites sleep up to six people with a full kitchen. There's also a heated pool, a marina, and a sandy beach on premises.

Ramada Limited   990 North Homestead Boulevard, Homestead (305) 247-7020   Despite the Homestead address, this hotel is no closer to the track than the Florida City hotels previously listed and has fewer amenities.

Travelodge   409 SE First Avenue, Florida City (305) 248-9777   One of the most affordable places in Florida City, this hotel sells out year after year for race weekend. Call early if you hope to get a room here.

Wellesley Inn   11750 Mills Drive, Kendall (305) 270-0359   Surrounded by a mall and several franchise restaurants, this moderately priced hotel has well-appointed rooms and a heated pool, and has been known to have rooms available up until race weekend.

Westin Beach Resort   97000 South Overseas Highway, Key Largo (305) 852-5553   A luxury resort on the water with two exceptional restaurants, a sandy beach, a host of watersports to choose from, a gorgeous pool, a secluded Jacuzzi, and nicely appointed rooms and suites.

CAMPSITES

The **Florida City Campsite and RV Park**, at 601 NW Third Avenue, has a reputation for being "ground zero" for race fans camping out during race week. They fill up fast, so call (305) 248-7889 to reserve a spot in advance. The **Southern Comfort RV Resort**, also in Florida City, is actually closer to the track at 345 East Palm Drive. For reservations call (305) 248-6909. The **Miami/Everglades KOA** campground, 11 miles north of the track, has tent and RV sites, as well as a limited number of cabins and lodges. The cabins and lodges are very reasonably priced and sell out quickly for race weekend. Call (800) 562-7732 for reservations.

HOUSEBOATS

For something completely different, call the **Flamingo Lodge** about houseboat rentals. Houseboats are completely stocked and sleep six to eight people. The only things you'll need are food, beverages, and to gas up the boat. Prior boating experience is preferred but not mandatory. Call (800) 600-3813 for details.

Good to Know

- To charge tickets or for additional race information, call (305) 230-7223.
- Mail orders can be sent to Homestead-Miami Speedway, Attn: Ticket Office, 1 Speedway Boulevard, Homestead, FL 33035-1500.

- The Tropical Everglades Visitor Center, on U.S. 1 in Florida City, can be reached at (800) 388-9669. The Miami Convention & Visitors Bureau also has a toll-free number, (800) 283-2707 or you can call them at (305) 539-3100.
- A worthwhile city Web site is www.tropicaleverglades.com or visit www.tropi cool.com for Greater Miami information.
- ➤ The official racetrack Web site is www.homesteadmiamispeedway.com.

NEARBY WINSTON CUP RACE CITIES

Daytona: 260 miles (four hours, thirty minutes)
Darlington: 660 miles (eleven hours, twenty minutes)
Atlanta: 665 miles (eleven hours, thirty minutes)

IN THE VICINITY

Key West, about 150 miles from Miami, is the southernmost point of the forty-eight contiguous states. The drive southwest on U.S. 1 takes about three and a half hours, crosses forty-four bridges linking the islands of the Gulf of Mexico, and is one of the most scenic and distinctive in the country. Key West is famous for its sunsets viewed from Mallory Square, and its laid-back yet lively nightlife. It also offers some of the country's best snorkeling, scuba diving, and deep-sea fishing.

There are dozens of restaurants and bars along Duval Street. My favorite bars include **Jimmy Buffet's Margaritaville** and **Hog's Breath Tavern**, both on Duval. Restaurants such as the **Pier House**, **Louie's Backyard**, and **Square One** are all worth checking out. The **Key West Cigar Factory**, a block off Duval near Mallory Square, is another personal favorite for outstanding hand-rolled cigars at a reasonable price. We stayed at the **Conch House Heritage Inn**, a wonderful yet affordable bed-and-breakfast place just off Duval at 625 Truman Avenue.

Key West is the site of the **Ernest Hemingway Home and Museum** at 907 Whitehead Street. Tours of this circa 1850 Spanish Colonial–style home and its tropical garden cost $4.50. It is said to be where several of Hemingway's greatest works were written. **Conch Tour Trains** are a fun way to see the island and learn about Old Town and the waterfront. The narrated ninety-minute trip leaves every half hour from Mallory Square or the depot at 3840 North Roosevelt Boulevard and costs $18 for adults. Call (800) 868-7482 or (305) 294-5161 for details. For additional information on lodging, restaurants, attractions, and nightlife, call the **Key West Chamber of Commerce** at (800) 527-8539 or (305) 294-2587.

▪ *INDIANAPOLIS MOTOR SPEEDWAY* ▪

Indianapolis, Indiana

"Indy is special, not because of what we made it into, but because of what it was when we got there."

— RICKY CRAVEN

NASCAR fans may not agree, but Indy is still the nation's foremost racetrack. More than ninety years ago, Indianapolis became the racing capital of the world, but the "Brickyard" has been part of the Winston Cup circuit for less than a decade. Despite its recent introduction to Winston Cup racing, the Brickyard 400 has become one of the most significant races for drivers and fans alike. The purse for the Brickyard 400 is among the largest in Winston Cup racing, exceeding $6 million, and the race has sold out every year since its inception in 1994.

The 2.5-mile layout has low 9-degree banked turns and is shaped like a giant rectangle. The identical flat straightaways are 3,300 feet each, while the short straights are both 660 feet long. The straights are 50 feet wide, often accommodating four- and five-wide racing, while the turns are 60 feet wide. Unlike Daytona and Talladega, Indy was not built with stock cars in mind, so drivers find it a difficult track to negotiate. In addition to being flat and tough for cars to handle through the turns, the track is unusually weather-sensitive and becomes slick with warmer temperatures. It's also hard for drivers to complete a clean pass, so much of the track position gained during a race is done in the pits or through pit strategy—taking on fuel only or changing two tires instead of four late in the race. Pit road is treacherously narrow at Indy, and sheet metal is often crumpled during mass pit stops as drivers try to gain an edge on the competition.

As an illustrious event, the Brickyard 400 ranks among the biggest and best in racing. My apologies to fans of the Coca-Cola 600, the Southern 500, and both Bristol races, but only Daytona surpasses the prestige of a stock car race run at the

The field negotiates the flat turns in the 2001 Brickyard 400. *(Photo by Dan Kaegebein)*

Brickyard. More than 300,000 fans show up each year to see the best NASCAR drivers take on this historic track, and there's a very real chance that the Brickyard 400 could one day outdraw the Indy 500. Folks show up with their coolers, blankets, and lawn chairs on race day at 5:30 in the morning, hoping to occupy the very best infield spots along the backstretch spectator mound. The boom of a cannon shot signifies the opening of the spectator gates at 8 A.M. and the fans begin pouring into the 224-acre infield.

A tall, four-sided scoring tower sits near pit road and lists the miles and laps completed as well as the top thirty-three drivers. Another four-sided scoring board, this one short and wide, is located just inside turn three and lists the top ten drivers. Several major additions to the track debuted in 2000. The pagoda building, situated to overlook the start/finish line from the infield side of the track, is a 160-foot-tall steel-and-glass building that offers nine viewing decks. Digital message boards atop the pagoda list the race leaders during the race. Beside the pagoda, closer to turn one, the Pit Road Terrace and Gasoline Alley Suites are available to team members, officials, and VIP guests.

Brickyard Crossing, an eighteen-hole golf course that was recently redesigned by Pete Dye, occupies a portion of the infield and has even hosted the PGA Senior Tour on more than one occasion. The **Hall of Fame Museum**, in the infield near turn two, is home to countless vintage vehicles including an 1886 Benz three-wheel motorcar, a Harley Davidson from the early 1900s, Richard Petty's 1992 STP Pontiac Grand Prix, and dozens of Indy cars. It is among the best racing attractions in the nation and well worth the $3 price of admission. The grandstands are not as antiquated as you might expect for a vintage track, and the infield amenities—garages, concessions, rest rooms, video screens, and paved parking lots—are the nicest in all of stock car racing. One pleasant surprise was concessions, which are reasonably priced throughout the speedway.

From a fan's perspective, however, Indy is not among my favorite tracks. Daytona and Talladega are as big or bigger, but you can still see most of the track from the better seats at these classic stock car ovals. At Indy, the infield structures, including the media tower, pagoda building, and grandstands on both sides of the frontstretch, are so tall that they completely obstruct the view from grandstands along the outside of the track as cars head into turn one and proceed around the track. There are about eighteen giant video monitors strategically placed about the track, so you can watch those when the cars are not directly in front of your seat, but that's not really the point of attending a race in person. One simply has to believe that the spectacle of a race at Indy is the main reason so many folks show up year after year.

Ticket prices for the Brickyard 400 are surprisingly reasonable and range from $35 to $140. Seats high in the Northwest Vista section in turn four may offer the most complete view of the track, as they permit fans to see down the frontstretch, where much of the passing occurs, and also offer a good perspective of the short chute between turns three and four. Most frontstretch seating sections offer aluminum benches with seatbacks while some areas have individual chairs. Other, less expensive sections have simple bleachers with no seatbacks. Individual cushioned seats with backrests are available for rent at the speedway for just $7. Many seats in the highest row of the frontstretch have a canopy overhead to protect fans from the heat and rain. There's also a nice view of the downtown Indianapolis skyline as you look beyond turn two from these seats.

Unlike most Winston Cup tracks, once you are inside the gates at Indy, you are not allowed to leave and return. If you want to shop at the souvenir trailers you can go to the area between gates 6 and 7 along Georgetown Road outside the gates on the frontstretch or to the driver merchandise trailers inside turn two, near the GM Experience and Hall of Fame Museum. The area inside the track offers a better diversity of souvenirs.

HISTORY

On May 30, 1911, the nation's first 500-mile automobile race was held at Indy. That first race offered a $10,000 first prize and may be the first time a pace car was used to start a race, as the forty-car field was too large to start safely from a dead start. The race was won in six hours and forty-two minutes. On his way to victory, Ray Harroun averaged 74.602 mph in a Marmon passenger car.

The track earned its nickname of the Brickyard in 1910, as 3.2 million 10-pound paving bricks were laid on their sides in a bed of sand. Mortar was added to ensure that the track was as smooth and durable as possible. The bricks lasted more than a quarter of a century before the track was partially asphalted in 1936. In 1961, the track was completely covered in asphalt except for a 3-foot strip (a yard of bricks) at the start/finish line.

The first eight Winston Cup races at Indy have not been classic, door-to-door clashes that fans will remember for the ages. However, the five drivers who have found their way to victory lane are all among the best in the business. As the season reaches the point where drivers converge on Indy, the teams that are at the top of the points chase are hitting their stride and tend to continue their success at Indy. In fact, the winner at Indy has gone on to win the points championship for four consecutive years, from 1998 through the 2001 season.

On August 6, 1994, Jeff Gordon won the inaugural Brickyard 400 by .53 of a second over Brett Bodine. Neither Bodine nor Gordon could keep up with Ernie Irvan that day, but a flat tire took Irvan out late in the race and Gordon, the local favorite, went on to earn a $613,000 payoff. The first Brickyard 400 was the site of another Winston Cup first. Geoff, Todd, and Brett Bodine all led at least one lap during the race. A trio of brothers had never done that before at any track in the modern era of NASCAR. A day earlier, John Andretti became the first driver to qualify for both the Brickyard 400 and the Indy 500 in the same year.

Gordon earned the pole the following year, but Dale Earnhardt took the checkered flag by leading the last twenty-seven laps. Earnhardt started the race in the thirteenth position, endured a rain delay of more than four hours, and held off Rusty Wallace, Dale Jarrett, and Bill Elliott for his only Brickyard victory. Dale Jarrett improved on his 1995 third-place performance by winning the 1996 Brickyard 400. Jarrett started twenty-fourth but overcame his poor position to lead just eleven laps on the way to victory. Jarrett traded positions with teammate Ernie Irvan twice in the final sixty-two laps, but took the lead for good in turn two on lap 154. Robert Pressley hit the wall in turn four on lap 159, so the race ended under yellow for the first time. Jeff Gordon set the Indy record for the worst finish by a pole sitter, coming in in thirty-seventh place.

Ricky Rudd became the fourth Brickyard winner in as many years on August 2,

1997. Rudd opted not to pit when the leaders stopped to top off their fuel cells. Dale Jarrett and Jeff Gordon made strong runs at the end but came up short as Rudd ran the final forty-six laps without stopping for fuel or tires. Rudd beat Bobby Labonte by .183 of a second, still the narrowest margin of victory at the speedway. The next season, Jeff Gordon became the track's first two-time winner. Gordon beat out Mark Martin and Bobby Labonte as the race ended under caution when a four-car crash occurred in turn four on a restart on lap 158. That race is listed as the slowest in track history, taking three hours, nine minutes, and nineteen seconds. Not surprisingly, that race also set the record for most caution flags and tied the 1996 race for fewest cars running at the finish. Gordon earned an extra $1 million for his win as part of the Winston No Bull 5 bonus.

Dale Jarrett became the track's second two-time winner on August 7, 1999. Jarrett led a track-record 117 laps to beat out Bobby Labonte, Bill Elliott, and Jerry Nadeau. Jarrett qualified third to become the third winner to start from the inside spot of the second row. Jeff Gordon had done it twice before. Gordon finished third in 1999 to earn the best finish of any pole sitter at Indy. Through the 2001 season, no pole winner has ever won at Indy. Bobby Labonte, who in the three previous years had finished second twice and third once, finally won at Indy on his way to the Winston Cup points championship. Labonte beat out Rusty Wallace and Bill Elliott, as Pontiac won for the first time at Indy. Labonte averaged 155.912 mph, the fastest average speed at Indy to date. Rusty Wallace led 100 laps that day, the most laps led by a driver who did not win at Indy.

On August 5, 2001, Jeff Gordon became the first driver to win the Brickyard 400 three times. Gordon led just twenty-nine laps all day and won the race despite starting the race in the twenty-seventh position, the worst starting position ever to win a race at Indy. Gordon took the lead from Sterling Marlin on lap 136 of 160 and won by .943 of a second in a race that took three hours, three minutes, and thirty seconds. Gordon averaged a relatively slow 130.790 mph in a contest that featured eighteen lead changes. Three rookies, Kevin Harvick, Kurt Busch, and Ryan Newman, led at least one lap during the race to set a track record. Jeff Gordon, however, truly rules at Indy, having earned three poles, three victories, and more than $4.2 million in the first eight races there.

GETTING TO THE TRACK

The track is about 6 miles northwest of downtown, and the folks at Indianapolis Motor Speedway have learned a thing or two over the years about moving traffic along on race day. With 300,000 fans attending a single event, you expect traffic jams, especially after the race, but the Indianapolis authorities do a stellar job of keeping traffic flowing. The main routes to the track from the east are Thirtieth,

Sixteenth, and Tenth Streets, although as you get close to the track several local roads are open only to buses, media, and credentialed VIPs on race day.

Traffic is heaviest from the east, especially on Sixteenth Street, so if at all possible it's best to circle the track and approach from the south or west. From the south, Lynhurst Drive may be a worthwhile alternative route. On our way home, trying to take Lafayette Road to I-65 South, we stumbled upon Guilon Road, a terrific shortcut off Georgetown Road that led directly to I-65 South and downtown Indianapolis. Once we cleared the traffic immediately surrounding the track, we were back at our hotel in twenty minutes.

Very little of the parking at the track is free. Expect to pay $10–30 for a spot. The closer you are to the track, the more you'll pay. The Coke lot, at the corner of Georgetown Road and Thirtieth Street, is the largest public lot near the track. The track is huge, so make an effort to determine where your seats are located and park nearby, or you could spend a great deal of time walking around the track to the gate near your seats.

The **IndyGo Shuttle** offers round-trip service to the race from the airport and downtown at the RCA Dome, and the corner of Illinois and Market Street, near Monument Circle. Shuttle service begins at six in the morning, runs every fifteen minutes, and continues until three hours after the race ends. Round-trip transportation costs just $15. Buses are given a priority route and the trip takes about twenty minutes each way. Call (317) 635-3344 or use their Web site at www.indygo. net for more information or to reserve tickets.

WHAT TO SEE AND DO

The city of Indianapolis astonished me in many ways, but the diversity and quality of local attractions and museums may have been the biggest surprise. Many of the landmark attractions are in the heart of downtown or within a short drive. Indianapolis is home to the NFL Colts and the NBA Pacers, both of whom play their home games in state-of-the-art downtown arenas. As a result, the areas immediately surrounding the RCA Dome and Conseco Fieldhouse have experienced an impressive urban renewal over the past decade or so.

The **Indianapolis Zoo** is spread out over 64 acres on the edge of downtown at 1200 West Washington Street. This cageless zoo is home to 2,000 animals, including elephants, tigers, lions, polar bears, and giraffes, in natural settings. There's also an aquarium with dolphin shows. Admission is $9.75 for adults and $6 for kids. The adjacent **White River Gardens** is a 3.3-acre botanical garden and conservatory.

The **Indianapolis Indians** play their home games at Victory Field. Considered one of the best AAA ballparks in the nation, this stunning downtown ballpark is home to the Brewers farm team that won the 2000 AAA World Series. You don't have to be a baseball fan to appreciate the **NCAA Hall of Champions** at 700 West Washington Street. Relive your favorite moments in college sports at this new facility with countless interactive displays highlighting championship student athletes, a turn-of-the-century basketball court, and four theaters. The Hall of Champions is open daily until 5 P.M. and admission is $7 for adults.

Race fans may want to spend some time on the track racing their buddies on a local go-kart track. Indy is home to at least three quality indoor go-kart centers. **Racers**, downtown at Union Station, **Fast Times**, at Ninety-sixth Street and Keystone Avenue, and the **Stefan Johansson Karting Center**, on Lafayette Road, all feature top-notch go-karts, challenging tracks, and fast and furious racing fun. Find the one near you and see who among you can drive like a pro. If you'd rather leave it to the pros, **Indianapolis Raceway Park**, at 10267 U.S. Highway 136, hosts a Busch Series race on the same weekend as the Brickyard 400. In addition to a smooth paved half-mile oval, IRP hosts NHRA drag races, USAC races, the Craftsman Truck Series, and road course races. Call (317) 291-4090 for schedule and ticket information.

The **Indianapolis Museum of Art**, at 1200 West Thirty-eighth Street, is home to acres of gardens, fountains, sculptures, and walking paths. Inside you'll find hundreds of works of art, including paintings, photographs, sculpture, drawings, and prints from Asia, Europe, Africa, and America. The **Indiana Soldiers' and Sailors' Monument** is an impressive tribute to the soldiers who fought and died in the Civil War. The monument was completed in 1902 and is located at Monument Circle in the heart of downtown. You can climb to the top of the 284-foot monument via thirty-two flights of stairs or take the elevator. Either way, you'll be rewarded with a spectacular view of downtown Indianapolis. At the monument's base, you'll find the **Eli Lilly Civil War Museum**. Admission is free, but the museum is closed Monday and Tuesday.

Broad Ripple Village is a quaint area of shops, galleries, and cafés about twenty minutes north of downtown. Walk, run, or bike through Broad Ripple Park or along the newly completed **Monon Trail**. This area transforms into a festive dining and nightlife district after dark. **India Garden** is one of the standout restaurants in the area, but there are plenty of other ethnic and traditional American eateries to choose from, as well as some of the area's best local nightlife.

NIGHTLIFE IN INDIANAPOLIS

On the southern edge of the downtown nightlife district, at the corner of Meridian and South Street, the **Slippery Noodle Inn** is the city's oldest standing bar. Said to be a hideout for gangster John Dillinger years ago, this place offers live blues every night and serves a pretty mean dinner. The outdoor patio is a nice retreat from the smoke and crowd, while the music rooms and bars fill up early. Don't expect your beers to come often or inexpensively on race weekend, but the local blues bands play late into the night and the enthusiastic crowd gets into the tunes.

Just a short walk back toward downtown at 234 South Meridian Street, the **Claddagh Irish Pub** is a good-sized drinking hole with an agreeable atmosphere, a streetside patio, a typical Irish pub menu of sandwiches, stews, and shepherd's pie, a helpful staff, and a handsome crowd. Next door you'll find **Ike and Jonsey's**, a fifties-style dance club that features the dance music of every decade from the fifties to the present. They also offer an outdoor patio, dozens of beers to choose from, and a solid menu. **Rock Bottom Brewery** and their basement billiard room "Under the Rock" are also located downtown at 10 West Washington Street. Open for lunch, dinner, and late-night fun, this upscale brewery/restaurant offers a sidewalk café, billiards, live entertainment, and a selection of beers brewed on site.

Jazz fans will want to head to the **Chatterbox Tavern**, a small, smoky music room with great acoustics and a friendly staff. Get there early or you'll miss out on a table with a view of the stage. The patio offers a nice respite from the noise and smoke. There's live music nightly, and you should expect a cover charge on weekends. Just up the street, **Rathskellar** is another favorite with the locals. The German entrees are top-notch, but the biergarten out back and live bands are the main attraction here. The atmosphere is a sight to behold and the crowd is as unpretentious as you'll find in downtown Indy.

Alcatraz Brewing Company at the Circle Centre is a worthwhile place to watch a game, grab a bite to eat, and sample microbrew beers. The San Francisco atmosphere is a bit manufactured, but the handcrafted beers are worthy, the service engaging, and the massive hot pretzels an absolute bargain. **World Mardi Gras Entertainment Complex** offers several nightclubs under one roof. Located on the fourth floor of the Circle Centre Mall, you'll find Flashbaxx and Gators, a pair of dance clubs; Brewski's, a sizable sports bar with 120 types of beer to choose from; and the World Mardi Gras Music Hall, which hosts live entertainment Thursday through Saturday.

To get a feel for Indy nightlife with the locals, don't be afraid to venture north of downtown toward the canal at Broad Ripple. There are too many outstanding clubs, pubs, and bars to explore in a single evening, but this area is worth the short cab ride to hang with the Butler University crowd. Start at the northern edge of Broad Ripple and work your way south. The **Broad Ripple Brew Pub**, at 840 East Sixty-fifth Street, is a beer lover's paradise where you'll find quality lagers and ales, charming servers, a nice outdoor patio, and a relaxed setting. **Average Joe's** is a Broad Ripple institution with plenty of pool tables, darts, a foosball table, a satisfying jukebox, giant-screen TV, and a formidable collection of racing and sports memorabilia. Located at 814-16 Broad Ripple Avenue, you can grab some quick munchies while you're there. **Old Pro's Table** is another billiard and sports bar on Broad Ripple Avenue that packs them in on the weekends. Beer aficionados should also check out **Chumley's**, just up the street from Average Joe's. They offer a nice outdoor patio and nearly 150 types of beer to choose from. In what used to be a theater, **The Vogue** has become the area's predominant live music venue. The marquee out front lists local, regional, and occasional national-caliber musicians. It gets cranking a little later than the surrounding drinking holes, but you can count on a decent-sized weekend crowd as the night wears on.

If you are fortunate enough to find a room near the track, **Union Jack's Pub** at 6225 West Twenty-fifth Street in Speedway is just minutes away. This intimate restaurant has some of the best pizza in the city, a sizable collection of racing helmets, several gallery-quality racing paintings, and oodles of racing memorabilia. You'll also find more than fifty imported drafts on tap and another fifty bottled imported beers. They have a second location at Broad Ripple.

WHERE TO EAT

Ask anybody in Indy where to eat, and chances are they will mention **St. Elmo's Steak House** and their legendary shrimp cocktails. The shrimp cocktails are certainly the best I've ever had, but the steaks are also outstanding, and the service is top-notch. You're likely to see several race teams, celebrities, and race broadcasters enjoying a meal here throughout the race weekend. This place, located downtown at 127 South Illinois Street, has been an Indianapolis institution since 1902. Take the time to check out the photos of classic sporting venues, athletes, and celebrities that line the dark paneled rooms that make up this outstanding eatery.

As St. Elmo's becomes better known, **Dunaway's** has become a spot for sports celebrities and the well-to-do to enjoy a terrific meal away from the crowds. This fine dining establishment is off the beaten path in the historic Indiana Oxygen Building at 351 South East Street. In most race towns **Ruth's Chris Steak House**, at the corner of Keystone and Ninety-sixth Street, would be the finest place in town for steaks and a great place to run into your favorite driver or celebrity. In Indianapolis, Ruth's still serves a mean steak but has to settle for also-ran when it comes to places to "see and be seen" during race week. For a diverse selection of seafood, pasta, rotisserie entrees, and regional American cuisine in a stylish atmosphere check out **Palomino** at 49 West Maryland Street.

Sometimes, all you want is exceptional pizza. If that's the case, head to **Bazbeaux** at 334 Massachusetts Avenue. The pizza is made fresh and they offer more than fifty toppings—as if cheese and pepperoni weren't enough. The streetside patio can get crowded at lunch and dinner, so get there early. For what several people described to me as "the best breakfast place in Indy," check out **Le Peep**. There are six locations to choose from. I ate breakfast at their downtown location, at 301 North Illinois, and wish I had discovered it earlier in my trip. They're open only for breakfast and lunch but certainly worth stopping by.

LOCAL MEDIA

The local paper, *The Indianapolis Star*, does a terrific job of covering NASCAR Winston Cup racing. *Nuvo*, the local entertainment weekly, is helpful in choosing nightlife and entertainment options during race week and has a Brickyard Party Guide section with race-related entertainment and a listing of driver autograph sessions. *Indianapolis* magazine is among the best in the nation and well worth purchasing in advance of your visit. Race broadcasts can be heard on IMS Radio carried locally by WIBC 1070 AM as well as on MRN Radio, WNDE 1260 AM.

WHERE TO STAY

HOTELS

I was completely surprised by the number of quality hotels in downtown Indianapolis. With the track less than 6 miles from downtown and the lion's share of restaurants, nightlife, and attractions downtown, there's really no reason to stay elsewhere. Hotels do sell out quickly on race weekend, so book a place as soon as you have secured tickets to the race.

Brickyard Crossing Golf Resort and Inn   4400 West Sixteenth Street (317) 241-2500   Located at the track, there is no more convenient place to stay on race day. Staying here will require a short drive to downtown restaurants and attractions, but the convenience on race day may outweigh that fact.

Canterbury Hotel   123 South Illinois (317) 634-3000   This historic downtown hotel is where celebrities are likely to be staying for race weekend. Located in the midst of nearly everything worth doing in downtown Indy.

Courtyard by Marriott   501 West Washington Street (317) 635-4443   Conveniently located near the ballpark, zoo, NCAA Hall of Champions, and several museums, this affordable hotel sells out quickly for race week.

Crowne Plaza Union Station   123 W. Louisiana St. (317) 631-2221   I found this place to be a steal of a deal on race weekend. Located within walking distance of nearly everything in downtown Indy, the rooms are outstanding and the service is first rate. Even parking at the adjacent underground lot was reasonable.

Embassy Suites North   3912 Vincennes Road (317) 872-7700   On the north side about thirty minutes from the track. This reasonably priced hotel offers a pool, complimentary happy hour, and cooked-to-order hot breakfast. Whispers, an on-site lounge, offers a pool table, jukebox, and darts.

Super Eight West   2602 North High School Road, Speedway (317) 291-8800   A modest hotel about a mile and a half from the track. Amenities include an indoor pool and hot tub.

Omni Severin Hotel   40 West Jackson Place (317) 634-6664   Deluxe accommodations in the heart of downtown within walking distance of nightlife, shopping, and restaurants. It's not cheap, especially on Brickyard 400 weekend, but no place worth staying is what I'd consider inexpensive for race week.

Good to Know

- To charge tickets or for additional race information, call (317) 484-6700.
- Mail orders can be sent to Indianapolis Motor Speedway, P.O. Box 24512, Speedway, IN 46222.
- The Convention & Visitors Association can be reached at (317) 237-5200.
- Indianapolis Downtown Inc. can be reached at (317) 237-2222.
- A worthwhile city Web site is www.indy.org.
- ➤ The official racetrack Web site is www.brickyard400.com.

NEARBY WINSTON CUP RACE CITIES

ChicagoLand: 190 miles (three hours, forty minutes)
Michigan International Speedway: 250 miles (four hours, thirty minutes)

IN THE VICINITY

Louisville, Kentucky, is across the Ohio River, just a few hours south of Indianapolis. Louisville is home to the Kentucky Derby and Churchill Downs. Tickets to the big race, that first Saturday in May, are not easy to come by, but horse racing fans will enjoy the **Kentucky Derby Museum** at gate 1 of the venerable racetrack. In addition to a historic look at races and championship horses from years past, a thirty-minute walking tour of the Derby grounds is included in the $7 admission fee. East of the track, near I-65, **Six Flags Kentucky Kingdom** is home to some killer roller coasters and more than 100 rides and attractions.

The **Louisville Slugger Museum**, in downtown Louisville at the corner of Eighth and Main Streets, is tough to miss because of the giant baseball bat leaning against this museum dedicated to the game's most prodigious hitters. After a quick tour of the museum, you can tour the bat factory and see how today's big-league bats are manufactured. Baseball fans will find it well worth the $5 entry fee. Louisville is a reasonable option if hotels in Indianapolis are completely booked on race weekend, but the college towns of Terre Haute, Bloomington, and West Lafayette are much closer to Indy.

▪ *KANSAS SPEEDWAY* ▪

Kansas City, Kansas

"What a great racetrack! Kansas City, this was a lot of fun. My car was driving itself out there. I wasn't putting any pressure on it or anything. It was just going round and round."

—DALE EARNHARDT JR.

Five years and $224 million in the making, this veritable clone of Chicago and Las Vegas is among the finest facilities in the sport. Designers seem to have thought of every nuance to make this a fan-friendly track, and drivers generally agree that it's among the best they race on. The race surface is smooth and wide. In the very first race drivers were able to go three wide at various points of the track, so side-by-side racing should become commonplace as the track matures. The track has tremendous grip on the bottom, and drivers expect the track to age well as a second groove began to develop about two-thirds of the way through the first race.

Like several newer tracks, Kansas Speedway is a 1.5-mile tri-oval, but it's different from Chicago, Las Vegas, Texas, and Homestead in a number of ways. The banking is 15 degrees in all four turns, steeper than Homestead and Vegas, yet not quite as angled as Chicago and Texas. The tri-oval is sloped at 10.4 degrees while the backstretch is banked at just 5 degrees. In the track's first sanctioned race, Winston Cup drivers exceeded 190 mph and 9,000 rpm on the 2,685-foot frontstretch, so fans can expect to see the high speeds they crave. The track may turn out to be tough on engines and tires even though races are just 400 miles or 267 laps long. Only time will tell, but Johnny Benson and Bill Elliott left the race with failed engines, and several accidents were the result of blown tires, in particular right

Action from the Inaugural NASCAR Winston Cup Series Protection One 400 at Kansas Speedway, Sept. 30, 2001. *(Photo by Jim Compton, courtesy of Kansas Speedway)*

front tires. The backstretch is 2,207 feet long, and during the inaugural race, drivers reached 190 mph before heading into turn three. Even through the turns, drivers can go all out and rarely dip below 150 mph during green flag laps. Drivers also like the state-of-the-art garages and pit road, which is quite wide, so there should be relatively few mishaps during mass pit stops.

From the fans' standpoint the track is absolutely world class. The infield was dug out and the backstretch is slightly higher than the frontstretch, so those fans in the very bottom rows have a decent view of the entire track. The four infield garage buildings, with their arched blue roofs, are unobtrusive despite being built parallel to the frontstretch. All seats have chairbacks, many have cup holders, and, because current seating sections overlook the tri-oval portion of the frontstretch, they all present a good view of the action. A wide roadway sits between the stands and the race surface, minimizing the amount of dust and rubber being blown into the faces of fans.

All told, there are 75,000 seats at the track, and plans are in place to expand to 150,000 seats. Initial expansion will result in 10,000 seats on either side of the current grandstand, but is not expected to be completed in time for the 2002 season. Given that the first Winston Cup race sold out months before the event, despite the requirement of buying a season ticket package of IRL and NASCAR truck races, expansion of the grandstands is sure to happen soon. Grandstands have two tiers of seating. The 100 level is a section of green seats that stretch from one end of pit road to the other. The 200 level is a section of purple and yellow seats located directly behind a wide walkway above the green seats. The massive press box and luxury suites sit above the 200 level sections creating a nice shady area late in the race. Concession stands and rest rooms are located every 300 feet and each concession stand has a TV monitor, so you don't have to miss the race while standing in line.

The track has a nice symmetry to it. Aside from the hospitality area overlooking turn one, there seem to be two of everything at the track. From the air, the north end of the track is practically a mirror image of the south end. A "Fan Walk" plaza in the infield has benches, concession stands, shade tents, slot car racing, and a stage. If you are lucky, you may even be able to take on one of the drivers in a slot car race. Driver Jason Leffler was seen competing with fans just after winning the pole. In the middle of it all stands a mammoth four-sided scoring tower listing the top ten drivers and the current lap. In a nod to Pocono, the owners have installed their own "Autograph Alley" near the garages that allow fans to seek driver autographs before a race. The fences here have holes strategically placed so fans can pass their hats, programs, and other items through to be signed by their favorite drivers. The inspection garage has clear doors and is visible from concrete risers that allow fans a glimpse of the prerace inspection process. A limited number of infield passes to the "Fan Walk" area are sold for just $15 per person.

The track is surrounded by mounds and trees, giving it the sense of being in the middle of nowhere despite its location near the largest highway intersection in the state. Wide pedestrian walkways allow fans to easily negotiate the hills between the parking lots and the track. The Midway Plaza outside the grandstands allows fans with or without tickets to partake in the race-day fun. A stage is set up for bands, souvenir trailers, and concessions are available. Concessions at Kansas Speedway are among the best in racing because area restaurants have a number of food stands offering a nice variety of menu items. Two worth looking for are the barbecue from Oklahoma Joe's and the sandwiches from Mr. Goodcents.

A pedestrian tunnel is located under turn one, and crossover gates are at the start/finish line and in turn one. The vehicle tunnel, with a pedestrian lane, accessing the infield runs under turn three. An infield RV area near turns three and four allows campers to park facing the track. Additional RV parking on the hill overlooking the backstretch and turns three and four presents a sweeping view of the track. The view from turn four offers a nice view down the frontstretch and entry to pit road. A modest collection of billboards lines the track in turns two and three. Wide grassy areas between the infield and track allow drivers to recover in the event of losing control of their cars exiting turns two and four.

The track does have a few minor flaws. The giant tri-oval places the pit road and victory lane a long way from the grandstands. Likewise, the grassy areas between the infield and track diminish the intimacy infield fans can get at older tracks. Some would argue that the track is too symmetrical and pristine, but as more grandstands are added and the years create a sense of wear, that criticism will subside. Except for Bristol, the grandstands here are as vertical as any in racing. While this allows fans in the upper rows to be close to the action, it does make for a fairly rigorous hike to the better seats. On the whole, however, this is a tremendous racetrack. Just like Chicago, the greatest criticism I have for this track is the rule against bringing in your own food and beverages.

HISTORY

Prior to the 2001 Protection One 400, Winston Cup had never raced in the state of Kansas. Jason Leffler earned the pole in the inaugural race and Jeff Gordon sat on the front row beside him. The experts feared that the most exciting part of a race at Kansas Speedway was going to be the start as drivers raced to the inside of the track for position along the bottom groove because the track has less bank and grip than similar facilities. Early in the race, single-file, nose-to-tail racing was the norm when it became apparent that cars that tried to pass on the outside were often left out to dry and passed by small groups of cars drafting along the bottom of the track.

Yellow flags came early and often as drivers got used to the track. In fact, there were two cautions within the first ten laps and thirteen overall, which marked the most cautions at a speedway all season. Every restart was an adventure as track position became key to finishing well. Another key was pitting quickly as several lead changes and position shuffles occurred in the pits.

Rusty Wallace took the lead for the first time on lap 79 and led 118 laps on the day. Still most of the passing was happening on the inside groove. After about 100 laps drivers started to test the outside with Wallace having the most success. Most drivers found it difficult to move through the pack and were content to maintain position, hope their cars held together, and let their pit crews improve their position by outpitting their competitors.

A few drivers, including Dale Earnhardt Jr., experienced tire blowouts and hit the wall hard. As a result of the caution for Earnhardt's wreck, the leaders pitted and Rusty Wallace, battling Ricky Rudd for first, was penalized for exceeding the 45-mph speed limit on pit road. Wallace was sent to the back of the longest line of traffic and started fifteenth instead of first. Late in the race, drivers took their cars three wide with varying degrees of success. Gordon, Rudd, and Mark Martin traded positions a number of times late in the race, but on lap 248, a three-wide situation resulted in Dale Jarrett and Bobby Labonte tangling and Jarrett hit the wall hard between turns one and two.

On the ensuing restart, Wallace made a bold outside pass of several cars to gain fifth position. Jason Leffler crashed on the frontstretch with ten laps to go and the race was red flagged. The race resumed with six laps to go and an all-out rumble ensued between Jeff Gordon, Ricky Rudd, Ryan Newman, Mark Martin, Sterling Marlin, and Rusty Wallace. Gordon pulled away with Rudd and Newman in hot pursuit. On lap 262, Wallace, Marlin, and Martin went three wide in turn one, and Newman passed Rudd in turn two of the next lap to take second place.

Gordon hung on to beat rookie Ryan Newman. Rudd settled for third and Wallace pulled off an amazing fourth-place finish. Marlin and Martin were side by side for fifth and sixth place. The victory was Gordon's third at an inaugural race, the most of any active driver. It's safe to say that the track remained a mystery to many teams, as the list of drivers who did not finish the inaugural race because of accident or equipment trouble was a veritable "who's who" of veterans and hot shot youngsters. That list included Dale Jarrett, Dale Earnhardt Jr., Ward Burton, Bill Elliott, Johnny Benson, Matt Kenseth, Bobby Labonte, John Andretti, Casey Atwood, Terry Labonte, Todd Bodine, Michael Waltrip, and pole sitter Jason Leffler among others.

GETTING TO THE TRACK

Contrary to several media reports, the track is in Wyandotte County, Kansas. The track is close to the Kansas/Missouri border, about 10 miles west of downtown Kansas City, Missouri, near the intersection of I-435 and I-70. Unlike ChicagoLand, traffic to and from the inaugural race was considered to be tolerable by most accounts. Of course, the grandstands accommodate only 75,000 fans at this point. When the grandstands expand to handle 150,000 fans, traffic may become more of a problem, but the infrastructure surrounding the track seems to be well suited for large crowds.

From Kansas City, Missouri, and points east of the track, take I-70 West to 110th Street. Alternate routes favored by locals are State Avenue (also known as Highway 24) and Route 32 to Edwardsville Drive North. Approaching from the south via I-435, take the Riverview Avenue exit west to Edwardsville Drive North. From the north, on I-435, take Parallel Parkway or State Avenue West and follow the signs.

WHAT TO SEE AND DO

Kansas City, Kansas, is not nearly as happening as its Missouri counterpart, but there are quite a few things to see in the immediate area. And Kansas City, Missouri, is just a short drive to the east.

Lakeside Speedway is a half-mile asphalt oval that has been hosting Friday-night races of various racing series in Kansas City for years. Gates open at 5 P.M. and admission is just $10 for adults. The track is located at 5615 Wolcott Drive. Call (913) 299-2040 for racing schedule. **Harley Davidson** has a new Final Assembly Plant in Platte County, Kansas. Tours are available during the week from 8 A.M. to 11 A.M. by calling (888) 875-2883 in advance to schedule a time. Dress as if you were touring the pit and garage area of your favorite track. A virtual film tour and gift shop are also on site.

The Woodlands is a combination thoroughbred, quarter horse, and greyhound racing facility in the rolling hills of Wyandotte County. Just off I-435, at 9700 Leavenworth Road, the track hosts horse races Wednesday through Sunday at noon and dog races at 7 P.M. Wednesday through Saturday. General admission is just $1.50 or clubhouse entrance is $3.50. Call (800) 695-7223 for details. **Sandstone Amphitheatre** is an open-air concert facility that has been presenting nationally known entertainers for more than fifteen years. Located at 633 North 130th Street, in Bonner Springs, this is a terrific place to enjoy an outdoor concert.

Just across the river in Missouri, Kansas City is a wonderfully clean city with plenty to do during the day and a good variety of nightlife. If you want to get a quick sense of what there is to do, board the **Kansas City Trolley** at one of the downtown hotels, or call to find the stop nearest you. For a modest fee of $4 per day, you can get on and off as often as you like and see the sights as the driver tells you a little about Kansas City's storied past. The **Nelson-Atkins Museum of Art**, in addition to works by Rembrandt, Seurat, Monet, Van Gogh, Gauguin, Renoir, Degas, and Cezanne, has the largest collection of Henry Moore's bronze sculptures in the United States. This is one of the most impressive art museums near a Winston Cup track and admission is just $4. The museum is closed on Monday.

Ask somebody what there is to do in KC and they're likely to mention the **Country Club Plaza**. The plaza is an outdoor area of shops, restaurants, and galleries near downtown Kansas City. The fourteen-block area is modeled after the Spanish city of Seville, one of Kansas City's sister cities, and features Spanish architecture, with a number of handsome statues and fountains. Built in 1922, it is reportedly the world's first shopping center.

Baseball fans will want to check out the **Negro League Baseball Museum**, the only museum of its kind. The museum offers a glimpse of baseball before Jackie Robinson broke the major leagues' color barrier by signing to play with the Brooklyn Dodgers in 1947. It's located in the historic Eighteenth and Vine Street section of town at 1601 East Eighteenth Street. The collection of Negro League memorabilia is the largest in the nation and includes uniforms, photos, film footage, and autographs of Negro League stars. The museum's powerful centerpiece is the Field of Legends with life-size statues of ten Hall of Fame ballplayers. The Kansas City Royals play at **Kauffman Field**, one of the best ballparks in the big leagues. The stadium features a show with lights, fountains, and waterfalls beyond the outfield wall and was recently converted to a natural grass playing surface. Call (816) 921-8000 or (800) 676-9257 for schedule and ticket information. The NFL Kansas City Chiefs play next door at **Arrowhead Stadium**. For Chiefs tickets call (816) 920-9300 or (800) 676-5488.

The **Liberty Memorial** is a 217-foot memorial tower built to honor soldiers who fought and died in World War I. It was dedicated in 1921 by Calvin Coolidge in the presence of all five allied commanders. The top of the tower offers a dramatic panoramic view of the city and can be reached by elevator. Admission is a $1 donation. At the base of the tower is a museum featuring weapons, uniforms, and other war memorabilia of the era. There's also a full-scale replica of a World War I battle trench. Across the street is **Union Station**. The second-largest train station in the United States, it was renovated to the tune of $253 million and houses a number of restaurants, shops, and bars. Union Station also hosts traveling exhibits. My favorite destination is **Fitz's**, a two-story place specializing in a local brew—Boulevard Beer—with a sports bar upstairs and a root beer brewery below.

Worlds of Fun is an amusement park at I-435 and Parvin Road, offering more than 140 rides, shows, and attractions including the world's largest steel roller coaster and one of the finest wooden roller coasters in the nation. Next door you'll find **Oceans of Fun**, a 60-acre water theme park. Combination tickets are available. South of downtown KC, just off Interstate 435 in Swope Park, you'll find the **Kansas City Zoo**. A few years ago the zoo underwent a $71 million expansion and renovation to become one of the largest metropolitan zoos in the country. Admission is just $6 for adults, parking is $2 more. Admission is free on Tuesdays from 9 A.M. until noon.

NIGHTLIFE IN KANSAS CITY

Chappell's Restaurant and Sports Museum at 323 Armour Road in North Kansas City is said to have the largest collection of sports memorabilia in the Midwest. The collection is mind boggling and the food and drink are worth the trip as well. Don't be surprised if you encounter a few celebrities while you are there.

Westport Square is an ideal place to barhop near downtown Kansas City. A popular spot is **Kelly's**, an Irish pub housed in the city's oldest building. They offer a genuine pub atmosphere with a friendly staff and a menu of inexpensive entrees. If you are in the mood for live music, **The Lonestar** hosts a wide variety of national-caliber acts from folk to heavy metal. Located at 4117 Mill Street, they are certainly worth a phone call in advance, as they tend to sell out many of their more renowned shows. Other worthwhile Westport stops include **The Beaumont Club**, a country dance club with the area's only mechanical bull, **Harry's**, a classic cigar bar, and **Harpo's**, another casual place with a comfortable courtyard and live entertainment.

The **Grand Emporium** is Kansas City's home of live blues. It has twice been named the W. C. Handy Best Blues Club in America and honored for years as Kansas City's Best Live Music Spot. The atmosphere is that of a classic blues dive: dark, smoky, and intimate. On Mondays they offer alternative music, attracting more of a college crowd, and Wednesdays are slated for reggae music. Thursday through Saturday you're likely to see some of the great blues legends. As you stroll about the place, checking out the posters of past performers, you'll see that almost all the greats played here at one time.

Kansas City also has a great jazz heritage and a number of fine jazz establishments. The leader of the pack seems to be the **Phoenix Piano Bar and Grill** at 302 West Eighth Street, a cozy place with a casual-to-dressy atmosphere and extensive, yet remarkably inexpensive menu. A few years ago, *New Yorker* magazine named it one of the best jazz and blues bars in the country. The Phoenix offers live jazz six nights a week (Monday to Saturday) and is open only for dinner. Get there early if you want a good table; the place gets packed not long after they open.

WHERE TO EAT

As you might suspect, there's an abundance of steak, rib, and barbecue places in Kansas City. Locals insist that **Arthur Bryant's**, at 1727 Brooklyn near Eighteenth Street, is the best in town and **Gates Barbecue**, with locations in both Kansas and Missouri is said to be a close second. Other indigenous places include **K.C. Masterpiece** at 4747 Wyandotte, **Papa Lew's BBQ and Soul Food** at 1504 Prospect, and **Marty's Bar-B-Q** at 2516 NE Vivion Road. You can't go wrong at any of these places, so find the one near you and enjoy. Better yet, check out a few of them and decide which is your favorite.

On the Kansas side of the border, check out the **Frontier Steakhouse**, not far from the track at 9338 State Avenue. In addition to a solid lunch and dinner menu, they have a collection of racing memorabilia and racing gift shop. A little farther from the speedway, at 8441 State Avenue, **Wyandot Bar-B-Q** has been serving ribs, beef and pork barbecue, turkey, beans, and slaw in a friendly atmosphere for more than twenty-five years. On one side there's a full-service restaurant, on the other a lounge with racing memorabilia plastered all over the walls. **R & J Barbeque**, at 8401 Parallel Parkway, just north of the track, is a humble place with a fun atmosphere and friendly staff serving lunch and dinner. **Oklahoma Joe's**, at 3002 West Forty-seventh Street, is a barbecue place within a combination gas station and liquor store that has become a local institution and is sure to be a hit with visiting race fans.

On the Missouri side of the river, check out the **Hereford House** at the corner of Twentieth and Main Streets. This place has been serving fine cuts of beef in a friendly atmosphere since 1957. **Colony Steakhouse and Lobster Pot** has a seafood buffet of crab, shrimp, oysters, sushi, and more on Friday and Saturday nights, but the steaks are what has kept the place at the top since 1953. Located at Eighty-ninth Street and State Line Road, you may want to call ahead for reservations.

Ruth's Chris at 700 West Forty-seventh Street is an upscale steak house that packs them in on race weekend. Reservations are suggested. **McCormick and Schmick's**, at 448 West Forty-seventh Street, is as good a seafood place as you'll find in the Midwest. This upscale Seattle-based institution has consistently good food while the atmosphere and service are top-notch.

LOCAL MEDIA

The *Kansas City Star* is the local daily newspaper. The *New Times* and *Pitch Weekly* are worthwhile free entertainment weeklies. Race broadcasts can be heard via the Motor Racing Network on KFKF 94.1 FM.

WHERE TO STAY

Between the two states, there are plenty of hotel rooms near the track. That may change in the years to come as the track is expanded to accommodate more fans. Places in Kansas offer the convenience of being close to the track, while those in Missouri have the advantage of being in the heart of a truly world-class city. Hotels near the track sell out quickly, so if you prefer to stay close to the speedway, call up to a year in advance to reserve a room. The track and the area Convention and Visitor Bureau have teamed up to form "Places to Stay for the Races," a group of area hotels that have pledged not to jack up their rates on race weekend. Call (800) 767-7700 for details.

KANSAS HOTELS

Best Western Flamingo   4725 State Avenue (913) 287-5511   Less than 6 miles from the track, this humble motel offers free continental breakfast and local calls.

Best Western Inn   501 Southwest Boulevard (913) 677-3060   Not as close to the track as their sister property mentioned above, but this is the newer and nicer of the two. This place offers a free shuttle to nearby attractions and is located next door to Applebee's, and a short drive from a few other notable restaurants.

Comfort Inn   234 Seventy-eighth Street at I-70 (913) 299-5555   A brand-new hotel that also happens to be one of the closest name-brand inns to the track. In addition to a free continental breakfast, they offer an indoor pool, spa, and exercise facility.

Days Inn   3930 Rainbow Boulevard (913) 236-6880   This moderately priced chain hotel is not particularly convenient to the track; in fact, it's almost in Missouri.

Holiday Inn Express   13031 Ridge Avenue in Bonner Springs (913) 721-5300   Located just west of the track, this clean, comfortable hotel offers a heated pool and whirlpool, as well as complimentary continental breakfast.

KANSAS CAMPSITES

Campers will want to check out the **Cottonwood RV Park**, at 115 South 130th Street in Bonner Springs, which is not far from the track and offers dual shower houses, laundry facilities, a swimming pool, horseshoes, a convenience store, and tent camping spots. Call (913) 422-8038 for reservations.

MISSOURI HOTELS

Adam's Mark Hotel   9103 East Thirty-ninth Street (816) 737-0200   A massive high-rise hotel with a lounge, restaurant, indoor pool, and health club on site. Walking distance from the Chiefs and Royals stadia, this is a convenient, albeit pricey, place to stay unless you plan to spend most of your time in downtown Kansas City, Missouri.

Drury Inn   3830 Blue Ridge Cutoff (816) 923-3000   Directly across from the Truman Sports Complex, this place is also convenient for Chiefs and Royals games. A modest drive to downtown Kansas City and the speedway, this is a relative bargain compared to surrounding hotels.

Embassy Suites   220 West Forty-third Street (816) 756-1720   Nice accommodations within a short walk of Country Club Plaza and Westport Square. There are plenty of things to do nearby, and a lounge, restaurant, indoor pool, and health club are all located on the property.

Hyatt Regency Crown Center   2345 McGee (816) 421-1234   Deluxe downtown hotel connected to the Crown Center via a covered walkway. If you are not concerned with being close to the track, this place, in the middle of everything, is a fine choice for race week.

Marriott Downtown   200 West Twelfth Street (816) 421-6800   Very nice accommodations. Convenient to nightlife and cultural district. There's also a lounge, restaurant, indoor pool, and health club on site.

The Raphael   325 Ward Parkway (816) 756-3800   Small, luxurious European-style hotel across the street from the Country Club Plaza. This hotel and restaurant are among the finest in town.

Good to Know

- To charge tickets or for additional race information, call (913) 328-7223. At the time of publishing, there was a waiting list for grandstand seats.
- For RV camping information call (913) 328-3300.
- Mail orders can be sent to 1333 Meadowlark Lane, Suite 201, Kansas City, KS 66102.
- To contact the Kansas City/Wyandotte County Convention and Visitor Bureau, call (913) 321-5800 or (800) 264-1563. The Greater Kansas City Convention & Visitors Bureau can be reached at (800) 767-7700.
- A worthwhile city Web site is www.kckcvb.org.
- ➤ The official racetrack Web site is www.kansasspeedway.com.

NEARBY WINSTON CUP RACE CITIES

ChicagoLand: 505 miles (eight hours, forty-five minutes)
Michigan: 715 miles (twelve hours, twenty minutes)

IN THE VICINITY

The Harry S. Truman Library and Museum is one of the most often visited presidential libraries in the country. Truman led the nation during the final months of World War II, made decisions to drop nuclear weapons on Japan, sent troops to Korea, and fired General Douglas MacArthur. His terms were far from uneventful and the museum built in his honor, located in Independence, Missouri, at Highway 24 and Delaware, is worth a visit. Admission is just $5 for adults. For more information, call (816) 833-1400.

▪ *LAS VEGAS MOTOR SPEEDWAY* ▪

Las Vegas, Nevada

"Drivers still love to run at Las Vegas Motor Speedway. It's fairly easy, it's smooth, and it's wide."

— BENNY PARSONS

This is a modern racetrack in every sense of the term. It's also among the best-kept facilities on the Winston Cup circuit. It's a flat track with 12-degree banking in all four turns, a 9-degree slope through the 2,275-foot frontstretch, and just 3 degrees in the 1,572-foot back straightaway. At 66 feet across, the track is wide enough that three-wide racing is not impossible if there is enough grip on the track for more than a single groove of racing. Located just 17 miles northeast of the Las Vegas strip, the track is an oasis of asphalt and green grass amid the arid sands between I-15 and Las Vegas Boulevard North. To accentuate the effect, there are 6,000 palm trees scattered throughout the 1,600-acre complex.

The 1.5-mile tri-oval speedway has seating for 107,000 fans on two tiers of seating. The lower section has three grades of seats. The red seats make up the first ten to fifteen rows and offer a limited perspective of the opposite side of the track. The white seats comprise the next fifteen rows or so and allow a decent view of the entire track. The blue seats occupy the top few rows of the first tier and continue upward beyond the second-level walkway for about fifteen rows, up to the press box and skybox suites. Needless to say, the blue seats, in rows 35 and higher, just above the second walkway, are among the most desirable and highest priced at the track. Not only do these seats offer a terrific view of the track, they also overlook the Sunrise Mountain Natural Area beyond the backstretch. This view is only slightly marred by the two dozen billboards that start near turn two and extend more than halfway through the backstretch.

Seating at Las Vegas Motor Speedway is very simplified. All sections have forty-nine rows of seats, and sections are alphabetized from left to right. Grandstand One overlooks the first turn and the exit from pit road back onto the track. This is my favorite section of seats at the track, simply because these seats are closest to pit road, allow a good view of the frontstretch and entry to the first turn, and are more moderately priced than those overlooking the start/finish line. The only downfall of seats here is that you can be looking into the sun as it sets. Tickets here cost $65 in the red section, $90 in the white rows, and $115 for blue seats.

Grandstand Two is situated over the start/finish line in the tri-oval portion of the track. Seats in the upper rows here are among the most expensive at the track. They can be a long way from pit road because the grassy area between the start/finish line and pit road seems to be as big as a football field. Grandstand Three is near the scoring tower in turn four and offers a view of the entrance to pit road

Wide turns and a smooth surface make Las Vegas an ideal track for Winston Cup races. *(Photo by Tom Donoghue, courtesy of Las Vegas Motor Speedway)*

as well as a handful of pit stalls. These tickets are also cheaper than those on the tri-oval. Grandstand Four sweeps around to turn three and offers a long look down either straightaway from the outermost seating sections. Seats here are the least expensive at the track and have the advantage of the sun setting behind them.

Bruton Smith bought the track in 1998, and like most Speedway Motorsports facilities, Las Vegas Motor Speedway offers all the amenities a fan could possibly want and some they may never have conceived. What is said to be the world's longest escalator transports fans through a tunnel that runs from beneath the grandstands to the pit area. The track is lighted, so in the event of a second date's being added to the Winston Cup schedule, a race could be run at night to avoid the sweltering heat of a Las Vegas summer. All seats are aluminum benches with seatbacks; walkways are sufficiently wide to facilitate easy movement, while the concession areas and rest rooms are more than adequate. A pair of scoring towers, one at each end of pit road,

lists the top fifteen cars and current lap. The infield media center is not so tall that it blocks the view from the grandstands, and team garages are perpendicular to the backstretch, so as to minimize interference with fans' view of the action.

The track's greatest flaw is the fact that you are not allowed to bring your own beer into the track, which race fans in the Southeast consider to be something akin to a birthright. Another imperfection is the enormous distance between pit road and the stands. While many tracks allow fans in frontstretch seating sections to be right on top of the pit road action, the pits here are a long way from the stands. It's also unfortunate that there is almost no protection from the sun in the grandstands, so fans must retreat to the concourse area to beat the heat. Race-day traffic at LVMS is also among the most brutal on the circuit. The first year NASCAR drivers raced here, many fans who were not savvy to the concept of leaving home early in the morning on race day missed the first third of the race as they waited in traffic on the highway. Since then, ownership has made several infrastructure changes, such as widening Las Vegas Boulevard North, to improve that situation, and the local highway patrol has become more adept at directing traffic toward the track.

In addition to grandstand seating and 102 luxury suites, the track has eighty-seven RV spots on a hill overlooking the backstretch that offer a sweeping view of the track and sell for $2,900. An on-site RV park, the El Monte RV Corral, is outside the track near turn four and rents to self-contained motor homes for just $99 for the weekend. There's also infield RV parking near the backstretch that ranges from $400 to $800. The vehicle tunnel to the infield is beneath turn two and can be best accessed from gate 3 off North Las Vegas Boulevard. The infield is for RV traffic only, although an individual wristband can be bought for $75. Fans who want to experience the pits can purchase a $25 pit pass good for Friday only.

The track is home to the University of Motorsports with ten training schools from BMX to stock car racing. Fans will find more than a dozen tracks of varying length and style on the property. In addition to the mile-and-a-half paved oval, the speedway complex has a world-class 4,000-foot dragway with seating for more than 30,000 fans. There's also a half-mile dirt track that hosts World of Outlaws, monster trucks, IMCA modified cars, and an occasional demolition derby. The "Bullring" is a 3/8-mile, paved oval that hosts NASCAR's lower division series races with seating for 5,000 fans.

HISTORY

The city of Las Vegas hosted its first NASCAR race on October 16, 1955, at Las Vegas Speedway Park, a 1-mile dirt track. Norm Nelson won that race as darkness ended the race after 111 of 200 scheduled laps. It was the last time NASCAR drivers competed in a sanctioned race at LVSP.

The current track opened on June 25, 1996, but it wasn't until March 1, 1998, that NASCAR Winston Cup drivers took the green flag for the inaugural Las Vegas 400. Dale Jarrett earned the pole for the first Winston Cup race in the Vegas desert, but Mark Martin took the honors with an average speed of 146.554 mph, a speed that remains the track record. Martin started seventh that afternoon, but led five times for eighty-two laps, including the final twenty-three laps, to hold off Jeff Burton, Rusty Wallace, Johnny Benson, and Jeremy Mayfield as Ford swept the top five finishing positions. Dale Jarrett blew an engine and finished fortieth.

Bobby Labonte took the pole the following year, but Jeff Burton, who started nineteenth, was not to be denied, as he bested his older brother Ward, Jeff Gordon, Mike Skinner, and Bobby Labonte. It was one of three one-two finishes for the Burton brothers in the 1999 season—Rockingham and Darlington were the others—all of which Jeff won. Labonte's fifth-place finish in 1999 is still the best for a pole sitter.

On March 3, 2000, Ricky Rudd set the track qualifying record with a speed of 172.563 mph, completing his lap in just 31.293 seconds. Rudd's blistering qualifying pace did not prevent Jeff Burton from becoming the track's first repeat winner, as Ford and Jack Roush made it three wins in a row at Vegas. Burton started eleventh but was in the right place at the right time when rain shortened the race to 148 laps. Burton outpaced Tony Stewart, Mark Martin, Bill Elliott, and Bobby Labonte for the victory.

Jeff Gordon won the UAW-DaimlerChrysler 400 to end the Roush and Ford streaks at Las Vegas on March 4, 2001. In addition to being Chevrolet's and car owner Rick Hendrick's first win at Vegas, it was Gordon's first win of the 2001 season.

GETTING TO THE TRACK

Traffic here can be ugly on race day. A good friend spent four hours in traffic to travel less than 20 miles for the inaugural race. There are basically two routes to the track: I-15 and Las Vegas Boulevard North. I-15 can be absolutely horrendous. Las Vegas Boulevard has been widened near the track but bottlenecks as you get toward the strip, especially after the race. Depending on where you are staying, Nellis Boulevard may be a convenient shortcut. Locals avoid the Interstate and use a handful of back roads including Lamb Boulevard and Pecos Road, both of which run north and south from downtown to I-15 or Las Vegas Boulevard, or Craig Road that runs east and west.

Parking at the track is free, but lots surround the track, so be sure to park as close to your seats as possible or you will be in for a long walk. The north lot off I-15 is nearest to frontstretch seats. The west parking lot, off Las Vegas Boulevard, is convenient to Grandstand One and offers the quickest egress back to the strip after a race. The south and east lots are also off Las Vegas Boulevard and are a reasonable walk from seats in Grandstand Four.

One good way to get to the track is by hotel bus. Buses, taxis, and limos have priority parking along Hollywood Boulevard and are allowed to exit before anybody else. The best way to get to the race is via helicopter. Several hotels and independent operators offer service from the strip to the track and back for as little as $250 per person. Ask your hotel concierge for information on helicopter shuttles.

WHAT TO SEE AND DO

When it comes to worthwhile attractions in Winston Cup cities, only Chicago comes close to Las Vegas. This place is packed to the gills with entertainment options. It is also the one town on the circuit where you are most likely to see drivers and their families out and about. This is partially because they may be staying at an area hotel instead of in their coaches, but also because Las Vegas has become a haven for family entertainment.

The Las Vegas **NASCAR Café**, at the Sahara Hotel & Casino, is a step above others I've visited. Featuring Speed, an indoor/outdoor roller coaster that accelerates from 0 to 45 mph in two seconds, this place also features race simulators, video games, and the obligatory restaurant and gift shop. Simulators cost $8 per ride. The roller coaster is just $6, but serious fans jump on the $14.95 all-day pass. The café offers cold beer and soft drinks and a menu that includes Talladega Tenders, the Rockingham Ribeye, and a Speedway Salad. Sadly, you won't find any $2 Martinsville Hot Dogs.

Treasure Island presents an action-packed sea battle between a pirate ship and the HMS *Britannia* in Buccaneer Bay. The show is performed every ninety minutes, six times a day, starting at four in the afternoon. This daredevil production is free for everyone and entertaining for kids and adults alike. **Race for Atlantis** at Caesars is billed as the only IMAX 3-D ride on earth. Recommended for adults and kids twelve and older, this high-paced chariot ride adventure takes place inside the nation's largest IMAX dome.

Circus, Circus's **Adventure Dome** is another family-oriented attraction with rides, shows, and games within the glass-domed 5-acre indoor theme park. The New York, New York Hotel and Casino offers the **Manhattan Express** an exciting throwback roller coaster with twists and loops through the big-city skyline.

Adults will appreciate shows such as **Blue Man Group** at the Luxor, Cirque du Soleil's **O** at the Bellagio or **Mystere** at Treasure Island, and impressionists **Danny Gans** at the Mirage and **Andre-Phillipe Gagnon** at the Venetian. These were just a few of the incredible ongoing shows when I last visited Las Vegas. The Bellagio was exhibiting Steve Martin's phenomenal collection of twentieth-century paintings at that same time. The MGM Grand has a reputation for booking top-rate comedians, as does the Comedy Stop at the Tropicana, and there are more magic acts in town than you'll ever need to know about.

Paris, Las Vegas is home to a casino re-creation of that famous French city, complete with an Eiffel Tower, L'Arc de Triomphe, streetside cafés, bakeries, and shops. The **Imperial Palace** casino is owned by the original owners of the speedway and is home to an incredible automobile collection of more than 700 cars. **Sam's Town** casino, on Boulder Highway, is not on the main strip, but they are big sponsors of the speedway and offer live, nationally known country music acts.

Several organizations offer helicopter tours of Vegas at night or the Grand Canyon by day. The strip is incredible at night, while the Grand Canyon is among the most amazing natural wonders in the world. Reputable operators include Maverick Helicopters, Las Vegas Helicopters, Sundance Helicopters, and Papillon Grand Canyon Helicopters. Trips range from $69 for a tour of the strip to $499 to the Grand Canyon. A round-trip ride to the track on race day is about $250–300. If you are traveling with a group, you can even reserve the entire chopper.

The **Freemont Street Experience**, at 425 Freemont Street, is a downtown pedestrian area with shops, restaurants, and an incredible display of lights that begins at dusk. **Wet 'n Wild**, near the Sahara Hotel at 2601 Las Vegas Boulevard, is a 26-acre water park with a number of refreshing flume rides, a roller coaster, and a wave pool. For a more radical experience, check out **Flyaway Indoor Skydiving**, an indoor vertical wind tunnel that simulates a parachute free fall. Located just off the strip at 200 Convention Center Drive, they offer a fifteen-minute "training flight" that costs just $45. They are open daily at 10 A.M. but do not accept reservations. Call (877) 545-8093 for details.

Las Vegas Mini Gran Prix, at 1401 North Rainbow Boulevard, has four tracks to choose from: high-banked oval sprint karts, open-wheel adult Gran Prix cars, go-karts, and kiddie karts. These are not the souped-up, high-tech carts you'll find at tracks in some Winston Cup cities, and crowds can be significant, but the tracks are long and families will have a blast here.

NIGHTLIFE IN LAS VEGAS

House of Blues at Mandalay Bay books national acts in its 2,000-seat music hall. They also offer a dance club, an indoor courtyard with acoustic shows, and a pair of restaurants: the Soul Kitchen and the Foundation Room, the latter of which offers an incredible view of the strip. Their Fabulous Gospel Brunch is held every Sunday. Call (702) 632-7600 for upcoming shows and cover charge information. **The Joint**, at 4455 Paradise Road in the Hard Rock Hotel, is another outstanding music venue that books nationally known concert acts. Call (702) 693-5000 for upcoming acts. **Baby's**, also at the Hard Rock, is a dance club with thumping dance tunes and outgoing DJs. Ladies are generally admitted free.

Studio 54 at the MGM Grand is a tribute to the halcyon days of New York's most famous disco. This three-level club has several dance floors and bars and a fun, nostalgic crowd. They open at 10 P.M. Tuesday through Saturday. Expect a cover charge from $10 to $20. The crowd at the **VooDoo Café & Lounge** is dressed to impress. High atop the Rio, this swank club is accessed via high-speed glass-enclosed elevators that make the thirty-eight-story trip in less than thirty seconds. The Voodoo opens earlier than most other clubs and stays open late. A $10 cover charge is imposed after 8 P.M. on the weekends.

Catch a Rising Star at the Excalibur features up-and-coming comedians. A little off the beaten path, **Tommy Rocker's Cantina** is a beach bar at 4275 South Industrial Road. The **Crown and Anchor**, a British pub that stays open until 6 A.M. and serves a mean plate of fish and chips, is also off the strip at 1350 East Tropicana Avenue. **The Beach**, at 365 Convention Center Drive, is an enormous casual club that hosts occasional live music. This place is popular with locals as well as folks who spend a good deal of time in Vegas. The **Monte Carlo Pub & Brewery** is a noteworthy microbrewery in the Monte Carlo Hotel and Casino.

The casinos provide their own forms of nightlife in Vegas. My favorites, mainly for the shows because I'm not much of a casino gambler, are Bellagio, Venetian, Paris, Luxor, Mandalay Bay, Mirage, New York, New York, Treasure Island, and Circus, Circus. There are dozens more casinos that are probably every bit as good, and each one appeals to a different crowd for different reasons. Before you sit down to gamble, be sure to join their casino clubs to earn comps, cash, or merchandise.

WHERE TO EAT

Every hotel and casino on the strip has its own variety of restaurants to choose from, so there is no shortage of quality places to eat in town. Nearly every casino offers an all-you-can-eat buffet, but frankly, I don't understand the attraction. Listed below are a few places that are worth checking out.

Bertolini's Trattoria   9500 West Sahara Avenue (702) 735-4663   The same folks who run Morton's of Chicago offer this fancy Italian eatery with pasta, wood-fired pizza, and a solid wine list.

Harley Davidson Café   3725 Las Vegas Boulevard South (702) 740-4555   Nestled among the hotels and casinos on the strip, this place stands out because of the giant Harley crashing out of the building. By Vegas standards, the burgers, sandwiches, steaks, and salads are reasonably priced. The staff is friendly, the bar is well stocked, and the food is quite good.

McCormick & Schmick's 335 Hughes Center Drive (702) 836-9000 This upscale steak and seafood restaurant will spoil you rotten. The food is meticulously prepared and presented, the service incredible, and the atmosphere downright opulent. It all adds up to a sumptuous dining experience.

Memphis Barbecue 4379 Las Vegas Boulevard North (702) 644-0000 Just around the corner from the track, this is a great place to pick up tailgate supplies. The casual sit-down restaurant has kicking pork and beef barbecue, ribs, chicken, and burgers.

P. F. Chang's 3667 Las Vegas Boulevard South (702) 836-0955 I know there's nothing indigenous about this place, but they offer some of the finest, consistently good Chinese food in the country. The crowd is always looking good, the service is attentive, and the atmosphere is inviting. In addition to this bistro at the Aladdin Hotel and Casino, they have two other locations in town.

Z Tejas Grill 3824 South Paradise Road (702) 732-1660 This casual southwestern-style bistro is minutes from the strip and a nice diversion from the casinos. Open for lunch and dinner, the food is terrific and the atmosphere is completely comfortable.

LOCAL MEDIA

The *Las Vegas Review-Journal* and *Las Vegas Sun* are the local newspapers. *Where* magazine, *What's On*, and *Showbiz Weekly* are all good sources for entertainment options. Race broadcasts can be heard on MRN via KKLZ-FM, 96.3.

WHERE TO STAY

HOTELS

Thirty-six million people visit Las Vegas every year, so a NASCAR race does not overwhelm this city as it does many other Winston Cup towns. That's not to say that places don't jack up their prices on race weekend. Consider looking for deals directly with hotel chains via their Internet site, through a travel agent, or a major hotel discounter such as the Hotel Reservation Network at www.hoteldiscounts.com.

Aladdin 3667 Las Vegas Boulevard South (877) 333-9474 As hotels on the strip go, this moderately priced giant offers a significant savings over the superswank hotels that surround it, but it is not nearly as customer-service-oriented as the biggest and best places in Vegas.

Bellagio   3600 Las Vegas Blvd South (702) 693-7111   This place is the daddy of all strip hotels. The service is first-rate, the atmosphere is astounding, and the rooms are unbelievable. If you are willing to pay top dollar for these amenities, there's no better place than this. The nightly laser light and fountain show in the lake out front is an absolute treat.

Caesars Palace   3570 Las Vegas Blvd South (702) 731-7110   Recently renovated, this place remains among the biggest and best old guard hotels on the strip. They still have one of the best sports books in the area, while the shows, restaurants, shops, and casino are all outstanding.

Fitzgerald's   301 Fremont Street (800) 274-5825   This Holiday Inn property is among the more affordable quality places to stay near the strip. This place is not overly fancy, but the view of the Freemont Street Experience light show from your room is a highlight.

Hard Rock Hotel   4455 Paradise Road (800) 473-7625   It's not on the strip, but this is a surprisingly well-kept and fairly priced place to stay. The crowd tends to be younger and hipper than at the megahotels on the strip, while the restaurants and pool are outstanding.

Venetian   3355 Las Vegas Boulevard South (702) 733-5000 or (888) 283-6423   This is another remarkable hotel and casino. No expense was spared on this re-creation of the Italian city of Venice, complete with gondola rides on the Grand Canal. Expect attentive, friendly service, and quality amenities.

Paris, Las Vegas   3655 Las Vegas Boulevard South (702) 946-7000 or (888) 266-5687   Another recent addition to the strip, this place has scaled-down versions of several Paris landmarks including a fifty-story Eiffel Tower with an observation deck overlooking the strip. A trip to the top via a glass-enclosed elevator will set you back $11.

Luxor   3900 Las Vegas Boulevard South (702) 262-4000 or (800) 288-1000   This phenomenal thirty-story pyramid has more than 4,400 rooms of its own. The replica Egyptian landmarks—some are actually full-scale—are remarkably well done. The guestrooms occupy the outer edges of the pyramid and are accessed by innovative elevators that travel diagonally up to the room levels.

Mandalay Bay   3950 Las Vegas Boulevard South (702) 632-7777 or (888) 632-7000   This luxurious tropical hotel features eleven restaurants and an 11-acre lagoon with waterfalls, a sandy beach, several outstanding pools, and a swim-up shark reef.

Mirage 3400 Las Vegas Boulevard South (702) 791-7111 or (800) 627-6667
Step inside the lobby for a look at the 20,000-gallon aquarium. This world-class
hotel and casino also features a rainforest, a 50-foot volcano, and a 2.5-million-
gallon saltwater pool with bottlenose dolphins.

New York, New York 3790 Las Vegas Boulevard South (702) 740-6969 or (800)
693-6763 If the Big Apple were as clean as Disneyland, this is what it might
look like. The Brooklyn Bridge, Empire State Building, Statue of Liberty, and
Chrysler Building are all painstakingly re-created here, as is the harbor, complete with tugboats.

Treasure Island 3300 Las Vegas Boulevard South (702) 894-7111 or (800) 944-
7444 An elegant resort with some of the best restaurants and celebrity shows
on the strip. It's also home to the outdoor Buccaneer Bay, which hosts what may
be the most popular free show in town.

Circus, Circus 2880 Las Vegas Boulevard South (702) 734-0410 or (800) 444-
2472 This massive place has more than 3,700 rooms, three stellar casinos, a
half dozen upscale restaurants, and a carnival atmosphere.

The Maxim 160 East Flamingo Road Las Vegas Boulevard South (702) 731-4300
or (800) 634-6987 This affordable hotel is just a block off the strip within walking distance of many of the major casinos and attractions.

Good to Know

- To charge tickets or for additional race information, call (702) 644-4443.
- For information on RV camping spots in the infield or outside the track, call
  (702) 644-4444.
- Mail orders can be sent to 7000 Las Vegas Boulevard, Las Vegas, NV 89115.
- The Convention & Visitors Authority can be reached at (702) 892-0711.
- Worthwhile city Web sites are www.lasvegas.com, www.vegas.com, and
  www.lvol.com. The Las Vegas Convention and Visitors Authority's site is
  www.lasvegas24hours.com.
- ➤ The official racetrack Web site is www.lvms.com.

NEARBY WINSTON CUP RACE CITIES

California/Fontana: 230 miles (four hours)
Phoenix: 295 miles (five hours, fifteen minutes)
Sonoma/Sears Point: 625 miles (ten hours, forty-five minutes)

IN THE VICINITY

The **Hoover Dam** is a miracle of American ingenuity. This concrete dam and others like it provide the electricity for Las Vegas and a host of southwestern cities. Built in 1936, Hoover Dam is more than 725 feet tall and created one of the planet's largest man-made lakes. The visitor center offers a short yet informative film on the building of the dam. Fascinating guided tours take visitors into the base of the dam where hydroelectric generators are housed. Guided tours cost just $8 to $25 and can take from thirty minutes to an hour. For tour reservations call (702) 294-3524.

The **Grand Canyon** is just a few hours to the southeast. A helicopter tour is certainly an option, but nothing beats a trip to the edge, a night in a canyonside cabin, dinner at the lodge, and observing a sunrise or sunset from the rim of this incredible natural wonder. See the Phoenix chapter for additional information on the canyon.

A Dozen Favorite Racing Attractions

12 Darlington-Winston Walk of Fame/NASCAR SpeedPark, Myrtle Beach

11 Daytona USA

10 Hendrick Motorsports Museum and new Jeff Gordon shop

9 Talladega-Texaco Walk of Fame in Talladega

8 Joe Weatherly Museum/Hall of Fame

7 NASCAR Café, Las Vegas—the best of the bunch because of the roller coaster

6 The Rock—NASCAR's "Stanley Cup" permanently situated outside North Carolina Speedway

5 Race City, USA—the diversity of team garages in Mooresville, NC

4 Thunder Road USA/Georgia Racing Hall of Fame

3 International Motorsports Hall of Fame/Talladega

2 Dale Earnhardt Experience

1 Indianapolis 500 Racing Museum

▪ *LOWE'S MOTOR SPEEDWAY* ▪

Charlotte, North Carolina

"The team that's able to be diverse and run a lot of differ-ent tracks at a high level, that's the kind of team that has success. The more of these mile-and-a-half, cookie-cutter racetracks we build, it takes some of that away."

— JEFF BURTON

LMS, just north of Charlotte, in Concord, hosts two Winston Cup points races and has become the epicenter of NASCAR Winston Cup racing. The high-banked oval speedway is a mile and a half long and is considered one of the circuit's best tracks. Bruton Smith and Humpy Wheeler have spared no expense in providing race fans with all the amenities. From the Speedway Club restaurant and luxury condomini-ums to the infield facilities and family grandstands, Lowe's Motor Speedway is a top-notch facility that draws rave reviews from first-time visitors year after year. Drivers also rate Charlotte among the best and appreciate the fact that the 60-foot-wide track has been resurfaced four times in the last forty years. The long straight-aways and 24-degree banked turns can be counted on to provide some of the most intense racing of the Winston Cup season. Lowe's Motor Speedway is also home to the circuit's best prerace shows and postrace fireworks and festivities.

Reserved seating is currently a whopping 167,254, and the infield can accom-modate more than 50,000 fans, for an overall capacity exceeding 217,000. Smith is said to have plans to expand capacity to more than 300,000 once the track is entirely surrounded by grandstands in 2007.

The **Coca-Cola 600**, the season's longest race, is run at Charlotte every Memo-rial Day weekend. Starting in early evening and finishing under the lights, the 600 is a test of endurance for fans and drivers alike, often lasting more than four and a

Fans settle in for the marathon Coca-Cola 600. *(Photo by Tracy Allen)*

half hours. Tickets range from $109 for rows 32–51 of the General Motors and Chrysler Grandstands along the frontstretch and rows 1–28 of the Fourth Turn Terrace, to $37 for bleacher seats in the East Grandstand and the Family section along the backstretch. Kids 12 and younger can get in for just $5 in these two sections.

The three-level Ford Grandstand, added in 2000, created 10,860 new seats overlooking pit row as it merges with the frontstretch and race traffic heads into turn one. These seats also offer a view of the start/finish line, scoring tower, and winner's circle. The Upper Terrace is the highest deck of seats at the track—110 feet above the concourse level—and seats here go for a premium as they present a sweeping view of the race, comfortable stadium-style seats with armrests, and a convenient new concession area. Tickets available in the Ford Grandstand, for either of the two big races, range from $57 for trackside bleachers to $102 for benchback seats in rows 22–26 of the Upper Terrace.

The **UAW-GM Quality 500**, held late in the Winston Cup season, consistently plays a part in deciding the points championship. The track's qualifying record, Ward Burton's 185.759 mph in 1994, and the race speed record of 154.537 mph, set by Ernie Irvan in 1993, were both set in the October race. Despite the shorter format, ticket prices for the 500 are the same as the Coca-Cola 600.

Seats above row 26 in any section generally offer a view of almost the entire track. The upper rows of the Grand National Tower, just below the condos, present a great view of the cars as they leave the pits and offer some welcome shade for a portion of the race. If you can't find good seats on the frontstretch, the $66 seats in Diamond Tower rows 23–75 are a worthwhile seating option for either race. Camping for either race is $60 for a reserved spot and $40 for an unreserved camping spot. Infield camping spots are so popular that there is a five-year waiting list.

Charlotte is also home to one of the sport's most intriguing races, **The Winston**, a nonpoints, all-star race of seventy green flag laps run under the lights. The first and second segments are thirty laps each and the final ten laps are an all-out, balls-to-the-wall sprint for the cash. The rules seem to change nearly every year, but after the first segment, between three and twelve cars are inverted in order of finish. The Winston was first run in 1985 but has become a tradition among die-hard fans because its unique format often makes for a terrific finish. Tickets for the Winston range from $29 in the East Grandstand and Family section to $76 in rows 41–51 of the General Motors or Chrysler grandstands and rows 1–28 of the Fourth Turn Terrace.

In 1992, Charlotte Motor Speedway became the first lighted superspeedway. The $1.7 million Musco lighting system consists of 1,200 fixed lights and uses mirrors to reflect light onto the track without producing the glare that most stadium lights create. This one-of-a-kind setup eliminates the need for giant light poles that can also create blind spots and obstructed views.

Charlotte added a new scoring tower in 1999 that shows the position of the top twenty drivers. The old scoreboard, which is still in place, shows the top five cars. Corporate amenities include the Speedway Club, an exclusive restaurant with a sweeping view of the race from above the frontstretch, and two Hospitality Villages outside the track with closed-circuit TV coverage of the races. There are even dozens of year-round, luxury condominiums overlooking the first turn. Inexpensive track tours include a behind-the-scenes peek at the facilities with a visit to the "Court of Legends" where fans will find the signatures as well as hand and foot imprints of retired drivers in the cement just in front of the entrance to the main ticket office.

You'll also see the infield, check out the winner's circle, and do a quick lap around the track in a shuttle van. Despite being able to conduct tours only when the track is not in use, the facility was toured by more than 35,000 folks in 1999.

HISTORY

On June 19, 1949, in Charlotte, NASCAR held their first sanctioned race of "strictly stock" cars. The sport of racing automobiles whose namesakes could be bought by average Americans at their local car dealer became famous that day. On that same date in 1960, Joe Lee Johnson drove his 1960 Chevy to victory at an average speed of 107 mph. The Memorial Day weekend race was 400 miles long until becoming a 600-mile marathon in 1968. Later that year, in the National 400, a predecessor to October's UAW-GM 500, Speedy Thompson upped the ante with an average speed of 112 mph as he wheeled his Ford to the winner's circle.

Over the years, Charlotte has been especially kind to Dale Earnhardt, Jeff Gordon, David Pearson, Bill Elliott, and Darrell Waltrip. Pearson, Gordon, and Bobby Labonte all won their first Winston Cup races at Charlotte. Darrell Waltrip practically owned the place in the late seventies and eighties, and had six victories in fifty-five races at Charlotte. Bobby Allison also had six wins in Charlotte and twenty-three top-five finishes. Pearson had four victories, including three wins in the 600, and qualified to drive from the pole position fourteen times in Charlotte. He earned a dozen straight pole positions at one point and won the 600 from the pole in 1974 and 1976. The King, Richard Petty, also had four victories and thirty top-ten finishes.

In 1991, Geoff Bodine led the way as Ford swept the top three positions, with Davey Allison and Alan Kulwicki finishing second and third. Chevy struck back in 1993, as Dale Earnhardt won his second consecutive Coca-Cola 600 and Chevrolet completed a rare sweep of the top five finishing positions. The Coca-Cola 600 has been won from the pole just seven times, and Jeff Gordon has three of those wins, in 1994, 1997, and 1998. Gordon's win in the Coca-Cola 600 on May 29, 1994, was his first Winston Cup victory. Bobby Labonte has also had some success in Charlotte. He set the Coca-Cola record of 151.952 mph with his first Winston Cup victory on May 28, 1995, and has earned the pole three times since then. Labonte has had one third and two second-place finishes since his 1995 victory. On May 28, 2000, in just his eighteenth Winston Cup start, Matt Kenseth earned his first career Winston Cup victory in the Coca-Cola 600.

NASCAR's all-star race, the Winston, has been the scene of some incredible racing action. In 1987, Dale Earnhardt pulled off his remarkable "pass in the grass" to take a race that Bill Elliott had otherwise dominated. Earnhardt also won in 1990, starting from the pole and leading all seventy laps in a caution-free race that was over in less than thirty-nine minutes. Earnhardt's third and final Winston victory was in 1993. Davey Allison won the first Winston run under the lights at Charlotte in 1992. It was his second consecutive Winston victory, winning both from the pole. In 1995, Jeff Gordon started in the seventh spot and won all three segments of the race, a feat that was never duplicated. In 2000, Dale Earnhardt Jr. drove the hometown crowd wild by winning the first time he ever qualified to run in the Winston. Junior earned a whopping $516,410 for his efforts. The following year, Gordon won the Winston in his backup car. A wreck caused by a wet track forced him and several other drivers to the garage before the first lap was completed. Gordon started at the back of the field and worked his way to a most improbable victory.

GETTING TO THE TRACK

Just 12 miles north of Charlotte, off I-85, Lowe's Motor Speedway can be challenging to get to during race weeks. Experienced fans often show up early Thursday morning and camp out at the track. Out-of-towners generally use exits 45 or 49 from I-85, while locals take advantage of a handful of back roads that include Highway 49, U.S. 29, and Route 601 when coming from the east. If you are arriving from the north on I-77, consider taking exit 28 (Cornelius) or 25 and going east on Route 73 to Highway 29 South (Salisbury Road).

It costs $5 to park in official lots along Speedway Boulevard and surrounding the track. Shuttle buses are available from the more remote parking lots. Some entrepreneur lots along Morehead Road charge $10 to park. One way to beat the traffic is to take advantage of Saber Executive Helicopter service from Charlotte Airport. For $175 per person they fly you to and from the race. Call (704) 359-8456.

WHAT TO SEE AND DO

The "Queen City," as locals often refer to their hometown, is fast becoming one of the nation's worst-kept secrets. The addition of NBA and NFL franchises to the center of the NASCAR universe has resulted in a nightlife and entertainment scene that rivals that of much larger cities. For years, Charlotte was thought of as a buttoned-down banker city located in the heart of the Bible Belt. As such, a visitor's options could be somewhat limited.

Charlotte jumped onto the national radar screen when the Hornets joined the NBA in 1988. The NFL Panthers came to town a few years later, and suddenly Charlotte was no longer a sleepy little burg but a genuine city with world-class aspirations. Those aspirations have manifested themselves beyond pro sports in the form of an influx of regional and national restaurants, significant cultural institutions, and a nightlife scene that stays up until the wee hours of the morning.

Charlotte has become one of several NASCAR cities that can keep fans not just occupied but busy for an entire week. The annual **600 Festival** in May features a parade of drivers and race cars on Tuesday and **Pole Night** on Wednesday, and culminates with **Speed Street** held in downtown Charlotte on Thursday, Friday, and Saturday before the race. Fans will find show cars, race simulators, nationally known musicians on two main stages, occasional visits from NASCAR and Grand National drivers, fireworks displays, and thousands of avid race fans. **Founders Hall**, an indoor mall located in the heart of downtown, hosts a number of Speed Street-related activities, including driver appearances.

The **Hendrick Motorsports Museum** is practically around the corner from the track, at 4400 Papa Joe Hendrick Boulevard. Fans will find famous Hendrick team cars from the past and present, a working race shop, Winston Cup Championship trophy displays, and the remarkable mangled remains of Kenny Schrader's infamous 200-mph crash at Talladega in 1995. The complex is open Monday through Saturday and free to the public. Fans of racing artist **Sam Bass** will want to check out his main gallery at 6104 Performance Drive, just across from the speedway. The gallery boasts a massive collection of Bass's work and offers some terrific deals throughout race week. Jeff Gordon fans will want to check out his new shop at the Hendrick Complex.

In Mooresville, the **Dale Earnhardt Experience** is a state-of-the-art showroom that serves as the nerve center for Dale Earnhardt Inc. The building itself is a work of art and may be as close as it gets to a race fan's Graceland. Exhibits constantly change, but you can expect to see a collection of cars, photos, trophies, and film footage of the seven-time Winston Cup champion's illustrious career. You'll also find a growing collection of Dale Earnhardt Jr. memorabilia. The facility is free to the public and offers extended hours during race week. Also in Mooresville, fans will find the **N.C. Auto Racing Hall of Fame**. Highlights include more than thirty-five past and present racecars and a fifty-five-minute film shown in the Goodyear Mini Theater. The Hall of Fame is open seven days a week and costs just $5.

Straddling the North Carolina/South Carolina border is **Paramount's Carowinds**, a 100+ acre family amusement park with five outstanding adult roller coasters, a massive family water park, games of chance, live shows, and countless top-notch kids' rides. The park's premier ride, the Top Gun Jet Coaster, is a thrilling roller coaster that glides through twists, loops, and turns as your feet dangle below you. Other rides worth waiting for include Drop Zone Stunt Tower, which simulates a sixteen-story free fall that's over before you have time to scream; Vortex, a top-flight steel, stand-up roller coaster; and Thunder Road, a long, old-fashioned wooden roller coaster that you can ride forward or backward. Admission to the park is $39.95 per day and includes all major rides and shows.

The **Mint Museum of Craft & Design**, located in the heart of downtown at Tryon and Sixth Streets, is one of the nation's premier craft museums. Its sister museum, the **Mint Museum of Art**, a short drive away on Randolph Road, has a fine permanent collection of paintings and sculptures and often hosts impressive traveling exhibits. A ticket to either Mint Museum gets you free admission to the other on the same day. **The Museum of the New South** celebrates regional heritage and accomplishments since the Civil War. This relative newcomer to Charlotte's downtown cultural scene is at the corner of College and Seventh Streets.

Discovery Place is the region's leading hands-on science and learning museum that is a big hit with kids. Adults and kids will enjoy the state-of-the-art **Omnimax Theater** that shows a diverse selection of larger-than-life educational films and laser light shows. Discovery Place, located downtown at Tryon and Sixth Streets, also hopes to develop a state-of-the-art aquarium nearby.

If you want to catch the NFL Panthers in action at **Ericsson Stadium** while you are in town for a race, you may have to show up a week before the October races or stay until the following Sunday, as the NFL and NASCAR generally don't go head to head for the attention (and dollars) of fans. Ericsson is one of the NFL's finest stadiums and has become one of the new standards by which modern football stadiums are measured. Tickets may be available through the box office or outside the stadium on the day of the game, especially when the Panthers are not playing a marquee team.

Charlotte is also home to the Charlotte Knights, the AAA baseball farm team for the Chicago White Sox. The Knights play April through September at **Knights Castle**, just over the South Carolina border in Fort Mill. The ACC baseball championship, featuring perennial powerhouse teams from Florida State and Georgia Tech, is played here, often on the same weekend as the Winston in late May.

Victory Lane Karting, near the intersection of I-85 and I-77 at 2330 Tipton Lane, is a serious indoor go-kart track that's open seven days a week. There are others in town, but this is where the pros go on their days off to tool around on the challenging road course or wide-open oval. Call (704) 377-FAST for details. Ken Shrader's **Seekonk Grand Prix** is a more family oriented go-kart track with a slick track and a road course, as well as an indoor game arcade with pool tables, video games, and air hockey. The area's preeminent outdoor concert venue is **Verizon Wireless Pavilion**. The pavilion seats more than 19,000 fans and hosts dozens of shows each year. The season runs from spring though fall and includes the best acts in country, rock, urban, pop, and alternative music.

Concord Motorsport Park, at 7940 Highway 601 South, is a short drive from Lowe's Motor Speedway. The half-mile, high-banked asphalt tri-oval is popular with families and fans of all ages on Friday and Saturday nights throughout the year.

For race week, NASCAR fans converge on this place to watch late model stock cars, trucks, bandleros, and legends cars battle it out. The complex also features a quarter mile, slightly banked asphalt track. Call (704) 782-4221 for schedule and admission prices.

Also not far from the track is **Concord Mills** Mall, where NASCAR fans will want to check out the billiards, horseshoes, neon bowling, dance floor, and video game hall chock-full of interactive race simulators at **Jillian's**. Four fully stocked bars, a diverse menu, plenty of televisions, and a separate hibachi grill offer something for everyone. Jillian's has a streetside entrance but is also accessible from inside the mall in Neighborhood One. Serious race fans will also want to head across the hall to **NASCAR Silicon Motor Speedway**, where fourteen .85-scale simulators allow fans to compete against each other on one of four simulated Winston Cup racetracks. A twenty-minute experience, including a brief driver's meeting costs $8.50 per person. Concord Mills, the nation's second-largest mall, offers an immense food court, a 24-screen movie theater, and more than 140 stores, including a massive **Bass Pro Shop Outdoor World**.

The Charlotte area also boasts some remarkable golf courses designed by the likes of Arnold Palmer, Tom Jackson, Hale Irwin, and Donald Ross. Several public courses manage to stand out. **Rocky River** is a well-maintained eighteen-hole course with a nice blend of woods and water, minutes from the Speedway in Concord at 6900 Speedway Boulevard. This course is actually closer to the track than many of the area parking lots. Golfers can park here free on the day they play. **Highland Creek**, not far from Mallard Creek Church Road and I-85, offers one of the more picturesque and daunting local layouts. **Birkdale Golf Club** is a wonderfully scenic, Arnold Palmer–designed course in Huntersville, and **Regent Park**, just over the South Carolina border near I-77, is another local favorite that's well worth the drive.

Whether you want to fish, walk, jog, play tennis, or just soak up the natural surroundings, Charlotte has no shortage of parks to choose from. **Freedom Park**, near Dilworth, hosts a number of festivals, offers a jogging path around a scenic man-made lake, and has an abundance of tennis and volleyball courts. **Reedy Creek Park**, on Rocky River Church Road off W. T. Harris Boulevard, offers hundreds of acres to wander, a wooded eighteen-hole disc golf course, picnic facilities, and fishing ponds. **Latta Plantation**, in nearby Huntersville, offers canoe rentals, fishing, and 2,000 acres of wooded space on the edge of Mountain Island Lake.

Charlotte has two sizable lakes for boating enthusiasts to choose from. **Lake Norman**, the larger of the two, is to the north, and **Lake Wylie** is to the south on both sides of the North Carolina/South Carolina border. Both lakes have at least a dozen public boat launches with nearby water-skiing and fishing opportunities. Outfitters offering fully equipped pontoon boats, jet skis, and fishing boats for rent can be found on both lakes.

NIGHTLIFE IN CHARLOTTE

Visitors are often taken aback by North Carolina laws mandating that nightclubs that sell more alcohol than food require memberships. Theoretically, in order to gain access to such a club, you must be a member or be the guest of a member. This baffling rule is loosely enforced and should not deter you from checking out the local nightlife scene.

The granddaddy of Charlotte nightlife is the **Double Door Inn**. Since 1972 the Double Door has brought blues greats like Stevie Ray Vaughn, Buddy Guy, Koko Taylor, and Roy Buchanan to Charlotte. Eric Clapton actually stopped by after a concert one night in 1982 and played a set. This intimate, friendly club has the most dedicated staff in Charlotte and has never outgrown its roots while expanding and improving amenities over the years. You'll find live music here seven days a week, so be sure to call to see who is playing while you are in town.

Another live music club is the **Tremont Music Hall** in the SouthEnd area. Little more than a gutted warehouse with a stage, a bar, and a handful of pool tables, this club introduces Charlotte to countless progressive and alternative bands as they tour the Southeast. For a reasonable cover charge, you're likely to see an up-and-coming band in a moderate-sized venue, with great sight lines and adequate acoustics. Country music fans will want to check out **Coyote Joe's** on Wilkinson Boulevard. This massive place hosts major country acts and packs 'em in on the weekends. The **Palomino Club**, on Albemarle Road, is Charlotte's oldest country-and-western bar. This is another giant club, albeit a little more rustic, that hosts national-caliber country and rock shows.

Downtown has become the epicenter of Charlotte nightlife with a fairly diverse array of clubs and restaurants to choose from within an easy walk of one another. The revival was solidified with the addition of dance clubs to an old warehouse district along College Street near Seventh. **Mythos, BAR, Have a Nice Day Café**, and **The Hut** generally get kicking a little later in the evening, and you can expect to wait in line on weekends. Mythos is the most intriguing of the group, with an eclectic crowd, thumping techno tunes, and a massive dance floor. **Dixie's**, a relative newcomer to the scene, offers a Louisiana menu with reasonably priced beverages and has become one of the more popular places along the College Street Entertainment District, especially after work and in the evenings. **RiRa** is an outstanding authentic Irish pub with a loyal clientele. After work and on weekends, you're sure to find an exuberant crowd hoisting a few pints and soaking in the pub's atmosphere. Nearby you'll find **Rock Bottom Brewery**, a Colorado-based franchise that offers a number of microbrew beers, top-rate bar chow, and a white-collar crowd. The **Fox and the Hound** is a new downtown sports bar that's sure to pack them in during Speed Street. This three-level bar/restaurant has plenty of TVs, killer food and a friendly staff.

If Charlotte has a "hometown" bar, it must be **Alexander Michael's**. Tucked away among small houses and condos in the shadows of Charlotte's big bank towers in the Fourth Ward District, you'll find Al Mike's. A singular destination if ever there was one, this cozy place serves some of the city's best burgers and is invariably home to some of its best bartenders. **Selwyn Pub**, off the beaten path near Queens College on Selwyn Avenue, is another hometown establishment with a great staff, friendly atmosphere, and a festive crowd. In the SouthPark area, **Village Tavern** offers a huge outdoor patio and a strong singles scene on the weekends.

SouthEnd, just below downtown, has also become an entertainment district in its own right, with a decent concentration of nightlife and restaurants. The original SouthEnd establishment, **Vinnie's Raw Bar**, has become an after-work institution famous for $1 beers, fresh seafood, and legendary crowds. Weekends also pack 'em in, especially for races, football games, and basketball games. **Jillian's**, the massive arcade/restaurant chain, has two locations in the Charlotte area, but the city's original is located in SouthEnd. With pool tables, interactive video games, Ping-Pong tables, and a full bar and restaurant, there's something for everyone. **SouthEnd Brewery** is a good-sized place with live music on the weekends, a substantial menu, and an ample selection of local microbrewed beers. They have a second location on Jetton Road near Lake Norman.

Perhaps the funkiest, most urban section of town is the Central Avenue/Plaza-Midwood area. Clubs and restaurants like **Swing 1000**, **Thomas Street Tavern**, **Elizabeth Billiards**, **The Penguin**, and **Fuel Pizza** have turned this into one of the hipper places to eat, drink, and be merry.

Just southwest of the Plaza-Midwood area, near downtown, you'll find the Elizabeth neighborhood. Mainstays like **Cajun Queen** and the **Bayou Kitchen** have been the backbone of Charlotte dining and nightlife for years. If you are looking for a sampling of indigenous Charlotte establishments, this is a great place to start. They are within walking distance of each other and offer outstanding entrees and appetizers.

There's no shortage of quality sports bars in town to catch up on the latest race news. **Coach's** is a good-sized place near Pineville, with an impressive collection of sports memorabilia, plenty of TVs, pool tables, a friendly staff, and loads of interactive video games. **Champps**, near the corner of Woodlawn and Park Road, offers exceptional food, a giant TV wall, and a fun atmosphere during big races. **Picasso's Pizza** is one of the area's most established sports bars with a new location on East Boulevard in Dilworth. **Jocks & Jill's**, a swanky sports bar owned by, among others, a group of current and former athletes, is opposite the new Coliseum on Tyvola Road.

The **Stock Car Café**, in Cornelius at Shops on the Green near the intersection of Highway 73 and I-77 (exit 28), is about equidistant from team garages in Mooresville,

Harrisburg, and Concord. This place is a race fan magnet offering a simple menu of sandwiches, steaks, and southern fare, cold beverages, and a solid collection of racing memorabilia. They produce a complimentary map with phone numbers and addresses of area race shops. There is a second location at the airport.

Despite the city's conservative status, Charlotte is not devoid of gentlemen's clubs. The **Men's Club**, located near Tyvola Road and I-77, has sister clubs in Dallas, Reno, and Houston. This upscale place offers a full lunch and dinner menu and can generally be counted on for a boisterous time, especially on race weekends. The **Uptown Cabaret** is another reputable adult establishment, conveniently situated between SouthEnd and downtown Charlotte, at the corner of South Tryon and Morehead Street.

WHERE TO EAT

It wasn't all that long ago that a nice dinner at a restaurant in Charlotte meant crossing town to one of just a handful of very worthwhile eateries. That's not to say they didn't exist; they were just few and far between. Indigenous establishments such as **Beef & Bottle**, **Cajun Queen**, **Manzetti's**, **Rheinland Haus**, **Wan Fu**, **Villa Antonio's**, **Hereford Barn**, and **Fishmarket** have been setting the standard in Charlotte for years. To sample Charlotte cuisine at its best, plan a meal at any or all of these fine bistros. Recently, however, nationally known places like **The Palm**, **Morton's**, **Melting Pot**, **Sullivan's**, and **Bistro 100** have rolled into town and given the locals a run for their money. The Palm and Bistro 100 offer the best bang for your buck, but they are all outstanding.

McIntosh's, in the trendy SouthEnd District, is an upscale place with tremendous steaks and seafood, a first-rate wine list, and attentive service. Nearby, you'll find **La Paz**, a Mexican place with a nice atmosphere, hearty portions of Americanized entrees, and tasty margaritas. Another, more moderately priced choice for authentic Mexican fare is **Azteca** on Woodlawn near I-77.

Palomino Euro Bistro, a Seattle import, downtown on North Tryon Street, has a warm, inviting atmosphere and serves some of the finest entrees and most creative appetizers to be found in the city. Also nearby is **Capital Grille**, an ultra-swank, dark-paneling-and-white-linen steakhouse chain with restaurants in New York, Boston, and Washington, D.C. **LaVecchia's** is another fancy downtown eatery specializing in seafood. It's located in **Seventh Street Station** and the wait can be significant on weekends, but the food and ambiance are well worth it.

More moderately priced fare can be found at mainstay establishments such as **Lupie's**, **Moosehead Grille**, **Bayou Kitchen**, **Village Tavern**, **Mert's**, and the **Comet Grill**. Among the city's favorite lunch spots, you can't go wrong at any of these casual eateries. They all provide monster servings, friendly service, and reasonably priced beverages. The Village Tavern is the most upscale place of the group, Moosehead and Mert's the most eclectic, but locals will tell you that Lupie's is the most beloved. Expect a line for lunch at several of these places, with tables somewhat easier to obtain for an early dinner.

A number of outstanding pizza places have sprouted up in Charlotte. **Wolfman Pizza** has been around for about a decade and has several locations—from the University area to Selwyn Road, Cotswold to Pineville, and South Charlotte—all with calzones and pizzas piled high with gourmet toppings and a fresh crust. **Fuel Pizza**, a relative newcomer with three locations, has its own special flair with pizza by the slice or whole pies and a funky gas-station motif at their downtown Trade Street, Central Avenue, or Davidson location. If all you want is a New York–style pie, **Avanti's**, located in the Arboretum shopping center, may have the city's best cheese and pepperoni slices in town. Their meat lover's stuffed pizza is as close to Chicago style as it gets in Charlotte.

Castaldi's Marketplace is an authentic Italian eatery with a full-service bar and take-out market that's worth the trip to Huntersville at the Northcross shopping center. **Mickey & Mooch's**, located in the same shopping center, is a more upscale eatery. The dark interior with a mobster motif contributes to an enjoyable, upscale dining experience. They have another location at the Arboretum in southeast Charlotte near Matthews. Castaldi's also has a second location at University Place not far from the Hilton University Place.

LOCAL MEDIA

The *Charlotte Observer* is the only local daily newspaper and does a terrific job covering NASCAR. *Creative Loafing* is the area's entertainment weekly and a particularly good source for nightlife listings. It's free at stores and restaurants all over town. *Trip* magazine is a convenient-sized visitors' guide with several handy maps. It's also free in many area hotels, restaurants, and attractions.

For in-depth descriptions and a more complete listing of local eateries, nightlife, and events, pick up a copy of *Charlotte* magazine, a full-color monthly available at local newsstands and supermarkets.

Radio station formats and ratings change all the time, but as of press time, the dominant local sports/talk radio station is WFNZ 610 AM. WBT 1110 AM broadcasts games of several local sports teams and occasional sports/talk shows. WRFX 99.7 FM is the local album-oriented rock station. DJs John Boy and Billy, whose morning show is syndicated throughout the Southeast, are huge racing fans and have all the major drivers and crew chiefs as guests on their show. WSOC-FM, 103.7, is a local country station that carries MRN broadcasts of races as well as related pre- and postrace coverage.

WHERE TO STAY

HOTELS

There are a few hotels to choose from near the track, so make your reservations as soon as you have secured tickets to the race. Lodging options are pretty limited on the north side of town. If you want to avoid traffic hassles and don't care about being close to downtown Charlotte, the brand-new **Wingate Inn**, with an impressive collection of race photos and memorabilia in the lobby area, is one of the hotels closest to the track, at 7841 Gateway Lane, and sure to be booked up early on race weekends. **Hawthorne Suites, Sleep Inn, Holiday Inn Express**, and **Comfort Inn** have all opened at this same intersection of I-85 and Speedway Boulevard. **Bob Evans, Hooters, Roadhouse Steakhouse**, and **On the Border** restaurants are also nearby.

The **Hilton at University Place** is one of the city's larger hotels and is surrounded by a number of clubs and restaurants, plenty of shops around an artificial lake, with paddleboats available and a scenic walking path. Not far from the track, near the intersection of Harris Boulevard and I-85, this place has been a favorite of NASCAR fans for years. The newer **Drury Inn** just across the street is also a bargain.

The **Adam's Mark** is a downtown institution. This reasonably priced hotel has a fine Italian restaurant, **Bravo!**, complete with a singing wait staff, plenty of rooms, and a terrific location on the edge of downtown. The **Dunhill** is a smaller, decidedly more upscale place with handsome rooms, attentive service, and a California-cuisine restaurant, **Monticello**, set in the heart of downtown within a short walk of nightlife and cultural attractions.

The **Holiday Inn Downtown** is just across the street from the College Street Entertainment District and has a great view of the surrounding area from its rooftop patio and pool. Nearby, at the Trade & Tryon Square, you'll find one of Charlotte's premier business traveler hotels, the **Marriott City Center**. This well-appointed hotel offers a number of restaurants to choose from, shopping in the adjoining Overstreet Mall, as well as **Cutter's Cigar Bar** and **Champions** sports bar on the lobby level. Other quality downtown hotels to consider are the **Omni** at 101 South Tryon Street, the **Hilton**, and the **Hampton Inn**, near the convention center.

The **Hampton Inn** at Phillips Place is as nice a Hampton Inn as you will find anywhere. Adjacent to **The Palm** restaurant, at one end of the city's most upscale outdoor shopping mall—with a theater, several fine restaurants, and remarkable high-end shops, galleries, and boutiques—it is in Charlotte's toney SouthPark neighborhood. On the opposite side of **SouthPark Mall** you'll find other upscale hotels, including the **Park Hotel, Hyatt**, and **SouthPark Suites**. All three are exceptional.

One of the area's newest hotels is the **Renaissance Charlotte Suites**. Just 2 miles from the airport, adjacent to the Coliseum, this mid-sized hotel offers spacious rooms and a convenient location. Just down the street, near I-77 and Tryon Street, you'll find the **Embassy Suites**.

There are also a number of moderately priced chain hotels such as Holiday Inn Express, Fairfield Inn, Courtyard by Marriott, Comfort Inn, and Residence Inn along the outer belt and in the surrounding suburbs of Charlotte. Two areas with a concentration of this type of accommodations are Pineville, to the south of Charlotte near the **Carolina Place Mall**, and the Tyvola Road exit of I-77 not far from the airport. A handful of more modest hotels can be found at the Carowinds Boulevard exit of I-77 along the North Carolina/South Carolina border. Huntersville, north of Charlotte and not far from the track, offers a Hawthorne Suites, Ramada, Country Inn, Courtyard by Marriott, Holiday Inn Express, and a Fairfield Inn to choose from. In north Charlotte, the **Hilton Garden Inn**, at 9405 Statesville Road just off I-77, is a moderately priced newcomer that shares their parking lot with a **Bob Evans** restaurant.

Good to Know

- To charge tickets or for additional race information, call (704) 455-3200.
- To get on the campsite waiting list, call (704) 455-4445.
- Mail orders can be sent to Ticket Manager, Lowe's Motor Speedway, P.O. Box 600, Concord, NC 28026-0600.
- For information on the 600 Festival, Speed Street, and UAW-GM Teamwork parade, call (704) 455-6814 or visit www.600festival.com.
- For more detailed information on Charlotte sights, attractions, and hotels, call the Convention and Visitors Bureau at (704) 331-2700 or (704) 331-2701. Or write them in advance at 330 South Tryon Street, Charlotte, NC 28202.
- For a list of hotels in Concord, call the Cabarus County Visitors Center at (800) 848-3740.
- Worthwhile city Web sites include:
  - ➤ www.charlotte.com
  - ➤ www.gocarolinas.com
  - ➤ www.visitcharlotte.org

NEARBY WINSTON CUP RACE CITIES

Darlington: 74 miles (one hour and twenty minutes)
Rockingham: 105 miles (two hours)
Atlanta: 235 miles (four hours)
Bristol: 177 miles (four hours)
Richmond: 292 miles (five hours, five minutes)

IN THE VICINITY

Nowhere else in the country can race fans visit so many race team garages in such a concentrated area. Mooresville, a.k.a. **Race City, USA**, is home to more than a dozen Winston Cup garages alone. The Bodine, Roush, and Wallace teams are among a dozen garages conveniently located in a pair of industrial parks near the intersection of I-77 and Highway 150. One of my favorite places to visit is **JR's Garage** where fans can buy scraps of sheet metal and other used parts from Roush Racing Winston Cup cars. The **Memory Lane Motorsports Museum**, at 769 River Highway, is the newest addition to an area that has plenty of racing attractions. The collection ranges from moonshine runners to modern day stock cars. Racecars driven by Richard Petty, Dale Earnhardt, Junior Johnson, Alan Kulwicki, Jeff Gordon, Cale Yarborough, and many others are on display. Call (704) 662-3673 for operating hours and admission price.

Drivers switch teams regularly, but just a short drive from the track you can generally see crews working on cars for Dale Jarrett, Mark Martin, Jeff Gordon, Bill Elliott, Dale Earnhardt Jr., Bobby Labonte, Tony Stewart, and other top drivers. The **Petty Enterprises Museum**, another worthwhile stop for race fans, is at the team's race shop complex in Level Cross, NC. Most team garages allow you to watch as they prepare cars for competition and are open to the public from 8 A.M. to 5 P.M., Monday to Friday. Many garages close for lunch from noon to 1 P.M. Just before lunch, some crews run a simulated pit stop practice behind their shops. If you want an up-close look at your favorite pit crew in action, it's the next best thing to being in the pits on race day.

For a free guide to local team garages, stop by the **Mooresville Visitor Center** at 119 Knob Hill Road, or call them at (704) 663-5331. For a guided tour with a behind the scenes glimpse of some of the best racing attractions in Concord, Huntersville, and Mooresville, call Trisha with **Race Shop Tours** at (704) 788-8802. Tours cost just $35 per person and are available throughout the race season. Your group may even get lucky and have lunch at some of the same places as your favorite drivers and crews. Advanced booking is suggested. Visit them on the Internet at www.raceshoptours.net.

■ *MICHIGAN INTERNATIONAL SPEEDWAY* ■

Brooklyn, Michigan

"This place is aggravating. It's an easy track to drive. It's big, it's very frustrating. You can go high, you can go low . . . you can't get away from anybody."

—DARRELL WALTRIP

Drivers like this track because it's long and wide with lots of room to race. Aside from the occasional fuel-mileage victory, races here are generally determined by the crew's ability to put a good car on the track and the driver's capacity to outperform his peers. Opened in 1968 and created by the same designer who produced Daytona, the 2-mile D-shaped oval's turns are banked at 18 degrees. The frontstraight is 3,600 feet long and arced at 12 degrees through the tri-oval, while the backstraight is 2,242 feet long and banked at 5 degrees. The transitions from the turns into the straights are among the smoothest on the Winston Cup circuit, while the 73-foot-wide turns and 45-foot-wide straights allow for side-by-side racing that has been known to go five cars wide in the closing laps. The racing surface, a polymer-enhanced asphalt that was put down in 1995, is considered one of the surest and fastest on the circuit.

As a result, MIS is a fast track. Winston Cup drivers at the front of the pack accelerate to nearly 190 mph at the start/finish line and regularly surpass 200 mph before they enter turn one. Even on the backstretch, cars exceed 190 mph and seldom slow down to less than 155 mph through turns three and four. Despite the high speeds, MIS is also considered one of the most forgiving tracks on the circuit. Cars tend to sort out quickly, there are often long runs without caution flags, and relatively few mishaps occur once the drivers run a dozen or so green flag laps. In the track's first thirty-two years, three races here have actually been run without a caution flag. An expansive grassy area between the track and infield allows drivers who spin out ample opportunity to recover without hitting the inside retaining wall. A wide stretch of asphalt along the inside of the backstretch, near turn two, is even more effective in helping drivers maintain control through spins that occur exiting the second turn. Because things happen fast at Michigan, it's been referred to as a "spotter's track" and is a particularly good track for fans to listen to a scanner because strategy is key and conversation between driver and crew is nearly constant.

MIS is similar to Fontana in that it's moderately banked and long. Running well at Michigan requires a balanced setup. Horsepower is needed to establish the pace but cannot come at the expense of fuel conservation. A solid aerodynamic package is essential to maintaining that high velocity and achieving good fuel mileage, while significant downforce is needed to keep drivers in control at high speeds. Pit strategy is also critical, as the race's 400-mile/200-lap format requires a minimum of three well-spaced pit stops for gas. Drafting at these speeds enables cars to slingshot around each other, so races here tend to feature a good deal of passing back and forth.

There's a rule of thumb in NASCAR Winston Cup racing that the better the competition, the less fan-friendly the facility, and vice versa. While that is certainly not always the case, it seems to hold true with Michigan. The track provides outstanding competition, but the hassle of getting to a race here, finding a nearby place to stay, and dealing with the antiquated grandstands and facilities at the track is unfortunate. MIS was added to the Winston Cup circuit the same year as Dover and Talladega but has not held up particularly well, nor has track ownership done as diligent a job of improving the facilities. Aside from expanded grandstands and adding wide pedestrian bridges that cross Brooklyn Highway, few renovations seem to have been made to benefit everyday blue-collar fans. There are far too many backless bleachers, roads and infrastructure surrounding the track are inadequate, and the stands almost look like they were slapped up as an afterthought. Infield suites and grandstands obscure the view from several seating sections on the frontstretch, and the safety fence is among the most obtrusive in Winston Cup racing. There are too few giant-screen TVs in the infield to help fans follow the race when cars are clear across the track, while fan facilities are run-down and entirely too scarce. To illustrate this point, there are only four rest rooms in the entire 150-acre infield.

The track's rickety appearance doesn't discourage folks from showing up. MIS seats 136,384 fans, and tickets can be somewhat hard to come by, especially for the earlier of the two Winston Cup events. Races here are especially well attended by automotive industry executives from the not-so-nearby Detroit area, because a win in Michigan holds the added benefit of bragging rights within the domestic-car-manufacturing community.

Seating sections at MIS are fairly simple to understand. The numbered sections start at the start/finish line and start with section one. Odd-numbered sections proceed through the first turn, while even-numbered sections head back through turn four all the way into the entrance of turn three. Seats in turn three and four are fairly well elevated, so seats in row 30 and higher offer a decent perspective of the track. Seats in the lower rows of the center grandstand, near turn one, have to contend with infield structures that block your view of racing action on the backstretch. Some of the finest seats at the track are those in rows 31–54 of the even-numbered sections 28–56. These are among the highest seats on the front side and they overlook the treacherous exit from turn four. Stands 1, 3, and 5 in turn one offer a good look down the frontstretch, as well as a view of pit road, and are not as hindered by the infield grandstands along pit road.

A water tower sits beyond the first turn, while dense trees and sponsor billboards sit beyond the retaining wall of the backstretch. A pair of three-sided scoring towers, one at each end of the infield, lists the top ten drivers and the number of laps completed. A horizontal scoreboard sits in the infield and lists the top five cars. For vehicle and pedestrian access to the infield a three-lane tunnel crosses under the track near the entrance to turn one. Infield guardrail sites cost $175 for Winston Cup weekends, while interior sites cost $125. Individual infield tickets can be bought in advance for $80. They go up to $100 on race weekend. Sunday-only tickets are $40. A pedestrian tunnel crosses under the track near section 1 of the center grandstand. Vehicle crossovers leading to Michigan 50 and U.S. 12 are also near the turns on the backstretch. If you forget to bring something, the **Pit Stop Party Shoppe**, a trackside convenience store at 13342 Michigan 50, has got everything you might need at reasonable prices.

HISTORY

The very first NASCAR race at Michigan, the Motor State 500, was held in 1969, a year after the track opened, and was an indication of things to come. Cale Yarborough and LeeRoy Yarbrough, both driving Mercurys, exchanged the lead five times over the last thirty laps. They crossed the start/finish line side by side for the white flag lap and got into each other going into turn one. LeeRoy Yarbrough, running on the outside, ended up in the wall while Cale Yarborough recovered to take the checkered flag. It was the first and only 500-mile Winston Cup race held at MIS and the first of Yarborough's eight wins at the track. That fall, MIS hosted the Yankee 600, which David Pearson won from the pole. Rain and darkness shortened the race to just 330 miles. The following year races at MIS were shortened to 400 miles and have been run at that distance ever since.

Bobby Allison swept the races in 1971, winning the spring race from the pole. Not to be outdone, David Pearson won the next three races. All told, Pearson won nine points races and ten poles at Michigan, all between 1969 and 1979. From 1976 to 1978, Pearson earned the pole position five straight times and won twice. In the mid- to late seventies, Michigan was the site of several exciting last-lap passes to take the checkered flag. Pearson was the victim as Richard Petty grabbed the lead from him on the final lap of the 1975 Champion 400, but Pearson pulled a last-lap pass of his own in 1978, sliding by Darrell Waltrip in turn three to win for the ninth time at Michigan. The following year, Petty, driving a Chevrolet, repeated his last-lap magic with a nifty pass of Buddy Baker on the white flag lap of the Champion 400. That race also marked the first time a manufacturer swept the top three positions at Michigan; in fact, Chevy earned the top five spots that afternoon.

Benny Parsons earned his only Michigan checkered flag in 1980. Parsons won from the pole and edged out Cale Yarborough and Buddy Baker as Chevy swept the top three spots once again. Yarborough dominated the early eighties at Michigan, with five wins in four years through 1983. Interestingly, from 1970 through 1983, Yarborough won at Michigan driving a Mercury, Chevrolet, Oldsmobile, and Buick for four different car owners. He only earned the pole once, in 1975, a year that he did not win at Michigan. The late eighties at Michigan belonged to Bill Elliott. "Awesome Bill from Dawsonville" earned his first Michigan checkered flag in the 1984 Miller 400. That fall, Darrell Waltrip won the Champion 400 in a race that was run without a caution flag. Elliott proceeded to win the next four races at MIS and added wins in the fall of 1987 and spring of 1989. All told, Elliott won seven races in six seasons.

Dale Jarrett won the Champion 400 for his first Winston Cup victory on August 18, 1991. The win also marked the first time a race was ever won at Michigan from outside the top ten qualifying positions. Harry Gant's eighteenth and final victory came in the Champion 400, beating out Darrell Waltrip and Bill Elliott in August of 1992 at the age of fifty-two, making Gant the oldest driver to win a NASCAR Winston Cup race. Remarkably, Gant won from the twenty-fourth starting position. Bobby Labonte swept the 1995 season races at Michigan and set the fall race record with an average speed of 157.739 mph.

During a Saturday morning practice run for the Goodwrench 400 on August 20, 1994, Ernie Irvan slammed his car into the retaining wall. Thought to be driving at 190 mph at the time, Irvan suffered massive injuries to major organs and was lucky to be alive. Irvan defied the odds and not only lived but returned to race again. In June of 1997, Irvan won the Miller 400 at Michigan. Lightning struck twice, however, as Irvan suffered another devastating wreck at Michigan, in August 1999. The wreck ended Irvan's career but spared him his life.

In the 1999 Kmart 400, Dale Jarrett led every lap on his way to victory. This was the third race in the track's history that was run without a caution flag and set the track record of 173.997 mph in a race that lasted just two hours, seventeen minutes, and fifty-six seconds. Tony Stewart won the Kmart 400 from the twenty-

Dale Earnhardt fans paid homage to "The Intimidator" by signing the DEI souvenir trailer at Winston Cup races throughout the 2001 season. *(Photo by Author)*

eighth qualifying position to set the record for winning from the worst starting position. On August 18, 2000, Dale Earnhardt Jr. set the track qualifying record with a 37.667-second lap and a speed of 191.149 mph.

The 2001 season saw a pair of noteworthy races at Michigan. Jeff Gordon won the 2001 Kmart 400 in a hotly contested, back-and-forth battle with Ricky Rudd. Rudd passed Gordon to take the white flag, but Gordon retook the lead on the final lap and held off Rudd for his fifty-fifth Winston Cup checkered flag and the 100th win for Hendrick Racing. It was also the first time in twenty consecutive starts that a cup race was won by the pole sitter. Sterling Marlin won a rain-shortened Pepsi 400 on August 19, 2001, that returned Dodge to the winner's circle for the first time since November 20, 1977. Marlin took the lead on lap 145 and a steady rain halted the race on lap 162. It was Dodge's first win of the season and fiftieth victory in the modern era of Winston Cup racing.

GETTING TO THE TRACK

Roads leading to the track—U.S. 12, Michigan 50, and Vicary/Taylor Road—are converted to one-way roads to and from the speedway, but none of these routes handle the volume of traffic well. Be certain to leave very early in the morning to get to the race. Parking lots open at 6:30 A.M. for the Winston Cup race. If at all possible stay south of the track or pitch a tent at a campsite adjacent to the track because traffic here is among the worst on the circuit and the track is a long way from any city of significant size. MIS is actually 9 miles closer to Toledo, Ohio, than it is to Detroit, which is 67 miles northeast of the track. Lansing, Michigan, is 55 miles to the north.

If you are staying southeast of the track, in or around Adrian, take U.S. 223 toward the track. Go north on Onsted Highway, west on Stephenson Road, right on Hawkins Highway, left on Laird Road, and right on Brix Road. The last portion is a dirt road that puts you out between turns one and two, right next to the track. This may be the best shortcut I have ever been made privy to in all of Winston Cup racing. The Brooklyn–Irish Hills Chamber of Commerce produces a wonderful, free map of the area that shows all kinds of back roads that are not on the map provided by rental car companies.

Parking at the track is free. The track is practically surrounded by parking lots, so no matter which direction you approach from, you'll find a lot. Free tram service makes it easy to get to the track from track-owned lots. Lots 11, 12, and 14 offer the easiest egress after a race, but you should still plan to spend a great deal of time in traffic.

WHAT TO SEE AND DO

I thought Pocono was the cheesiest resort area to host Winston Cup races until I visited Irish Hills, Michigan. Attractions such as the Prehistoric Forest, Mystery Hill, and the Stagecoach Stop are too ridiculous to even consider unless you have young children or a big buzz and an urge to throw away your money.

W. J. Hayes State Park is a scenic 654-acre park, just minutes from the track. The prime attraction is the recreational waters of Wamplers Lake. A modest lakeside beach and boat ramp make this a popular destination through the summer months. A fishing pier on Round Lake is also convenient. You can also rent rowboats, canoes, and inner tubes. The park offers a concession stand, horseshoe pits, and picnic shelters. There are 185 campsites near Round Lake. Each site has electricity and a fire pit. These sites are suitable for RVs or tent camping. Fishing in Wamplers Lake can yield pike, crappie, and bass. Call (517) 467-7401 or (800) 447-2757 for additional park information and campground reservations. **Hidden Lake Gardens**, 7 miles east of Brooklyn on Michigan 50, offers 5 miles of hiking trails, or you can take a winding 6-mile scenic drive through the property. The gardens occupy 775 acres surrounding Hidden Lake. The gardens are open daily. Admission is $3 per person.

The **Walker Tavern** was a popular stopping point in the days when folks took stagecoach rides from Detroit to Chicago. These rides would take five days, and in the years between 1825 and 1855, the Walker Tavern served meals and allowed folks a chance to stretch their legs and rest the horses before getting back on the road. The complex, located at the intersection of Michigan 50 and U.S. 12, features an 1840s-era parlor, barroom, dining room, and kitchen. You'll also see a barn with stagecoach exhibits. Admission is free.

Port to Port Adventure Golf has a nineteen-hole miniature golf course, several baseball and softball batting cages, and an indoor arcade. Located at 5768 U.S. 12, this is among the better-maintained "tourist attractions" in the area. **Victory Lane Speedway**, at 13501 Michigan 50, has a quarter-mile Grand Prix go-kart track and bumper boats. They are open seven days a week and are located next door to Shooper's Grill.

Hunting and fishing fans may want to check out the **Cabela's** store in Dundee. This massive store has everything you could possibly need in outdoor gear, but the store itself is worth a look. Inside you'll find a 65,000-gallon aquarium with twenty-four species of fish. There are several viewing windows to the tank, the largest of which is 28 feet long, 6 feet high, and 3 inches thick. A 40-foot mountain, complete with wildlife panoramas of bison, coyotes, elks, and other animals, has three waterfalls that drop 28 feet into a beaver pond and eventually reaches a pond stocked with live trout. The store is at the junction of U.S. 23 and Michigan 50.

NIGHTLIFE IN THE BROOKLYN AREA

Your choices are somewhat limited, but as long as you don't expect to stay out until the wee hours of the morning, there are some worthwhile places to grab a beer with friends and family. Most of the places listed below are equal parts restaurant and bar.

The **Eagle's Nest** is tucked away on Clark Lake. About 7 miles from the track on Eagle Point Road, this rustic place has a full bar and a comfortable outdoor patio. They also serve steaks, seafood, chicken, burgers, sandwiches, and Mexican food. **Shooper's Grill and Pub**, at 11551 Brooklyn Road, is a friendly, modest-sized rib place with a bar and a couple of TVs. They also serve affordable steaks, burgers, fish, and pizza. **Cruise Inn**, at 6400 U.S. 12 in Tipton, is a genuine sports bar with TVs, a pool table, and a few video games. This humble place gets busy during race week and offers reasonably priced sandwiches, pizza, and appetizers.

Jerry's Pub and Restaurant, at 650 Egan Highway on the south shore of

Wamplers Lake, offers live music on the weekends. You can dock your boat right beside the place while you dine outdoors on the deck overlooking the lake. The **Beach Bar and Restaurant** is another place on Clark Lake, at 3505 Ocean Beach Road, that offers some semblance of nightlife overlooking the lake. They offer live music and stay open until midnight on the weekends. They also serve pizza and sandwiches.

WHERE TO EAT

Maria's Garden Café, inside the Brooklyn Hotel on the square in downtown Brooklyn, doesn't look like much from the outside, but the southern Italian cuisine is outstanding for lunch or dinner, while the service is friendly and attentive. **Pappa's Place** is a country-style eatery that serves breakfast all day. There's nothing fancy about the place, but if all you're looking for is an affordable breakfast, lunch, or dinner in a comfortable setting, this is the place.

Harold's Place, at the corner of Onsted and U.S. 12, is open for breakfast, lunch, and dinner. Harold's has the feel of a country lodge with a handsome fireplace, Native American art on the walls, and a substantial collection of model trains. For more than twenty years race fans have been showing up here for the all-you-can eat fish fry on Thursday and Friday nights and the steaks, seafood, chicken, and chops the rest of the week. **Bahlan's Golden Nugget** is one of the area's largest establishments. This restaurant and saloon, at 7305 U.S. 12 in the Irish Hills, specializes in ribs and is open for lunch and dinner. They also feature live music on the weekends through the summer months.

Lyon's Tavern is a bit of a drive from the track at 735 Manitou Road in Manitou Beach. On the south side of Devils Lake, they offer occasional live music, nightly home-cooked dinner specials, a handful of TVs scattered about, and an outdoor beer garden. They are open until 11 P.M. on the weekends, but the kitchen generally closes an hour earlier.

If you are not the type to try local fare, you'll also find fast food franchises including Subway, McDonald's, Big Boy, and KFC.

LOCAL MEDIA

The local newspaper is the *Brooklyn Exponent*. Other papers include the *Adrian Daily Telegram*, the *Jackson Citizen Patriot*, and the *Toledo Blade*. They are all valuable for local entertainment and dining options, but the *Detroit Free Press* does the most thorough job of covering local and national sports. Race broadcasts can be heard on MRN Radio WTKA 1050 AM or WKHM 970 AM.

WHERE TO STAY

HOTELS

There are very few brand-name hotels in Brooklyn and Irish Hills, so unless you get lucky, you should expect to drive at least 10 miles to get to the track. Other towns to consider for hotels include Ann Arbor, about 40 miles from the track; Jackson, about 20 miles away; Lansing, 50 miles north of the speedway; and Battle Creek, which is 65 miles to the west. Toledo and Detroit are the closest big cities. While a long way from the track, they may offer the best hotel and rental car bargains. The drive from Toledo is more direct and generally easier.

Carlton Lodge   100 White Tail Drive, Dundee (734) 529-5100   Located near Cabela's, this is a fairly new hotel that features a wildlife-themed lobby and clean, comfortable rooms. They offer a heated indoor pool and complimentary breakfast.

Carlton Lodge   1629 West Maumee Street, Adrian (517) 263-7000   About 20 miles south of the track, this is another fine place to stay on race weekend.

Chicago Street Inn   219 Chicago Street, Brooklyn (517) 592-3888   This quaint bed-and-breakfast inn is minutes from the track and within a short drive of all area attractions.

Hampton Inn   2225 Shirley Drive, Jackson (517) 789-8696   Among the better properties in town. They offer a well-maintained pool and comfortable rooms. Located within a mile or so of several worthwhile restaurants.

Holiday Inn   2000 Holiday Inn Drive (517) 783-5744   A popular place on race weekend. In addition to a heated pool and hot tub, this hotel features exceptional guest rooms, a putting green, mini-golf, and a game room. Convenient to a number of notable restaurants.

Holiday Inn Express   1077 West U.S. 223, Adrian (517) 265-5873   Quality accommodations about 25 miles southeast of the track and a short drive from a number of franchise restaurants.

Super 8 Motel   Michigan 50 South, Brooklyn (517) 592-0888   This is the newest name-brand hotel in the area. Their fifty-two guest rooms will sell quickly, but there is no more convenient hotel in the area.

Super 8 Motel   1091 U.S. 223, Adrian (517) 265-8888   This new hotel offers affordable accommodations a short drive from Adrian Mall and worthwhile restaurants.

CAMPSITES

This is an ideal track at which to camp. There are well-positioned campsites right at the track and others not far away. Track-owned campgrounds open at 7 A.M. on the Saturday before the Winston Cup race. There are two track-owned camping areas to choose from. The **Coleman Campground** is on Brooklyn Highway, across from the speedway. Sites here are reserved in advance for Winston Cup races by calling the track. Oversized spots for RVs and trailers cost $125. Smaller spots suitable for tents cost $100. The Coleman Campground offers primitive campsites without electric hookups. There are shower facilities, portable rest rooms, running cold water, an RV dump station, a picnic shelter, firewood for sale, and Buddy's Convenience Store for other needs. The Michigan 50 campground is first come, first served, and sites cost $100.

In addition to track campgrounds and W. J. Hayes State Park, nearby campgrounds include **JaDo Campground**, at 5603 U.S. 12 in Tipton, (517) 431-2111, **Bernie's Campground**, at 14335 U.S. 12 in Brooklyn, (517) 592-8221, and **Track Side Campground** at 10510 U.S. 12 in Brooklyn, (512) 467-7107. For a more complete list of campgrounds call the Brooklyn/Irish Hills Chamber of Commerce.

Good to Know

- To charge tickets or for additional race information, call (800) 354-1010.
- For campsite information call (517) 592-6666.
- Mail orders can be sent to: 12626 U.S. Highway 12, Brooklyn, MI 49230.
- The Jackson Convention & Tourist Bureau can be reached at (517) 764-4400 or call the Lenawee County Conference & Visitors Bureau (800) 536-2933.
- City Web sites include www.brooklynmi.com and www.irishhills.com.
- ➤ The official racetrack Web site is www.mispeedway.com.

NEARBY WINSTON CUP RACE CITIES

ChicagoLand: 230 miles (four hours, ten minutes)
Indianapolis: 250 miles (four hours, thirty minutes)

IN THE VICINITY

Detroit, Michigan, will surprise you. The Motor City area has a bunch to do, and Detroit is among the nation's elite sports towns. Race fans will want to stop by the **American Motorsports Museum and Hall of Fame** in nearby Novi, which features race cars, trucks, motorcycles, memorabilia, uniforms, and video presentations. Admission is just $3 for adults. The museum, located in the Novi Expo Center at I-96 and Novi Road, is open daily during race season.

The **Henry Ford Museum & Greenfield Village** have an incredible collection of artifacts that are a testament to American ingenuity and inventiveness. Spread out over 93 acres, you may not get to see it all in a single day. You'll see countless automobiles, planes, locomotives, and unusual historical items. The village features historic buildings, including the actual Menlo Park laboratory in which Thomas Edison conceived and invented the phonograph and lightbulb. There's also the Wright Brothers' bicycle shop, Henry Ford's house, a 1913 carousel, a working steamboat, and a steam engine train. A two-day pass to both the museum and village costs $24. Admission to the IMAX theater is not included. The **Walter P. Chrysler Museum** is all about cars, trucks, jeeps, and other vehicles. With more than seventy automobiles, you'll see muscle cars, race memorabilia, concept cars, and gain a better understanding of automotive technology and manufacturing. The **Detroit Institute of Arts** is the fifth-largest fine arts museum in the nation and an absolute jewel. The building itself is incredible and the permanent collection is one of the finest in the Midwest.

Belle Isle, the **Detroit Zoo**, and the casinos of Windsor, Canada, are also worth a visit. **Comerica Park** is one of the finest new big-league ballparks in the nation. The area surrounding the park offers a wealth of pubs, clubs, restaurants, and attractions within a short walk. The baseball stadium has a nostalgic main entrance plaza and gets even better on the inside. The city skyline and a massive scoreboard, complete with roaring tigers, dominate the outfield, while a throwback carousel and Ferris wheel thrill kids of all ages inside. About a half dozen remarkable stainless steel statues of past Tiger greats adorn the concourse walkway beyond center field.

Nearby pubs and sports bars include the **Town Pump**, a warm, enthusiastic place with sensational "pub grub" and eighteen beers on tap at 100 West Montcalm. A block or so closer to the ballpark, **Hockeytown Café** is a formidable, three-story shrine to hockey. Outside of Canada, you will never see a more impressive tribute to the game. **Second City**, next door to Hockeytown at 2301 Woodward Avenue, is only the third in the nation. The performance comedy troupe started in Chicago and brought us Dan Aykroyd, Gilda Radner, and John Candy. The Detroit gang is not as well known but performs timely skits based on national events that are sure to make you laugh. Reservations are suggested on weekends.

Lindell AC is a classic beer joint, at 1310 Cass Avenue, with photos of hundreds of athletes and celebrities who have spent time here since 1948. Said to be the nation's first sports bar, the beers are reasonable and the burgers are near legendary. The **Rock-n-Bowl**, at 4120 Woodward Avenue, combines music, bowling, and a happening bar. **Old Shillelagh** is a notable Irish pub with an enthusiastic crowd and live entertainment nightly. Oddly, you'll find this well-established watering hole in the heart of Greektown, at 349 Monroe Street.

There's plenty more to do in Detroit. For additional attraction, restaurant, and hotel information, call the Convention and Visitors Bureau at (800) DETROIT.

▪ *NEW HAMPSHIRE INTERNATIONAL SPEEDWAY* ▪

Loudon, New Hampshire

"They just weren't thinking when they designed this track. . . . I'd run ten Bristols in a row to this one race. It's nothing against the people up here. Its just a track that needs a lot of work on it."

— STERLING MARLIN

It's been said that New Hampshire resembles a big Martinsville, with long, flat straightaways, 12-degree banking in the turns, and a paper clip shape. Another common feature is that single-file racing along the bottom of the track is the preferred line of attack. That, however, is where the tracks' similarities end. Martinsville has a long, distinguished history in stock car racing, and drivers often speak of it in reverent terms. Despite its being a new track, drivers do not hold New Hampshire in as high regard, nor do many fans I've met who have visited more than a handful of tracks. Nevertheless, the track has no problem selling more than 100,000 tickets to each of its Winston Cup races.

From the drivers' standpoint, the track has not changed dramatically since they first ran here in 1993, and it certainly can't be said that one particular driver or manufacturer has a significant advantage here. It's simply a challenging place to drive and, unless the track is reconfigured someday, it's up to the drivers and teams to figure out how to win a race under the circumstances presented by the current layout.

The track, nicknamed "The Magic Mile," is unique among Winston Cup speedways because it is 1.058 miles long and has identical 1,500-foot-long straightaways with 2-degree banking. The track is 65 feet wide through the straights and widens to 80 feet in the turns but is traditionally thought of as a one-groove racetrack with flat corners. As such it requires good balance in setting up a car on race day. Braking is important at New Hampshire because the long straights lead to flat turns that require drivers to slow down to less than 100 mph from speeds often exceeding 150 mph. It's also critical for drivers to be able to keep their rear wheels from spinning so they can accelerate out of the corners. Passing is difficult here, so superior horsepower is essential as it occasionally enables a driver to take advantage of the long straights and pass opponents before heading back into the turns.

In years past, the track was bumpy and had slick patches in the turns that needed to be avoided. Sealer was put down in 2001 and while the track was infinitely smoother, new problems arose as the sealer marbled up and clumps of rubber accumulated in the turns. Without the new sealer, the track tends to be slick early in a race, until tires become a little worn and develop better grip, so be sure to get to your seats before the green flag drops as races here can be eventful in the opening laps.

Surrounded by the New Hampshire hills of birch and pine trees, the speedway is certainly easy on the eyes once you get to your seat. Grandstand seating consists of aluminum benches with backrests and will set you back a healthy sum for higher rows. Most areas are nicely elevated and set well back from the track, offering a good perspective of the entire speedway. The Concord Grandstand, overlooking turn one, was recently expanded to fifty-four rows, the tallest section at the track. Seats in the higher rows of sections A through E offer a good look down the frontstretch and the exit of pit road. As sections swing around toward section X near turn two, the view becomes somewhat less compelling. Because the track is just over a mile long, most of the track can be seen from the grandstands, and giant-screen TVs are conspicuously absent. Inoffensive smatterings of billboards are situated near the backstretch in turns two and three. In the years to come, these may give way to grandstands as expansion curls around toward the backstretch.

Seats in the main grandstand, rows 21 and higher, are among the most sought-after tickets at the track. Aside from the very lowest rows, spots here offer a good perspective of the race, pits, and victory lane. Seats here also offer the advantage of more concession stands and rest rooms. Directly beneath the press box and luxury suites a sizable shaded area develops as the race goes on.

The Laconia Grandstand is near turn four and has the opposite perspective of seats in the Concord section. Seats here are fairly elevated, so rows 10 and higher are worthwhile. Sections in or near section A offer the best view down the frontstretch and the challenging exit from turn four. Early in a race, however, fans in the Laconia section may find themselves looking into the sun. Another interesting area of seating is along the grassy hill overlooking the backstretch below a hilltop RV area. Folks here spread out their blankets and lawn chairs near the apex of the mound for a more relaxed day of racing. Spots here face directly into the sun as the race nears the finish.

(Photo by Howie Hodge, courtesy of New Hampshire International Speedway)

A modest-sized RV village is in the infield near turns one and two, but close enough to the middle that the vehicles do not obstruct the view of the track for fans in the grandstand. A four-sided scoring tower, listing the top seven cars and the current lap, is situated in the middle of the infield. Infield fans will want to stop by the Checkered Flag Restaurant, a 120-seat cafeteria near the garages that opens at 6 A.M. on race weekends. A two-lane vehicle tunnel to the infield runs beneath turn two and can be accessed via the south gate.

HISTORY

Winston Cup drivers competed in the track's first sanctioned race on July 11, 1993. That date is significant for several reasons. In addition to being the return of NASCAR racing to New England, drivers Jeff Burton and Joe Nemechek were making their first career Winston Cup starts. It also turned out to be the final race of Davey Allison's spectacular career. Allison died in a helicopter crash later that week at Talladega.

Mark Martin earned the pole for the inaugural race. Martin led for much of the day but finished second as Rusty Wallace, who started thirty-third, drove his Pontiac toward the front of the pack and took the lead with a quick pit stop late in the race. Allison came in third that afternoon.

The following year, Ricky Rudd steered his Ford to victory lane, edging out Dale Earnhardt, Rusty Wallace, and Mark Martin. Rudd started in the third qualifying position and set what remains the record for the slowest average speed of 87.599 mph in a caution-marred 300-lap race. Rudd is the only driver to win at NHIS as a driver/owner. Mark Martin earned the pole again in 1995, but Jeff Gordon took the checkered flag for his first win at New Hampshire. Gordon started twenty-first and set a track record with an average speed of 107.029 mph.

Ernie Irvan won the 1996 Jiffy Lube 300 starting from the sixth position. Irvan beat out Dale Jarrett, Ricky Rudd, and Jeff Burton as Ford swept the top four positions, the only time a sweep has occurred at New Hampshire. The following season saw a second race added to the schedule at New Hampshire. On July 13, 1997, Ken Schrader started from the pole, but just four years after his first career start, Jeff Burton won from the fifteenth position with a track record average speed of 117.194 mph. Dale Earnhardt and Rusty Wallace rounded out the top three. Schrader took the pole again in the second race at the track that season to become the first and only driver to sweep the poles in a single season at New Hampshire. Schrader did not manage a top-five finish in either race, and Jeff Gordon earned the win in the season's second race at New Hampshire, despite starting thirteenth.

Jeff Burton returned to the winner's circle in 1998 with his second consecutive Jiffy Lube 300 victory. Burton easily outpaced Mark Martin, Jeff Gordon, and Rusty Wallace with a 7.5-second margin of victory. Later that same season, Mark Martin finished second again, despite leading 192 laps, as Jeff Gordon won his second straight CMT 300. This time Gordon won from the pole to become the first and only driver to accomplish the feat at NHIS.

Burton made it three in a row by winning the Jiffy Lube 300 again in 1999. Burton started out in the thirty-eighth position, a record for worst starting position to win at New Hampshire. On August 19 of that season, Joe Nemechek won his first Winston Cup race at the Magic Mile. In keeping with track history, Nemechek started outside the top ten but managed to pull off the victory by holding off Tony Stewart, Bobby Labonte, Jeff Burton, and Jeff Gordon.

New Hampshire has seen more than its share of tragedy in the track's brief history. Adam Petty, the fourth generation of racing Pettys, was killed when he crashed into the wall of turn three during a Grand National practice in May of 2000. Kenny Irwin lost his life in nearly the same spot, in July of that year, when he crashed during a Winston Cup practice. Tony Stewart, who grew up racing against Irwin, returned Pontiac to victory lane at New Hampshire with a rain-shortened win that weekend. Stewart dedicated the win to Irwin's memory. Stewart was in the right place that afternoon as Nemechek and Mark Martin completed the top three. This race was a landmark of sorts because it was the first New England sporting event to be attended by more than 100,000 fans. Providing further evidence that New Hampshire is a difficult place to pass, Jeff Burton led all 300 laps in the fall of 2000 on his way to his fourth win at the speedway, a feat that is becoming nearly unheard of in Winston Cup stock car racing.

In July 2001, Jeff Gordon and Dale Jarrett went into the race, the nineteenth of the season, tied in Winston Cup points. Gordon earned his third pole at the Magic Mile, but it was Dale Jarrett who visited victory lane at NHIS for the first time. Jarrett started ninth and held off Gordon and Ricky Rudd after passing Rudd, his teammate, with a controversial pass on lap 297. The race was somewhat marred by new sealer that was put down just prior to race weekend. The sealer caused tires to spew rubber that balled up in clumps and made it difficult for drivers to maintain speed through the corners.

New Hampshire's second race for 2001 was postponed until the Friday after Thanksgiving because of the tragic events of September 11. Nearly everyone, including the drivers, expected blizzard-like conditions, but fans and drivers were blessed with unseasonably warm weather and a wild race ensued. Jeff Gordon, who had already clinched his fourth Winston Cup championship, dominated the race. Gordon started on the pole and looked like a runaway winner until Robby Gordon unceremoniously nudged him from behind as they exited turn four on lap 285. Uncharacteristically, Jeff Gordon took offense and rammed Robby Gordon under caution. The DuPont Chevrolet was black flagged and lost any chance to finish his championship season with another victory. Robby Gordon held on for his first Winston Cup victory, beating Sterling Marlin and Dale Jarrett. Jeff Gordon settled for a fifteenth place finish.

GETTING TO THE TRACK

New Hampshire International Speedway is located on Route 106, just 14 miles north of Concord. There are more than 400 acres of parking to accommodate in excess of 70,000 vehicles. All track-owned parking is free.

The track has a reputation for heinous traffic jams before and after a race because there is essentially only one route to the track. Traffic from Concord and Manchester, to the south, is among the most time-consuming in the sport. To avoid the worst of it, leave early in the morning if you plan to arrive on the day of the Winston Cup race. Most fans will take I-93 North to I-393 East to Route 106 North. These are the directions that race programs and local papers push most, so the route can be painfully slow. It may help to travel farther north on I-93 to exit 17 or 20 and head east to the track. From the east, Routes 140 and 129 lead to Route 106.

Stay north of the track and you'll be better off. Lake Winnipesaukee is a popular spot about 30 miles north of the track. Laconia, just 15 miles away, is another option.

WHAT TO SEE AND DO

Few areas welcome race fans as warmly as New Hampshire. In addition to a host of quaint inns and restaurants, the region is home to a wealth of outdoor activities. The entire state of New Hampshire has a little more than 1.2 million people but has 770,000 acres of national parks and forests as well as 15,544 miles of rivers, and 13,000 lakes and ponds.

Mount Washington, the highest peak in New England, is a popular hiking destination but can also be traversed by car. The view from the top is nothing short of spectacular. **Weirs Beach** and the **Boardwalk** at Lake Winnipesaukee are popular in the summer months. The lake is the largest in the state and is home to more than 270 islands. **Mount Washington Cruises** offers a relaxing two-and-a-half-hour narrated tour of the lake. Tours are available at 10 A.M. and 12:30 P.M. daily during race season and cost $18 for adults and $9 for kids. Family packages are available. Call (603) 366-BOAT for additional information. The lake is also a favorite with fisherman and hikers with 240 miles of shoreline. For additional information on fishing and boating in New Hampshire, contact the **Fish and Game Department** at (603) 271-3421.

The **Christa McAuliffe Planetarium** is southwest of the track near Concord. The planetarium, a tribute to the teacher who died aboard the space shuttle *Challenger* in 1986, features outer-space-related exhibits, displays and shows. Admission is just $8 for adults and $5 for kids. Shows last about an hour, and the planetarium is open daily. The **Canterbury Shaker Village** is just north of the track on the way to Laconia. The village was originally built in 1792 and features twenty-five original buildings that have been restored and brought back to life by local craftspeople and artisans. Narrated tours are available and admission is $10 for adults. Family packages are also available.

The state motto is "Live Free or Die," which may explain New Hampshire's remarkably liberal alcohol policies. Aside from New Orleans, this is the only place I've encountered drive-in liquor stores. No sense in getting out of your car, just pull up to the window, order your beer, liquor, or lottery tickets, and be on your way. What more could a race fan ask for?

NIGHTLIFE

When it comes to standout local nightlife options, there are only a handful of places to choose from, and most of those are in Concord. **Barley House Tavern** is located in a brick building just across from the state building at 132 North Main Street in Concord. This casual place has a friendly staff, more than a dozen beers on tap, a solid bar menu, and live music. They also have a newly added sports room with pool tables, darts, foosball, and pinball games. **Chantilly's**, a.k.a the Speedway Lounge, is at 89 Fort Eddy Road, just off I-393. Possibly the only genuine pool hall in town, this place has been around forever and draws a good crowd on race weekend. It's a good-sized place with sixteen regulation pool tables, a smattering of race car hoods on the walls, and live music at night. Cover charge varies.

Cheers is as much a restaurant as a bar, but it stays open later than most area eateries and has a decent bar crowd during race week. Located at 17 Depot Street in Concord, the bar is downstairs while the restaurant above serves wings, burgers, steaks, sandwiches, seafood, and pasta.

Hermano's Cocina Mexicana at 11 Hills Avenue in Concord is located in a turn-of-the-century brick building in downtown. This two-story Mexican restaurant has a pretty happening lounge upstairs with live jazz music Sunday through Thursday. There's never a cover charge, and the margaritas are as good as you'll find in the city. **Margarita's**, at 1 Bicentennial Square, is another worthwhile Mexican eatery with a better-than-average bar upstairs. Just up the street, **Penuche's Ale House**, at 16 Bicentennial Square, is an affable place with a tremendous selection of area microbrewed beers on tap and thirty-six bottled beers to choose from. They have some of the most affordable ice-cold beer in town, as well as foosball, bumper pool, video games, and live music on the weekends.

In Manchester, **Billy's Sports Bar and Grill** is a happening stop for televised sports and a casual meal. A little out of the way, at 34 Tarrytown Road, this place welcomes race fans and offers a sizable collection of sports memorabilia, plenty of TVs, and an affordable menu of burgers, wings, sandwiches, and salads.

WHERE TO EAT

Angelina's, at 11 Depot Street in downtown Concord, is an intimate, upscale bistro that offers some of the finest Italian food in town. **The Cat 'n Fiddle** is a family-oriented Greek and Italian place at 118 Manchester Street in Concord. The generous entrees range from steak or chicken to pasta and seafood. **Makris Lobster and Steakhouse** is among the premier family-owned lobster places in Concord. This rustic eatery has affordable New England–style entrees in addition to their trademark lobsters. They offer outdoor seating and affordable beverages in the ninety-seat, full-service lounge that features satellite sports on TV. At 354 Sheep Davis Road in Concord, this is among the largest and closest restaurants to the track. Other outstanding seafood places include **Sandy Point** in Alton and **Weathervane Seafoods**, on Route 4 in Chichester.

Shibley's at the Pier, on Route 11 in Alton Bay, is one of the most popular eateries located right on the lake. They offer indoor and outdoor seating and American-style seafood, including salmon, trout, swordfish, and halibut, as well as wild game entrees at dinner or fried seafood and wrap sandwiches at lunch. Boat owners can pull right up to the dock and spend some time enjoying the casual to upscale atmosphere. **Cherrystone Lobster House**, near the lake at 40 Weirs Road in Gilford, has been around for twenty years and is one of a handful of outstanding seafood places worth seeking out when you are nearby for a race. This casual place caters to the resort crowd and features a friendly staff, reasonably priced entrees, and a casual atmosphere.

The **Capitol Grill** is a casual place with an intimate setting at 1 Eagle Square across from the State Building. They offer three dining rooms and a full-service lounge. The menu features steaks, burgers, sandwiches, and salads. Just around the corner, **Brianna's Bistro** is another place with an amiable staff and a candlelit setting to enjoy a nicely presented meal prepared with Mediterranean flair. **The Common Man** is a good-sized place that serves a traditional American menu with a variety of specialties usually consisting of meat and two vegetables. Located at 29 Water Street in Concord, they also have a full bar and go out of their way to ensure that race fans will feel right at home. **The Red Blazer**, at 72 Manchester Street in Concord, is a moderately priced place that also serves traditional American fare of steaks, roast beef, and chicken as well as a handful of Italian specialties. Their Sunday brunch is especially worthwhile.

The **Kansas City Steakhouse**, in the Holiday Inn, offers a rustic atmosphere, Wild West artwork, and country music playing in the background. Located at 172 North Main Street in Concord, this place attracts a crowd of race fans on the weekends and offers moderate to expensive cuts of beef as well as seafood and pasta entrees. **Ginger Garden** is a good choice for oriental cuisine and is one of the few places in the area to serve sushi. Located at 161 Loudon Road in Concord, they have a comfortable atmosphere, attentive service, and a diverse menu. **Oliver's** is less than ten miles from the track in Tilton and has been serving lunch and dinner for more than a decade. This casual place specializes in seafood, steaks and pasta. They've won best seafood chowder six out of the last eight years. Their English-style pub has a horseshoe bar and offers live acoustic music on the weekends.

LOCAL MEDIA

The *Concord Monitor* is the local daily newspaper. Race broadcasts can be heard on WKXL-FM, 107.7, via the Motor Racing Network.

WHERE TO STAY

HOTELS

There are very few hotels near the track in Loudon, so race fans tend to stay in the capital city of Concord or farther south in Manchester. Regulars insist that you are better off staying north of the track to avoid traffic and to take advantage of the attractions in and around Lake Winnipesaukee. Laconia is another town, north of the track, with a number of hotels and restaurants to choose from. Listed below are a few places worth checking out. Some of these places require a three-night minimum. If you find that these hotels are sold out for race weekend, don't forget to ask for a recommendation of alternative accommodations from the person working at the front desk.

1875 Inn   42 Main Street, Tilton (603) 286-7774   A short drive from the track, this vintage inn has just eleven rooms to choose from. The Patriot's Tavern adjacent to the inn stays busy during race week.

Best Western Inn   97 Hall Street, Concord (603) 228-4300   A decent-sized place by Concord standards, with a pool, sauna, whirlpool, and workout room.

The Centennial Inn   96 Pleasant Street (603) 227-9000   This Victorian-style building was originally built in 1892 but has been restored in recent years to become one of the most charming area inns. It's not the well-kept secret it used to be and it's not inexpensive, but if you want to stay in style this should be your first choice. The inn's **Franklin Pierce Dining Room** is among the finest restaurants in town. Even if you are staying elsewhere, it's worth a visit.

Comfort Inn   71 Hall Street, Concord (603) 226-4100   Conveniently located near downtown and the highway, this moderately priced hotel has a heated indoor pool and whirlpool.

Courtyard by Marriott   70 Constitution Avenue (603) 225-0303   A clean, comfortable place that is not far from area restaurants and attractions. This is one of the first places to sell out, so be sure to call in advance.

Fairfield Inn   4 Gulf Street, Concord (603) 224-4011   Among the nicer and newer places in town, they offer the same amenities as those places listed above.

Hampton Inn   515 South Street, Bow (603) 224-5322   This place offers well-appointed rooms and a full array of amenities. It's located just south of Concord but close enough that it's an easy trip to town for restaurants and nightlife.

Holiday Inn   172 North Main Street, Concord (603) 224-9534   Located in the heart of downtown, this hotel is very convenient to the area's better restaurants and nightlife.

Margate Resort   76 Lake Street, Laconia (603) 524-5210 or (800) 627-4283   A four-building complex with a pool and restaurant on the lake. Like many places on race weekend, they have a three-night minimum. Expect to spend $550–750 for the weekend. **Blackstone's**, a restaurant at the Margate, offers fine dining with a diverse menu served in an upscale atmosphere.

Red Roof Inn   519 Route 106 South, Loudon (603) 225-8399   As close to the track as brand-name hotels get. This moderately priced place packs with race fans on race weekend and is among the most affordable places to stay.

Sheraton Four Points   55 John E. Devine Drive, Manchester (603) 668-6110   Among the better places to stay in Manchester (the Holiday Inn and Ramada are equally nice and worth a call if this place is sold out). This place is convenient to the highway and has a restaurant, heated pool, and whirlpool on site.

CAMPSITES

Camping is very popular near the track on race weekend. I have not found any places in Loudon, but there are a number of campgrounds within a reasonable drive of the track. These include the **Circle Nine Ranch** in Epsom (603) 736-9656; **Clearwater Campground** on Lake Pemigewasset in Meredith (603) 279-7761; **Hack-Ma-Tack Campground** in Laconia (603) 366-5977; **Thousand Acres Family Campground** on Route 3 in Franklin (603) 934-4440; and the **Twin Oaks Campground** on Route 28 in Allenstown (603) 485-2700. These places fill up quickly, and amenities vary from complimentary shuttles to the race to live entertainment, so be sure to call in advance to reserve a spot for race week and ask about shortcuts to the track.

Good to Know

- To charge tickets or for additional race information, call (603) 783-4931.
- For camping information call (603) 783-4744.
- Mail orders can be sent to New Hampshire International Speedway, P.O. Box 7888, Loudon, NH 03307.
- The New Hampshire Office of Travel and Tourism can be reached at (603) 271-2666. The Concord Chamber of Commerce is at (603) 224-2508. Call the Greater Laconia–Weirs Beach Chamber of Commerce at (603) 524-5531.

- A worthwhile city Web site is www.concordnhchamber.com.
- ➤ The official racetrack Web site is www.nhis.com.

NEARBY WINSTON CUP RACE CITIES

Pocono: 360 miles (six hours, twenty minutes)
Watkins Glen: 385 miles (six hours, forty-five minutes)

IN THE VICINITY

Boston, Massachusetts, is about 85 miles south of Loudon. Boston, especially in the spring and summer months, is one of the nation's most visitor-friendly cities. There is plenty to do and see, a wealth of hotel rooms, wonderfully diverse nightlife, and a terrific mass transit system. The **New England Aquarium** features a unique 187,000-gallon cylinder-shaped tank that you can view from different levels and perspectives. The aquarium is home to more than 2,000 marine animals and has become one of the city's most visited attractions.

Historical attractions include **Faneuil Hall**, an important meeting hall during the Revolutionary War, the **Bunker Hill Monument**, the **Paul Revere House**, and the **Old North Church**. All are worth checking out, especially for Revolutionary War and history buffs. The **USS *Constitution*** is the oldest commissioned ship in the Navy. Docked at the Charleston Navy Yard, north of downtown, along the Boston Inner Harbor, guided tours are available and a museum is adjacent to the ship on shore. Admission is just $3 for adults.

Other Beantown attractions include the **Quincy Market**, **Boston Commons**, and the **John Hancock Tower**. Baseball fans will want to check out **Fenway Park**. If the Red Sox are playing in town, it is definitely worth the trip to see this venerable old ballpark before it meets the wrecking ball.

▪ *NORTH CAROLINA SPEEDWAY* ▪

Rockingham, North Carolina

"This racetrack is real coarse. It's like sandpaper. It just eats up tires."

—MIKE WALLACE

"The Rock," as North Carolina Speedway is affectionately known, is a classic track that has been hosting sanctioned races since 1965. Originally built as a flat, 1-mile track, the Rock was reconfigured with the help of a computer to its current configuration in 1969. The goal of the state-of-the-art redesign was to create a track that would increase speeds and lessen engine wear and tear.

Today, the track is 1.017 miles long and has 22-degree banks in turns one and two, 25-degree banking in the third and fourth turns, and 8-degree banking through the straights. The backstretch, at 1,367 feet, is slightly longer than the 1,300-foot frontstretch and allows for wide-open racing action. Phoenix is the only other track on the Winston Cup circuit where the backstretch is longer than the frontstretch. The pits used to be located along both straightaways, but in 1999 pit road was reconfigured to start at the beginning of the frontstretch and continue through the first turn. Drivers re-enter the track from pit road near the start of the second turn.

While Rockingham has been the site of some remarkable races over the years and offers terrific side-by-side racing on its 50-foot-wide straightaways and through the 55-foot-wide turns, the facility shows its age more than most tracks. Infrastructure surrounding the track is woefully inadequate, many of the grandstands are less than ideal, and some of the concession and rest room facilities, especially on the frontstretch, are downright nasty.

NCS has just 60,113 grandstand seats and a modest infield capacity, but there are many fine places to sit. Most seating sections along the frontstretch have just twenty rows of seats. Seats in rows 10 or higher offer a good perspective of the entire track.

A look at the tri-oval from the frontstretch grandstands. *(Photo by Bill Rider)*

Since pit row was extended through turn one, seating sections in this area offer a good view of pit action, as well as the frontstretch and the entry into turn one. If possible, avoid seats in section 33 and 35, but anywhere else near the first turn is a good place to sit. Seats in the upper rows of sections 37, 39, and 41 offer a particularly good view of the entire track.

The frontstretch at Rockingham has a simple seating system. Seats overlooking the start/finish line are in sections 1 and 2. Even-numbered sections go up in number toward turn four, and odd-numbered sections increase toward the first turn. The higher your section, the farther you are from the start/finish line. The good news is that the most expensive seats in the whole place are just $80, reasonable by Winston Cup standards. Seats along the backstretch, in rows 3–32, and in the first three rows of the frontstretch, between sections 1 and 31, are only $45, but I generally try to find seats elsewhere.

A scoreboard listing the current lap and top five cars sits between turns three and four. The board is easiest to see from the backstretch and frontstretch seats in section 27 and lower. Fans in turns one and two may have a tough time seeing the board, nearly half a mile away. There are no tall buildings in the infield to obscure the view and infield RV camping is limited, so the track can be easily viewed from nearly any seat in the house. The Pontiac stands near turn four are the highest section of seats on the front side; sections 30–34 have twenty-two rows of seats, while sections 36–40 have twenty-three rows. Turn four is one of the more challenging portions of the track, so seats here can be close to a lot of the action. An added advantage to sitting here is that these newer sections have their own concession stands and rest rooms.

In 1998, 28,021 seats were added to the backstretch. This section has fifty-eight rows of seats and from those near the top, fans can see the entire track. Drivers find the track to be slickest coming out of turn two early in the race, so seats here are often right on top of some of the hairiest race action. Seats in row 33 and higher sell for $65 during Winston Cup races.

A two-lane tunnel under turn four is accessible from Highway 1 and North Carolina Highway 177 and allows fans to get to the 25-acre infield area with concession stands, rest rooms, reserved parking, first aid center, and a cafeteria. There's also a transporter crossover at turn three that closes just before the race begins. There are 21 acres of camping sites at gate E behind the Hamlet grandstands along Richmond Road and North Carolina Highway 177. Camping outside the track is $40 for the week. Shower, phone, and rest room facilities are on site and a ham-and-sausage-biscuit breakfast is provided for all campers from 7 to 9 A.M. on race Sunday.

You'll also find one of racing's finest symbols at this classic racetrack. The Rock has its own "Stanley Cup" of auto racing, a massive boulder located near the main office that has the names of past winners etched into it.

Every October, the **Union 76/Rockingham Pit Crew Competition** is held at Rockingham, the only NASCAR sanctioned pit crew competition where the top 25 crews try to change all four tires and add 22 gallons of gas in the quickest time without penalties. The competition is held Saturday morning before the Busch race, on the same weekend as Sunday's Winston Cup race. Rockingham is also home to the **Buck Baker Racing School** with half-day, full-day, and multiday courses that allow you to strap into a Winston Cup–style race car and zoom around one of the circuit's most challenging tracks. Call (800) 529-2825 or (704) 596-8930 for details.

Wayside Grill is a temporary store that's open on race weekends, just west of the track on U.S. 1. Keep in mind, they are not allowed to sell beer until noon on Sundays and supplies run low as the weekend goes on, but if you need to fill up on camping supplies, ice or beverages this is a handy place within a short walk of the track.

Souvenir row, with the driver souvenir trailers, is located along Richmond Road outside turn two, to the west of the track. The fourth turn tunnel is how drivers access the helipads east of the track, so this is a spot to look for driver autographs after a race.

HISTORY

The big boys of stock car racing journey to Rockingham twice a year. Every spring the Rock hosts a race that generally follows the Daytona opener, while the fall Winston Cup race has seen its share of championship-clinching contests over the years. Curtis Turner, returning from what was supposed to be a lifetime suspension for trying to unionize the drivers, took the checkered flag in the track's inaugural race. Turner held off Cale Yarborough as Ford swept the first four positions in a 500-mile race that took four hours and fifty-four minutes. It was the seventeenth and final win of Turner's tragically short career.

Richard Petty leads all drivers with eleven North Carolina Speedway victories. In 1967, Petty earned his first checkered flag at the track, guiding his Plymouth to the win while averaging 104.682 mph. Richard Petty became the first driver to sweep both of the track's points races in 1971 and repeated the feat in 1976. Not surprisingly, given the track's slick surface, there has never been a caution-free race at Rockingham. In 1974 Petty won the Carolina 500, a race that featured just two caution flags, the fewest in track history. In 1992, the AC Delco 500 matched the record for fewest cautions, in a race won by Richard's son Kyle Petty.

In June 1968, Donnie and Bobby Allison finished first in second in the Carolina 500, the first one-two finish for brothers in more than a decade. David Pearson won the Carolina 500 in 1969, and earned five wins at Rockingham throughout his career, including both races in the 1973 season. In the 1973 Carolina 500, Pearson started from the pole and led a remarkable 491 of 492 laps to set a track record. There were only two lead changes the entire race, setting another Rockingham record.

Cale Yarborough is the second-winningest driver at Rockingham, with seven victories. Yarborough first conquered the Rock in 1970 and swept the points races here in 1975 and 1980. With two races left on the season schedule, Yarborough clinched the 1977 Winston Cup Championship with a fourth-place finish in the American 500 on October 23 of that year. Almost exactly a year later, Cale won the American 500 to clinch his third consecutive points championship. Yarborough is still the only driver to win three consecutive Winston Cup points titles.

In 1976, Bill Elliott made the first start of his illustrious Winston Cup career at Rockingham. It was an inauspicious beginning as Elliott started thirty-fourth in a thirty-six-car field and blew an engine after just thirty-two laps. It wasn't until 1984 that Elliott finally earned the checkers at Rockingham, his first of three wins there. Darrell Waltrip was also a three-time winner at Rockingham. In a Junior Johnson–owned Buick, Waltrip swept the 1981 races, taking over where the Johnson/Yarborough team had left off the previous season. The Carolina 500 that season featured thirty-six lead changes, a track record. That record was matched in the 1983

American 500, in which Terry Labonte earned his first win at Rockingham and his only victory of the season.

Dale Earnhardt clinched the 1987 points championship with a second-place finish in the AC Delco 500 that fall. Neil Bonnett earned his eighteenth and final career win at Rockingham on March 6, 1988. Rusty Wallace is among the top three drivers at Rockingham with five victories. His first win at the the Rock came in the 1988 AC Delco 500. Wallace made it back-to-back wins by claiming the Goodwrench 500 in 1989. Mark Martin edged out Rusty Wallace for his first career Winston Cup win in 1989. Kyle Petty, who has three victories at Rockingham, won the Goodwrench 500 on March 4, 1990, from the pole and claimed $228,000 for his efforts. That remains the largest first-place prize won at Rockingham. Rusty Wallace returned to his winning ways by sweeping the points races in the 1993 season and extended his streak to three in a row by winning the spring race in 1994.

The following spring, Jeff Gordon earned the first of his four Rockingham wins in the final 500-mile race held at NCS. In the summer of 1994 the track was repaved and races were shortened to 400 miles, as Ward Burton won his first career Winston Cup race by holding off Rusty Wallace in that fall's AC Delco 400. In the 1994 AC Delco 500, Dale Earnhardt won the race and clinched his record-tying seventh points championship.

On February 23, 1997, Mark Martin set a new qualifying record on his way to one of five poles he has earned at Rockingham. Only Kyle Petty, David Pearson, and Cale Yarborough have as many poles at NCS. On October 24, 1999, Jeff Burton set the track record with an average speed of 131.103 mph in a race that lasted just three hours, two minutes, and fifty-five seconds. On February 25, 2000, Rusty Wallace set the qualifying record with a 23.167-second lap, achieving a speed of 158.035 mph.

GETTING TO THE TRACK

There is no easy way to get to Rockingham on race day. U.S. 1, on which the track is located, is shown on maps as a major thoroughfare running from Raleigh, North Carolina, almost all the way to Columbia, South Carolina, but in truth it is a two-lane road winding through countless small towns along the way. Interstate 177 also borders the track to the east and can be helpful if you are approaching from points east and south, but it's also a minor artery that clogs up as you get near the track. I-74 is your best bet traveling from Charlotte and points to the west. The new U.S. 74 Rockingham Bypass alleviates some beach traffic on race weekend but is marginally helpful getting to the track itself.

Your best bet may be to arrive very early in the morning or consider camping out before and after the race. The majority of public parking lots are located along 177. Parking outside the facility in track-owned lots is free. There are also entrepreneur lots, west and across the street from the track, that allow for easier exiting. These lots cost $10 for parking and some discourage grilling, but I've found them to be worthwhile, especially after a race when traffic can be maddening.

WHAT TO SEE AND DO

On the Thursday before either race weekend at the Rock, **Thunderfest** is held at the square in downtown Rockingham near the courthouse. Thunderfest is a festival that runs from 11 A.M. until 9 P.M. and features driver autograph sessions, show cars, Winston Cup simulators, live entertainment, and a plethora of merchandise and collectibles vendors. Admission is free, and a complimentary shuttle is offered from the main office at the track to the festival. Rockingham is the epitome of a small-town racing destination, but there are a handful of things to do while you are in town. The **Rockingham Dragway** features NHRA races and a regular schedule of events February through November. For schedule information call (910) 582-3400. The **National Railroad Museum and Hall of Fame**, in a temporary home at 23 Hamlet Avenue, is home to an extensive model train layout, train artifacts, maps, and historic photos. Call (910) 582-3337 for hours of operation. Nearby, the **Hamlet Train Station**, once listed among the National Register of Historic Places, has been renovated to an active depot, museum, and visitor center.

The **Rankin Museum of American Heritage**, in Ellerbe, has a modest collection of historical artifacts relating to the area's development. Ellerbe is also known for its antique shops and produce markets. Outdoor enthusiasts will want to check out Blewitt Falls, the Great Pee Dee River, and McKinney Lake National Hatchery. Golfers should bring their clubs and take on the **Richmond Pines Country Club**, a challenging, Donald Ross–designed golf course.

NIGHTLIFE IN ROCKINGHAM

Rockingham passed a liquor-by-the-drink ordinance in September 2000, so night-clubs will become more commonplace in the years to come, but until then you may want to consider heading to Southern Pines, which is just twenty minutes away. Bars in Rockingham are predominantly private clubs that require guests to arrive with members, but rules are often loosely enforced.

The Bar is just a few miles from the track on Fayetteville Road. Located in a strip mall shopping center, this dark club serves beer only but offers televised sports, three pool tables, and darts. **Fat Boys** at 416 East Broad Avenue is a modest, race-fan-friendly place with a pair of pool tables and three TVs. They also offer darts, a jukebox, and karaoke on Friday nights.

Rock N Jams is a dance club that attracts a younger crowd at 122 East Washington Street. Just up the street, **Hugo's**, at 303 East Washington Street, is open Wednesday, Friday, and Saturday nights and offers occasional live music. Call (910) 895-8244 for band listing and cover charge information.

SOUTHERN PINES

Squires Pub at 1720 U.S. 1 South is a casual British pub with traditional pub grub, including an outstanding fish-and-chips basket. There's also a terrific selection of imported beers to choose from. **J. Albert's** is a moderately upscale, beach music club with a mature crowd. Located at 1420 U.S. 1 South, at the Days Inn, you can count on an enthusiastic crowd here during race week. Just around the corner, the **Broad Street Bar & Grill** is a small neighborhood pub with a comfortable deck and a rooftop patio.

The Back Alley, formerly Bucketheads, is a good-sized place on U.S. 1 with a respectable beer selection, a dance floor, and three pool tables. Race fans will want to check out the giant vintage photo of North Carolina Speedway on the wall.

PINEHURST

The 726 Pub   Located at the Magnolia Inn, this quaint English pub gets a good-sized, fun-loving crowd on race weekend. The pub is also the more casual of the inn's eateries; you can order off the main dining hall menu or from the more modest pub menu.

WHERE TO EAT

Alonzo's   503 Rockingham Road (910) 997-4414   One of the newest, and easily the best, eatery I've come across in Rockingham. Near the intersection of I-74 and U.S. 1, this place is sure to pack them in during race week.

Becky's   Highway U.S. 1 (910) 895-0207   A modest lunch place that also offers Friday-night dinners. Located about 2 miles from the track, at Richmond Pines, an eighteen-hole golf course that has been around since 1926.

Little Bo Steak House   127 Little Bo Lane (910) 997-2171   One of the finer places in town to grab a steak, chops, ribs, or pasta. They offer a full bar and are open Wednesday through Saturday only.

MiCasita Restaurant   1201 East Broad Avenue (910) 895-2222   A popular, affordable Mexican eatery that has been around for years.

Rockingham Fish Camp & Steak   532 East Broad Avenue (910) 997-4006   A good-sized place about 10 miles southeast of the track that specializes in grilled and marinated seafood. Voted "Best of the Best" Seafood by readers of the local newspaper, but they pride themselves on the fresh-cut steaks. In years past, this place was a favorite of Davey Allison and a number of other drivers on the Friday night before the race.

SOUTHERN PINES

The Barn   305 Rothney Avenue (910) 692-7700   A rustic, two-level steakhouse with chicken, ribs, fresh fish, homemade soups, and desserts. A pleasantly furnished bar accommodates folks waiting to be seated.

Beefeaters   672 SW Broad Street (910) 692-5550   A fancier steak place with a good-sized bar. They're open for dinner only Monday through Saturday. Call for reservations.

John's Barbeque   1910 U.S. Highway 15/501 (910) 692-9474   This is the place to go for lunch or dinner. The barbecue is absolutely out of this world, and the folks in charge are always happy to see you.

Outback Steakhouse   100 Southern Road (910) 695-7000   I prefer to list indigenous places, but this national chain is popular with race fans. You can't go wrong with their steaks and a blooming onion.

Raffaele's   1550 U.S. Highway 1 South (910) 692-1952   One of the original area restaurants specializing in continental Italian dishes, but also quality steak and chicken dishes. Everything is made fresh and it's all very affordable. They also offer a sizable bar with a big-screen TV showing sports.

Ragazzi's   1640 U.S. Highway 1 South (910) 692-4626   A commendable Italian restaurant with specialties that include pasta, lasagna, rib eye steaks, and a bottomless salad bowl. Across from the Hampton Inn, this casual eatery seats more than 200 people and still gets crowded for race week.

Vito's Ristorante   311 SE Broad Street (910) 692-7815   One of Southern Pines' original fine dining restaurants. Open for dinner only Tuesday through Saturday. Be sure to call ahead for reservations.

LOCAL MEDIA

The *Richmond Daily Journal* is the local newspaper, and race broadcasts can be heard on the Motorsports Radio Network carried by WKML 95.7 FM.

WHERE TO STAY

ROCKINGHAM HOTELS

Comfort Suites   307 Green Street (910) 410-0077   Possibly the finest place to stay in town. They are just 10 miles from the track and within walking distance of several fast food restaurants. This is generally one of the very first places to sell out on race weekend.

Holiday Inn Express   U.S. Highway 74 (910) 692-8585   Another clean, comfortable place to stay in Rockingham, just 8 miles from the track. Within a short drive of several worthwhile restaurants. Like the Comfort Suites, they sell out quickly.

Regal Inn   (910) 997-3336   Affordable accommodations less than 10 miles from the track and within walking distance of a handful of fast food franchises. Because there are so few places to stay this close to the track, this place also sells out quickly.

SOUTHERN PINES HOTELS

Comfort Inn   9801 U.S. Highway 15/501 (910) 215-5500   Worthwhile accommodations with a pool and a lounge on site. Several solid restaurants are just a short drive away.

Days Inn   1420 U.S. 1 South (910) 692-7581   Affordable establishment with an outdoor pool and complimentary breakfast. The adjacent J. Albert's nightclub packs them in on race weekend.

Hampton Inn   1675 U.S. Highway 1 South (910) 692-9266   Quality accommodations in the heart of the Sandhills. Within walking distance of Ragazzi's, they offer an outdoor pool and complimentary breakfast.

Holiday Inn   U.S. Highway 1 at Morganton Road (910) 692-2240   Another nice place to stay for race week. They offer an outdoor pool and tennis courts on property. Within a short drive of several fine restaurants.

PINEHURST HOTELS

Magnolia Inn   65 Magnolia Road (800) 526-5562   A historic, 106-year-old inn with eleven rooms, a fine dining restaurant, and the 726 Pub, an old English tavern. They offer golf packages and often host a race team during race week.

Manor Inn   5 Community Road (910) 295-2700   A quaint hotel with forty-five rooms that do not come inexpensively. Expect Old World service, quality rooms, and a pleasant stay.

Microtel Inn   205 Windstar Place (910) 693-3737   Easily the most affordable place to stay within a reasonable drive of the track. Short on amenities, but if all you need is a place to crash, it will certainly do.

Springhill Suites   (888) 287-9400 or (910) 695-0234   By Pinehurst standards, this place is a steal of a deal, about 18 miles from the track and 2 miles from Pinehurst. Clean, comfortable rooms, and a helpful staff.

Good to Know

- To charge tickets or for additional race information, call (910) 582-2861.
- Mail orders can be sent to P.O. Box 500, Rockingham, NC, 28380-0500.
- The Richmond County Chamber of Commerce/Tourist Development Authority can be reached at (800) 858-1688 or (910) 895-9058.
- A worthwhile city Web site is www.richmondcountychamber.com.
- ➤ The official racetrack Web site is www.northcarolinaspeedway.com.

NEARBY WINSTON CUP RACE CITIES

Darlington: 47 miles (one hour)
Charlotte: 75 miles (one hour, thirty minutes)
Martinsville: 135 miles (two hours, thirty minutes)
Bristol: 250 miles (five hours)
Richmond: 275 miles (five hours, thirty minutes)

IN THE VICINITY

The village of Pinehurst is the golfing capital of North Carolina. There are more than forty golf courses to choose from including **Pinehurst Number Two**, which hosted the Men's U.S. Open in 1999 and will host it again in 2005. Call the **Pinehurst Area Convention and Visitors Bureau** at (800) 346-5362 for a complete list of golf courses, hotels, and restaurants.

One of my favorite places to play in the area is the **National Golf Club**, designed by Jack Nicklaus. This wonderfully scenic course is semiprivate, but they do allow the public to play on occasion. Call (910) 295-5340 for tee times or more information.

■ *POCONO RACEWAY* ■

Long Pond, Pennsylvania

"Pocono is a different animal. We don't race anywhere else that is remotely like it, and that makes it fun. It's like a speedway and a short track. It's really fun to drive at Pocono, and that's a big part of it. I think every driver in the garage likes to run up here."

— MICHAEL WALTRIP

Nestled in the piney woods of Long Pond, Pennsylvania, Pocono Raceway is unlike any track in the nation. It's isolated from surrounding towns by acres of trees that create the sense of being in the middle of nowhere, despite the fact that 60 million people live within a 200-mile radius of the track. My first impression was that it had been built in a haphazard manner until it all finally came together to its current configuration. The more I research the track's history, the more I realize that my first impression is not far from being accurate.

The track is a giant 2.5-mile triangle with seemingly no rhyme or reason to the straightaway lengths or the banking of the turns. The frontstretch is the second longest on the Winston Cup circuit at 3,740 feet. For the sake of perspective, this single straightaway is nearly as long as the entire .750-mile Richmond International Raceway. The 3,055-foot backstretch is longer than either Bristol or Martinsville. All told, Pocono Raceway is .7 miles longer than Bristol, Richmond, Martinsville, and the old .625-mile track at North Wilkesboro, combined.

It's been said that Pocono features one turn each from a superspeedway, a short track, and a road course. The turns are all relatively flat, but to make matters even more interesting they are all banked differently. Turn one is the steepest at 14 degrees. Turn two, the "tunnel turn," is 8 degrees, while turn three is just 6 degrees.

Consider that the other two Winston Cup superspeedways longer than 2 miles, Daytona and Talladega, offer banking of 31 and 33 degrees in the turns, respectively. Even the tri-ovals at Daytona and Talladega have 18-degree banks.

All this adds up to a setup nightmare for crew chiefs, who must provide adequate gearing for the long straights and also consider the difference in the modestly banked turns when choosing a chassis setup. Drivers, on the other hand, all seem to enjoy racing at Pocono. The track has been described as a superspeedway that drives like a road course. The 100-foot-wide frontstretch easily accommodates five-wide racing as drivers exceed 200 mph before heading into the first turn, the tightest of the three turns here at Pocono. Turn two, the tunnel turn, is the most treacherous and is often the scene of some major mishaps, with drivers reaching 170 mph as they approach the turn and slow down to set up their exit from the turn. Another reason turn two is tough to negotiate is that cars are generally set up for turn one or turn three, but almost never for turn two. The grandstands near turn

View from the pits of the frontstretch grandstands, flagstand and finish line. *(Photo by Author)*

three are my favorite place to watch a race at Pocono, as drivers come out of the turn and bunch up three, four, and sometimes five wide. A great deal of passing takes place as the cars exit turn three.

Pocono's pit road is the longest and widest on the Winston Cup circuit and is overlooked by the paddock area and some of the most distinctive grandstands in the sport. **The Paddock** is an area where fans with $30 prerace pit passes (over and above the cost of their grandstand ticket) can view the cars up close and queue up in hopes of getting drivers' autographs before the race begins. This area also features the **Pacesetter's Club**, a set of infield grandstands facing the track and pits. These seats sell for $200 and include admission and a prerace pit/paddock pass, as well as food and beverages. The **Victory Circle Club**, situated between the Pacesetter's section and the corporate pit suites, is a three-tiered section overlooking the winner's circle and the start/finish line. The first two levels are available to the public for $250 on a limited basis and include food and beverages, as well as a prerace pit/paddock pass. The rooftop level is for corporate clients only. **Autograph Alley** is a fenced area beside the walkway leading from the garages to the pits. Drivers occasionally stop along the way to sign autographs for fans.

The Winston Cup races at Pocono are generally just six weeks apart, the shortest break between races for any track that hosts two events. Perhaps it's appropriate for the track that hosts a race on Father's Day to create a family atmosphere on race day. Nearly everything is painted with wide black and white stripes, and buildings at the track are reminiscent of a classic horse track. A giant midway area, just inside the gates, behind the main grandstand, features a state fair atmosphere with clowns, jugglers, musicians, and a petting zoo. This is also where you'll find Long John, the world's largest bathroom facility at 1,100 feet long, with 1,000 stalls and virtually no lines. A convenient pedestrian tunnel runs from the grandstands to the paddock area in the infield. There are also 200 picnic tables situated under pine trees and handsome gazebos spread about the area behind the main grandstands, so finding a place to enjoy a meal is not difficult.

Pocono Raceway does not release official attendance numbers, but they sell in excess of 100,000 tickets for cup races. Tickets sell quickly, so buy early if you want a good seat. The grandstand offers more than fifty rows of seats, which vary greatly. Seats in the concourse, concourse vista, terrace, and terrace vista sections are bleachers without seatbacks. Prices range from $45 to $80. Spring for the second tier, $75 to $80 terrace sections, if you hope to see much of the track beyond the frontstretch. The grandstand is divided into north and south at the start/finish line. Seats start at N1 and go up to N24 near turn three and S1 through S22 as they approach turn one. Pocono regulars try to get seats near the top, as close to turn one or three as possible. These seats will have higher section numbers and, of course, higher row numbers. Rows 25 and higher offer the best perspective of the track, but even these seats can be blocked somewhat by the three-story Victory Circle Club, if for only a second or two of racing all the way across the 2.5-mile track.

If you really want to blow it out, seats in the air-conditioned **Sky Box Club** sit atop the stands and cost $375. **Terrace Club** seats, in the shade just below the skybox area, cost $200. Seats in both these sections come with pit/paddock passes, food, and beverages. I was surprised to see that Terrace Club seats are simple aluminum bleachers with seatbacks. I was also dismayed that support beams at the front of each section can obstruct the view of the track from some seats here. RV owners will want to consider the trackside RV area. For $500 plus $50 per person, you can park your RV along the straightaway between turns two and three and watch the race from the comfort of your captain's chairs. One fan described it as "like pulling up to the drive-in theater and watching a race." Other RV spots outside the track are $150, plus grandstand tickets for each person.

Infield RV spots range from $100 to $200, plus $50 per person. One-day infield tickets are just $40 per person. A restaurant, souvenir stand, and rest rooms are available to infield fans. Infield fans will want to check the Davey Allison flagpole memorial and the half dozen black boulders with gold numbers painted on them to pay tribute to great drivers of the past. The most recent addition is the number 3, in memoriam to Dale Earnhardt. A short, three-sided scoring tower, showing the top four cars and current lap, is near the start/finish line. A horizontal scoreboard on the backstretch lists the top five cars and laps completed. The antiquated scoreboards, unique 2.5-mile triangular layout, dearth of big-screen TVs, and massive infield structures make Pocono one of the toughest tracks at which to follow an entire race in person, but the atmosphere and crowd enthusiasm don't seem to be at all diminished by these obstacles.

HISTORY

Pocono opened in 1974, during the height of Richard Petty's dominance in stock car racing, and Petty did not disappoint his fans in attendance at that year's Purolator 500. Petty started in the third position and won the rain-shortened contest by pacing his Dodge around the track at an average speed of 115.593 mph. Petty became the track's first two-time winner by taking the checkered flag again in 1976. Darrell Waltrip is tied with Tim Richmond, Bill Elliott, and Rusty Wallace as the winningest drivers at Pocono with four victories each. Waltrip earned his first Pennsylvania checkered flag in the Coca-Cola 500 in 1978. Waltrip beat the track record for best average speed by more than 14 mph, when he achieved a mark of 142.540 mph, a record that stood for thirteen seasons and twenty-three races. Three seasons later, Waltrip became the first driver to win from the pole at Pocono.

After years of waiting, Pocono finally received a second race on the Winston

Cup schedule in 1982. Dave Marcis may not be a household name, but on June 6, 1982, he made a name for himself as a good sport. Bobby Allison was leading the Van Scoy 500 but ran out of gas. Tim Richmond assumed the lead as Marcis nestled in behind Allison and pushed his car into the pits. Allison managed to fuel up and return to the track without losing a lap. Allison eventually regained the lead and won the race. Richmond finished second. Ironically, Marcis and Richmond drove for the same car owner, J. D. Stacy. Bobby Allison went on to sweep the two races that season with a win over Tim Richmond, the only other driver to finish on the lead lap. Allison became the first driver to win three consecutive races at Pocono with a victory in the 1983 Van Scoy 500. They were his only three wins at Long Pond. Richmond became just the second driver to win from the pole at Pocono in the second Pocono race of the 1983 season. It was his first Winston Cup win at a superspeedway.

Bill Elliott swept the Pocono races in 1985, starting from the pole in the first race. Tim Richmond extended his dominance by winning the next three races at Long Pond, including a sweep of the 1986 season races. In 1987, Dale Earnhardt ended Richmond's reign and found his way to victory lane in the second race at Pocono. Earnhardt started the race in the sixteenth position, becoming the first driver to win from outside the top twelve qualifying positions. On the first lap of the 1988 AC Sparkplug 500, Bobby Allison was involved in a near-fatal wreck in turn two. It was the last race of his illustrious career.

Dale Earnhardt was not generally recognized for his kindness and good nature on the racetrack. Late in the season, during the 1991 Miller Genuine Draft 500, Rusty Wallace was leading the race but running low on fuel as the race was flagged for a rain delay. As the race resumed under caution, Earnhardt, who was uncharacteristically several laps down, pushed Wallace around the track for a few laps to help Wallace conserve fuel. As the rain started again, Wallace restarted his engine to run a lap under power and was awarded the win after just 447.5 miles, when the race was called due to rain. According to NASCAR rules only the final lap must be completed without the aid of a competitor, so it was all perfectly legal. It was Wallace's first of four wins at Long Pond.

On June 14, 1992, Alan Kulwicki broke Bill Elliott's track record with an average speed of 144.023 mph, as Ford swept the top three spots in the Champion Sparkplug 500. It was the last win of Kulwicki's brief career. On June 13, 1993, a fan at Pocono scaled an infield fence and sprinted across the track in front of race leader Kyle Petty during the Champion Sparkplug 500. Petty managed to avoid a mishap and went on to win the race. The fan, who needless to say had been drinking, was apprehended and charged with several felony offenses and two misdemeanors. Pocono is not particularly kind to pole sitters; through the first Pocono race of 2001, only seven drivers have won from the pole and nobody has done it twice. In 1994 the pole sitter won twice, as Rusty Wallace and Geoffrey Bodine each accomplished the feat.

The following season, Terry Labonte broke his own track record by winning despite starting from the twenty-seventh position. Six years earlier he set the record by winning from the twenty-third spot. On July 21, 1996, Rusty Wallace established the track's best average speed with a mark of 144.892 mph in a race that lasted just three hours, twenty-seven minutes, and three seconds. Jeremy Mayfield visited victory lane for the first time by outdueling the field of the Pocono 500 on June 1, 1998. Mayfield started in the third position and beat out pole sitter Jeff Gordon by .340 seconds. Mayfield won again in 2000, beating out Dale Jarrett and Ricky Rudd, as Ford swept the top three spots in a race that was delayed until Monday by rain. Rudd broke an eighty-eight-race drought with a victory in the 2001 Pocono 500. Rudd became just the seventh driver to win from the pole as he dove inside to complete a three-wide pass of leader Dale Jarrett, who was battling Dale Earnhardt Jr. on the 177th lap. Rudd held off Jeff Gordon by 1.11 seconds for the win. On July 29, 2001, Bobby Labonte earned his first victory of the season by passing Dale Earnhardt Jr. with just four laps remaining.

GETTING TO THE TRACK

Insiders will tell you that traffic here is among the worst in all of Winston Cup. Only Vegas and Loudon, New Hampshire, come close. The nearest major highway is I-80, which slows to a crawl on race day. The main entrance to the facility is on Highway 115, three miles from I-80 at exit 43, but Highway 115 is a two-lane road that often backs up to a stop. Long Pond Road leads from the main entrance to the track parking lots and can be a nightmare in its own right. If you are entering from 115, park in the very first open lot on your left to shorten your wait upon exiting.

From the south, you can take I-476, the NE extension of the Pennsylvania Turnpike, to exit 95, which is I-80 East, drive to the next off-ramp, exit 284 (Route 115), and proceed south for three miles. The track will be on your left. U.S. 209 is a back road that runs east and west between the Turnpike and State Road 33. U.S. 209 intersects with Route 115, south of the track. Leaving the track, locals often take Stoney Hollow Road, north to 940, which leads back to I-80. Unfortunately, so many folks have learned about this "shortcut" that it is almost as congested as the main road. A new access road leading directly to I-80 is planned for upcoming years, but it's not expected to be completed by the 2002 season.

In keeping with the family atmosphere, hayrides are offered from the parking lots to the track entrances. For fans heading to the infield, the vehicle tunnel runs under the track at turn two. The infield opens to cars at 5 A.M., but the line develops around 4 A.M. on Sunday. To stay overnight in the infield you must be in a self-contained recreational vehicle.

WHAT TO SEE AND DO

There are several modest racetracks in the area surrounding Pocono Raceway. Popular favorites that host races throughout race week include **Mountain Speedway**, about 34 miles west in St. Johns, and **Borger's Speedway**, around twenty miles south in Saylorsburg. Mountain Speedway, a semi-banked asphalt oval, claims to be the "fastest 1/3-mile track" in the country and hosts modifieds, late model, pro stocks, street stocks and factory stocks on Saturday nights. Admission is $15 for adults. Call (570) 788-7544 for a race schedule. Borger's is a unique 1/7-mile dirt track with long straights and hairpin turns that host micro-sprints, slingshots and karts on Tuesday, Friday and Saturday nights under the lights. Admission is just $6 for adults. Call (570) 992-8131 for details.

The Poconos are home to 150 lakes, including the man-made, 5,600-acre Lake Wallenpaupack, countless streams, more than a dozen waterfalls, a wealth of wildlife, and some great fishing. So bring your outdoor gear. Call the **Fish & Boat Commission** at (717) 657-4518 for information on the best fishing spots, licenses, and motorboat registration. The Appalachian Trail runs through the Poconos and there are dozens of state-maintained hiking trails to check out. The **Delaware Water Gap Recreation Area** is a 70,000-acre park that runs on either side of the Delaware River for 37 miles. The park is home to nearly every conceivable outdoor activity. Call (570) 588-2451 for details.

Bushkill Falls has eight natural waterfalls along a moderately easy hiking trail, paddleboat rides, fishing, and a wildlife exhibit of eighty stuffed and mounted animals that live and breed in the Poconos. Admission is $8 per person. A better way to get back to nature might be to take a horseback ride, whitewater rafting or canoe trip, go mountain biking, or even play some paintball. There are a number of stables in the area that offer horseback riding trails. **Pocono Adventures Riding Stable** and **Mountain Creek Riding Stable** are two that are relatively close to the track. **Jim Thorpe River Adventures**, in Jim Thorpe, Pennsylvania, just south of the track, has mountain bike rentals and guided whitewater rafting trips. They do require reservations in advance so call (570) 325-2570. Paintball enthusiasts will want to check out **Splatter Paintball Games** at Jack Frost Mountain. More than 2,500 acres of battlegrounds make this a great place to play. Call (800) 468-2442 for details.

The **Camel Beach Water Park**, in Tannersville, has eight water slides, including the 800-foot Titan, kids' play zones, a swimming pool, the new Kahuna Lagoon wave pool, an adventure river, bumper boats, and miniature golf. Fun for families with small children, especially during the second Pocono race week. **Thunder Creek Quarry**, at Mountain Manor Inn and Golf Club, offers go-karts, bumper boats, and miniature golf. **S&S Speedways**, on Gilbert Road in Effort, claims that Tony Stewart and other drivers have stopped by for a race in years past.

Summertime in the Poconos presents a surprising number of big-name entertainers. The **Coors Light Amphitheatre** at Montage Mountain features live music from the biggest names in rock, country, and pop musicians. Upcoming shows are listed on concerthotline.com and tickets can be charged at (560) 693-4100. If all else fails, there's always shopping. **The Crossing Factory Stores** off I-80 at exit 45 has 100 stores and the added benefit of no state tax on clothes and shoes.

NIGHTLIFE IN POCONOS

The good folks at **Barley Creek Brewing Pub** brew their own ales and lagers on site. They offer outstanding pub food from fish and chips to ribs in a comfortable, casual setting. The pub has an outdoor patio and its own Wiffle ball stadium. Located off exit 45, at the corner of Sullivan Trail and Camelback Road in Tannersville.

Alaska Pete's Roadhouse Grill & Moondog Saloon is a relatively new place in Marshall Creek. It's not particularly close to the track, but for folks staying nearby it's one of the few places to offer casual dining and nightlife. The saloon offers a dozen beers on tap, a pair of giant-screen TVs, and a friendly atmosphere. **Werry's Pub**, just across the street, offers live music on the weekends, an outdoor deck, and better-than-average "pub grub" from burgers to crab legs.

The **Deer Head Inn** is a classic country inn on Main Street in Delaware Water Gap. They feature live jazz at night during the summer months. Call (570) 424-2000 for upcoming acts and cover charge information. Sports fans tend to migrate to the **Goal Line** at 279 South Courtland Street in East Stroudsburg. This intimate place offers a giant-screen TV and two smaller monitors, darts, air hockey, and a kitchen that stays open until eleven at night for late-night noshing.

McGurk's Tavern, at 1946 West Main Street on the outskirts of Stroudsburg, is a friendly place that serves sandwiches, wings, and other assorted pub grub. A pair of televisions grace the place, and they offer live music on Friday and karaoke on most Saturday nights. The **Pocono Pub**, established in 1923, offers live music on Saturday nights, sports on their giant-screen television, as well as food and drink specials nightly. There's also pool and darts, an outdoor patio, and a convenient location across from the Holiday Inn on Route 611, at exit 46B off I-80.

Caesars Pocono Resorts has four hotels in the area, and they often host national-caliber musicians and stand-up comedians. Call (800) 522-5071 to see who is booked at the four resorts.

WHERE TO EAT

Woody's Country House is a tiny place on Route 115, minutes from the track. The food is outstanding, affordable pub fare, the beverage selection is somewhat limited, but the friendly service and convenient location are tough to beat. A back patio nearly doubles the seating capacity. Just across the street and up the road about 1 mile from the track, **Murphy's Loft** is really two places in one. The main bar and dining room are housed in a cabin built in 1934. It's not much to look at, but the drinks are very reasonably priced and the service attentive. The newer glass-enclosed patio offers a pool and bar that looks oddly out of place, but it's a great place to eat and drink among race fans. Don't be fooled by the decor; this place has terrific meals. Dale Earnhardt Jr. and his crew are said to have taken over the place when they came to Pocono for testing in June 2001.

Edelweiss, not far from the track, on Route 940 between Blakeslee and Mount Pocono, has been offering Swiss and German specialties for forty years. They also serve American dishes and are open for breakfast, lunch, and dinner. Bring an appetite and feel free to dress casually. A little farther up the street you'll find **Robert Christian's**. They claim to be "casual, country dining at its best" and may be much more than that. The atmosphere is more fine dining than country, and the menu ranges from crab cakes to New York strip. Specials vary daily, while all entrees come with soup and salad. The **Chateau at Camelback**, in Tannersville at 300 Camelback Road, is an exclusive place that is popular with drivers, team owners, and race officials. They specialize in prime rib and chops. Reservations are required.

Beaver House is an upscale seafood place with five dining rooms, just north of Stroudsburg at 1001 North Ninth Street. They specialize in live Maine lobsters but also serve a mean prime rib. They are open seven days a week for dinner only. **Bailey's Grille & Steakhouse**, in Mount Pocono, has an inviting atmosphere that's kid-friendly. They offer everything from burgers and wings to pasta and seafood in a casual setting. They are open for lunch and dinner every day. **Andrew Moore's Stone Bar Inn** is an upscale place with fine food and extensive wine and beer selections. This place has been around since 1936 and specializes in prime Angus steaks, North Atlantic seafood, and wild game.

For simpler fare, check out the **Snydersville Diner** for breakfast, lunch, or dinner. They offer hearty chow, such as roast beef sandwiches and mashed potatoes with gravy, served in huge portions and moderately priced. This place has been in business since I vacationed in the Poconos as a kid. They are open every day from 6 A.M. to 11 P.M. and open twenty-four hours on Friday and Saturday. **Van Gilder's Jubilee**, in Pocono Pines, is another outstanding breakfast spot that has been around for ages. They are open every day for breakfast, lunch, and dinner but are renowned for their massive breakfasts, which are served every day until 3 P.M. The adjacent pub, **Pub in the Pines**, has fifteen beers on tap and a 10-foot projection TV for major sporting events.

The **Red Rooster**, on Route 715 just north of Tannersville, serves Italian and American seafood dishes, as well as steaks and chops in a casual atmosphere. Open for dinner Tuesday through Saturday, and for lunch on Friday and Saturday, you'll find a nice variety of menu choices at reasonable prices. On Lake Harmony, **Nick's Lake House** offers waterfront dining, indoors or on the deck. They feature seafood, steaks, and gourmet pizza. They're open for lunch and dinner every day and offer breakfast on the weekends. **Shenanigans** is another fine dining restaurant on Lake Harmony that offers entertainment nightly. They serve lunch and dinner seven days a week. The adjoining dance club **Baby Boomers** features music of the fifties and sixties.

LOCAL MEDIA

The *Pocono Record* is the local newspaper. Race broadcasts can be heard via Motor Racing Network on WZZO-FM, 95.1, or via the track's 99.5 FM, which also carries a MRN feed. Folks in RVs will want to check out channel 20, which provides low-power television coverage of the race.

WHERE TO STAY

HOTELS

The Pocono Mountains have been a resort area since long before Winston Cup races came to town, so there are quite a few worthwhile places to stay. It's estimated that 59 percent of fans travel from out of state, however, so the better hotel rooms—as far away as Scranton, Allentown, and Wilkes-Barre—book weeks in advance. With this in mind, reserve a room as soon as possible.

Best Western at the corner of I-80 and 115 in Blakeslee (800) 780-7234 or (570) 646-6000   This brand-new hotel has a pool, continental breakfast, and free parking and it's just 3 miles from the track.

Blue Berry Mountain Inn   Thomas Road in Blakeslee (570) 646-7144   A handsome bed-and-breakfast inn with a heated pool, whirlpool, and billiard room, as well as access to canoeing, fishing, and hiking trails.

Clarion   1220 West Main Street, Stroudsburg (570) 424-1930   A well-kept establishment with an indoor pool, restaurant and lounge, and game room just 10 miles from the track.

Comfort Inn   I-80 and Route 940 (570) 443-8461   About 10 miles from the track in Whitehaven, this motel has an indoor and outdoor pool, whirlpool, game room, and a handful of restaurants within walking distance.

Howard Johnson I-80 and Route 611, Bartonsville (570) 424-6100 Near the Crossing Outlet Mall and a handful of restaurants, about 30 miles from the track, this modest place offers an indoor heated pool, game room, restaurant, and lounge on site.

Pocono Ramada Inn 809 Route 940, Lake Harmony (570) 443-8471 Just 10 miles from the track, this is one of the nicer chain hotels in the area with two restaurants and a lounge on site. There's also a volleyball court, basketball, and hiking trails. The Stable, an adjacent restaurant, is a favorite of Winston Cup teams staying in the area.

Resort at Split Rock 1 Lake Drive (800) 255-7625 or (570) 722-9111 This is about as nice as it gets in the Poconos. Accommodations range from simple rooms to four-person villas, but they are all top-notch and require a minimum three-night stay. Three pools on site and all the activities you could ask for, just 6 miles from the track. They tend to book solid by December for the following race season, so call as soon as you have secured tickets.

Caesars Resorts has four properties in the Poconos. They are all-inclusive type resorts where your meals and activities are included. They may not be your typical race fan accommodations, but if you enjoy heart-shaped tubs, round beds, mirrored ceilings, and champagne glass hot tubs, these are the places for you. They also offer nationally known entertainers and a host of activities, such as golf, tennis, archery, hiking, biking, fishing, and billiards, as well as all-you-can-eat breakfast and dinner buffets. Call (800) 522-5071 for details.

CAMPSITES

W.T. Family Campground is a kid-friendly place to camp with a heated pool, slot car racing on a re-creation of Pocono Raceway, hiking trails, and wooded sites. They also offer RV rentals on site, but they tend to sell out early. Call (570) 646-9255 for details. **Fern Ridge Campgrounds**, across from the Best Western just 5 miles from the track, offers tent and RV camping, as well as cabin rentals. There's a heated swimming pool, basketball, volleyball, horseshoes, and a trout stream on site. Call (570) 646-2267 or (800) 468-2442 for reservations.

Good to Know

- To charge tickets or for additional race information, call (800) 722-3929.
- To get on the campsite waiting list, call (570) 646-2300.
- Mail orders can be sent to Pocono Raceway Ticket Office, P.O. Box 500, Pocono, PA 18334-0500.

- The Pocono Mountains Vacations Bureau can be reached at (800) 762-6667. They offer a free vacation guide with a helpful list of hotels, restaurants, attractions and campgrounds.
- A worthwhile city Web site is www.800poconos.com.
- The official racetrack Web site is www.poconoraceway.com.

In Pennsylvania you cannot buy beer or wine at the grocery store. Wine and liquor are sold in specialty shops, while beer is available at distributors and, oddly, pizza places. **Pizza Nut** is on 115 between I-80 and the track, but for better prices, quantity, and selection go to **Harmony Beverage**, just west of the track on Route 940. Nearby on 940, you'll find **Ahart's**, the closest grocery store.

NEARBY WINSTON CUP RACE CITIES

Dover Downs: 165 miles (three hours)
Richmond: 335 miles (six hours)
New Hampshire: 360 miles (six hours, thirty minutes)
Martinsville: 515 miles (eight hours, thirty minutes)
Bristol: 540 miles (nine hours, fifteen minutes)

IN THE VICINITY

Less than two hours to the south, **Philadelphia** is one of our nation's truly great cities. If you've never been, be sure to visit the historical sites such as the **Liberty Bell**, **Independence Hall**, **Congress Hall**, and **Old City Hall**. The "City of Brotherly Love" is home to several outstanding museums—the **Pennsylvania Academy of the Fine Arts**, **The Franklin Institute**, **Philadelphia Museum of Art**, **Norman Rockwell Museum**, the **Rodin Museum**, and the **Barnes Foundation** in nearby Merion.

For an authentic Philly cheese steak, try Pat's or Geno's in South Philly, or Campo's in the Old City area, but Philadelphia is also known as a terrific restaurant city, especially the world-class eateries along Walnut Street. While you are in town, check out the diverse array of nightclubs along South Street and the Delaware River Waterfront.

For more information on Philadelphia sights, attractions, restaurants, and hotels call the **Philadelphia Visitor's Center** at (800) 537-7676.

▪ *TALLADEGA SUPERSPEEDWAY* ▪

Talladega, Alabama

*"Move the grandstands back, throw the plates away, and
let us run, no matter if we go over 200 again."*

— DALE EARNHARDT

Not everybody is a fan of restrictor plate racing, but the longest track on the
NASCAR/Winston Cup circuit has become legendary in the eyes of its fans. At 2.66
miles long, Talladega is considered to be the fastest, widest, and most exciting stock
car track currently in use. Drivers regularly exceeded 200 mph in qualifying before
Bobby Allison's terrifying 1987 crash in which his car almost flew through the
retaining wall and into the stands. Restrictor plates were mandated for safety in
1988, and many drivers insist they have felt less safe since then, because cars tend
to bunch up all race long and a single mistake can result in a horrific multicar
wreck, a.k.a. the Big One.

In addition to being long and fast, Talladega is known for its 33-degree banked
turns and a narrow 18-degree tri-oval where drivers reach incredible speeds on the
4,300-foot frontstretch. The backstretch, a true straightaway, is not quite as long at
4,000 feet, but it remains the longest in NASCAR. Despite the backstretch's subtle
2-degree banking, drivers regularly exceed 190 miles per hour between turns two
and three.

The first thing that strikes you as you walk into the facility is the sheer size of the
place. More imposing than Daytona, Talladega features four lanes of asphalt where
side-by-side-by-side racing is commonplace, even in the turns. Teams generally feel
it's easier to get a car set up to handle well for Talladega than Daytona and that Talladega is a less weather-sensitive track. No other racetrack presents four-wide racing
as often as Talladega. In recent years, races here have gained a reputation for suf-
fering one big wreck that often eliminates a quarter of the field in spectacular fash-

Four wide through the turns at Talladega is a common occurrence. *(Photo by Author)*

ion. This place is so big that even the spotters are said to have portions of the track they can't see along the backstretch.

Despite the track's size, there are a surprising number of worthwhile seats at Talladega. Tower seats along the frontstretch, especially in rows 26 and higher, offer a tremendous view of nearly the whole track. In sections along the tri-oval and into turn one, the very back rows of the lower level offer shade and a decent view of almost the entire frontstretch, but my favorite seats were those in the Birmingham Tower. On my most recent visit, I sat in row 42 (of fifty) between the end of pit row and the start/finish line and could see practically every square foot of track. Seats here offer comfortable metal chairs and the sections are only thirty-four seats across, so you can get from the middle to an aisle quite easily. Seats in the upper rows of Tri-Oval Tower, the highest section at the track, the O. V. Hill South Tower, overlooking victory lane, and Talladega Tower, situated above the flagstand, are more expensive, and arguably better, but for my money, I like the Birmingham and Moss-Thornton Towers.

Another pleasant surprise was that concessions, programs, and tickets can be downright reasonable at Talladega. Comparable seats and souvenirs at Daytona, a track that folks generally compare to Talladega, cost considerably more. Unlike Daytona, Talladega seems to have few unused tickets for sale on race day. Scalpers congregate off-property along I-20, but a handful of fans looking to break even on an extra ticket can be found after parking your car. I even had a cute ticket taker offer to sell me a "comp" infield ticket for $35. I thanked her but found an even better deal on the frontstretch. A system of not-so-convenient trams carry ticketed fans from one side of the track to the other, so backstretch fans can partake of the souvenir vendors and entertainment area on the front side of the track. Fans sitting on the frontstretch won't miss much if they don't bother venturing to the backside of Talladega. A shuttle van offers rides to the Motorsports Hall of Fame, located at the speedway, east of the north tunnel between turn four and Speedway Boulevard.

The Coleman Camping area outside turns one and two offers an enclosed area of reserved campsites, rest room, and shower facilities. Spots here cost $250 for the week, and while I was at the track, Coleman sponsored driver autograph sessions nearby. Across Speedway Boulevard from the track, unreserved, primitive camping spots are free. A second area offers reserved weekend spots for $50.

Talladega has its flaws. Race action can be a long way from your seat for considerable stretches of the day because the track is so big, and lap times can easily exceed forty-five seconds—as compared to sixteen- to twenty-second laps run at short tracks. A race here can often have more than twenty lead changes, and even if you pay attention to the race leaders, you'll be fortunate to see a third of them happen from your seat. If you want to see the race action, many infield and backstretch seats are barely worth having. Infield fans at Talladega are legendary for being hard-core party fans that can get downright crude. This is no place for the meek, but if you can hold your own in a sloppy Mardi Gras atmosphere, this is the place to be.

Also, for much of the day, races at Talladega can have limited communication between drivers, crew chiefs, and spotters, so scanners are not nearly as helpful here as they are at shorter tracks. I certainly don't want to discourage fans from making the trip to Talladega, because I hoped races at the sport's biggest track would be as exciting as my Daytona experiences, but I wonder if a race here is, in some ways, better watched on TV.

HISTORY

Completed in 1969, Talladega has a remarkable history of high speeds and close finishes. The first race at Talladega almost didn't happen. Drivers were not comfortable with the way tires wore down at the track, and many big-name drivers boycotted the race in 1969, including Charlie Glotzbach, who had qualified his car for the pole. Richard Brickhouse inherited Glotzbach's Dodge and went on to win the race as Dodge swept the first four spots. It was Brickhouse's first career Winston Cup victory.

Since 1970 Talladega has hosted two Winston Cup races per season. Pete Hamilton, the 1968 Rookie of the Year, won both races at Talladega in 1970, beating out Bobby Isaac twice. Isaac settled for second twice that season, despite earning the pole for both races.

Donnie Allison won the Winston 500 from the pole in 1971. Allison earned the pole again that fall, but Bobby Allison, who started beside Donnie, took the checkered flag while Richard Petty came in second. The 1973 Winston 500 had sixty cars start the race, and a track-record forty-three cars did not finish. David Pearson won as the only car on the lead lap. One of the season's most remarkable upsets happened in the 1973 Talladega 500. Dick Brooks, a substitute driver, was a lap down with thirteen laps to go when race leader Buddy Baker experienced engine trouble. Brooks beat Baker back to the caution flag to make up his lap and proceeded to hold off Baker and Pearson to score his only NASCAR victory.

Richard Petty earned his first Talladega victory in 1974, while his second (and last) Talladega checkered flag came nine years later. The illustrious DeWayne "Tiny" Lund died in a seventh-lap, multicar crash on the backstretch at Talladega in 1975. Lund's good friend Buddy Baker swept the races at Talladega in 1975 and made it three races in a row with a victory in the 1976 Winston 500. Baker earned four career Winston Cup wins at Talladega with another Winston 500 win in 1980. Darrell Waltrip, who also had four career wins at Talladega, swept the 1982 season to give him two wins in each race.

Cale Yarborough earned four consecutive poles from 1983 to 1984 but won just one race in that time frame. Bill Elliott did Cale one better by earning five straight poles from 1985 to 1987, and took the checkers in the 1985 Winston 500 and the 1987 Talladega 500. Elliott set the all-time track qualifying record, completing a 2.66-mile lap in 44.998 seconds on April 30, 1987. His time trial lap of 212.809 mph still stands as the fastest qualifying speed at Talladega. Bill Elliott's high-speed records did not translate into more wins at Talladega, as his 1987 victory was his last at the superspeedway. Davey Allison beat Elliott in the 1987 Winston 500 that was shortened to 178 laps because of darkness, for his first career victory. The hometown hero won three times at Talladega, in a career that was tragically cut short when he crashed his helicopter trying to land at Talladega Superspeedway on July 12, 1993. The following day he died from head injuries suffered in that crash.

The track has a history for first-time winners, as eight drivers earned their first career victory at Talladega. Phil Parsons earned his first and only Winston Cup win at Talladega, beating out Bobby Allison and Geoff Bodine in the spring of 1988 despite falling to last place when he pitted under green early in the race. The most recent first-time winner at Talladega was Kenny Schrader, who beat out Geoffrey

Bodine and Dale Earnhardt as Chevrolet took the top three spots in the 1988 DieHard 500. Dale Earnhardt swept the 1990 season at Talladega, winning from the pole that fall. Enhancing the track's reputation for exciting finishes, ten races have been won with final lap passes. Ernie Irvan was the last to do so in 1993. It was Irvan's second straight victory at the track and his last ever win at Talladega. Sterling Marlin has enjoyed some success at Talladega with back-to-back wins in the fall of 1995 and spring of '96. Marlin won from the pole in 1995 and has fourteen top-ten finishes in thirty-seven career starts. On May 10, 1997, Mark Martin set a track record with an average speed of 188.35 mph in the first caution-free race ever run at Talladega Superspeedway.

Surprisingly, the track has a short list of multiple winners. The "Man in Black," Dale Earnhardt, is at the top of that list with ten victories, six in the spring and four in the fall race. Waltrip, Baker, and Bobby Allison each had four wins. Davey Allison, David Pearson, and Cale Yarborough finished their careers with three wins each. Among active drivers, only Sterling Marlin, Terry Labonte, Mark Martin, and Jeff Gordon had more than one Winston Cup win at Talladega through the 2001 season.

Dale Earnhardt's final career victory, in the 2000 Alabama 500, is considered to be one of the greatest comebacks in all of racing, as he won despite being in eighteenth place with just five laps remaining. Jeff Gordon has developed a reputation as a dominant restrictor plate driver, winning the 1996 DieHard 500 in a race called after 129 laps because of rain and darkness. He won the 2000 Talladega 500 despite starting in the thirty-sixth position, the worst starting position ever to win at Talladega. In a race that saw ten drivers swap the lead twenty-seven times, Gordon avoided a sixteen-car wreck on lap 132 and took the lead on lap 183.

The 2001 Talladega 500 was the track's second-ever caution-free race. The race featured thirty-seven lead changes among twenty-six drivers. Never before had more than half the field led at least one lap of a race here. Twenty-eight cars finished on the lead lap, another track record. Bobby Hamilton took the checkered flag by leading just three laps all day, yet another race record. Hamilton's average speed was 184.003 mph and the race lasted just two hours, forty-three minutes, and four seconds. Hamilton was in tenth place with eleven laps to go but learned a thing or two from Dale Earnhardt's win the previous fall and earned his first Talladega win in his nineteenth start at the track. It was also his fourth career Winston Cup victory.

Dale Earnhardt Jr. continued his dominance in restrictor plate races with a thrilling win on October 21, 2001. Junior led the race eleven times for sixty-seven laps and was in front when Bobby Labonte and Bobby Hamilton got tangled up on the backstretch of the final lap causing the Big One that everyone feared was inevitable at Talladega. Junior held off Tony Stewart and Jeff Burton for his first win at Talladega. The good news is that nobody was seriously injured and the massive wreck resulted in a significant change in "aero" package rules for restrictor plate tracks.

GETTING TO THE TRACK

Talladega is among the easiest tracks to get to in all of Winston Cup racing. Located just off Interstate 20, 105 miles west of Atlanta and 40 miles east of Birmingham, the traffic is remarkably well managed considering that 180,000 to 200,000 fans are converging on this giant track in the middle of nowhere. Traffic tends to be more of a problem coming from Birmingham than from Atlanta, or better yet, Anniston, Alabama.

Parking is ample and free. If you want to exit quickly, your best bet is to turn left into the very first lot you see that will allow you to make a right turn back in the direction you want to leave in. Folks with private planes should consider flying into Talladega Municipal Airport, adjacent to the track.

For those folks who, like the author, travel by car, the track publishes a helpful guest guide with entry and exit "hot tips" outlining traffic patterns, construction updates, and potential shortcuts. The guide also presents parking options that allow for easier access no matter which direction you approach the track from. This guide is revised annually and is available by calling the ticket office well in advance.

WHAT TO SEE AND DO

The **International Motorsports Hall of Fame** is located at the track and is home to more than $20 million worth of vehicles. Three enormous showrooms hold more than 100 cars that date back 100 years. More than just stock cars, you'll see Indy cars, drag racers, muscle cars, motorcycles, and even the Budweiser Rocket Car, which was the first land vehicle to travel faster than the speed of sound, reaching 739.6 mph in 1979. A separate hall hosts the plaques and histories of more than sixty inductees from all ends of the racing spectrum. The hall did not waive the five-year minimum for Dale Earnhardt upon his death in 2001, so we can expect him to be nominated and inducted in 2006. A formal induction ceremony is held each spring at the Hall of Fame on the Thursday evening before race weekend. Call (256) 362-5002 for more information.

Also of interest to race fans is the **Talladega-Texaco Walk of Fame**, a sidewalk shaped like the tri-oval speedway that allows fans to see plaques dedicated to drivers at Davey Allison Memorial Park in downtown Talladega. On the Saturday evening before the fall Winston Cup race, two inactive drivers and one active driver are inducted in a ceremony that is open and free to the public. Buses shuttle fans to the park from the track for the ceremony. In recent years, World of Outlaw and Super Late Model races have been held about a half-mile east of the track on Friday and Saturday nights at the **Talladega Short Track**. Located on Speedway Boulevard close to I-20, this one-third mile, high-banked clay oval has become a popular place for race fans to gather on nights leading up to the Winston Cup race. Races are generally held at 8 P.M., but call (256) 831-1413 for a complete track schedule. For reserved seats to World of Outlaw races, call (515) 987-1220 in advance.

Moore's Family Fun Center, a go-kart track in Oxford, just off I-20 near Anniston, is also popular with fans and race crews. This wide oval track is reminiscent of Indy, with a rectangular track surrounded by used tires that serve as retaining walls. For race week, they run what they call super-karts, ten to fifteen at a time, and charge $10 for an eight-minute session. This place also offers softball batting cages and an indoor arcade with pool tables and video games.

DeSoto Caverns Park, just south of Talladega in Childersburg, features the Great Onyx Chamber, an onyx and marble cavern that's 120 feet tall and more than 300 feet long. Special laser light shows and fountain displays within the cave are a highlight of any visit here. The caves were considered sacred ground by the Creek Indians, played a role in the Civil War, and actually became a popular speakeasy during Prohibition. Tours and kids activities are available daily. Call (800) 933-2283 for details. Alabama is a haven for outdoor activities and fishing. The **Alabama Mountain Lakes Association** offers a complimentary brochure with information on area sights and outdoor attractions. Contact them at (800) 648-5381.

Six Flags over Georgia, an amusement park in Austell, Georgia, has more than 100 rides and attractions spread out over 330 acres. Highlights include the Ninja and the Georgia Scorcher, two of the finest roller coasters in the Southeast. A little more than an hour east of the track and half an hour from Atlanta, Austell has a variety of moderately priced chain hotels—Days Inn, La Quinta, and Sleep Inn—and a handful of restaurants to choose from. If you are coming from the east and can't find accommodations closer to the track, this is a fine place to stay for a race at Talladega.

Huntsville, Alabama, about an hour and forty-five minutes north of Talladega, is home to the **U.S. Space and Rocket Center** and the **NASA Marshall Space Flight Center**. The collection of rockets and space exploration vehicles is among the world's largest. The center's hands-on displays allow participants to simulate many of the sensations of space travel. A full-size space shuttle replica, the Spacedome IMAX theater, and the Space Station Development Center are among the highlights of the guided tour. Admission, including all the above and more, is just $14.95. Call (800) 637-7223 or (256) 837-3400 for additional information.

Be sure to bring along your golf clubs when you visit Talladega. The **Robert**

Trent Jones Golf Trail has fifty-four holes of extraordinary public golf within an hour of the speedway. All told, the RTJ Golf Trail is a network of twenty-one public courses designed by Jones. Call (800) 949-4444 for more information and tee times at courses near the track.

NIGHTLIFE IN TALLADEGA

Talladega regulars will tell you that local nightlife does not exist, nor would you want it to. There are a few exceptions in Anniston. **Alabama Show Palace** is a live music and dance club that's open all day, everyday, just seventeen miles from the track at 1503 Hillyer Robinson Parkway, near I-20. This casual honky-tonk has eight pool tables in the main bar, live music on the weekends, karaoke during the week, an extensive menu of appetizers and entrees, ice-cold beer, and a full bar. The back bar has another pair of pool tables. The **Peerless Saloon**, in downtown Anniston at 13 West Tenth Street, is a former brothel dating back to 1899 that has been turned into a comfortable bar. They offer live music in an intimate setting, a full bar, a pool table, and foosball.

Winner's is a relatively new place at 221 South Quintard. This is a good-sized sports bar with plenty of televisions, including a pair of big-screen TVs, two pool tables, a handful of video games, a diverse menu for lunch and dinner, a full bar, and a tremendous selection of domestic and imported beers. **City Limits** is a two-level club on Noble Street with a young dance crowd downstairs and a more laid-back setting upstairs with pool tables and televisions. The **Platinum Club**, at 263 Weatherbrook Lane, is a strip club that is popular with race fans.

The majority of fans I spoke with camped at the track and hung out with friends and family. Others stayed in western Georgia and counted on Atlanta for their nightlife options. Still others I talked to, who came to the track from the west, spent the night in Birmingham and partied there.

Another Talladega nightlife option is **Race Fever Night**, a formal charity dinner held at the track on the Friday evening before the spring races. Tickets are $60 per person and allow fans to meet drivers, participate in a memorabilia auction, and rub elbows with the stars of racing. Call (256) 761-3317 for more information.

WHERE TO EAT

Talladega is situated between Atlanta and Birmingham, so depending on which direction you are approaching the track from, your best bet for lodging, nightlife, and restaurants may be either of these big cities, but there are a handful of worth-while eateries in the smaller towns surrounding Talladega. Two of those towns are Anniston and Oxford, Alabama, about 15 miles east of the track.

Anniston

Betty's Bar-B-Q   401 South Quintard Avenue   This affordable establishment features fast, friendly service, outstanding barbecue, surprisingly good fried chicken, and an entree I did not try: a barbecue salad.

Goal Post Barbecue   1910 Quintard Avenue   Another solid choice for barbecue, this intimate, inexpensive, casual eatery also serves great baked beans as a side dish.

House of Chen   4 East 43rd Street (256) 236-0305   In the Saks neighborhood of Anniston, this moderate-sized place offers authentic Chinese fare, courteous service, and intimate booths in a cozy setting.

Los Mexicanos   1101 South Quintard Avenue   As good as it gets for Mexican food in the area, this humble restaurant offers good-sized portions at a fair price served in comfortable surroundings.

Mata's Greek Pizza & Grinders   1708 Quintard Avenue   Don't let the name throw you: this pizza parlor has the best pizza in town and an incredible Greek salad, a friendly staff, and an ultra-casual atmosphere.

Mikado Japanese Steakhouse   McClellan Plaza (256) 236-1616   This is a terrific place to take a group during race week. Chefs prepare your meal at your table and put on a wonderful show in the process. The teriyaki steak is exceptional, but you really can't go wrong here.

Old Smokehouse Bar-B-Q   631 South Quintard Avenue (256) 237-5200   This affordable, family-oriented place has been around for decades. They specialize in ribs and chicken and everything is hickory-smoked, the old-fashioned way. Their Brunswick stew is also exceptional.

Top o' the River   3220 McClellan Boulevard (256) 238-0097   In years past this was a popular spot with officials, drivers, and their crews. It's still among the finest places to eat in the area, and you may very well encounter racing celebrities on nights leading up to the race.

Victoria Inn   1604 Quintard Avenue (256) 236-0503   About as fancy as it gets in Anniston, this historic mansion turned country inn is home to an upscale restaurant specializing in attentive service and fine dining. This seems to have become the hotspot with teams and officials. Call for reservations.

Oxford

Brad's Bar-B-Q   U.S. Highway 78 East (256) 831-7878   A popular place with a relatively new location, this easygoing eatery has excellent barbecue and if you're feeling a bit daring, order the fried catfish sandwich.

China Luck   503 Quintard Avenue (256) 831-5221   Generally thought of as the area's best Chinese bistro, this well-lit, airy restaurant could hold its own in much larger cities.

Logan's Roadhouse A casual steakhouse that serves baskets of peanuts and encourages you to toss the shells on the floor. They specialize in steaks and chops but also serve burgers, chicken, and a solid kids' menu.

Zack's Mesquite Grill 1613 East Snow Drive This newly remodeled place serves lunch and dinner Tuesday through Saturday. They specialize in steaks, shrimp, and lobster, but their trademark entree is the filet mignon. Call (256) 831-9334 for reservations.

Oxford also offers a number of franchise restaurants to choose from including **Applebee's** on Highway 78 at the intersection of 21 South; **Cracker Barrel** at 220 Morgan Road; **Lone Star Steakhouse** at 171 Colonial Drive; **O'Charley's** on Highway 21 South; and an **Outback Steakhouse** located at 196 Springbranch Drive.

LOCAL MEDIA

The local newspaper is the *Anniston Star*. Motorsports Racing Network carries races at Talladega on WTDR-FM, 92.7.

WHERE TO STAY

HOTELS

Your best bets for quality lodging are in or near Atlanta and Birmingham, but there are also a number of name-brand hotels closer to the track in Carrolton, Georgia, or even closer to Talladega in Oxford and Anniston, Alabama. Adventure Travel, with locations in Atlanta, Birmingham, and Huntsville, is the official travel agency of the speedway and is very helpful in finding rooms within a reasonable drive of the track. Their toll-free number is (888) 673-3499.

Best Western Anniston-Oxford Highway 78 and Alabama 21 (256) 831-3410 One of the first area hotels to sell out on race weekends, this place offers an outdoor pool, a kids' playground, and an advantageous location.

Best Western Crossroads 1202 South Park Street, Carrolton (770) 832-2611 A convenient, clean hotel just south of I-20 near the Alabama/Georgia border about equidistant from the track and Atlanta.

Colony House on Highway 77 is about it for lodging in Talladega. This modest motel offers a swimming pool, restaurant, and lounge. Call (256) 362-0900 for reservations.

Hampton Inn 1600 Highway 21 South, Oxford (256) 835-1492 Another fine place to stay in nearby Oxford with limited amenities but clean, comfortable rooms within a short drive of several worthwhile restaurants.

Holiday Inn Express 850 Speedway Industrial Drive, Lincoln (256) 763-9777 Just 3 miles from the track, this is one of the most convenient and reasonably priced hotels in the area.

Holiday Inn Express 160 Colonial Drive, Oxford (256) 835-8768 One of the newest hotels to spring up in the area, this is where several race teams stay for race week. Lone Star Steakhouse next door also provides room service for the hotel.

Jameson Inn 700 South Park Street, Carrolton (770) 834-2600 A more modest hotel with the same convenient Carrolton location as the aforementioned Best Western Crossroads.

Jameson Inn 161 Colonial Drive, Oxford (256) 835-2170 Fewer rooms than other area hotels, but they offer the same convenience.

Wingate Inn 143 Colonial Drive, Oxford (256) 831-1921 An unassuming motel with few amenities, but a worthwhile location and comfortable rooms.

CAMPSITES

There are a number of campsites within a short drive of the speedway, especially to the west in Pell City, but the closest campground I discovered was the **Dogwood Meadows Campground** about 3 miles north of the track at Highways 77 and 78. They welcome tent and RV campers on the 70-acre campground. Reservations are accepted for trailers and RVs by calling (205) 763-7454. Be sure to ask about the backroads to the track that allow you to avoid most of the traffic on race day.

Good to Know

- To charge tickets or for additional race information, call (256) 362-RACE.
- For camping at the track, call (256) 362-2261.
- Mail orders can be sent to P.O. Box 777, 3366 Speedway Boulevard, Talladega, AL 35161.
- The Talladega Chamber of Commerce can be reached at (256) 362-9075. The Calhoun County Visitors Center can be reached at (800) 489-1087 or (256) 237-3536.
- Worthwhile city Web sites include www.calhounchamber.com and www.talla dega.com.
- ➤ The official racetrack Web site is www.talladegasuperspeedway.com.

NEARBY WINSTON CUP RACE CITIES

Atlanta: 105 miles (one hour, fifty minutes)
Charlotte: 335 miles (six hours)
Daytona: 405 miles (seven hours, thirty minutes)

IN THE VICINITY

Birmingham, Alabama, is a good-sized city with plenty of hotels and restaurants, just 45 miles west of the track. Many folks who attend a race at Talladega fly into Birmingham, stay at an area hotel, and take advantage of the city's hospitality during long race weekends. Birmingham's **Southside** district is home to a number of outstanding nightclubs, including **Studio** and **Bellbottom's**, a pair of dance clubs. Nearby, race fans may want to check out the microbrew beer selection at **The Mill**, a worthwhile brew pub/restaurant, or head to **Dave's Pub** for the comfortable outdoor patio and casual setting.

NASCAR Silicon Motor Speedway offers race simulators at the Riverchase Mall. The **Alabama Sports Hall of Fame**, built in 1992, has inducted more than 170 native sons and daughters. You may be surprised to see the impressive collection of memorabilia and the diversity of sports heroes who have called Alabama home, including NASCAR stars Bobby, Donnie, and Davey Allison as well as Neil Bonnett. Located in Birmingham, this fine facility is open seven days a week, and adult admission is just $5. Call (205) 323-6665 for details and directions. The **Southern Museum of Flight** presents nearly ninety years of aviation history from the Wright Brothers' experimental field at what is now Maxwell Air Force Base near Montgomery to a modest collection of military planes; from Delta Airlines' first plane to homebuilt aircraft and seaplanes. Admission is $3 for adults. For more information call (205) 833-8226.

In addition to chain hotels, consider the **Mountain Brook Inn** at 2800 U.S. Highway 280. Located about five minutes from downtown, this good-sized inn offers a pool, the Savannah Café, and a lounge on site with live entertainment and, perhaps most important, no minimum stay on race weekends. Just up the street you'll find **Ralph & Kacoo's**, an intriguing seafood establishment with New Orleans roots and a Cajun flair. **Ali Baba's**, in nearby Hoover at 110 Centre at Riverchase, offers exceptional Middle Eastern food. For a more complete list of attractions, hotels, nightclubs, and restaurants contact the **Greater Birmingham Convention and Visitors Bureau** at (800) 458-8085 or (205) 458-8000.

■ *TEXAS MOTOR SPEEDWAY* ■

Fort Worth, Texas

"It's a real fast racetrack. . . . It's a real tight corner coming off four. The people who get to the front straightaway the best is usually who puts the show on."

— BOBBY HAMILTON

Touted as "The Great American Speedway," TMS has been hosting the big boys since 1999, so the book on how to win at Texas is still being written. Drivers generally agree that a race here is fast and furious, and they are thrilled with the first-place prize money exceeding $400,000, but nobody claims to have mastered this track yet. After the second Winston Cup race in 1998, the surface at Texas was deemed unsafe because of water seepage problems on the track, so Bruton Smith wasted no time in resurfacing the speedway. While he was at it, he established a Texas-sized speedway with all the amenities a Texas tycoon could ask for. TMS does an astounding amount of corporate suite and hospitality business on race day, but everyday race fans can also have fun here, as nearly every seat in the house has a terrific view of the track.

"Massive" does not begin to describe the magnitude of this place. In fact, TMS is the third-largest sporting facility in the world, and the Winston Cup race held here each spring is the sixth-largest sporting event in the United States. This 1.5-mile quad-oval with 24-degree banks, 147,000 seats, and a monstrous infield may very well be the "cookie-cutter" model for all future speedways. Home to 15,000 camper spots, more parking spaces than Disneyland, and in excess of 210,000 fans on race day, it's no wonder the overall prize purse exceeds $5 million on race day. The track was just repaved after the 2001 Winston Cup race, so once again it's lightning fast. Until the surface has been raced on a few times, however, there will be just one groove, which may limit drivers' opportunity to pass.

Looking down the frontstretch at Texas Motor Speedway. *(Photo by Author)*

If at all possible, purchase a ticket for a seat high up on the frontstretch section, which has sixty-six rows of seats, but don't feel like you have to be right on the start/finish line. Seats near turn four offer the excitement of watching drivers battle with the difficult re-entry to the frontstretch, while seats near the start of turn one have a nice perspective of the approach into a bumpy banked turn that barely seems to slow the cars down. Seats here also have a good look at cars as they exit pit row. The scoring tower, which lists the top twenty drivers and current lap, is near the end of pit row, as is a giant-screen TV. A second scoring tower is in the infield near the start of turn three. Additional giant-screen TVs are situated at the start/finish line and facing seats in turn four.

During a race, cars travel more than 190 mph on the 2,250-foot frontstretch, maintain 155 mph into turn one, and exceed 180 mph on the 1,330-foot backstretch. Drivers will tell you that this track is so fast and skinny, just 58 feet across at its narrowest point, that it's difficult to determine setups for the car, so it can take nearly the whole race to get the car to do what they want. The track presents countless challenges to race teams as they learn their way around at high speed.

Drivers face flat entries into the turns, a bump in the middle of turn one, brutal handling coming out of turn four, and a tight squeeze at the start/finish line. Crew chiefs know that the track is notoriously tough on tires and engine attrition is extraordinary because cars are running at higher than normal speeds for 500 miles, so pit strategy and fuel mileage are generally critical at the end of the race.

Fans will want to get to the track early, as this place has a reputation for horrendous traffic and early mistakes. Many compare Texas Motor Speedway to Atlanta and Charlotte, a pair of 1.5-mile speedways with traffic hassles of their own, but Texas has some significant differences. Transitions in the corners are said to be more difficult at TMS, and three out of five Winston Cup races here have seen the yellow flag wave within the first five laps. In 1999, the caution flag waited until lap 18 to appear. Drivers often start the day searching for setups at Texas, and as they get up to speed something invariably gets loose and at least one driver's day is over before it really got going. You simply hope it's not the guy you drew in this week's race pool.

As the day goes on at TMS, drivers say the bottom of turn two gets slicker and it becomes harder to get off that corner and keep the car out of the fence. On top of all the other challenges at Texas, track position becomes paramount, especially with sixty to seventy laps to go, because there is only one groove with good grip and it is difficult for cars to get back to the front of the pack. From a fan's perspective, the track's dominant flaw may be that side-by-side racing action is rare as drivers are often reluctant to get out of the groove until the very last laps.

Camping facilities at the track are among the nicest on the circuit. The campsite has two 5,100-square-foot rest rooms with forty-four showers. Campers heading to the infield should use the south tunnel. Infield camping facilities include a pair of rest rooms with twenty-nine shower stalls in each building. Texas Motor Speedway also has a .40-mile dirt track with 12-degree turns that hosts World of Outlaws series races on the weekend of the Winston Cup race. The dirt track seats 13,000 fans and generally sells out for Thursday and Friday nights of race weekend. Fans of artist Sam Bass will want to check out his gallery on the eighth floor in the Speedway Club at TMS.

HISTORY

The story of TMS to date can be summed up in five words—five races and five faces. Jeff Burton won the inaugural race in 1997, edging out Dale Jarrett, who started on the pole because qualifying was rained out. It was Burton's first career victory. He started in the fifth qualifying position and took the checkered flag before an enthusiastic, sold-out crowd. Texas was a turning point for Burton, who visited the winner's circle twice more that season, on the way to eighteen top-ten finishes, and ended the season among the top five drivers in the Winston Cup points chase. Texas has been relatively kind to Burton, as he has earned three top-ten finishes in five races. Mark Martin won the following year by the ever-so-slim margin of .573 seconds, enabling Jack Roush Racing to repeat as winners and lead Ford to a sweep of the top three spots.

"Texas" Terry Labonte, who grew up in Corpus Christi and started racing quarter-midgets thirty-five years earlier, did his fans proud as he took the checkered flag in 1999. Dale Jarrett took second place again as Labonte started on the outside of row two and set a track record in his Rick Hendrick Chevrolet with an average speed of 144.276 mph in a race that took just three hours, twenty-eight minutes, and twenty-one seconds. In qualifying the following year, Terry set another track record with a speed of 192.137 mph and lap time of 28.105 seconds in his Chevrolet Monte Carlo. Terry's younger brother, Bobby, has taken third place three times at Texas. Through four races at Texas, the Labonte brothers finished no worse than eighth place. That changed in 2001 as Terry came in thirteenth while Bobby's engine failed on lap 149 and he had to settle for forty-second place and $94,552 in winnings.

On April 2, 2000, Lone Star race fans went wild as Dale Earnhardt Jr. outdueled Jeff Burton to become the second driver to win his first career Winston Cup race at Texas. Junior won the Coca-Cola 300 here two years earlier for his first career Busch Grand National victory. In his rookie Winston Cup season, Earnhardt Jr. went on to win at Richmond, tying the late Davey Allison's modern-era record of two wins in his first sixteen races. Junior also earned two poles and a sixteenth-place finish in the points standings in his rookie campaign. Dale Earnhardt Sr. was said to be particularly proud of Junior's success here, as Dale Sr. started four races at Texas but never managed a top-five finish.

In 2001, Dale Jarrett finally got that elusive Texas victory by outrunning Steve Park and Johnny Benson. After finishing second in 1997 and 1999, Jarrett found his way to victory circle for his second win of the season after pitting on lap 316 for four fresh tires. With his win at Texas, Jarrett became the first driver of the 2001 season to lead the most laps and win the same race. The win also marked the twenty-sixth time he visited victory lane, tying him with Fast Freddy Lorenzen for twentieth all-time. He moved ahead of Lorenzen with a win at Martinsville the following week and became the first three-race winner of the 2001 season. Also significant was Jeff Gordon's fifth-place finish at TMS in 2001. In the four prior races at Texas he had never done better than twenty-fifth place. Texas remains as one of three established tracks currently on the Winston Cup circuit at which Gordon has not won.

In five races there have been five different winners in Texas. Who will be the first to repeat is anybody's guess. Through 2001, the race at Texas has yet to be won from the pole. Each winner had started among the top ten qualifying positions, however.

GETTING TO THE TRACK

The speedway is 20 miles north of Fort Worth, and traffic can be a nightmare. We got to the track at seven in the morning and had to battle with it at that time. As we got inside the track, we could see the roads around the track were backed up for miles. The drive home was no picnic either. We stayed after the race for several hours and still found ourselves mired in some serious traffic on the way home. This is definitely a place to grill out afterward and let the rest of the crowd get a jump on things.

The primary highway is I-35 West, which for reasons I can't explain runs north and south. There are a few worthwhile minor arteries surrounding the track that allow you to avoid the mess on I-35. Highway 377 runs north and south, parallel to I-35, and Route 114 leads east toward Dallas or west to Route 81, but they are predominantly four-lane roads that also get bottled up with local race fans. Route 26 is well east of the track and runs directly toward I-35 just above Fort Worth and can be a good alternate route if you are stuck in the bulk of postrace traffic.

A new road being built from an exit on I-35 will be named Dale Earnhardt Way and should help alleviate some of the traffic hassles. Parking is not terrible at Texas. It can cost $10–20 and you should expect to walk a long way. The souvenir vendor area at Texas is among the largest on the circuit and well worth checking out. Tunnels leading to the infield are at either end of the track and allow access during the race. The pit area at Texas is one of the biggest and newest around. It's worth checking out if you can purchase a pass.

WHAT TO SEE AND DO

This is one NASCAR Winston Cup destination that has no problem keeping fans entertained for a week-long excursion. Fort Worth, Dallas, and Arlington have a wealth of cultural attractions to choose from. The **Fort Worth Stockyards District** is a ten-block historic area that was once one of the largest cattle markets in the world. Today, it's a huge entertainment and shopping complex, where you can take a ride on the **Tarantula Steam Train**, down a few cold ones at the **White Elephant Saloon**, or learn to two-step at **Billy Bob's Texas**, the world's largest country-and-western honky-tonk. The Tarantula is a restored 1896 steam engine that rides the rails from Fort Worth to the historic Cotton Belt Depot in Grapevine. The forty-two mile round-trip ride takes about two and a half hours. Call (800) 952-5717 for details.

The **Kimbell Art Museum**, at 3333 Camp Bowie Boulevard in the Fort Worth Cultural District, generally has free admission when it's not hosting special traveling exhibits. *The New York Times* calls the Kimbell "the nation's best small museum . . . every single picture in the building is worth seeing." In Sundance Square, the **Sid Richardson Collection of Western Art** features sixty paintings and bronze sculptures by Frederic Remington and Charles Russell. Located at 309 Main Street, this is among the nation's most significant collections on public display. Admission is free. The **Fort Worth Museum of Science and History**, at 1501 Montgomery Street, consists of six exhibit halls displaying everything from dinosaurs to computers. The museum is also home to the Noble Planetarium and the Omni Theater, which features an 80-foot domed screen and state-of-the-art sound system. Admission to the museum is $3; films cost extra.

Dallas has its own array of attractions. My favorite is the **Sixth Floor John F. Kennedy Museum** at 411 Elm Street. This is the site of the School Book Depository from which Lee Harvey Oswald is said to have shot President Kennedy. An effort has been made to keep the building laid out exactly as it was when Kennedy was assassinated, giving the place an eerie feeling. Admission is $4; for $2 more you'll be given a Walkman-type cassette player that describes what each exhibit is. The audio tour is well worth the extra couple of dollars, as it routes you through what might otherwise be a confusing, haphazard layout. The museum has become the city's most visited attraction and, to their credit, they do not completely dismiss theories that there may have been others behind Kennedy's assassination. **Speed-Zone**, at 11130 Malibu Drive, is the area's premier go-kart facility with four tracks to choose from. There's something for drivers of every skill level, including 300-horsepower dragsters, a video game room, and a full-service bar and restaurant.

A few miles northwest of downtown Dallas, in the town of Irving, Cowboys fans will want to tour **Texas Stadium** for a behind-the-scenes look at the home of "America's team." You'll see the team locker room, a luxury skybox, and, if you feel the urge, you can charge out of the tunnel onto the field, where you are welcome to run a few pass patterns or kick a field goal or two. Be sure to bring your own ball though. The tour costs $5 for adults. **Grapevine Mills** is a giant shopping and entertainment complex, at 3000 Grapevine Mills Parkway, in the town of Grapevine. The mall features hundreds of shops and a massive food court. The biggest attraction for race fans may be the enormous **Bass Pro Shops Outdoor World** store. There's also a few themed restaurants including Jeckyll & Hyde Club, Dick Clark's American Bandstand Grill, and the Rain Forest Café.

Six Flags over Texas is a 205-acre amusement park adjacent to the ballpark in Arlington with more than 100 rides, shows, and midway games. The park's feature ride is the Texas Giant, rated the number-one roller coaster in the world by *Fast Track* magazine a few years ago. The park is open daily in the summer and on weekends in the spring. The adjacent **Hurricane Harbor** is a water park with more than twenty-five rides spread out over 50 acres that offers a nice respite from the Texas heat. One of the area's more unusual attractions is the **Air Combat School** where you can strap into an actual jet fighter cockpit/flight simulator and dogfight bogey aircraft. Attending ground school and ejection training, donning your flight gear, and the "flight" itself take about an hour and a half. The entire experience costs about $40 per person.

NIGHTLIFE IN DALLAS/FORT WORTH

Billy Bob's Texas, at 2520 Rodeo Plaza in the Fort Worth Stockyards, is like a whole other country! I'm not much of a country music fan, but if all country-and-western bars are this much fun, I completely understand the attraction. With 122,000 square feet of space, this place is absolutely gigantic. A live music stage, dance floor, and main bar occupy the lower level that's surrounded by smaller bars, a second dance floor, pool tables, a gift shop, and a genuine indoor bull-riding arena. Weekends feature nationally recognized country music acts, the clientele is dressed to kill, and couples on the dance floor do whatever it takes to stand out from the crowd. Billy Bob's is open until 2 A.M. seven days a week and has a modest cover charge that varies with the caliber of the band booked. Nearby, at 106 East Exchange Avenue, you'll find the **White Elephant Saloon**, a 100-year-old Wild West bar that *Esquire* magazine lists as one of the 100 best bars in America. Open seven days a week, the White Elephant features live country music nightly.

In case you are not a country music fan, check out the **Pour House Sports Grill**, at 209 West Fifth Street in downtown Fort Worth's Sundance Square. This place has it all, live music, big-screen TV sports, dancing, and an affordable lunch and dinner menu. The **Flying Saucer Beer Emporium**, at 111 East Fourth Street in Sundance Square, is a beer lover's paradise. There are plenty of TVs scattered about the place and the food is outstanding, but the crowds keep coming back for the wonderful selection of handcrafted beers.

Dallas is the place for nightlife. On the edge of the West End Historic District at 211 North Record Street, the **West End Pub** is neither trendy nor fancy. It does have a friendly staff, excellent bar food for lunch or dinner, and a genuine pub atmosphere. **Deep Elum** is the area's premier cutting-edge nightlife district with between fifteen and twenty clubs and restaurants within walking distance of each other. **July Alley**, at 2809 Elm Street, is a dark, rowdy place with outstanding progressive music. **Club Dada**, down the street at 2720 Elm Street, is a solid choice for live music. Other notable clubs include the **Xpo Lounge**, **Adair's Saloon**, **Trees**, and **On the Rocks**. The **Deep Elum Café** is a worthwhile place for a good, inexpensive meal. For more information about Deep Elum happenings, call the **What's Up Line** at (214) 747-DEEP.

Dave & Busters is a massive place that features billiards, no-keeps blackjack casinos, shuffleboard, and video games galore. There's one at 8021 Walnut Hill and another at 10727 Composite. Chances are you'll see a bunch of race fans and an occasional race team hanging out at either location during race week. Blues fans may want to stop by **Blue Cat Blues**, on the edge of Deep Elum at 2617 Commerce. They book regional and nationally known blues acts. **The Improvisation**, at 4980 Beltline Road, is the area's preeminent comedy club.

Another area known for its nightlife is **Greenville Avenue**, between the LBJ Freeway and Ross Avenue, north of downtown. Upper Greenville offers a number of discos and fifties and sixties style clubs, while lower Greenville has its own diversity of pubs and sports bars. Below McCommas on Greenville Avenue, check out **Zubar**, an alternative club and restaurant with a patio overlooking the street that allows for great people-watching, or **Milk Bar**, which offers thumping dance music, a big-city nightclub atmosphere, and a rooftop patio.

West End Marketplace, in downtown Dallas, is a more trendy entertainment area with a Dick's Last Resort, Planet Hollywood, and a number of franchise eateries tucked away in an indoor/outdoor shopping complex. My favorite area watering hole is the **Dallas Brewing Company**, a handsome microbrewery with friendly service and good grub at 703 McKinney Avenue.

WHERE TO EAT

Cattlemen's Steakhouse, in the Fort Worth Stockyards District at 2458 North Main Street, has been serving great steaks since 1947. Reservations are recommended. The **Saltgrass Steakhouse** is not far from the track at 5845 Sandshell Drive in north Fort Worth. It looks like a chain but features fresh everything, from the remarkable thick-cut Angus steaks right down to the croutons in your salad. They pack 'em in on race weekends, so be sure to make a reservation early and bring a hearty appetite. It's not inexpensive, but they offer an excellent variety of steaks, a solid lounge, and attentive service. **Angelo's**, at 2533 White Settlement Road, is the home for inexpensive ribs, barbequed chicken, and beef brisket in Fort Worth. This humble place has a giant stuffed grizzly bear guarding the front entrance, ice-cold beers, and terrific side dishes.

Pappadeaux, at 2708 West Freeway, specializes in fresh seafood meticulously prepared with a Cajun flair and served by an attentive and helpful staff. Next door, **Pappasito's Cantina** offers the same expertise with traditional Mexican fare. They also make one heck of a frozen margarita. **Kincaid's**, at 4901 Camp Bowie Boulevard, offers some of the area's best cheeseburgers. This inexpensive eatery keeps it simple and gets it right. Just up the street, **El Fenix**, an affordable eatery at 6391 Camp Bowie Boulevard, is said to be the original home of Fort Worth Tex-Mex cuisine. A second location can be found at 1814 Green Oaks Road.

My favorite restaurant in Dallas is **Baby Doe's**, a wonderfully rustic place with remarkable American cuisine of steaks, chicken, pasta, and fresh fish. This two-level establishment sits on the side of a hill at 3305 Harry Hines Boulevard and has a terrific view of the Dallas skyline. If money is no object, **Ruth's Chris Steakhouse** prepares the finest cuts of beef, custom aged and hand cut at your table. They have two locations in Dallas, one at 5922 Cedar Spring Road, the other at 17840 Dallas Parkway. **Sonny Bryan's** has been serving ribs, chopped beef barbecue, and onion rings for more than forty years. There are several locations throughout the area, but the original is at 2202 Inwood Road.

LOCAL MEDIA

The *Fort Worth Star Telegram* and the *Dallas Morning News* are both outstanding daily newspapers. The *Dallas Observer* is a free entertainment weekly that can be very helpful in choosing area nightspots. Races are broadcast on the Performance Racing Network, 820 AM WBAP, and on the Motor Racing Network, 103.3 FM KESN.

WHERE TO STAY

HOTELS

There are plenty of places to stay in the Dallas/Fort Worth area. Few places are convenient to the track and the downtown attractions for either city because the track is a good way from both. Fort Worth is slightly closer and hotels near DFW airport are also convenient. In lieu of a place within a few miles of the track, Arlington hotels, farther south than Fort Worth, are still convenient. The town of Grapevine is very close to the track and another destination worth looking into.

Best Western Market Center 2023 Market Center Boulevard, Dallas (214) 741-9000 Convenient to area attractions, this clean, comfortable hotel offers complimentary breakfast, on-site lounge, and a shuttle van.

Candlewood Suites Hotel 5201 Endicott Avenue, Fort Worth (817) 838-8229 About 10 miles south of the track, this place offers good-sized suites with convenient, fully equipped kitchens.

Comfort Inn 2425 Scott Avenue, Fort Worth (817) 535-2591 Just 25 miles from the track, this reputable hotel offers complimentary breakfast, a pool, and tennis courts.

Comfort Inn and Suites 801 West Highway 114, Roanoke (817) 490-1455 Just 3 miles from the track, this is one of the most convenient area hotels. Amenities include an outdoor pool and complimentary breakfast.

Country Inn And Suites 4100 West Carpenter Freeway, Irving (972) 929-4008 Just 2 miles from the airport, this place features suites with full kitchens, as well as complimentary breakfast and social hour.

Drury Inn 4210 West Airport Freeway, Irving (972) 986-1200 One mile from the airport. Complimentary buffet breakfast and courtesy shuttle available.

Embassy Suites–Outdoor World 2401 Bass Pro Drive, Grapevine (972) 724-2600 Top-notch hotel adjacent to the Grapevine Mills Mall, it's actually attached to the Bass Pro Shops Outdoor World. Hotel features an indoor pool, sauna, Jacuzzi, and game room.

Hyatt Regency 300 Reunion Boulevard, Dallas (214) 651-1234 Upscale digs near several downtown Dallas attractions, restaurants, and nightlife options.

La Quinta Inn 825 North Watson Road (817) 640-4142 A reasonably priced place minutes from Six Flags over Texas and Hurricane Harbor.

Mansion on Turtle Creek 2821 Turtle Creek Boulevard, Dallas (214) 559-2100 This exquisite bed-and-breakfast-style inn was once the home of a local oil and cotton tycoon, so you can expect to stay in the lap of luxury and be spoiled rotten by the gracious staff during a stay here.

Ramada Hotel Downtown 1710 Commerce, Fort Worth (817) 335-7000 Nice hotel with an indoor pool and airport transportation available.

The **Cowtown RV Park**, west of Fort Worth in Aledo, about 30 miles from the track, has more than 100 paved, pull-through RV spots with full hookups. They also offer a laundromat, showers, and a pool. They sell out quickly for race weekend, so call (800) 781-4678 for reservations.

Good to Know

- To charge tickets or for additional race information, call (817) 215-8500.
- Mail orders can be sent to P.O. Box 500, Fort Worth, TX 76101-2500.
- The Fort Worth Convention & Visitors Bureau can be reached at (800) 433-5747. The Dallas Convention and Visitors Bureau is at (214) 571-1000. The Arlington Convention and Visitors Bureau can be reached toll free at (800) 342-4305.
- Worthwhile city Web sites include www.fortworth.com, www.dallascvb.com and www.arlington.org.
- ➤ The official racetrack Web site is www.texasmotorspeedway.com.

NEARBY WINSTON CUP RACE CITIES

Kansas City: 525 miles (nine hours and fifty minutes)
Talladega: 720 miles (twelve hours)

IN THE VICINITY

Austin is the state's capital city and offers a nice blend of history and nightlife. The atmosphere on Sixth Street is comparable to Beale Street in Memphis or, to a lesser degree, Bourbon Street in New Orleans. There are dozens of nightclubs and restaurants with just about every type of music you could hope for.

The PBS TV show **Austin City Limits** is taped August through February with 100 seats available to the public. Tickets are free but go quickly, so call (512) 471-4811 ext. 310 or 475-9077 well in advance. The **Lyndon B. Johnson Library**, at 2313 Red River Street, is the most visited presidential library in the nation. It's open from nine to five daily, and admission is free. For more information call (512) 482-5137.

The historic **Driskill Hotel** is a terrific place to stay, right in the heart of the action, at the corner of Brazos and Sixth Street. Call the Austin Convention and Visitors Bureau at (800) 888-8287 for a more complete listing of area attractions, hotels, and restaurants.

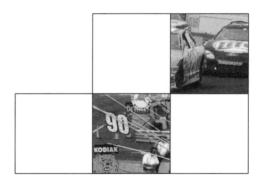

▪ *SEARS POINT RACEWAY* ▪

Sonoma, California

"My father's advice for [Sears Point] was 'just stay on the asphalt and you're going to do all right.' Don't get run over, stay on the pavement, and the ride home ain't too bad."

— DALE EARNHARDT JR.

Nestled in the arid hills of Sonoma, California, Sears Point was built in 1968 as a twelve-turn, 2.52-mile road course in 1968. Twenty-one years later, NASCAR drivers began racing here each year as a part of the Winston Cup circuit. Road course racing presents a number of challenges that NASCAR teams don't face from week to week, namely hills and right turns. One of those turns at Sears Point, turn 11, is a drastic right-hand hairpin turn that leads to the final short straightaway and the start/finish line. This turn has earned the nickname "Calamity Corner" and has been the make-or-break point of many a race at Sears Point. To best illustrate the track's elevation, turn 3 is actually thirteen stories higher than the start/finish line.

The track features other oddities for a NASCAR race: the race is run clockwise, and the pits at Sears Point are separated into two groups. The main pit road is accessed by exiting to the left of turn 11 and running outside the turn toward the start/finish line, but nine pit stalls are to the inside, in an area known as "Gilligan's Island." Drivers who pit here are assessed an eighteen-second wait after the crew finishes working on the car before they can return to the track, because the entrance to Gilligan's Island is much shorter than the entrance to the other pit stalls. In the coming seasons, pit road will be lengthened so all forty-three pit stalls will be on the same side. Another unusual aspect at Sears Point: the race is measured in kilometers, not miles, so the annual Dodge/Save Mart 350 consists of just 112 laps or 224 miles. That's 361.5 kilometers, which is conveniently rounded down to 350.

Tony Stewart ahead of Rusty Wallace in the hairpin turn. *(Photo by Author)*

Sears Point is considered to be the less demanding of the stock car season's two road course races. The track differs from Watkins Glen, the circuit's other current road course, in that it has more turns and hills, as well as fewer straights. As drivers became acclimated to racing at Sears Point, it was obvious that turn 11 provided the only real opportunity to pass without the benefit of a miscue by an opposing driver. Oddly, while turn 11 is the site of much of the action at Sears Point, very few of the seats overlook this portion of the track. In fact, Gilligan's Island and the grand-stands on the approach to turn 11 will be removed altogether before the 2002 race. Fans with garage passes often stand inside the garages and look out the rear win-dows with a view of the pits, the start/finish line, and the entire hairpin turn. This is an especially worthwhile place to be when it's hot outside.

In recent years, track officials set out to make some changes to keep fans—at the track and watching on TV at home—interested as their heroes take on the challenge of a road course. In the hopes of giving NASCAR fans better visibility of the entire course and creating a more competitive race, Sears Point was reconfigured in 1999 by creating "the chute," a straightaway between what was originally turn 4a and turn 7, thereby decreasing the total track length to 1.949 miles. This shorter layout allowed for more laps, hence more chances for fans to see their favorite drivers zoom by, but in the end, it did not present a more competitive race.

In 2001, Sears Point introduced some major changes that seem to have done the trick. The track was lengthened to 2 miles, as "the chute" between turns 4a and 7 was extended by 300 feet. This created an 870-foot straight that allows drivers to reach speeds of 110 mph. The trickiest part of the track is the approach to turn 10, where drivers can reach 140 mph before having to slow down to 40 mph through turn 11. These changes have resulted in the track's now having three primary passing zones: turn 11, turn 4a, and turn 7.

The new Earnhardt Terrace, a 34,000-seat section consisting of 22 rows of cement bleachers, was added overlooking turns 2 through 4. This is the highest seating section at the track and allows fans to see more than half of the entire track. A memorial to Dale Earnhardt, consisting of a monument and a flagpole with the #3 flag, sits just behind these seats. Similar sections of terraced bench seats will be added alongside turns 8 and 9 in 2002.

The lap/leader board is a short, three-sided tower, near turns 1 and 2, that lists the top five cars. It is easily viewed from the Earnhardt Terrace, as well as the grandstands near turns 7 and 9, but nearly impossible to see from the pits and start/finish area. For Winston Cup races, four giant-screen TVs are spread out among the track's many twists and turns. Three are inside the track, facing turns 2, 7, and 9, while the fourth is outside the track facing the tower suites and grandstands overlooking the start/finish line. Much of the seating at Sears Point is general admission, so folks show up early, spread a blanket high on the hills overlooking their favorite turn, and take in the race. This is particularly true of the hill overlooking turns 8 and 8a, but 30,000 hillside terrace seats will be constructed here for the 2002 race. In the infield, fans can be found seated on blankets and in folding chairs nearly everywhere within the large western loop at Sears Point.

Concessions and souvenir stands are plentiful at Sears Point, although rest rooms are somewhat scarce and lines can be ridiculously long. Massive groups of Porta Johns are scattered about the course and serviced by outdoor sinks, a luxury not always provided at Winston Cup tracks. Four pedestrian bridges allow fans to cross over the track at various points, and three more bridges will be added for the 2002 race. The current bridges have long lines before the race, especially the one near gate 2, so the addition of new bridges should provide some much-needed relief. A pedestrian tunnel under Highway 121 will also help ease traffic before and after races.

Sears Point has often been described as a driver's course because there are only so many changes a crew can make to a car once they get to the track. Setting up the transmission with the right gearing is essential, as are durable brakes, but because the race is relatively short at 224 miles, there are usually just two pit stops during a race and the drivers make do with the car essentially "as is" once the race begins. Worn tires and engine fatigue are uncommon, so qualifying well and maintaining track position are generally the keys to winning at Sears Point. In fact, all but three victories at Sears Point have come from the top five starting positions.

I have not always been a big fan of Winston Cup road course races, but I definitely enjoy the races at Sears Point in person much more than watching them on TV, despite television's technological advances in recent years. The changes made at Sears Point seem to be good ones, and additional improvements can be expected in the coming years as Bruton Smith and Steve Page continue to modernize and add fan amenities to this classic road course. If you've never been to a road course, I suggest you check one out in person before you dismiss it out of hand. Tickets are $60 for the Winston Cup race and most seating areas are general admission.

HISTORY

NASCAR/Winston Cup drivers haven't been racing at Sonoma long, but the track has been the site of some wild races. You won't experience the high-speed clashes of Talladega or Daytona. Nor will you witness the banging and rubbing of Bristol, Martinsville, or Richmond. You won't even see as many critical pit stop performances as you might encounter at more traditional race ovals. You will, however, gain a better understanding for the challenging conditions Winston Cup drivers face as they negotiate the hills and turns that make up Sears Point. Looking at the list of drivers who have won at Sears Point, the first thing that strikes you is the fact that they are all among the best in the business.

Ricky Rudd won the inaugural race at Sears Point, the 1989 Banquet 300, by a slim .05-second margin. Rudd averaged 76.088 mph in his Buick, edging out Rusty Wallace, Bill Elliott, and Dale Earnhardt. The 1989 win was the only time Rudd took the checkered flag at Sears Point, but he has qualified for the pole four times, more than any other driver. In addition to his victory, Rudd has placed second once, come in third twice, finished fourth three times, and ran fifth once, for eight top-five finishes in his first thirteen starts at Sears Point.

Rusty Wallace took the checkered flag at Sonoma, despite qualifying tenth in 1990. Wallace is another driver who has enjoyed considerable success at Sears Point. In 1996, Rusty revisited victory lane at Sears Point as Ford swept the top three positions. This is the only time a manufacturer has accomplished such a sweep at Sears Point. Wallace is one of the most consistent drivers at Sears Point with a second-place finish, a third, a fourth, and three fifth-place finishes through the 2001 season. Wallace also set the track qualifying lap record of 99.309 mph (70.652 seconds) on June 23, 2000.

Davey Allison earned his own track record by winning the 1991 race from the thirteenth position. Allison outran Rudd, Wallace, and Ernie Irvan that year. It was Allison's only Winston Cup road course victory in his brief but spectacular career. Ernie Irvan followed his strong '91 performance with a win the following season, despite being penalized early in the race and having to come back from last place. Irvan paced his Chevy at a track record of 81.413 mph, a mark that stands today as the best average race speed at Sears Point. In 1993, Irvan finished second to Geoffrey Bodine. Irvan won again at Sears Point in 1994, by the largest margin in track history, 9.56 seconds, and became the first driver to win twice in Sonoma. Bodine just missed claiming that distinction, coming in second place that year. Surprisingly, Irvan's win in 1994 was the first at Sears Point to come from the pole position.

Dale Earnhardt's only victory at Sears Point came in 1995. It was also his only career road course win. Remarkably, in twelve starts at Sears Point, Earnhardt had just two top-three finishes. Mark Martin finished second that year and again in 1996. Martin found his way to the winner's circle in 1997, by starting from the pole and holding off Jeff Gordon and Terry Labonte. Since his second place finish in 1995, Martin has never finished outside the top ten at Sears Point through 2001.

Jeff Gordon pretty much took over in 1998. Gordon won the first of three consecutive races at Sears Point that season. In just nine races here, Gordon has become the track's leading money winner, has led the most laps, and has finished no lower than sixth since 1995. Gordon's 1998 and 1999 races both began from the pole position. He has qualified for three poles at Sears Point, second only to Ricky Rudd. In 2001, Tony Stewart pulled out the win with a nifty pass of Robby Gordon and the lapped car of Kevin Harvick on turn 7 with just ten laps to go. It was Stewart's first career road course win, which came in just his fifth road course start.

GETTING TO THE TRACK

Traffic to and from races at Sears Point leaves a little to be desired. Located near the intersection of Highways 37 and 121, about 50 miles north of San Francisco, the track is south of Sonoma and west of Napa. Interstate 80 is the only major road that approaches the track, but it's quite a way to the east, so you can't help but spend a lot of time on two lane roads that back up for miles near the track. Highway 37, between I-80 and Highway 121, is particularly slow and narrow. It is being widened and may be better in time for the 2002 race.

Coming from San Francisco it may be best to take 101 North (just over 40 miles) to Highway 37 East (about 8 miles) to 121. The track is a quarter mile to your left. There are entrance gates surrounding the track, but avoid gate 9 off Lakeville Highway. This single-lane dirt road winds its way up the hill and will often come to a complete stop hours before the race. Parking lots here are a long way from the grandstands and are accessible only by shuttle bus. All parking at the track is free, but gates along Highway 121 offer the easiest egress after the race. Newly added pedestrian bridges and tunnels will ease traffic in the coming years.

WHAT TO SEE AND DO

There are plenty of things to do in northern California. Wine enthusiasts will want to check out Sonoma and Napa, just a short drive from the track. Some of the more recognizable wineries in the area include **Chateau St. Jean** in Kenwood, **Sebastiani Cask Cellars**, at 389 Fourth Street East in Sonoma, **Buena Vista**, one of the area's original vineyards, at 18000 Old Winery Road in Sonoma, and **Ravenswood**, at 18701 Gehricke Road, just north of Sonoma. There are probably as many vineyards in Sonoma as there are types of wine, so let your personal preferences dictate which to visit. The **Sonoma Valley Visitors Bureau**, at 453 First Street East, offers several free brochures and maps, so this may be a good place to start.

The town of Sonoma has a quaint downtown area of adobe-style buildings that house restaurants, shops, cafés, galleries, and historic attractions. City Hall, the Visitors Bureau, and a shaded park with picnic spots, monuments, and a duck pond center on Sonoma Plaza. Attractions here range from the borderline touristy— **Sonoma Cheese Factory**—to the genuinely historic—**Sonoma Barracks**, a Mexican fort built in 1836. In between you'll find a wealth of streetside cafés, shops, and galleries to enjoy.

The Sonoma Barracks, built by the Mexican army under the order of General Mariano Guadalupe Vallejo in 1836, is on the square at Spain Street and First Street East. Tickets are just $1 and also allow visitors to see the **San Francisco Solano de Sonoma Mission**, built in 1823, and **Lachryma Montis**, General Vallejo's home, just a short walk away. The **Swiss Hotel**, at 18 West Spain Street, was built in the 1850 by the General's brother Salvador, and converted into a popular hotel and restaurant.

As you walk the streets of Sonoma, don't forget to check out the side streets and alleys. **Place de Pyrenees**, an alley off First Street East, offers a handful of shops and restaurants tucked out of sight from the main drag. Other alleys around the square are home to a number of outstanding galleries and cafés. If you would like to pick up some wine, but don't have time to visit a bunch of vineyards, stop by **The Wine Exchange**, at 452 First Street East. They have a tremendous selection of California wines and more than 200 beers to choose from.

If shopping and eating is not your bag, check out the **Vintage Aircraft Company**. Minutes from the track, at 23982 Arnold Drive, Vintage Aircraft offers unforgettable rides in a Stearman PT 17 biplane or a World War II–era T-6 Texan. Rides vary from leisurely flights over the scenic Sonoma Valley to intensely aerobatic rides with loops, rolls, and other wild maneuvers. While you are there check out the airport's variety of antique and classic airplanes. Families traveling with small children will enjoy **Sonoma Train Town**. The Train Town Railroad offers a scale-model train ride through a 10-acre park with waterfalls, bridges, and tunnels. Train Town also features a Ferris wheel, carousel, petting zoo, and numerous train exhibits. Train Town is located on Broadway, 1 mile south of Sonoma's Town Square.

Napa may not offer the history and charm of Sonoma, but there is plenty to see and do in the area. The **Napa Valley Visitors Bureau**, at 1310 Napa Town Center, is a terrific place to start. Many wineries here offer guided tours from 10 A.M. to 4 P.M., while others have similar hours for self-guided tours. My favorite was the **Niebaum-Coppola Estate Winery** in Rutherford, at 1991 Saint Helena Highway. Fans of director Francis Ford Coppola will find this place absolutely remarkable. Not only is it one of the most scenic vineyards in the area, but there is a significant collection of movie paraphernalia from classic Coppola movies such as *Godfather* and *Deer Hunter*. A tasting of four wines costs $7.50 and allows you take home a souvenir glass.

Another excellent winery is **Domaine Chandon** in nearby Yountville. In addition to visiting a world-class vineyard, you can enjoy a hot-air balloon ride over Napa Valley. **Napa Valley Balloons** launch every morning from the winery giving passengers a once-in-a-lifetime perspective of the valley below. Tours cost $175 per person and include a continental breakfast and coffee before launching, as well as a champagne brunch afterward. Call (800) 253-2224 for reservations. The actual flight is about an hour long, so be sure to bring a camera and lots of film.

Another way to see wine country is aboard the **Napa Train Tour**. This upscale passenger train offers year-round gourmet dining excursions for brunch, lunch, and dinner. For reservations or details call (800) 427-4124 or (707) 253-2111. Outside of California they can be reached toll-free at (800) 522-4142. Folks staying near Vallejo should consider a visit to **Six Flags Marine World**, a combination theme park, wildlife park, and oceanarium. The park has more than thirty rides including the Medusa roller coaster, which zooms through seven complete loops, a killer whale and dolphin show, and dozens of wild animals on exhibit.

NIGHTLIFE IN SONOMA

Steiner's would be very easy to walk right by on First Street West, because there is no indication from the outside that it's a tavern. Mirrored windows belie the rustic interior of this friendly place. Established in 1927, Steiner's used to be located just down the street but moved when it became obvious that moving would be easier than closing to remodel. The new location is dark and cool, with plenty of televisions and a pair of pool tables. They also have reasonably priced beverages, by California standards. Don't be surprised to run into race crews here before the race weekend.

Murphy's Irish Pub is tucked away on Place de Pyrenees, but is worth seeking out. They offer ice-cold drinks, friendly service, better-than-average pub grub, and occasional live acoustic music. The patio is a great place to people watch, while the intimate indoor bar has a few televisions and an authentic pub atmosphere.

WHERE TO EAT

Meritage, at 522 Broadway, is one of the finer places near the Plaza. They specialize in southern French and northern Italian cuisine in a warm, inviting atmosphere. The solicitous staff will tend to your every desire, and the wine list is tremendous. They are open for lunch, dinner, and a stellar weekend brunch on the patio. If you are in the mood for a steak, head to **Saddles Steakhouse** at MacArthur Place, just south of the Plaza at 29 East MacArthur and Broadway. Expect giant cuts of prime steaks, fresh seafood, and top-notch service.

Just off the Plaza, across from Murphy's, you'll find **Feathers**, a casual eatery that offers a menu of strictly chicken entrees. So if you're craving poultry, this is the place for you. Open for lunch and dinner daily, the patio is a comfortable place to grab a bite. **Cucina Viansa** is a full-service wine bar with the atmosphere of a gourmet Italian marketplace. Located at 400 First Street East, just across from the Mission, this is one place that gets into the spirit on Winston Cup race weekends. They feature acoustic entertainers Thursday through Sunday.

If all you're looking for is a casual, down-to-earth place for breakfast, **Pearl's** is tough to beat. Off the beaten path at 561 Fifth Street West, Pearl's specializes in French toast and pancakes, but they also serve a pretty mean burger at lunch. Another place that is not in the heart of town, but worth the trek, is **Rob's Rib Shack** at 18709 Arnold Drive. Open for lunch and dinner only, they offer live music on the weekends and a casual outdoor patio.

There are plenty of Mexican restaurants in the area, but near the Plaza, **La Casa** is a worthwhile choice. Just a short walk from the barracks at 121 East Spain Street, La Casa offers an outdoor patio and serves generous portions. Around the corner, at 421 First Street East, **Zino's Ristorante** offers Italian and American fare at reasonable prices in a family-friendly, comfortable setting. They are open daily for lunch and dinner.

On the recommendation of a friend, I checked out **Rutherford's**. Across the street from the Niebaum-Coppola Winery, this is a terrific place for steaks, pasta, and salads. The ribs, as my buddy promised, were among the finest I've ever had. The outdoor patio and bar fills up quickly on sunny days, but indoor seating is just as desirable. The service is attentive, prices are surprisingly reasonable, and, most importantly, the food is outstanding. If you are staying northwest of the track, check out **Cattlemen's** in the quaint riverfront town of Petaluma. Cattlemen's is a rustic, friendly steakhouse, specializing in ribs, chops, and their own tumbleweed onion. They have a second location, farther north, in Santa Rosa.

LOCAL MEDIA

The local paper is the *Sonoma Index Tribune*, but for extensive NASCAR coverage you may want to pick up the *San Francisco Chronicle*. MRN Radio broadcasts the races on KTCT-AM, 1050. The Sonoma Valley Visitors Bureau publishes a helpful *Visitors Guide* annually. The guide can be picked up for free at area visitor centers.

WHERE TO STAY

HOTELS

Whether you are looking for a fancy inn and spa or simple accommodations, there are plenty of places to stay in the area. Nothing is near the track, but some places are easier to get to and from. Traffic from the north and west is least problematic, so you may want to choose to stay in Sonoma, Novato, or Petaluma. Petaluma, about 12 miles from the track, has a handful of reasonably priced name-brand hotels. For my first visit to Sears Point, I stayed in Vallejo—Jeff Gordon's hometown just east of the track—but there's absolutely nothing to do there, so I ended up kicking around in Sonoma all weekend. Here are a few places to consider in and around Sonoma.

Sonoma Hotel   110 West Spain, Sonoma (800) 468-6016 or (707) 996-2996   This quaint, historic place is right on the square in Sonoma, within walking distance of a wealth of restaurants, shops, and pubs. The hotel's sixteen rooms were remodeled in 1999.

Sonoma Valley Inn   550 Second Street West, Sonoma (800) 334-5784 or (707) 938-9200   This is as nice a Best Western property as you will find on the race circuit. It's not cheap, but it is convenient. They even bring you breakfast in bed and a local bottle of wine to your room each day.

Gaige House Inn   13540 Arnold Drive, Glen Ellen (800) 935-0237 or (707) 935-0237   If you're traveling with your significant other and want to do it up right, this fine bed and breakfast is the place. They have only fifteen rooms, but all are unbelievable, and the staff is world class.

The Lodge at Sonoma   1325 Broadway Avenue, Sonoma (707) 935-6600   A brand-new hotel that may still qualify as a well-kept secret in Sonoma. Don't be fooled by the name; this Renaissance property offers 182 gorgeous rooms just a mile from Sonoma Plaza.

MacArthur Place   29 East MacAthur Street, Sonoma (800) 722-1866 or (707) 938-2929   Another indulgent wine country spa and inn that prides itself on service and comfortable rooms. MacArthur Place has sixty-four rooms that start near $200 per night and go up considerably from there.

Best Western Petaluma   200 South McDowell Boulevard, Petaluma (800) 297-3846 or (707) 763-0994   An unassuming two-level motel with a heated outdoor pool, convenient location, and a helpful staff.

Courtyard by Marriott   1400 North Hamilton Parkway, Novato (800) 321-2211 or (415) 883-8950   A relatively new hotel, just 9 miles from the track. They offer comfortable rooms, as well as a heated outdoor pool and whirlpool.

Days Inn   300 Fairgrounds Drive, Vallejo (800) 329-7466 or (707) 554-8000   A clean, convenient hotel just half a mile from Marine World/Six Flags amusement park. It's also one of the closest hotels east of the track.

The **Bed & Breakfast Association of Sonoma Valley** offers a convenient Web site with pictures, information, and availability at www.sonomabb.com. They have more than fifteen B&Bs to choose from. Call (707) 938-9513 for details. **Accommodations Express** offers a reservation service for area hotels at (877) 484-5245.

Good to Know

- To charge tickets or for additional race information, call (800) 870-7223 or (707) 938-8448.
- Mail orders can be sent to Sears Point Raceway, Highways 37 and 121, Sonoma, CA 95476.
- The Sonoma Valley Visitors Bureau can be reached at (707) 996-1090.
- A worthwhile city Web site is www.sonomavalley.com.
- ➤ The official racetrack Web site is www.searspoint.com.

NEARBY WINSTON CUP RACE CITIES

California/Fontana: 420 miles (seven hours)
Las Vegas: 625 miles (ten hours, forty-five minutes)
Phoenix: 805 miles (fourteen hours)

IN THE VICINITY

San Francisco is just an hour to the south and has enough incredible things to do to keep you busy for a week or more. When people think of San Francisco, their first image is generally of the **Golden Gate Bridge** and the San Francisco Bay. The bridge is more than 8,900 feet long, and its twin towers are the highest in the nation at 746 feet tall. A walk across the bridge offers a great view of the city skyline, assuming it's not a cloudy day. Every year nearly a million people take the mile-and-a-half boat ride to **Alcatraz**, America's most famous maximum-security prison. You can catch the Red & White Fleet Ferry across San Francisco Bay (for $5.50 roundtrip) at Pier 41. Tickets should be purchased well in advance by calling (415) 546-2700. Once you are on the island, be sure to take the self-guided audio tour (an additional $3), narrated by ex-inmates and guards. You can also wait for a free ranger-led tour to get a good feel for the prison's short but colorful history.

No visit to San Francisco would be complete without a ride on a **cable car**. What used to be the main form of mass transit in San Francisco is now little more than a tourist attraction, as there are only three lines and 17 miles of track left these days. Nevertheless, more than 10 million folks ride the cable cars each year. The Powell-Hyde line, which takes you down Russian Hill, is my favorite. **Fisherman's Wharf** has become a serious tourist trap, with far too many souvenir shops, but it still offers some notable restaurants and nightclubs. **Lou's Pier 47** is a particularly good club to catch live music, ranging from rock to pop acts. The *SF Bay Guardian* is a helpful alternative weekly tabloid that lists area happenings.

Lombard Street, the world's crookedest street, **Chinatown**, **Golden Gate State Park**, the **California Palace of the Legion of Honor**, one of the West Coast's finest art museums, the **Museum of Cartoon Art**, and the **Ansel Adams Center** are all worth checking out. For an unforgettable meal, head to the **Cliff House**, at 1066 Point Lobos Avenue. The food is terrific, but the view of the Pacific Ocean and Seal Rock is the main attraction here. Baseball fans should try to catch a game at **Pacific Bell Park**, one of the newest and best ballparks in the big leagues. The Giants sell out regularly, but tickets can be ordered in advance by calling (510) 762-2277.

This list barely scratches the surface of Bay Area activities. Call the **San Francisco Convention and Visitors Bureau** at (415) 227-2603 for a more complete listing of attractions, restaurants, and lodging. The **Visitor Information Hotline** is (415) 391-2001.

▪ *WATKINS GLEN INTERNATIONAL* ▪

Watkins Glen, New York

"The late, great Dale Earnhardt taught me . . . stay on the course, don't get in the gravel pit, don't wear your brakes out, and don't break your transmission."

— STEVE PARK

The village of Watkins Glen had been known as a haven for sports car races through the streets of town until this upstate New York road course opened as a 2.3-mile serpentine in 1956. A year after the permanent track was built, surrounded by hillside fields of corn, the drivers of NASCAR took their turn. With few interruptions, they've been roaring through the Glen ever since.

The current Winston Cup configuration is 2.45 miles long and features eleven turns; seven of them are right turns. The turns offer slight banks ranging from 6 to 10 degrees. Unlike Sears Point, elevation changes throughout the track are not as significant, but Watkins Glen offers much greater speeds and is considered to be the more rigorous of the two Winston Cup road courses.

Turn one at Watkins Glen is called "the ninety" because it's a drastic right turn of roughly 90 degrees. It's the first opportunity for drivers to pass at the Glen. This is also a point on the course where cars that head down the hill into turn one too fast end up in the dreaded gravel pit, a giant sand trap that stops cars in their tracks before they hit the wall. Turn two is a less severe curve back to the right, while the third turn represents the first left pivot on the course. Along with turn four, this portion of the track comprises the uphill "esses" at Watkins Glen.

Turn four, a subtle right leading into the uphill backstretch, is another favorite place to pass with an inside move. Drivers take advantage of superior horsepower to pass on the 2,600-foot backstretch, the fastest stretch on the track, where cars can reach 170 mph. The backstraight is followed by the entrance to the inner loop,

View of pit road and frontstretch grandstands from the infield. *(Photo by Author)*

a right-left-left-right chicane that is considered the fourth place on the track to pass but can also be a good place to get in trouble if neither driver concedes position. The ninth turn is a looping right-hand arc, with a 10-degree bank, that heads back downhill and is the closest thing to a hairpin on the course. A 2,150-foot uphill straightaway leads to the track's final left-hand turn, of nearly 90 degrees, and on to turn eleven, a sharp right turn leads back to the start/finish line and the track's third straightaway. Turn eleven is another preferred position to outbrake the competition and pass on the inside before heading to the flagstand.

The keys to success at Watkins Glen are qualifying well, pitting quickly and as late as possible while maintaining good track position, and outbraking the competition through the track's primary passing zones. Of course, drivers also have to hope that their brakes stay firm through 990 turns and the transmission holds up as they shift more than 800 times during a race. Pit strategy—pitting out of sync with other drivers or getting lucky and being on pit road when the yellow flag is out—

has helped many a driver finish well at Watkins Glen. To illustrate the importance of qualifying well, nearly two-thirds of all races here have been won from within the top three starting positions, and nearly half of all winners started from the pole position.

Races here are ninety laps long, which usually translates to two scheduled pit stops generally near laps 30 and 60. Pit stops present a challenge, as cars drive clockwise at Watkins Glen, and pit crews are accustomed to counterclockwise stops for all but the two road course races. For this reason, fuel doors are placed on the opposite side of the chassis and a host of other changes are made to road course cars. Some pit crews even switch the positions of their tire changers from front to rear for road course races, so the transition is not as complicated. Costly equipment adjustments have become commonplace as teams chase points in the season championship, but they have also made it difficult for independent teams to compete with the multicar teams.

Watkins Glen has 130,000 seats, about 28,000 more than Sears Point, but they are not nearly as comfortable or well maintained. In fact, the short sections of bleachers overlooking the start/finish line are sorry-looking wooden structures with no seatbacks and very little legroom. Even from the very highest seats here, you do not see much of the track. We decided there was no way we could watch a ninety-lap/220.5-mile race from these seats, so we took a lap of our own around the infield. Now that's where the fun is at Watkins Glen. The grandstands inside turn ten offer a good view as cars roar up the frontstretch at speeds approaching 160 mph, make a left turn through ten, and head toward the track's final turn. Folks parked inside turn nine occupy what may be the loudest part of the track as drivers try to hang on through the swift, sweeping turn at 90 mph. The area near the chicane offers some of the best action at the track as cars decelerate and negotiate the switchbacks that open up into turn nine.

None of the track's seating sections allows you to see more than a fraction of the track. Giant-screen TV monitors are well positioned throughout the track, so fans can follow cars all the way around the course for laps that take about 75 seconds. The ninety, a section of seats near turn one, offers a great view of the cars as they head downhill into one of the track's trickiest turns. Seats along the inside of pit road present a terrific look at the pit action, as well as the frontstretch where cars reach nearly 150 mph. The very top rows of the orange section, outside the frontstretch, allow you to see cars head down into turn one and two, and a good deal more in either direction.

A vendor area with souvenir trailers, concession stands, sponsor exhibits, and an information tent is situated near the very center of the infield. As I mentioned earlier, folks in the infield at Watkins Glen know how to have a good time. The best seats we had all day were atop a converted school bus that occupied some prime trackside territory near turn ten. Our hosts were kind enough to let us climb up the ladder to join them for a few laps. Quite a few laps later, we took off before we wore out our welcome—or ran out of beer—and headed to our assigned seats outside the frontstretch between the flagstand and the entrance to pit road for the end of the race. Aside from being cramped and uncomfortable, these seats offered a great view of the finish.

HISTORY

Watkins Glen hosted its first NASCAR race on August 4, 1957. Buck Baker took the pole with a qualifying lap of just over 83 mph. Driving a Chevy, Baker led all 101.2 miles, just forty-four laps around the 2.3-mile circuit, to beat Fireball Roberts by half a second. It was the first and final road course win of Baker's illustrious career. NASCAR drivers did not return to Watkins Glen for a sanctioned race until 1964. Races were extended to sixty-six laps that season, and pole sitter Billy Wade beat LeeRoy Yarbrough by leading forty-one laps of the race and ran at an average speed of almost 98 mph. It was Wade's fourth consecutive win that season, but also the last of his career, as he died in testing at Daytona the very next season. Marvin Panch, driving a Ford, became the first driver to win at Watkins Glen without starting on the pole. The 1965 race was the last 151.8-mile Winston Cup race held at Watkins Glen.

When NASCAR drivers returned to Watkins Glen in 1986 for the first sanctioned ninety-lap race at the track, Tim Richmond took the checkered flag, beating out Darrell Waltrip, Dale Earnhardt, Bill Elliott, and Neil Bonnett. Rusty Wallace earned his first road course victory at Watkins Glen in 1987. Rusty won from the second qualifying position by edging out pole sitter Terry Labonte. Wallace finished second the next year as Ricky Rudd won for the first time at the Glen. That race marked the only time Buick has won here. In 1989, Rusty became the first two-time winner at Watkins Glen, holding off Mark Martin and Dale Earnhardt. Watkins Glen is one of very few tracks where Earnhardt did not win as a driver. In fact, Earnhardt finished no better than third at Watkins Glen, which he did three times for his only top-five finishes at the road course. Rudd won again in 1990 to become the second driver with two trips to victory lane at Watkins Glen. Brothers Geoff and Brett Bodine finished second and third that year.

On August 11, 1991, Ernie Irvan beat out Ricky Rudd, Mark Martin, and Rusty Wallace for the checkered flag at the last Watkins Glen race run on the 2.428-mile layout. It was Irvan's first road course victory, and at the time, his average speed of 98.77 mph was a track record. That race proved fatal for J. D. McDuffie as he lost control at the end of the backstretch and rolled his car on top of Jimmy Means's car and through the fence of what is now turn nine. The chicane at the exit of the backstretch was added the following season to prevent another such accident. Dale Earnhardt earned the first of his two Watkins Glen poles in 1992, but Kyle Petty won the first race at the new 2.45-mile layout in an event shortened to just fifty-one laps. At many tracks, two and sometimes three generations of Pettys have visited victory lane, but Kyle is the only Petty to have won at Watkins Glen.

Mark Martin became the first driver to win back-to-back-to-back races at Watkins Glen from 1993 to 1995. All three of his wins came from the pole. In 1993, Martin beat out Wally Dallenbach, Jimmy Spencer, and Bill Elliott, as Ford swept the top four spots, the only time in track history that a manufacturer swept even the top three positions. Martin's 1995 effort resulted in a track record speed of 103.030 mph in a race that lasted just two hours, eleven minutes, and fifty-four seconds. Dale Earnhardt earned his second pole in 1996, but Geoff Bodine, who grew up in nearby Chemung, New York, utilized an off-sync pit strategy to win the race from the thirteenth starting position. Jeff Gordon earned his first road course pole position for the 1997 race. He subsequently won the race and started a road course win streak. In addition to winning the next two Watkins Glen races in 1998 and 1999 to become the second driver to win three consecutive races at the Glen, Gordon won three straight contests at Sears Point for six consecutive road course victories.

Steve Park, another New Yorker, won the 2000 Global Crossing at the Glen from the eighteenth starting position. Not only was it the worst ever qualifying position for a driver to pull off a victory at Watkins Glen, it was Park's first win on the Winston Cup circuit. Jeff Gordon returned to victory lane at Watkins Glen in 2001 to become the track's all-time victory leader with four wins. He also became the winningest road course driver with a total of seven road course wins, surpassing Rusty Wallace, Bobby Allison, and Richard Petty who each had six victories.

GETTING TO THE TRACK

The track is 5 miles southwest of Watkins Glen on County Route 16, about 3 miles from Route 414. The track is 20 miles north of Elmira, New York, and 18 miles northeast of Corning, New York. There are not many worthwhile back roads or shortcuts that I am aware of, but traffic is not particularly bad on the way to a race, especially if you get there early. Depending on your approach, Beaver Dams Road and Bronson Hill Road are smaller, two-lane roads that lead toward the track and are perhaps less congested than Route 16 on race day, but may not be any quicker.

Track-owned parking lots are free, while entrepreneur lots can cost as much as $20. These lots tend to be a long way from the track but offer quicker egress. Free shuttles are available from gate 1, east of the track, and gate 7, to the south. We parked at a lot near Bronson Hill Road that was a fair walk to our seats. The lot was little more than a grassy field but was packed with tailgaters before and after the race. The rest room facility in this parking lot was as bad as I've seen anywhere. I turned around as soon as I got inside and can only hope that the facilities inside the track are better. I'm told they aren't, but that ownership has added a new rest room building each year for the past few years in an effort to replace the worst facilities. I was fortunate enough to have a pass to the hospitality area, which offered well-kept portable trailers, so I didn't venture into another permanent facility for fear of losing my lunch.

WHAT TO SEE AND DO

The Finger Lakes region of New York State is about as scenic as any Winston Cup destination. In addition to great boating and fishing, **Watkins Glen State Park**, also known as the Gorge, has nineteen remarkable waterfalls spread throughout its 1,000 acres of wilderness. The walking trail offers terrific views of the falls and many fascinating rock formations, and leads over a suspension bridge 165 feet above the glen. A giant granite wall serves as the screen for **Timespell**, a light and laser show that runs nightly at 8 and 9 P.M.; it highlights the history of the area and lasts about an hour. The park is about 4 miles from the track at the south end of Seneca Lake. Admission is free, but Timespell costs $6.50 for adults. This and other nearby parks offer the opportunity to explore this incredible countryside. To rent bikes, kayaks, and canoes for an adventure on or around Seneca Lake, stop by **Terrapin Outfitters**.

Winery tours have become a major tourist attraction for the Finger Lakes region. The **Seneca Lake Wine Trail** features twenty-one wineries along the lake's shore. Wineries vary from large, well-known vineyards to family-run places, and offerings range from simple tastings to extravagant places with fancy restaurants and lodging overlooking the lake. **Glenora Wine Cellars**, at 5435 Route 14 in Dundee, New York, offers daily tastings, an inn with handsome guest rooms, and a great view of the lake from the western shore. On the east side of the lake, at 5712 Route 414 in Hector, **Hazlitt 1852 Vineyards** offers a horseshoe-shaped tasting bar in a rustic barn and a fun atmosphere. **Wagner Vineyards**, also on the east side of the lake, has wine tastings daily and **Ginny Lee's**, a wonderful restaurant and their own micro-brewery. Call the Seneca Lake Winery Association at (877) 536-2717 for a complete list of participating wineries.

Racing Thunder in the Glen is a race-oriented festival held in the village of Watkins Glen, along Franklin Street, on the Friday night before the race. You'll see classic cars, show cars, drivers from other race series, vendors of all kinds, and live entertainment. Admission is free. While you're there, check out the **Walk of Fame** along Franklin Street. Stone tablets commemorate drivers who have raced at Watkins Glen. Many of the names are from the world of Grand Prix racing, but NASCAR drivers such as Lee Petty, Richard Petty, and Bobby Allison are among the names you'll find. A stone for Dale Earnhardt will be added in 2002. The local Chamber of Commerce provides a free brochure with a handy map.

The **International Motor Racing Research Center**, near downtown at 610 Decatur Street, has two floors of racing photos, films, uniforms, artwork, programs, and cars on display. The emphasis is on the town's storied road racing history, but you'll find plenty of stock car memorabilia also. Admission, including the theater, is free. Call (607) 535-9044 for current exhibit information. **Captain Bill's** offers 10-mile narrated cruises on Seneca Lake. Tours leave every hour from their Franklin Street pier. They also offer dinner cruises aboard the luxury vessel *Columbia*. Call (607) 535-4541 for reservations. **Seneca Grand Prix**, on Route 414 South, has a pair of go-kart tracks, bumper boats, mini-golf, and an arcade.

The **Corning Museum of Glass** has more than 35,000 pieces in its permanent collection spanning 3,500 years. Glassblowing demonstrations are given daily. This is a terrific place for kids and families to witness the technologies and skills used to create glass art and everyday artifacts. Call (800) 732-6845 for the cost of admission and operating hours.

NIGHTLIFE IN WATKINS GLEN

The **Crooked Rooster** is an Irish pub on North Franklin Street in downtown Watkins Glen. This popular place gets a good crowd with or without a race in town, but you can count on a full house on race weekend, especially after the Thunder in the Glen festival. **Victory Lane**, the lounge at the Glen Motor Inn, was a favorite of Bobby Allison and is packed with race fans on race weekend. Located about 5 miles from the track on the west side of the lake, the lobby of the hotel has a bunch of track photos and race memorabilia. The **Bench and Bar Tavern** at the Seneca Lodge has been a favorite of drivers since they started driving race cars at Watkins Glen in 1948. Racing memorabilia is displayed throughout and the walls are lined with racing photos.

Corning, New York, about 20 miles away, offers a few notable places of its own. The **Market Street Brewing Company**, at 63 Market Street, is a friendly brew pub with outdoor seating, live music on Friday nights, and a stellar bar menu. Across the street you'll find **Wet Goods**, a casual bar with a pool table, foosball, jukebox, and a decent dance floor. There's a DJ on weekends, and they serve wings, sandwiches, and appetizers until late in the evening. **Boomers Bistro**, a restaurant is next door at 58 West Market Street.

WHERE TO EAT

There are several places to eat within a short walk of each other along North Franklin Street in the heart of the village. They are likely to be packed on race weekend, but many of them are worth the wait. Several of the wineries on Seneca Lake have their own restaurants. These may offer a better chance to bump into a driver and their crews, especially on the nights leading up to a race. They also may require a reservation, as they are not the well-kept secret they once were.

Castel Grisch   3380 County Route 28 (607) 535-9614   Overlooking the lake in Watkins Glen, this is the closest winery to the track. Perhaps that's why drivers have been known to rent out the entire restaurant and manor for private events. Reservations are suggested.

Chef's Diner   Route 14–Watkins/Montour Road (607) 535-9975   Since the fifties, this family-owned diner has been serving hearty breakfasts and juicy cheeseburgers on the outskirts of town. This should be your first choice for affordable early-morning or late-night grub.

Franklin Street Grille   413 North Franklin Street (607) 535-2007   This is a terrific choice for lunch, dinner, or drinks in the midst of village happenings. A pit road racing mural depicts their history as a race day destination.

Ginny Lee Cafe   9322 Route 14 (607) 582-6574   A wonderful restaurant with a sweeping view from the east side of the lake at the Wagner Vineyards in Lodi. Needless to say, the emphasis here is on wines, but the on-site microbrewery is a welcomed addition.

Jerlando's Ristorante   400 North Franklin Street (607) 535-4254   Across the street from the Franklin Street Grill at Fourth Street and Franklin, this cozy place has authentic Italian fare, friendly service, and an excellent wine selection.

Mr. Chicken   106 South Franklin Street   This affordable cafeteria-style eatery has excellent food in a comfortable setting in the heart of the village.

Savaro's Family Restaurant   601 North Franklin Street (607) 535-4538   Another worthwhile breakfast joint that also serves affordable lunches and dinners. Situated in the heart of the village at the corner of Sixth and North Franklin Streets.

Season's Restaurant   108 North Franklin Street   Located at the Watkins Glen Hotel, this casual bistro offers solid fare and a host of classic racing photos on the walls. Like most local restaurants, they feature a sizable list of area wines.

Seneca Harbor Station   3 North Franklin Street (607) 535-6101   On the waterfront in a refurbished 1867 train depot, the inviting ambiance inside is as exceptional as the view of the lake from the deck. Seafood entrees are a highlight, as are the pasta, chowder, and gumbo.

Wildflower Café   301 North Franklin Street (607) 535-9797   One of the original upscale eateries on the main drag, they offer a multiethnic menu in a comfortable setting with high-backed booths, ceiling fans, and a quiet bar.

The Bistro at Red Newt Cellars   3675 Tichenor Road, Hector (607) 546-4100
Located at the Red Newt Wine Cellars, this upscale restaurant features Finger
Lakes cuisine and their own wines. The menu changes regularly, but guests can
expect innovative entrees and top-notch service.

LOCAL MEDIA

The local newspaper is the *Review & Express*. Race broadcasts can be heard on
MRN Radio via WPGI-FM, 100.9.

WHERE TO STAY

Because Watkins Glen is essentially a small village surrounded by several mid-size
towns, there is a dearth of available lodging in the area on race weekends. In addition to hotels in nearby cities such as Corning, Cornell, Ithaca, and Elmira, quality
lodging can be found at a handful of local wineries and a number of reputable bed-
and-breakfast inns. Call the Schuyler County Chamber of Commerce at (800) 607-
4552 for an up-to-date list of vacancies at area hotels, guesthouses, and B&Bs.
There are also some very worthwhile campgrounds in the area.

WATKINS GLEN HOTELS

Anchor Inn   Salt Point Road (607) 535-4232   An affordable motel with apart-
ments and cabins on the south end of Seneca Lake less than 2 miles from the village of Watkins Glen. On-site beach, picnic facilities, boat and jet ski rentals.

Idlewilde Inn   1 Lakeview Avenue (607) 535-3081   A massive inn built before
the turn of the century located on the lake. The rooms all feature private baths,
and the 2.5-acre grounds offer a nice view of the lake.

Glen Motor Inn   Route 14 North (607) 535-2706   On the west side of the lake,
across from the golf course, this humble place has just forty rooms, a great view
of the lake, and a pool.

Seneca Lodge   South Entrance to Watkins Glen State Park (607) 535-2014
A simple place, but you can't beat the location for a race weekend stay. The
shortcut to the track eliminates the need to get involved with track traffic.

Longhouse Lodge   Route 14 at Abrams Road (607) 535-2565   Two miles north of
the village, there are just twenty-two rooms, but the lodge and setting are quite
attractive. The place fills with fans for race week.

Longhouse Manor Bed & Breakfast   3137 Abrams Road (607) 535-2565
Tasteful decor sets this place apart. Shares a pool, gazebo, and grounds with the
lodge.

Seneca Lake Watch Bed and Breakfast   104 Seneca Street (607) 535-4490
This 1890 Victorian mansion is among the nicer bed-and-breakfast establishments in the area. The view of the lake from the porch is spectacular.

CORNING/PAINTED POST HOTELS

Comfort Inn   66 Pulteney Street (607) 962-1515   A nice place four blocks from the Corning Glass Museum. Offers a pool, fitness room, and free continental breakfast.

Days Inn   23 Riverside Drive (607) 963-9370   Another solid choice in Corning, just two blocks from the museum and five blocks to the nightlife district along Market Street.

Fairfield Inn   3 South Buffalo (607) 937-9600   Close to downtown Corning, this hotel offers spacious rooms, free local calls, an indoor pool, and complimentary breakfast.

Hampton Inn   9775 Victory Highway, Painted Post (607) 936-3344   Fairly new, well-kept accommodations minutes from everything you need to see in Corning.

Holiday Inn   Route 15 at 417 (607) 962-5021   An affordable place to stay with clean, comfortable rooms. Kids stay free, so this place is a bargain for families.

Radisson Hotel   125 Denisson Parkway East (607) 962-5000   Within walking distance of the Corning Glass Museum, this is one of the largest and nicest hotels in Corning, so it may be your best bet when places near Watkins Glen get scarce.

CAMPSITES

In addition to the camping facilities at Watkins Glen State Park, there are public RV and trailer campgrounds at **Clute Memorial Park**, east of the village on Seneca Lake, and RV camping hookups at **Montour Marina**, southeast of the track in Montour Falls. Call (607) 535-4438 for Clute Park information. To reserve a spot at the marina call (607) 535-9397. The **Hickory Hill Family Camping Resort**, well west of Watkins Glen in Bath, New York, is one of the largest area RV facilities. Call (800) 760-0947 for reservations. **KOA** in Watkins Glen has RV hookups and two dozen cabins. Call (800) 562-7430.

Good to Know

- To charge tickets or for additional race information, call (607) 535-2481.
- For information about camping at the track, call (607) 535-2481.
- Mail orders can be sent to Watkins Glen International, 2790 County Road 16, Watkins Glen, NY 14891.

- The Schuyler County Chamber of Commerce & Visitors Center is located at 100 North Franklin Street, Watkins Glen, NY 14891 and can be reached at (800) 607-4552.
- A worthwhile city Web site is www.schuylerny.com.
- ➤ The official racetrack Web site is www.theglen.com.

NEARBY WINSTON CUP RACE CITIES

Pocono Raceway: 155 miles (two hours, fifty minutes)
Dover Downs: 320 miles (five hours, forty minutes)
New Hampshire: 385 miles (six hours, thirty minutes)

IN THE VICINITY

The **Baseball Hall of Fame** in Cooperstown, New York, is a baseball fan's "magic kingdom" with hundreds of displays, statues, vintage equipment, theaters, baseball cards, and, of course, the brass plaques enshrining baseball's greatest players. More than 400,000 people visit this picturesque town of 2,100 citizens each year. Admission is $6 for adults. Call (607) 547-9988 for details.

Niagara Falls is another superb upstate New York attraction just 150 miles to the northwest. If you've never been, it would be a shame to be this close and not make the trip. There is no charge to view the falls, but rides aboard the *Maid of the Mist*, a boat that takes you out near the base of the falls, and narrated tours that take you behind the falls have separate admission charges. For more information about the Canadian Niagara Falls area, call (800) 563-2557.

Top Twelve Family-Friendly Winston Cup Race Cities

12 Dover—spend a few days at Rehoboth Beach, less than 50 miles south of the track and drive to the race mid-week, before the crowds show up on the weekend. You can stay at a hotel on the beach or camp at the scenic Delaware Seashore State Park. Rehoboth offers nature cruises, dolphin- and whale-watching tours, waterslides, golf, kayaking, a go-kart track, and a handful of museums. At the track, families enjoy the race from the infield while kids play soccer, fathers and sons play catch, or toss a football, and everybody seems to be grilling up a storm while the race roars on around them.

11 Darlington—same as previous, except the ocean waves can be found at nearby Myrtle Beach with an abundance of family attractions such as NASCAR SpeedPark, NASCAR Café, and Broadway at the Beach, an entertainment complex that offers laser light shows nightly. You'll also find a butterfly pavilion, Treasure Hunt: Pirates of the Carolina Coast, one of several amusement rides, Ripley's Aquarium, Dragon's Lair miniature golf, as well as a shuttle boat that ferries folks back and forth across the lake. The track itself is oozing with nostalgia and, unless there's a crowd, the adjacent Stock Car Hall of Fame and Joe Weatherly Museum is well worth the price of admission.

10 Pocono—the carnival atmosphere at Pocono is unlike any other track on the circuit. Jugglers, musicians, magicians, a petting zoo, and entertainers of all sorts occupy the midway out front of the grandstands on race day. The Camel Beach Water Park, in nearby Tannersville, has eight water slides, including the 800-foot Titan, kids' play zones, a swimming pool, the new Kahuna Lagoon wave pool, an adventure river, bumper boats, and miniature golf. Thunder Creek Quarry offers go-karts, bumper boats, and miniature golf. Race fans will marvel at Pocono's triangular 2.5-mile track, which is as unique as its circus atmosphere.

9 Indianapolis—I visited the racing museum and track as a kid, long before it hosted a NASCAR race, and my return trip as an adult was just as special. Car enthusiasts and race fans consider the museum a must-see attraction and the city of Indianapolis has a wonderful downtown zoo, a beautiful minor league ballpark, the NCAA Hall of Champions, and some of the finest go-kart facilities on the circuit. Racers, Fast Times, and the Stefan Johansson Karting Center, all feature top-notch go-karts, challenging tracks, and fast and furious racing fun.

8 Richmond—the night races alone are worth the trip, but the area amusement parks and historical sights make this a trip every family can enjoy. Paramount's Kings Dominion is a 400-acre theme park with more than 200 rides, shows, and attractions just half an hour north of Richmond. A little farther away, but certainly worth the drive, is Busch Gardens– Williamsburg, home to some of the nation's best amusement park rides. Families with young children should not miss the opportunity to spend an afternoon at Colonial Williamsburg, a genuine eighteenth-century village comprised of eighty-eight government buildings, homes, shops, and barns. Military re-enactors, costumed citizenry, and craftspeople perform daily.

7 **Kansas City**—this clean-cut Midwest town is home to one of the circuit's most innovative tracks and offers a surprising number of worthwhile attractions nearby. Worlds of Fun is an amusement park offering more than 140 rides, shows, and attractions including the world's largest steel roller coaster and one of the finest wooden roller coasters in the nation. Next door you'll find Oceans of Fun, a 60-acre water theme park. The Kansas City Zoo is among the largest metropolitan zoos in the country.

6 **Charlotte**—kids of all ages will enjoy the race team garages surrounding the track, the Hendrick Motorsports Museum, and the Dale Earnhardt Experience, in nearby Mooresville, which may be as close as it gets to a race fan's Graceland. Other family attractions include the N.C. Auto Racing Hall of Fame, the 18.5-scale race simulators at NASCAR Silicon in Concord Mills Mall, Paramount's Carowinds, a solid amusement park just across the South Carolina border, and Discovery Place, a hands-on science and learning museum in downtown Charlotte.

5 **Texas**—there's not a bad seat in the house at the "Great American Speedway," and there's plenty to see and do in the area. Six Flags over Texas is a 205-acre amusement park with more than 100 rides, shows, and midway games. The park's feature ride is the Texas Giant, rated the number one roller coaster in the world by *Fast Track* magazine a few years ago. The adjacent Hurricane Harbor is a water park with more than twenty-five rides spread out over 50 acres that offers a nice respite from the Texas heat. SpeedZone is the area's premier go-kart facility with four tracks to choose from.

4 **Daytona**—you can't beat the track for a sense of racing history, but the beach is the real attraction for families. Oceanfront Park is a popular beach that offers the Boardwalk Amusement Area, with a castle-shaped bandshell and the Salute to Speed consisting of more than thirty granite plaques recognizing Daytona's storied place in motorsports history. At the track, Daytona USA is billed as the ultimate motorsports attraction. Equal parts motorsports museum and arcade, this place allows fans to call a famous race in a simulated broadcast booth, race the clock in a pit stop challenge, take a virtual reality lap around Daytona Speedway, and so much more. The Kennedy Space Center and Walt Disney World are both within a modest drive of the track.

3 **ChicagoLand**—the track is nothing short of spectacular and you could easily spend a week with your family in Chicago. The Shedd Aquarium is the largest indoor aquarium in the world. It's home to sharks, dolphins, otters, sea turtles, and even a few beluga whales. The Navy Pier extends for half a mile into Lake Michigan and is home to several vintage amusement rides including a Ferris wheel and carousel. The Field Museum of Natural History is one of the finest in the nation. And while you're here, why not take the family to the friendly confines of Wrigley Field to see a ballgame.

2 **Las Vegas**—the track is absolutely pristine and offers some of the best RV camping on the circuit, but the city has gone out of its way to attract families. The Las Vegas NASCAR Café is a step above others I've visited. Featuring Speed, an indoor/outdoor roller coaster that accelerates from 0 to 45 mph in two seconds, this place also features race simulators, and video games. Treasure Island presents an action-packed sea battle between a pirate ship and the HMS *Britannia* in Buccaneer Bay. The show is performed every ninety minutes, six times a day, starting at four in the afternoon, and is free.

Circus Circus' Adventure Dome is another family-oriented attraction with rides, shows, and games within the glass-domed 5-acre indoor theme park. Wet 'n Wild is a 26-acre water park with a number of refreshing flume rides, a roller coaster, and a wave pool. Las Vegas Mini Grand Prix has four tracks to choose from. Choose from high-banked oval sprint karts, open-wheel adult Grand Prix cars, go-karts, and kiddie karts. Crowds can be significant, but the tracks are long and families will have a blast here.

1 **California**—you can sum up the family fun here in seven words— Disneyland, Knott's Berry Farm, and Universal Studios. Disneyland is the area's premier family attraction and occupies 82 acres. Disneyland is divided into eight different areas, with rides and attractions for both kids and adults. My favorite rides include the Matterhorn, a great indoor/ outdoor roller coaster with wild 45-degree turns that will scare the pants off you, and Space Mountain, an indoor roller coaster that features planetarium effects and a simulated space launch. The newest addition to Disneyland is California Adventure, a theme park with re-creations of several Golden State attractions.

Knott's Berry Farm is the area's other amusement park. The park offers hundreds of rides and attractions in six themed areas covering 150 acres. One of the park's more recent attractions is the Boomerang, a roller coaster that is more than 110 feet tall and turns you upside down six times. Not particularly close to the track, but well worth the drive,

Universal Studios has become equal parts amusement park and movie studio, attracting five million visitors a year. The studio occupies more than 400 acres, which you can see via guided tram and a walking tour. Along the way, you'll pass by several familiar backdrops and sets, see the star's dressing rooms, and come upon a number of catastrophes and calamities, re-creating scenes from some of Universal's more memorable movies and TV shows. The amusement park rides, especially Back to the Future and Jurassic Park, are some of the best I've ever been on.

BIBLIOGRAPHY

This book would not have been possible without referring to and being inspired by the following magazines, newspapers, books, programs, media kits, and guest guides as I traveled to Winston Cup cities and tracks.

AutoWeek 2001 Fan Racing Guide. Detroit: Crain Publications, 2000 and 2001.

Brown, Allen and Nancy. *National Speedway Directory*. Comstock Park, MI: 2001.

Charlotte (North Carolina) Observer. Numerous editions 1995–2001.

Dick Berggren's Speedway Illustrated. Rockport, ME: Performance Media, numerous editions 2000–2001.

Dickson, Paul. *Volvo Guide to Halls of Fame*. Washington, DC: Living Planet Press, 1995.

Fleischman, Bill, and Pearce, Al. *The Unauthorized NASCAR Fan Guide '99*. Farmington Mills, MI: Visible Ink Press, 1999.

Golenbock, Peter. *American Zoom—Stock Car Racing from the Dirt Tracks to Daytona*. New York: Macmillan, 1993.

———. *The Last Lap: The Life and Times of NASCAR's Legendary Heroes*. New York: Macmillan, 1998.

Hagstrom, Robert G. *The NASCAR Way: The Business That Drives the Sport*. New York: John Wiley & Sons, 1998.

Hoffman, Jim. *North Carolina Family Adventure Guide*. Old Saybrook, CT: Globe Pequot Press, 1997.

Johnson, Roy S. "Speed Sells—NASCAR Is America's New Favorite Sport—And Its Hottest Marketing Vehicle." *Fortune*, April 12, 1999.

Latford, Bob. *Built for Speed*. Philadelphia: Courage Books/Running Press, 1999.

———. *50 Years of NASCAR*. London: Carlton Books, 2000.

McCullough, Bob. *My Greatest Day in NASCAR*. New York: Thomas Dunne Books/St. Martin's Press, 2000.

McLaurin, Jim. *NASCAR's Most Wanted: The Top Ten Book of Outrageous Drivers, Wild Wrecks, and Other Oddities*. Dulles, VA: Brasseys, July 2001.

NASCAR Tech. Akron, OH: Babcox Publications, 2001.

NASCAR Winston Cup Scene. Charlotte, NC: Street & Smith, several editions 1997–2000.

NASCAR Winston Cup Series 2001 Media Guide. Winston-Salem, NC: Sports Marketing Enterprises, 2001.

Phillips, Benny, and Blake, Ben. *Dale Earnhardt—Determined*. Charlotte, NC: UMI Publications, 2001.

Teison, Herbert, and Dunnan, Nancy. *Travel Smarts: Getting the Most for Your Travel Dollars*. Old Saybrook, CT: Globe Pequot Press, 1995.

The Official NASCAR Handbook. New York: Harper Horizon, 1998.

The Official NASCAR 2001 Preview Guide. Charlotte, NC: UMI Publications, 2001.

UAW-GM Motorsports Industry Contact Book 2001. Concord, NC: Lowe's Motor Speedway, 2001.

Wolfe, Tom. "The Last American Hero, Is Junior Johnson—Yes!" *Esquire*, October 1965, p. 211.

I also acknowledge the city directories, race programs, guest guides, and media kits from convention and visitor bureaus and individual racetracks. The help of countless public relations people at the tracks and local tourism boards was also an invaluable contribution.

ACKNOWLEDGMENTS

To Steve, Jamie, and Tom (a.k.a. the Fink Brothers) who were such a big part of my track travels over the past few seasons. Thanks also to Jeff and Eric (a.k.a. the Williams Brothers) who, along with Jamie, dragged me kicking and screaming to qualifying almost seven years ago.

To Paul, Elizabeth, Scott, Angela, Tracy, Bill, Keith, Tom, Chris, Meribeth, Kevin, Darren, Carl, Dan, Karl, Mark, Rick, Joey, Dave, Norm, and all the good folks at Flag to Flag; Lanny, the Delta Chi fraternity in Daytona, and so many others who served as photographers, hosts, tailgate buddies, and co-conspirators along the way. To racing insiders including Joe, Walter, Robbie, David, Rob, Jerry, Mike, Jeff, Derrike, Tom, Brian, Eddie, Brad, countless PR folks, and all the amazing fans at the tracks who consented to be interviewed.

To Patricia, Mike, and Bruce for believing so strongly in my first book, as well as their encouraging words and deeds involved in the production of this one. To my editor, Richard, for helping turn a massive pile of notes, files, and photos into a coherent book.

To my parents, who instilled in me the unquenchable desire to travel, discover, and enjoy.

To my wife, Karen, who assisted in too many ways to list here, traveled with me to many of the cities herein, and kicked me in the rear when I needed to get busy writing.

ABOUT THE AUTHOR

Jay Ahuja, a former editor at *SportsWrap* magazine, has written articles for the *Charlotte Observer* and *Charlotte* magazine, as well as for national publications. He is a well-known Internet and radio interviewee, and the author of the best-selling *Fields of Dreams: A Guide to Visiting All 30 Major League Parks*. Originally from New York, he lives in North Carolina.